Public Feminisms

Member Institution Acknowledgments

Lever Press is a joint venture. This work was made possible by the generous support of Lever Press member libraries from the following institutions:

Amherst College
Berea College
Bowdoin College
Carleton College
Central Washington University
Claremont Graduate University
Claremont McKenna College
Clark Atlanta University
College of Saint Benedict & Saint John's University
The College of Wooster
Davidson College
Denison University
DePauw University
Grinnell College
Hamilton College
Harvey Mudd College
Hollins University
Iowa State University
Keck Graduate Institute
Knox College

Lafayette College
Macalester College
Middlebury College
Morehouse College
Norwich University
Penn State University
Pitzer College
Pomona College
Randolph-Macon College
Rollins College
Santa Clara University
Scripps College
Skidmore College
Smith College
Spelman College
Susquehanna University
Swarthmore College
Trinity University
UCLA Library
Union College
University of Idaho

University of Puget Sound
University of San Francisco
University of Vermont
Ursinus College
Vassar College
Washington and Lee University

Whitman College
Whittier College
Whitworth University
Willamette University
Williams College

Public Feminisms

FROM ACADEMY TO COMMUNITY

Carrie N. Baker and Aviva Dove-Viebahn, Eds.

Copyright © 2022 by Authors

Lever Press (leverpress.org) is a publisher of pathbreaking scholarship. Supported by a consortium of higher education institutions focused on, and renowned for, excellence in both research and teaching, our press is grounded on three essential commitments: to be a digitally native press, to be a peer-reviewed, open access press that charges no fees to either authors or their institutions, and to be a press aligned with the liberal arts ethos.

This work is licensed under the Creative Commons Attribution-NonCommercial 4.0 International License. To view a copy of this license, visit http://creativecommons.org/licenses/by-nc/4.0/ or send a letter to Creative Commons, PO Box 1866, Mountain View, CA 94042, USA.

The complete manuscript of this work was subjected to a partly closed ("single blind") review process. For more information, please see our Peer Review Commitments and Guidelines at https://www.leverpress.org/peerreview

DOI: https://doi.org/10.3998/mpub.12682117
Print ISBN: 978-1-64315-043-7
Open access ISBN: 978-1-64315-044-4

Library of Congress Control Number: 2022947916

Published in the United States of America by Lever Press, in partnership with Michigan Publishing.

Contents

Acknowledgments xi
Foreword by Dr. Beverly Guy-Sheftall xiii
Introduction: Back to Our Roots 1

Part I: Art, Media, and Public Programming 17

Chapter One: Red Carpet Radicals: Public Feminist
Scholarship and the Sexism|Cinema Film Series 19
*by Michael Borshuk, Don E. Lavigne, Elizabeth A. Sharp,
Jessica E. Smith, Dana A. Weiser, and Allison Whitney*

Chapter Two: "Las Doctoras": A Podcast for Community
Empowerment 37
by Cristina Rose and Renee Lemus

Chapter Three: From Classroom to Pavement: Creating a
Walking Tour of Calgary's Historic Sex Trade Industry 53
by Kimberly A. Williams

Chapter Four: The Day Angela Died: Imagining Violence and
Reclaiming Indigeneity through Collaborative Performance 81
by Zoë Eddy

Chapter Five: There Have Always Been Apocalypses: *Queer Apocalypse Solutions* for Liberation and Survival   105
by Helis Sikk, Lindsay Garcia, and José Roman

Part II: Activism and Public Education   127

Chapter Six: Take Back the Night: Feminism on the March   129
by Sharon L. Barnes

Chapter Seven: Public Feminism through Law and Policy Advocacy on Reproductive Rights   155
by Carrie N. Baker

Chapter Eight: Building Bridges: Researching with, and Not for, Students on Diversity and Inclusion Policy   173
by Gabrielle Rodriguez Gonzalez, Jack Kendrick, and Megan Nanney

Chapter Nine: Reflecting on Fat Activism as Research Methodology   191
by Calla Evans

Chapter Ten: "March into the Archives": Documenting Women's Protests   209
by Jessica A. Rose and Lynée Lewis Gaillet

Chapter Eleven: *Ma Beti ka Rishta*: Mother-Daughter Relationships as Public Feminist Archives   229
by Mariam Durrani, Nazneen Patel, and Zainab Shah

Part III: Public Writing and Scholarship   247

Chapter Twelve: A "Feminist Lens" on Activism and Inclusion in the Film and Television Industry   249
by Aviva Dove-Viebahn

Chapter Thirteen: Feminism, Faith, and Public Scholarship   263
by Susan M. Shaw

Chapter Fourteen: University Media Relations, Public
Scholarship, and Online Harassment   279
by Alex D. Ketchum

Chapter Fifteen: Translation as Feminist Activism:
Amplifying Diverse Voices through *Amargi Feminist Review*   299
by Begüm Acar, Nefise Kahraman, and Senem Kaptan

Chapter Sixteen: Love and Marriage and the
World's Best Editor   319
by Audrey Bilger

Chapter Seventeen: Scholar, Writer, Editor,
Publisher: Multifaceted Engagements in Feminist
Public Writing   335
by Julie R. Enszer

Part IV: Feminist Pedagogies for Community Engagement   347

Chapter Eighteen: The Activist Possibilities of
Wikipedia: Praxis, Pedagogy, and Potential Pitfalls   349
by Jenn Brandt

Chapter Nineteen: Teaching and Learning through
"Doing": Reflections on Using Open Access Digital Tools
for Feminist Pedagogy and Praxis   369
by Riddhima Sharma

Chapter Twenty: RBG, Public Pedagogy, and
Online Activism   387
by Suzanne Leonard

Chapter Twenty-One: There Is No Just Future without
Intersectional Sustainability: Feminist Pedagogy for Tackling
Privilege and Centering Praxis in Sustainability Education   403
by Michelle Larkins

Chapter Twenty-Two: Orienting Public Pedagogues:
A Black Feminist Approach to Community-Engaged
Writing Center Work 425
by Nick Sanders, Grace Pregent, Leah Bauer

Conclusion: Looking Forward 447

Author Biographies 461

Acknowledgments

We thank the former Director of Lever Press Beth Bouloukos for her generous guidance throughout the process of conceiving, developing, and completing this project. She convinced us early on that Lever's open access format was the perfect place for a book about community-engaged scholarship. By eliminating paywalls, open access publishing not only makes our book fully accessible to students and independent scholars without cost, but also enables us to freely share our work with our broader, non-academic communities—local, national, and global. We are eternally grateful to Beth for introducing us to this opportunity.

We also thank Lever's former Assistant Acquisitions Editor Hannah Brooks-Motl, current Lever Acquiring Editor Sean Guynes, and Digital Publishing Coordinator Carl Lavigne for their helpful editorial suggestions and the two anonymous reviewers for their detailed feedback on the manuscript. Smith College student Hazel Garrity was a tremendous help to us in reviewing the many excellent proposals we received and making the hard decisions about what to include in this anthology. And for writing the foreword, we are so grateful to Dr. Beverly Guy-Sheftall, who has for decades been an inspiring example of a community-engaged scholar. We dedicate this volume to our wonderful contributors who have shared their exemplary community-engaged work with all of us.

We met a decade ago as part of a Ford Foundation-funded fellowship to help train feminist scholars to write for the popular press run through Ms. magazine and have since continued to work together leading subsequent workshops and as members of the magazine's advisory Committee of Scholars. We will forever be grateful to the encouragement, guidance, and support we have received and continue to receive from the magazine, its parent organization (the Feminist Majority Foundation), and its individual editors, including Executive Editor Kathy Spillar, Managing Editor Camille Hahn, Digital Editor Roxy Szal, former editors Jessica Stites and Carmen Rios, and the late Michele Kort, a superlative editor who is sorely missed by all who knew her. In addition, the National Women's Studies Association has been incredibly supportive of our work on panels and workshops exploring public feminism through writing, activism, and education. Not coincidentally, it was at one of the NWSA conferences where we met Beth, bringing this whole venture, in many ways, full circle.

Foreword

By Beverly Guy-Sheftall

"From the very onset of my engagement with feminist practice, I was most excited about building a mass feminist movement ... I worked to envision ways of bringing the meaning of feminist thinking and practice to a larger audience, to the masses."
          bell hooks, *Feminism is For Everybody*, Preface to the new edition, 2015

While reading *Public Feminisms: From Academy to Community*, I thought deeply about the provocative, transgressive writings and teaching of bell hooks who has been perhaps the best example in our lifetime of the public feminist scholar/activist. I was motivated by *Public Feminisms* to reread bell hooks (having been saddened by her untimely death this past December) because, from my vantage point, it bears witness to the importance of her legacy. I imagined that the contributors were mindful of a frustration that bell spoke and wrote about often:

> Through the years as more diverse female and male voices have come to the table writing awesome feminist theory and cultural

criticism, academic settings became and have become the primary settings for the dissemination of feminist thought. This trend has had positive impact for college students as it provides greater opportunity for folks to learn the power and significance of feminist thinking and practice, but it has impacted negatively on the work of broadening the engagement of a larger public in feminist movement.[1]

bell hooks would likely feel the impact of her forty-year engagement with feminist theory and practice if she were able to read this book because it is the only anthology that showcases the significance and variety of public feminisms through its compelling case studies of feminist academics bridging the gap between theory and practice. I am convinced because of *Public Feminisms* that bell hooks' lifelong struggle—that began when she was a nineteen-year-old undergraduate to "communicate feminist politics to everyone"— has been embraced by countless scholar/activists, many of whom bear witness to the impact of her message here.

Reading *Public Feminisms* also reminded me of our own work at the Women's Center at Spelman College. I have been invigorated over our forty-year journey by our community service component which is evidenced by the number of women within the local Atlanta community, throughout the nation, and abroad who participate in our workshops, seminars, and conferences. These activities, like many showcased in the anthology, offer a diverse group of folks intellectual stimulation, support, fellowship, and the opportunity to discuss topics that impact their personal lives. Of special interest some years ago was the program for immigrant community women sponsored by the Center in collaboration with our Continuing Education Division. This program involved women from Africa, Asia, India, and the Caribbean, and was the first of its kind on the campus that specifically reached out to women from the Global South, most of whom were not professionals. The women were enrolled in two courses which were taught by

Spelman faculty. To accommodate the women who were mothers of small children, the College provided free-of-charge child care. Through social activities and informal discussions, the women shared experiences from different cultural contexts and developed a strong sense of cohesiveness as women from outside the United States This project, which culminated in a graduation exercise, won the Center and the College many friends and comrades among local immigrant communities in Atlanta. It also demonstrated the importance, like the examples in *Public Feminisms*, of bridging the gap between the academy and the community in our commitments to positive social change as we struggle to end white supremacy, heteropatriarchy, poverty, and the impacts of colonialism and imperialism around the globe.

Finally, the contributors to *Public Feminisms* are stellar examples of bell hooks' compelling ideas about visionary feminist thinkers who fundamentally understand the interconnectedness of all systems of oppression. They embrace intersectional feminism and believe that feminism is for everybody and must move beyond the confines of the ivory tower. Because of their projects, I am convinced that feminism is not dead and—remembering bell hooks—that "visionary feminism offers us hope for the future."

NOTE

1. bell hooks, *Feminism Is for Everybody: Passionate Politics, 2nd Edition* (New York: Routledge, 2014), viii.

INTRODUCTION: BACK TO OUR ROOTS

By Carrie N. Baker and Aviva Dove-Viebahn

A city walking tour that subverts tourists' assumptions about sex workers. Collaborative performances that offer participants a way to understand the stories of disappeared and murdered Indigenous women. Testimony before a state legislature on the harmful impact of parental consent laws for minors seeking abortion health care. A public film and discussion series encouraging intersectional feminist analysis. A Writing Center employing a Black feminist approach to teach writing to community members. These are just some of the stories told in this volume. Through art and public programming, activism and policy advocacy, public writing and community education, feminists in higher education are using scholarly methods and pedagogies to share academic knowledge and research with their communities at the local, national, and international levels. These scholars are advancing public knowledge about issues affecting women and girls,[1] racial and ethnic minorities, immigrants, Indigenous peoples, LGBTQIA+ individuals, and others facing discrimination, lacking resources, or experiencing economic, political, and social injustices. This book offers a selection of case studies, models, narratives, and tools from a diverse array of writers whose essays we have carefully curated to showcase myriad strategies for community engagement.

In the United States and transnationally, we are in a time of profound socio-political crises that calls for, among other things, the dissolution of long-imagined boundaries between academia and the public. The Carnegie Foundation defines community engagement as "collaboration between institutions of higher education and their larger communities for the mutually beneficial exchange of knowledge and resources in a context of partnership and reciprocity."[2] These communities can be local, regional, statewide, national, or international. Educational institutions are increasingly seeing public scholarship and civic engagement as relevant and fruitful complements to traditional academic study, research, and publishing. The Andrew W. Mellon Foundation, for example, recently created its Just Futures Initiative, which funds social justice-oriented projects that build paths between universities and various publics. The initiative recently awarded $72 million to scholars doing public engagement projects.[3] The Whiting Foundation has launched new public engagement programs to support "ambitious public-facing humanities projects." These programs include the Public Engagement Fellowship and the Public Engagement Seed Grant to "celebrate and empower humanities faculty who embrace public engagement as part of their scholarly vocation."[4] Feminist scholars from many disciplines are increasingly engaging their communities and providing students with real-world learning experiences through community-based learning and research.

In this collection of essays, scholar-activists write about the dynamic and varied ways we engage in public feminisms within our communities and with our students, via methods that extend beyond the traditional academic classroom and scholarly publications. This volume showcases the innovative techniques feminist scholars are using to amplify the voices of women, girls, and non-binary individuals, engage in activism, write or speak to a larger public, and promote social awareness in their communities. This book demonstrates the value of feminist research and scholarship as an important corrective to the general anti-intellectualism of U.S. culture in the early twenty-first century. This community-engaged work is crucial at this particular moment, yet these activities are part of a long history of feminist scholars engaging their communities.

WOMEN'S HISTORY OF COMMUNITY ENGAGEMENT

Feminist scholars and educators have for generations argued for the benefits of educated women engaging their communities to create social change. In 1792, English philosopher and women's rights advocate Mary Wollstonecraft published *A Vindication of the Rights of Woman*, a treatise urging for women's education to be as robust and comprehensive as that which was possible for men at the time. She argued that women will never be able to equal men in their abilities and place in society if they are not given an equal chance to be educated in ways both rational and challenging, noting the many merits of educated women and the need to allow women to thrive in all the arenas in which they were able: "For if it be allowed that women were destined by Providence to acquire human virtues, and by the exercise of their understandings, that stability of character which is the firmest ground to rest our future hopes upon, they must be permitted to turn to the fountain of light, and not be forced to shape their course by the twinkling of a mere satellite."[5] Wollstonecraft believed fervently both in the moral imperative to provide people equal rights and privileges regardless of gender and in the potential of women to achieve significant gains in society if only they were allowed equal access to education and the public sphere to exert their influence.

A century later and an ocean away, in her 1892 *A Voice from the South by a Black Woman of the South*, scholar, activist, and educator Anna Julia Cooper stressed how women's intellects and abilities have gone underserved and unappreciated, affirming that American women had a lot to offer the nation and the world in the spheres of politics, education, and culture if only they were given the chance. Cooper wrote,

> No plan for renovating society, no scheme for purifying politics, no reform in church or in state, no moral, social, or economic question, no movement upward or downward in the human plane is lost on [women]. [...] All departments in the new era are to be hers, in the sense that her interests are in all and through all; and it is incumbent on her to keep intelligently and sympathetically *en rapport* with all the great movements of her time, that she may know on which side to throw the weight of her influence.[6]

She offered further observations of the unique situation faced by women of color, influenced as they were by social assumptions about both their race and gender—an assertion predating Kimberlee Crenshaw's coining of the term "intersectionality" by a century.[7]

Cooper and Wollstonecraft were scholars who wrote to broad audiences and articulated a vision of community engagement by educated women to make the world better. They wrote from positions spanning the boundaries of public scholarship and academic inquiry, proposing interventions into the fabric of social life, culture, politics, and education in order to raise the prospects for women and girls of their time. Using logic suitable for a time in which many believed a woman's sole aim should be marriage and family, Wollstonecraft implored her peers to see how educated women would be better teachers of their children and more astute companions to their husbands, while also insisting on their ability to become more vibrant members of society even if they were to remain unmarried. Women's education, for Wollstonecraft, could only benefit everyone, just "as sound politics diffuse liberty, mankind, including woman, will become more wise and virtuous."[8] Cooper extolled the virtues of women as agents of a necessary influence on the world, without which "the world of thought moved in its orbit like the revolutions of the moon; with one face (the man's face) always out, so that the spectator could not distinguish whether it was disc or sphere."[9]

While much has changed in the intervening centuries, the essays in this collection similarly challenge readers to identify ways women and girls in their communities can and do exert their influence on the world, with the authors exploring, in part, how they make connections between their academic/scholarly work and community engagement. These connections and influences extend both ways, from academia to activism and from activism back into academia, as exemplified by the social justice movements of the 1960s and 1970s from which the earliest women's and gender studies programs germinated.

Feminist studies in the U.S. academy has deep roots in 1960s and 1970s social justice movements, and an imperfect but earnest conception of feminist potential and possibility emerges from the writing, speeches, and activist events of the era.[10] In the United States, these movements produced anti-discrimination laws that opened wide the doors of higher education to a more diverse array of people entering the academy as students, teachers, scholars, and researchers. Title VII of the Civil Rights Act of 1964 prohibited employment discrimination, and Title IX of the Education Amendments of 1972 barred sex discrimination in schools and universities. Women poured into colleges and universities, breaking barriers and asking new questions. Women historians asked where the women were in history, literary scholars searched for and found long-forgotten books written by women, and women scientists questioned traditional methodologies and assumptions about the natural world.

These inquiries were supported and spurred on from outside the academy by the women's movement participants, who were thirsty for the histories and writings of women of the past and determined to question male authorities in medicine, psychology, and other fields. Students began demanding classes on women— our history, stories, and politics. Women faculty created them, sometimes from whole cloth. If there were no scholarly studies available, teachers and students shared their own experiences. In a class on women and work at Cornell in 1974, for example, the teacher Lin Farley and her students discovered they all shared experiences of sexual coercion on the job. A year later, they joined with women from the community to name the experience "sexual harassment" and started a social movement that eventually made that behavior a federal civil rights violation.[11]

Since San Diego State University founded the first women's studies program in 1970,[12] the field has grown in size as well as breadth, with schools across the country developing interdisciplinary majors, master's degree programs, and, starting at Emory University in 1990, doctoral programs. The field expanded to include gender and sexuality studies and, albeit unevenly, to incorporate the perspectives of Black feminist theory and women of color feminisms. The field of women's, gender, and sexuality studies (WGSS) now has over twenty Ph.D. programs and many master's and certificate degree programs; over 500 universities and colleges across the United States offer WGSS majors, drawing on courses taught across the curriculum, from history, literature, anthropology, sociology, and psychology to communications, biology, and more. Many people doing feminist scholarly work are in WGSS, but they span the disciplines— only sometimes formally affiliated with WGSS programs. As the field has developed, some scholars and programs have become disconnected from social change movements, but for many, social justice and community engagement have remained important aspects of their work as teachers and scholars. In fact, the National Women's Studies Association describes the field as dedicated to promoting "synergistic relationships between scholarship, teaching and civic engagement in understandings of culture and society."[13]

Among college administrators, appreciation of the value of community engagement has grown over the years. In the mid-1980s, a group of higher education leaders came together to discuss their concerns about the future of American democracy and the increasing trend toward a focus on personal acquisition and personal advancement. These leaders created the organization Campus Compact to work together to advance the public purposes of higher education on their campuses. In 1999, Campus Compact promulgated the "Presidents' Declaration on the Civic Responsibility of Higher Education," a statement calling for renewed action to strengthen community engagement on college campuses.[14] In 2016, presidents and chancellors at more than 450 institutions committed again to these principles by signing Campus Compact's "30th Anniversary Action Statement," pledging a "renewed commitment to preparing students for democratic citizenship, building partnerships for change, and reinvigorating higher education for the public good."[15]

Nearly 1,100 institutions now belong to Campus Compact. There are at least ten scholarly journals dedicated to community engagement in higher education, such as the *Journal of Community Engagement and Scholarship* and the *International Journal of Research on Service-Learning and Community Engagement*. In addition to Campus Compact, other organizations promoting community engagement in higher education include the Civic Learning American Association of Colleges and Universities, the Engagement Scholarship Consortium, the National Service-Learning Clearinghouse, and the International Association for Research on Service-Learning and Community Engagement. The Scholars Strategy Network seeks to connect scholars with journalists, policymakers, and civic leaders to improve policy and strengthen democracy. Colleges and universities increasingly value public scholarship, encouraging more faculty to become publicly engaged, and faculty are now extolling the benefits of this work, both for themselves and their communities.[16]

The National Women's Studies Association (NWSA) has fostered a continuing commitment to civic engagement in the field. With a Teagle Foundation grant in 2011, NWSA created a working group on civic engagement, which produced a white paper arguing that the WGSS field is a leader in fostering civic engagement that will "deepen student learning, contribute respectfully to communities in which they become involved, and produce lifelong civic leaders."[17] The paper noted that WGSS centers on an understanding of how social problems emerge from interconnected systems of inequality and privilege, and simultaneously engages students to think about how to challenge those systems. This social justice framework influences how scholars and students engage communities in ways that are distinct from "service" or "volunteering," where too often issues of power and privilege go unquestioned.

The white paper focused on three areas: *activist scholarship, modes of inquiry,* and *engaged pedagogy.* Its writers, fifteen WGSS scholars from across the country, argued that *activist scholarship* draws on histories of radical politics to make both connections and distinctions between service and struggle, provides perspectives on deep democracy and informed reciprocity, counteracts both consumer and missionary models of community-based learning, and examines the possibilities of dissident citizenship. *Modes of inquiry* bring intersectional approaches to power, privilege, and inequality, examine local/global connections, acknowledge sexism and its relationship to other forms of oppression, and produce lifelong learners and critical inquiry toward social transformation. *Engaged pedagogies* encourage students to think about structures of inequality, teach students how to challenge norms of inequality, show students how private troubles can become public issues (and vice versa), and help students to enter communities with humility as well as an openness to learning and personal transformation.

The essays in this collection document many of these principles in action.

Contributors to this collection share how they have used their academic backgrounds, including scholarly knowledge, research methods, and pedagogical skills, in their publicly engaged work. They demonstrate how academic skills such as archival research, legal research, translation, and ethnography can be useful tools for scholars' public engagement. For example, Kimberly A. Williams in chapter three uses archival research and analysis of municipal records to understand the historic sex trade industry for her walking tour in Calgary. Lynée Lewis Gaillet and Jessica Rose in chapter ten explain how community archivists and special collection librarians collected and preserved materials from the 2017 women's protests. Susan Shaw in chapter thirteen explores how she uses her scholarly background and research on evangelical Christianity to write publicly and "make Christian, particularly evangelical, issues, attitudes, and behaviors intelligible for a feminist audience and to bring feminist perspectives to contemporary faith issues for Christian audiences." Begüm Acar, Nefise Kahraman, and Senem Kaptan in chapter fifteen describe how they used translation skills to make articles in a Turkish feminist journal accessible to international readers. These are just a few examples of the many ways that contributors to this volume have put their academic knowledge and skills to use in the public sphere.

Inside and outside the academy, regardless of disciplinary affiliation, feminist scholars have continued to foster civic engagement in our classrooms and communities through art, social media, community programming and education, activism, and public writing, responding to the particularly compelling need for scholarly public engagement at this current historical moment. The resurgence of misogyny, white supremacy, xenophobia, homophobia, and transphobia in politics over the last decade, as well as the attacks on science and truth, mean that feminist scholars' voices are needed now more than ever in the public sphere to bring to light marginalized perspectives and offer a thoughtful interdisciplinary and intersectional feminist analysis of current events. In an increasingly precarious and complicated political, social, and cultural landscape—in academia, in activist spaces, and in everyday life—feminist scholars are continuing to make both their teaching and writing relevant to a larger public. As a diverse discipline in the U.S. academmcy, with a core commitment to intersectional and transnational analysis, WGSS is uniquely positioned to contribute toward solving some of the most pressing and complex problems facing our nation and the world.

OUTLINE OF THE BOOK

This book is divided into four parts. Part one explores how scholars are sharing feminist scholarship and knowledge with broader audiences through art, media, and public programming. The essays include explorations of a public film and discussion series teaching intersectional feminist analysis of films; a podcast from Latina scholars discussing issues of reproductive justice, social justice, motherhood, sexuality, race, and gender; a city walking tour that subverts tourists' assumptions about sex workers; collaborative indigenous performance as a place for complex, embodied storytelling about gender-based violence; and the performance-based Queer Apocalypse Solutions collective that offers solutions for liberation and survival. In these projects, scholars use art, media, and public programming to teach feminist analysis of representation and discourse in the visual and built environment, as well as feminist strategies to survive oppressive systems.

Part two, on activism and public education, includes essays on "Take Back the Night" marches as a public feminist intervention; policy advocacy on reproductive rights and justice; student activism on institutional diversity and inclusion policies; fat activism using an activist-oriented research methodology; archiving the women's march protests; and a meditation on the meaning of "desi" Muslim mothering developed in women-run, women-first writing collaboratives in NYC. This part explores different ways that scholars can use their knowledge and skills in the broader world to create personal and social change.

Part three turns to public writing and scholarship, with essays on elevating the perspectives and voices of underrepresented creatives in the film and television industry; the challenges posed by writing for the public on feminism and Christianity; the obligations of institutions of higher education to protect scholars from online harassment; a group of scholars' experience translating Turkish feminist scholarship for an international audience; another scholar's relationship to her editor at *Ms.* magazine; and insights from an academic who edits a feminist magazine. Part three addresses strategies for public writing, as well as the benefits and challenges of feminist public scholarship.

Part four explores feminist pedagogies for community engagement, including how one scholar uses Wikipedia as an educational tool and platform for putting knowledge into practice; strategies for using open access social media tools; pedagogies for teaching public feminisms; an exploration of the intersection between feminism, sustainability, the environment, and climate change; and how a group of scholars are running a community-engaged writing center informed by Black feminist theory. This final section offers tangible suggestions for incorporating community engagement in the feminist classroom.

Contributors to this volume include senior, junior, and contingent faculty, graduate and undergraduate students, as well as independent scholars. They come from public and private institutions, large universities, small liberal arts colleges, and research institutes. The authors of this collection are located in many fields, including WGSS, Anthropology, African American Literature, Classics, Human Development and Family Studies, English, Film and Media Studies, Ethnic Studies, South Asian

Studies, Communications and Culture, American Studies, and Environmental Science and Studies. We title this collection *Public Feminisms* plural, because we recognize that although feminists generally share a belief in equality and justice for women, they define the term in multiple ways, with different emphases and priorities.

While we have sought to be inclusive and represent diverse identities, perspectives, and issues, we acknowledge some limitations. For example, we include a number of international scholars, but most of the scholars contributing to this collection are from or working now within North America. We have only one chapter focused explicitly on Latinx experiences (chapter two), one with the perspectives of Indigenous women (chapter four), and one grappling directly with transgender issues written from the perspective of non-binary/trans authors (chapter eight). We are grateful to include these essays, but believe these important perspectives need more attention. While the collection covers many important issues, we know there are more we were unable to include or which deserve more extensive attention, such as climate change, immigration, state violence, economic inequality, and poverty. We work within the constraints of the current moment and people's availability to contribute to this volume. We are thankful for those who were able to take the time to write for this collection.

In her book *Feminism Is for Everybody*, feminist and social justice activist bell hooks calls on feminist academics to make their work more publicly accessible, noting "Today in academic circles much of the most celebrated feminist theory is written in a sophisticated jargon that only the well-educated can read. Most people in society do not have a basic understanding of feminism." She continues, "Unfortunately class elitism has shaped the direction of feminist thought. Most feminist thinkers/theorists do their work in the elite setting of the university." As an antidote, hooks called for "mass-based feminist education for critical consciousness"[18] in 2000: the current political moment makes this call all the more urgent. The essays in this volume are a rich resource for scholars interested in answering hooks' call to infuse the public sphere with feminist knowledge. They also offer an opportunity to reflect on the meaning and importance of community engagement for scholars at a time when the larger world desperately needs their insights and knowledge. Finally, this collection archives some of the important work feminists are doing during a time of tremendous political division and upheaval.

NOTES

1. When we use the terms "women" and "girls," we mean all people who identify as women, including both cis-gender and transgender women and girls.
2. "Carnegie Community Engagement Classification," New England Resource Center for Higher Education, http://nerche.org/index.php?option=com_content&view=article&id=341&ltemid=618.
3. Andrew W. Mellon Foundation, Just Futures Initiative, https://mellon.org/initiatives/just-futures/.
4. Whiting Foundation, Public Engagement Programs, https://www.whiting.org/scholars/public-engagement-programs/about.
5. Mary Wollstonecraft, *A Vindication of the Rights of Woman: With Strictures on Political and Moral Subjects* [1792] (T. Fisher Unwin, 1891), 50.
6. Anna Julia Cooper, *A Voice from the South* [1892] (electronic edition, 2000), accessed on 17 December 2020, Documenting the American South, 142–43. https://docsouth.unc.edu/church/cooper/cooper.html.
7. See Kimberlé Crenshaw, "Mapping the Margins: Intersectionality, Identity Politics, and Violence against Women of Color," *Stanford Law Review*, 43, no. 6 (July 1991): 1241–1299.
8. Wollstonecraft, 73.
9. Cooper, 56.
10. *Persistence is Resistance: Celebrating 50 Years of Gender, Women & Sexuality Studies*, ed. by Julie Shayne (University of Washington, 2020), https://uw.pressbooks.pub/happy50thws/.
11. Carrie N. Baker, *The Women's Movement Against Sexual Harassment* (Cambridge University Press, 2007).
12. Temperance Russell, Lori Loftin, and Julie Shayne, "The History of San Diego State University's Women's Studies Program," in *Persistence Is Resistance: Celebrating 50 Years of Gender, Women & Sexuality Studies*, ed. by

Julie Shayne (University of Washington, 2020), https://uw.pressbooks.pub/happy50thws/.
13. National Women's Studies Association, "Our Mission," https://www.nwsa.org/.
14. Campus Compact, "Presidents' Declaration on the Civic Responsibility of Higher Education," March 23, 2009. https://compact.org/resources-for-presidents/presidents-declaration-on-the-civic-responsibility-of-higher-education/.
15. Campus Compact, "30th Anniversary Action Statement of Presidents and Chancellors," March 20, 2016, https://compact.org/actionstatement/statement/.
16. Carrie N. Baker, Michele Berger, Aviva Dove-Viebahn, Karon Jolna, and Carmen Rios, "Amplifying the Voices of Feminist Scholars in the Press," *Feminist Formations* 32, no. 2 (Summer 2020): 29–51; Laura W. Perna, *Taking It to the Streets: The Role of Scholarship in Advocacy and Advocacy in Scholarship* (Baltimore, MD: Johns Hopkins University Press, 2018); M.V. Lee Badgett, *The Public Professor: How to Use Your Research to Change the World* (NYU Press, 2017).
17. Catherine M. Orr, "Women's Studies as Civic Engagement: Research and Recommendations" (Teagle Foundation White Paper, 2011), http://www.teaglefoundation.org/Teagle/media/GlobalMediaLibrary/documents/resources/Womens_Studies_as_Civic_Engagement.pdf?ext=.pdf.
18. bell hooks, *Feminism Is for Everybody: Passionate Politics* (Pluto Press, 2000): 112–113.

WORKS CITED

Andrew W. Mellon Foundation, "Just Futures Initiative," https://mellon.org/initiatives/just-futures/.

Badgett, M.V. Lee. *The Public Professor: How to Use Your Research to Change the World*. New York: NYU Press, 2017.

Carrie N. Baker, Michele Berger, Aviva Dove-Viebahn, Karon Jolna, and Carmen Rios. "Amplifying the Voices of Feminist Scholars in the Press." *Feminist Formations* 32, no. 2 (Summer 2020): 29–51.

Campus Compact. "Presidents' Declaration on the Civic Responsibility of Higher Education." 1999.

Campus Compact. "30th Anniversary Action Statement of Presidents and Chancellors." 2016.

Cooper, Anna Julia. *A Voice from the South* [1892]. In Documenting the American South. 2000. https://docsouth.unc.edu/.

Crenshaw, Kimberlé. "Mapping the Margins: Intersectionality, Identity Politics, and Violence against Women of Color." *Stanford Law Review* 43, no. 6 (1991).
hooks, bell. *Feminism Is for Everybody: Passionate Politics*. London: Pluto Press, 2000.
National Women's Studies Association. "Our Mission." https://www.nwsa.org/.
Orr, Catherine M. "Women's Studies as Civic Engagement: Research and Recommendations." Teagle Foundation White Paper. 2011.
Perna, Laura W. *Taking It to the Streets: The Role of Scholarship in Advocacy and Advocacy in Scholarship*. Baltimore, MD: Johns Hopkins University Press, 2018.
Shayne, Julie, ed. *Persistence Is Resistance: Celebrating 50 Years of Gender, Women & Sexuality Studies*. Seattle: University of Washington, 2020.
Whiting Foundation. Public Engagement Programs. https://www.whiting.org/scholars/public-engagement-programs/about.
Wollstonecraft, Mary. *A Vindication of the Rights of Woman: With Strictures on Political and Moral Subjects* [1792]. London: T. Fisher Unwin, 1891.

PART I

ART, MEDIA, AND PUBLIC
PROGRAMMING

Chapters in this section offer dynamic approaches to the intersections of art, film, media, and activism in work for and with the public, examining the varied ways feminist scholars can engage with their communities and bridge the gap between academic knowledge and public spaces, history, media, and current events. In "Red Carpet Radicals: Public Feminist Scholarship and the Sexism|Cinema Film Series," a group of feminist scholars (Michael Borshuk, Don Lavigne, Elizabeth Sharp, Jessica Smith, Dana Weiser, and Allison Whitney) discuss their founding of a community-facing film series on sexism and cinema in West Texas as a response to racist and sexist events at their campus and beyond. "'Las Doctoras': A Podcast for Community Empowerment" chronicles the creation of Cristina Rose and Renee Lemus' podcast, in which they share knowledge that they have gained through their academic and personal experiences as Latinx scholars within their local community. In "From Classroom to Pavement: Creating a Walking Tour of Calgary's Historic Sex Trade Industry," Kimberly

A. Williams writes about her public walking tours, which combine historical knowledge about the sex tourism industry in Calgary with her understanding of her city's public and private spaces and communities, alongside issues of class and social inequality. Zoë Eddy's "The Day Angela Died: Imagining Violence and Reclaiming Indigeneity through Collaborative Performance" recounts the author's creation of a live-action role play event designed to allow participants to engage with the stories of Indigenous women who have been disappeared or murdered. Lastly, Lindsay Garcia, Helis Sikk, and Jose Roman's essay, "There Have Always Been Apocalypses: *Queer Apocalypse Solutions* for Liberation and Survival," considers their innovative Queer Apocalypse Solutions "art-life project," which merges performance art with community engagement and support.

CHAPTER ONE

RED CARPET RADICALS
Public Feminist Scholarship and the Sexism|Cinema Film Series

By Michael Borshuk, Don E. Lavigne,
Elizabeth A. Sharp, Jessica E. Smith,
Dana A. Weiser, and Allison Whitney

In 2015, two years before Hollywood A-listers exposed widespread sexual harassment and violence in the film industry and as the Black Lives Matter movement continued to gain momentum, a group of interdisciplinary feminist scholars at Texas Tech University created a community-based film series entitled "Sexism|Cinema" in partnership with a local movie theater, The Alamo Drafthouse, Lubbock. Since the series' inception, the programming team has grown to include the six co-authors, all current faculty members, although Smith was a doctoral student for the first three years of her participation. The purpose of Sexism|Cinema was to carve out a public space in which to engage in meaningful discussions about sexist, racist, classist, heterosexist, and other representations, attitudes, and behaviors that stand in opposition to social justice in our conservative city in West Texas. The particular impetus for the series was a nationally and internationally newsworthy sexist incident at an off-campus white fraternity party at our university.[1] The series was originally conceptualized as a single, semester-long event, but the response from the community was so enthusiastic, and the quality of our discussions so high, Sexism|Cinema became an established community touchstone. In February 2020, we marked our fifth anniversary, and not only do we expect to continue for the foreseeable future, but our model is also being adopted at other institutions.[2]

Flowing from bell hooks' and others' work,[3] the idea for the series emerged from a desire to make activism and pedagogy about draining and upsetting topics fun and engaging. Viewing a film collectively and discussing the work immediately afterwards offers opportunity for entertainment while also recognizing that the media plays a significant role in shaping cultural attitudes, beliefs, and social scripts with regard to gender, sexuality, race/ethnicity, nationalities, and socioeconomic class.[4] In the general set-up of our series, the film is introduced along with a brief rationale for the series, the film is shown, and a discussion follows the film. In our experience, a large portion of the audience (~ 75%) typically stays for the discussion, and of them, there is a roughly equal number of university-affiliated people (including faculty and staff but mostly students) and community members. Our promotional strategies include posters on campus and at community venues like coffee shops (designed by Sharp's former graduate student John Purcell), email notifications through campus systems, social media postings (Facebook, Instagram, Twitter), in-class announcements to students, advertising on the cinema's website, and occasional interviews and features on local television news as part of their arts programming. In order to prime audience members for the type of discussion we would like to stage, we provide attendees with a handout that provides information about the speaker, potential questions to ponder during the film, suggested readings, and a film fact, often pertaining to on- and off-screen inequities. Speakers are encouraged to share their work in the suggested readings of the handouts and the programming team have also included their academic work in the handouts. After each film the invited speaker offers brief remarks (five to seven minutes) and is tasked with offering an accessible and engaging entrée into selected feminist issues raised in the film. The speaker then leads the discussion, with occasional input from the series organizers. We have found this multi-pronged, graduated strategy to be quite successful in keeping the audience in the theater for an engaged discussion.

Multiple feminist frameworks inform the direction of the film series.[5] We draw on postmodern feminism and critical race feminism, emphasizing the racist, classist, and sexist conditions of wider social structures in which the films are embedded.[6] We also draw on post structural feminisms and queer feminist thought in order to trouble gender, racial, and sexual binaries.[7] We carefully integrate these theoretical concerns into our methodology by avoiding jargon and keeping the discussion approachable for a non-academic audience. When selecting films, we have one primary rule: the film must feature a woman-identified protagonist. We deploy a variety of strategies to ensure that the films we choose appeal to a broad constituency, making the series an attractive entertainment option for all members of our community. While we often present films that consciously challenge gender hegemony and employ progressive thematic and formal strategies, we also present problematic, even anti-feminist films, as a means of optimizing our opportunity for critical analysis.

One of the benefits of engaging with public feminism is that the theoretical and historical frameworks we develop in the academy can become immediately tangible when we try to put them into practice. In the case of Sexism|Cinema, our job as programmers is to identify appropriate films and consider how they will inspire and frame public discussions, but the practicalities of commercial exhibition often make the inequities of the media industry, and of society in general, highly visible. We are mindful to select films which feature protagonists with diverse sexualities, races/ethnicities, socioeconomic statuses, and nationalities. Among the top 100 domestic grossing films in 2019, 40% of films featured a female protagonist. However, of the top 100 films, 70% of major women characters were White, 18% were Black, 6% were Latina, and 5% were Asian.[8] Thus, while the number of women-identified protagonists hit a historic high, stark racial inequities persisted on-screen. With this disparity in mind, and the intersectional theoretical grounding of the series, we are intentional in showcasing and celebrating the art created by and featuring individuals with diverse identities. We also are intentional in choosing varied types of films, and have screened blockbusters (e.g., *Mad Max: Fury Road, Clueless, Easy A*), independent films (e.g., *Support the Girls, The Fits, Tangerine*), foreign-language films (e.g., *A Girl Walks Home Alone at Night, Blue is the Warmest Color*), and repertory titles (e.g., *Foxy Brown, Fame, Adam's Rib*). A full list of our past screenings and repository of handouts are available at sexismcinema.com. We select expert speakers from expansive disciplinary backgrounds and have featured faculty from the humanities, social sciences, legal studies, visual and performing arts, as well as staff from the LGBTQIA office, Student Counseling, and the Center for Campus Life. Author Becky Aikman and film directors Sean Baker, Andrew Bujalski, Julie Cohen, and Brigitta Wagner, have also participated in the series.

A strength of our interdisciplinary collaboration is that it synthesizes our diverse theoretical, methodological, and historical perspectives, while also energizing and informing our pedagogy. Allison Whitney brings her scholarship in feminist film history, genre, and exhibition studies to contextualize the norms of production, reception, and representation at the time of each film's production. Meanwhile, mediating public discussions has informed her teaching on film reception and audience studies. Dana Weiser was trained in Social Psychology and Human Development and Family Sciences, and as a social scientist, Sexism|Cinema has allowed her to see film as a site of analysis for sexuality and gender research. Further, it has allowed her to better utilize film in the classroom to discuss portrayals of gender and sexualities through the lens of social science research as well as the far-reaching influence of media for reinforcing gendered sexual scripts. As a literature professor, Michael Borshuk brings his critical reading practice to the film screenings, asking audience members to think past surface-level messaging. The series has had reciprocal benefits for his teaching, reminding him to engage students on the open-ended ways that culture and society interact, and the ideological stakes of textual interpretation. As a Classicist, Don Lavigne's work generally encompasses dusty old texts from the earliest period of ancient Greece, but he has found that his students are much more likely to understand critical gender theory when applying it to films, which in turn equips them for complex and careful textual analysis. Elizabeth Sharp, director of Women's and Gender Studies and professor in Human Development and Family Sciences, integrates her research on gendered family roles with her Sexism|Cinema programming. The film series has expanded her knowledge of the humanities, enhanced her activism and public feminist scholarship, deepened her relationships with colleagues from multiple disciplines, and encouraged other scholars and students within her program to engage critically with film. As a writer, Jess Smith's work explores gendered power dynamics and, more specifically, representations of intimate partner violence in popular media. Working on Sexism|Cinema has given her deeper insight into the way film in particular shapes attitudes toward gendered stereotypes. In her work as a professor of literature, she has been able to integrate film and scripts more readily into her classroom work based on the knowledge she's gained as a member of Sexism|Cinema.

We believe that this series has helped to create a sustained critical dialogue about gender, race/ethnicity, and sexuality in our conservative, small city, providing an engaging and open community space for feminist conversation. Below we describe in further detail our process in selecting three films and the critical feminist dialogues in which we engaged during the screenings. While space prohibits us from discussing each of the nearly fifty films we have screened, we chose to unpack these specific films in order to highlight three contrasting types of movies and the resultant discussions.

BRIDESMAIDS

The decision to screen 2011's *Bridesmaids* was driven by our desire to attract a broad audience. In addition, as the last film in the Spring 2016 season, we anticipated that there would be a fair amount of interest from students seeking extra-credit at the end of the semester. The film's mainstream success and popularity made it an excellent choice for filling the theater with audience members drawn from both our campus and civic communities (our screening sold out the 120-seat theater and several people had to be turned away). This screening was so successful, in fact, that when we embarked upon a collaboration with the University of Texas at Austin to help scholars there establish a Sexism|Cinema program, we chose this film as the pilot (again, it was very well attended).

At first blush, it may seem odd that a feminist film series would choose to screen a film produced and directed by men; however, the film was written by two women, Kristen Wiig (who also has the leading role) and Annie Mumolo. Our key criteria in choosing films is that they feature a woman-identified protagonist, so the film fit our baseline criterion. That it was written by women was also desirable, especially given the dearth of female voices in contemporary comedy and film, in general.[9] Nonetheless, a film featuring a largely female cast does not in and of itself imply a feminist message, much less a feminist ideology. Critics have been mixed in their assessment of the film on these grounds. As Ruth Franklin argued, the film offered an important intervention in the male-dominated world of Hollywood and simply seeing a comedy written by and starring women could be a political act showcasing audiences' desires for more women-driven productions. However, as Franklin points out, the film's basic narrative and characterization hew closely to patriarchal conceptions of femininity.[10] Rather than discount such ambiguities, we embraced them in order to generate a conversation about the issues raised, including discussions about social roles in contemporary America, the idea of internalized sexism, the role of women in comedy, and the role of women as writers, producers, and directors, among other pertinent issues.

The buzz generated by the film and its wide popularity make it an excellent vehicle for attracting audience members who might not otherwise attend screenings within a feminist film series, a fact that motivated our decision to feature it. By choosing a film so prominent in the public consciousness, we were able to engage our audience in a fairly sophisticated investigation of the controversial issues that swirled around the release of the film. We say "fairly sophisticated" because we are sensitive to the disparate levels of engagement with criticism (filmic, feminist, sociological, etc.) that members of our audience bring to the theater.

In the particular case of *Bridesmaids*, at our initial screening in the Spring of 2016, our featured speaker was one of our co-organizers, Elizabeth Sharp, who, among other things, researches single women, weddings, and new wives. To lighten the mood and integrate some fun into the serious business of analyzing the film, Sharp wore her wedding dress and invited several other colleagues to help her lead the discussion, all of whom were dressed in bridesmaid's gowns. This disarming move both relaxed the audience, who were not inclined to see this as an angry feminist intervention (a trope all too common in popular culture), and made the discussion an event to be anticipated. One of the attractions of the Alamo Drafthouse is that they often feature "movie parties" where patrons are encouraged to dress in costume and otherwise engage with the film, so it was both in keeping with the culture of the cinema to have a "wedding party" leading the event, while also framing a discussion grounded in feminist scholarship in an accessible way. The discussion addressed themes ranging from cultural variations in wedding rituals, the racial and class dynamics in the film, particularly regarding Maya Rudolph's casting as the bride, the wealth disparities among the main characters and how this influenced their experiences as members of the wedding party, and the social pressures on women to conform to heteronormative expectations. Given that one of the main goals of the series is to facilitate public discussions which model reasoned, critical, feminist analysis, the screening of *Bridesmaids* was a huge success, as it reached a very large and less ideologically aligned audience. Therefore, we see this screening as not only a model for using mainstream films to reach audiences who might not otherwise come to a feminist film series, but also a key aspect of our approach to accessibility and public engagement.

SAVING FACE

In Fall 2017, we screened *Saving Face*, a 2004 romantic comedy written and directed by Alice Wu, featuring a Chinese-American protagonist in a lesbian relationship. This choice reflects a number of the priorities in our programming, where we ensure that each season features women of color and LGBTQIA2S+ characters. We also draw upon a wide range of film genres, both to attract audiences with variable tastes, and because so many genre conventions and tropes are rooted in gender dynamics. During our planning meetings for Fall 2017 we noted that we had yet to feature an Asian-American protagonist, and while we were aware of their significant underrepresentation in American cinema, the consequences of that deficit became evident as we tried to identify an appropriate film. *The Joy Luck Club* (Wayne Wang, 1993) seemed an obvious choice, allowing us to address both an immigrant and multi-generational narrative, but it was not available for theatrical distribution. Problems with exhibition rights and print availability come with the territory in film programming, but in this case, nearly all the films we considered were unavailable. This logistical barrier demonstrated in vivid terms the implications of underrepresentation—when there are so few films featuring Asian-American women as main characters, the normal contingencies of exhibition help to perpetuate the problem. We were very glad to learn that *Saving Face* was available, but while the film had a glowing reception from critics and festival audiences during its initial release, it was now only accessible as a 35mm film print. Fortunately, due to the Alamo Drafthouse's emphasis on cinephilia, nostalgia, repertory titles, and cult movies, the cinema is both equipped and staffed for 35mm projection, but the fact that we needed to overcome so many industrial and technological hurdles to show such a film demonstrated the practical barriers to diversity in film culture.

In many respects, *Saving Face* is the kind of film one might expect to find in a feminist film series: an independent production written and directed by a Chinese-American woman, drawing upon the familiar tropes of romantic comedy but with the twist of a queer couple, extensive Chinese-language dialogue with subtitles, emphasis on an immigrant community, and produced as a result of Wu's winning a screenwriting award from the Coalition of Asian Pacifics in Entertainment. We quite deliberately program independent and less-seen films alongside their mainstream counterparts both to give those films more exposure and to draw upon audience expectations to cultivate discussion. *Saving Face*'s generic properties as a romantic comedy—the "meet cute," the sassy best friend, the humorous but poignant family relationships—each provided an opportunity to talk about gender, race, and sexuality in terms that were at once familiar and novel to our audiences. For example, the film's sub-plot where the main character Wil (Michelle Krusiec) learns that her widowed forty-eight-year-old mother (Joan Chen) is pregnant, only to then discover that the father is a much younger man (Brian Yang), allowed for a conversation about how women's desire is (or isn't) represented in mainstream culture, particularly for women over forty. On our handout, we primed our audience to think about how the film frames female sexuality in the video store scene, where the mother accesses two genres offering narratives of desire: Chinese soap operas and pornography.

One of the things that became evident during our screening of *Saving Face* is that it is a crowd-pleaser. Comedies are usually funnier with an audience as one benefits from the contagion of laughter, and much of the film's charm depends on that collective experience. Indeed, one of the benefits of using public screenings as a venue for discussion is that the experience of watching with an audience highlights not only collective pleasure, but also audience discomfort, and in many cases moments of crowd resistance inspire the most productive conversations. While *Saving Face* is in many ways a progressive text, our screening it thirteen years after its initial release created enough historical distance to highlight how much the discourses on gender, race, and sexuality have shifted in the last decade. For example, our audience raised questions about the representation of Wil's friend and neighbor Jay (Atoh Essandoh), a Black man who fulfils the "sassy best friend" role one expects of a romantic comedy, but who also becomes a foil for Wil's mother's racist attitudes. Audiences noted the awkwardness of these scenes, and pursued a conversation about the complexities of race and representations, in that the film both calls out racism within the Chinese-American community, but at the same time doesn't entirely undermine it. Meanwhile, as our handout question on heteronormativity suggested, the film's end-credits scene, where the lesbian couple are celebrating their forthcoming marriage, and where the final joke is a question about when they will be having a baby, offers what appeared to a 2017 audience as an affirmation of heteronormative relationship models. The ensuing discussion was emblematic of a useful function of showing films from varied historical periods, for even though it was just over a decade from the film's production, there had been significant social and legal changes concerning marriage equality, as well as queer critiques of traditional family structures. At the same time, it is fair to note that as a 2004 film, *Saving Face* was released in the midst of the legal and cultural struggle for marriage equality in the United States, so its allusion to marriage as a relationship goal was more radical in its time.

SIXTEEN CANDLES

The Alamo Drafthouse brand is committed to screening independent and foreign-language, or just generally more obscure, films that otherwise might not make their way to a mainstream cineplex, or in our case, to West Texas. The Alamo also regularly hosts movie parties, including sing-alongs, quote-alongs, and other similarly nostalgia-driven events. When we screened the 1984 John Hughes megahit *Sixteen Candles*, some attendees arrived assuming our event would be in this vein. At times, the tension was palpable between our intended feminist critique of the film and the benevolent place the movie still maintains in many viewers' memories.

One of the reasons we selected this film to screen was to interrogate the nostalgic glow *Sixteen Candles* entices. For what, exactly, are audiences nostalgic when we watch this film? How does it play racism, sexual violence, and toxic masculinity for laughs, and how might we have let these elements go unquestioned in the service of "humor" in years past, particularly within the coming-of-age teen comedy genre for which Hughes has long been so revered?

In a 2018 *New Yorker* article, Molly Ringwald reassessed her relationship to the three Hughes films she starred in—including

Sixteen Candles—in light of the #MeToo Movement. "Back then, I was only vaguely aware of how inappropriate much of John's writing was," she writes. "I was well into my thirties before I stopped considering verbally abusive men more interesting than the nice ones. I'm a little embarrassed to say that it took even longer for me to fully comprehend the scene ... when the dreamboat, Jake, essentially trades his drunk girlfriend, Caroline, to the Geek, to satisfy the latter's sexual urges."[11]

She refers here to a series of events at the end of the film, when the object of her character's affection, Jake (Michael Schoeffling), passes off his incapacitated girlfriend to a libidinous and awkward freshman, Farmer Ted (Anthony Michael Hall) (Indeed, Hall's character is so far from the film's social center, he is referred to only as "The Geek" by other characters in the film.) Let loose with a blackout-drunk senior, Ted shows her off to friends as a trophy, and photographs her body as a sexual memento. In the film's morning-after resolution, we are led to believe the two have had sex sometime in the night. Though she has little to no memory, Caroline (Haviland Morris) says to Ted that she has a "weird feeling" she enjoyed their sexual encounter. The entire sequence is meant to joke away the ethical implications of her absolute inability to consent.

In our discussion, we emphasized the transgression the film asks us to laugh at here: the school's most desirable woman stripped of the power to consent, and made sexually submissive to the whims of the most ungainly male representative. And yet, while the filmmakers ostensibly endorse the sexual assault, they also seem critically aware of Ted's questionable ethics, which they joke away with the tacked-on punchline about Caroline's purported "enjoyment." This film is merely one among many teen comedies from the 1980s that delight in toeing the moral line between male sexual entitlement and female vulnerability. We referenced, in our discussion, the boys-will-be-boys voyeurism of the "shower scene" in *Porky's* (Bob Clark, 1981), or a similar violation of consent in *Revenge of the Nerds* (Jeff Kanew, 1984), when the film's geeky protagonist seduces his dream girl while wearing a mask and fooling her into thinking she's partnered with her boyfriend. And did these permissive comedies of raucous male misbehavior have repercussions well beyond their own morally ambivalent representations? We screened *Sixteen Candles*, for instance, just six months after Brett Kavanaugh's confirmation hearings for the Supreme Court. We asked our audience to consider the question: How was the sexual violence of which Christine Blasey Ford accused Kavanaugh from the summer of 1982 related to the persistent rape scenarios that American filmmakers played for laughs around that same time? Indeed, Kavanaugh mentioned 1980s teen comedies in his testimony to contextualize his behavior—a rhetorical choice that itself motivated a public debate on the significance of these films.[12] How does our laughing at, or our waxing nostalgic for, these films contribute to a culture that laughs off violence against women?

This is not the only egregious and dangerous narrative choice in *Sixteen Candles*. We went on to discuss the notoriously racist representation of foreign exchange student Long Duk Dong (Gedde Watanabe), whose entrance into every scene is accompanied by a gong sound. He becomes sexually involved with a physically larger woman and the gender-role swapping is not only meant to play his femininity for laughs, but also makes it clear that the gender-role swapping is weird and othered. Any non-white characters in *Sixteen Candles* are othered, as with the "oily bohunk" Eastern European whom Ringwald's character's sister is marrying. Whiteness is centered, the default, and we asked our audience to consider this before the screening even began with a question on our handout, pointing out the frequent use of ethnic and racial stereotypes and jokes, including comments on whiteness. During our post-screening discussion, some members of the audience expressed feelings of tension, having expected a lighter experience attuned to sentimental attachment to the

1980s, and remarking on how seeing the film in the context of Sexism|Cinema made them revisit their past acceptance of racist and sexist humor. This conversation was generative and useful, as it gave our expert speakers even more opportunity to explore what, exactly, moviegoers feel attached to in this film, and what that feeling of attachment obscures.

FILM PUBLICS AND PUBLIC FEMINISMS

As our discussion of these three films shows, our goals for the Sexism|Cinema series are grounded in our intersectional feminist perspective. Through this methodology of embedding theory (through our handouts, speakers, as well as our choice of films) in organic and audience-centered discussions, we have been very successful in modeling respectful, critical explorations of issues of gender, race/ethnicity, class, and sexuality, among others. Our ongoing conversations with community members, colleagues, and students who have attended these events demonstrate that they are having an impact on their understanding of the range of social issues evoked in the films and our discussions. Furthermore, by having these public conversations, we have learned more about the issues themselves and how to create the kind of environments conducive to critical, public intellectual exchange.

As we were preparing this essay in the summer of 2020, a *New York Times* opinion piece by Racquel Gates entitled "The Problem With 'Anti-Racist' Movie Lists"[13] led us to reflect on our series and, in particular, on our commitment to fostering critical analysis of the depiction of gender, race/ethnicity, class, and sexuality in film. Gates suggests that the social awakening on racial injustice sweeping the nation and, indeed, the world has given rise to a series of ineffective interventions in the world of film. As groups and individuals try to engage with the Black Lives Matter and related movements, lists of "anti-racist" films have proliferated, reducing, in Gates' view, Black filmic achievement to a pedagogical exercise, especially for white people. While Black artists' work can be a vital component of social change, simply diversifying one's media consumption habits is not enough to effect cultural and political transformation. One of the things we believe is most successful about our series is that, while there is a prominent pedagogical aim, we do not simply provide a commodified package of films that gives the ticket holder unexamined access to the experience of "the oppressed." Of course, our series, as its title indicates, has at its center the critical assessment of the depiction of sexism and an analysis of the ways in which those representations interact with the sociopolitical sphere. However, the series is also, and has been from its inception, dedicated to showing how sexism is bound up with all other power structures and, therefore, cannot be adequately critiqued without a simultaneous critique of representations (or lack of representations) of other marginalized groups. In fact, the essence of an intersectional feminist commitment entails this very idea—all oppression is bound together in service to power. In attempting to both illustrate and critique this idea through the public and inclusive analytic discussion of a series of films whose single uniting factor is the existence of a main woman-identified protagonist, we have tried to create the kind of space wherein audience members can come to terms with the way gender, race/ethnicity, class, and sexuality contribute to our reality. We want our audiences to feel discomfort at the history of oppression and their roles in its propagation, while also understanding and appreciating the artistry and intellectual contributions of the films, to learn to use film to access the experience of others. Moreover, we want our audiences to develop a habit of critique that foregrounds the way those in power use gender, race/ethnicity, class, and sexuality to maintain their positions. Finally, we also want our audiences to learn that challenging these systems of oppression can be done in an accessible and engaging manner.

NOTES

1. Tyler Kingkade, "Texas Tech Investigating Frat For 'No Means Yes, Yes Means Anal' Sign," *The Huffington Post,* September 23, 2014; Elizabeth A. Sharp et al., "From Furious to Fearless: Faculty Action and Feminist Praxis in Response to Rape Culture on College Campuses," *Family Relations* 66, no. 1 (2017): 75–88.
2. In March 2020 our university and the Alamo Drafthouse closed due to the COVID-19 pandemic. We canceled screenings for April and May 2020 and hosted Sexism|Cinema virtually throughout the 2020–2021 academic year. We asked attendees to view the selected film on their own and then we conducted the conversation live on Zoom. While we were saddened to be apart, two positives came out of this transition to a virtual format. First, we were able to screen films we were unable to exhibit in the theater, including *The Joy Luck Club* and Disney's *The Princess and the Frog*. Second, in the virtual format we were able to invite more non-local speakers and broadened our community audience; indeed, family, friends, and colleagues from across the country were now able to join our lively Sexism|Cinema discussions.
3. bell hooks, *Teaching to Transgress* (New York: Routledge, 1994); bell hooks, *Reel to Real: Race, Class, and Sex at the Movies* (New York: Routledge, 1996).
4. hooks, *Reel to Real.*
5. John BK Purcell et al., "Lights, Camera, Activism: Using a Film Series to Generate Feminist Dialogue about Campus Sexual Violence," *Family Relations* 66, no. 1 (2017): 139–153.
6. Patricia Hill Collins, *Black Feminist Thought: Knowledge, Consciousness, and the Politics of Empowerment* (New York: Routledge, 1990).
7. Ramona Faith Oswald, Katherine A. Kuvalanka, Libby Balter Blume, and Dana Berkowitz, "Queering 'the Family,'" in *Handbook of Feminist Family Studies,* eds. Sally A. Lloyd, April L. Few, and Katherine R. Allen (Thousand Oaks, CA: Sage, 2009), 43–55.
8. Martha M. Lauzen, "The Celluloid Ceiling: Behind-the-Scenes Employment of Women on the Top 100, 250, and 500 Films of 2019," Center for the Study of Women in Television and Film, San Diego State University, 2020, https://womenintvfilm.sdsu.edu/wp-content/uploads/2020/01/2019_Celluloid_Ceiling_Report.pdf.
9. Martha M. Lauzen. "It's a Man's (Celluloid) World: Portrayals of Female Characters in the Top Grossing Films of 2019," *Center for the Study of Women in Television and Film*, San Diego State University, 2020, https://womenintvfilm.sdsu.edu/wp-content/uploads/2020/01/2019_Its_a_Mans_Celluloid_World_Report_REV.pdf.

10. Ruth Franklin, "You'll Laugh, You'll Cry, You'll Hurl," *The New Republic*, May 17, 2011, https://newrepublic.com/article/88547/bridesmaids-movie-judd-apatow-kristen-wiig-feminism.
11. Molly Ringwald "What about 'The Breakfast Club'? Revisiting the Movies of My Youth in the Age of #MeToo," *The New Yorker*, April 6, 2018, https://www.newyorker.com/culture/personal-history/what-about-the-breakfast-club-molly-ringwald-metoo-john-hughes-pretty-in-pink.
12. Wesley Morris, "In 80s Comedies, Boys Had it Made. Girls Were the Joke," *New York Times*, October 4, 2018, https://www.nytimes.com/2018/10/04/movies/brett-kavanaugh-80s-teen-comedies.html.
13. Racquel Gates, "The Problem With 'Anti-Racist' Movie Lists: Black Films Should Be Valued for More than What They Can Teach White Viewers about Race," *New York Times*, July 17, 2020, https://www.nytimes.com/2020/07/17/opinion/sunday/black-film-movies-racism.html.

WORKS CITED

Collins, Patricia Hill. *Black Feminist Thought: Knowledge, Consciousness, and the Politics of Empowerment*. New York: Routledge, 1990.

Franklin, Ruth. "You'll Laugh, You'll Cry, You'll Hurl." *The New Republic*, May 17, 2011. https://newrepublic.com/article/88547/bridesmaids-movie-judd-apatow-kristen-wiig-feminism.

Gates, Racquel. "The Problem With 'Anti-Racist' Movie Lists: Black Films Should Be Valued for More than What They Can Teach White Viewers about Race." *New York Times*, July 17, 2020. https://www.nytimes.com/2020/07/17/opinion/sunday/black-film-movies-racism.html.

hooks, bell. *Teaching to Transgress*. New York: Routledge, 1994.

hooks, bell. *Reel to Real: Race, Class, and Sex at the Movies*. New York: Routledge, 1996.

Kingkade, Tyler. "Texas Tech Investigating Frat For 'No Means Yes, Yes Means Anal' Sign." *The Huffington Post*, September 23, 2014. https://www.huffpost.com/entry/texas-tech-no-means-yes-fraternity-phi-delt_n_5865606?guccounter=1&guce_referrer=aHR0cHM6Ly93d3cuZ29vZ2xlLmNvbS8&guce_referrer_sig=AQAAAM3BCeuCSX0UCkyWDXsfI2ALH0Ymmmld290GA7R3Be6dTQZJxK0M_P-bvPptlE14VSvPJFBx-y9emIoCM2ubipwXRZDQbKU5UXsx5YilNa9-W1SGdeMbltOxBuk4keI3QJn1HcKrTA8UvArQCvYQ8yfkT7u3sCp002nYXClhMw8e.

Lauzen, Martha M. "The Celluloid Ceiling: Behind-the-Scenes Employment of Women on the Top 100, 250, and 500 Films of 2019." Center for the Study of Women in Television and Film. San Diego State University, 2020.

https://womenintvfilm.sdsu.edu/wp-content/uploads/2020/01/2019_Celluloid_Ceiling_Report.pdf.

Lauzen, Martha M. "It's a Man's (Celluloid) World: Portrayals of Female Characters in the Top Grossing Films of 2019." Center for the Study of Women in Television and Film. San Diego State University, 2020. https://womenintvfilm.sdsu.edu/wp-content/uploads/2020/01/2019_Its_a_Mans_Celluloid_World_Report_REV.pdf.

Morris, Wesley. "In 80s Comedies, Boys Had it Made. Girls Were the Joke." *New York Times*, October 4, 2018. https://www.nytimes.com/2018/10/04/movies/brett-kavanaugh-80s-teen-comedies.html.

Oswald, Ramona Faith., Katherine A. Kuvalanka, Libby Balter Blume, and Dana Berkowitz. "Queering 'the Family'." In *Handbook of Feminist Family Studies*, edited by Sally. A. Lloyd, April. L. Few, and Katherine. R. Allen, 43–55. Thousand Oaks, CA: Sage, 2009.

Purcell, John BK, C. Rebecca Oldham, Dana A. Weiser, and Elizabeth A. Sharp. "Lights, Camera, Activism: Using a Film Series to Generate Feminist Dialogue about Campus Sexual Violence." *Family Relations* 66, no. 1 (2017): 139–153.

Ringwald, Molly. "What about 'The Breakfast Club'? Revisiting the Movies of My Youth in the Age of #MeToo." *The New Yorker*, April 6, 2018. https://www.newyorker.com/culture/personal-history/what-about-the-breakfast-club-molly-ringwald-metoo-john-hughes-pretty-in-pink.

Sharp, Elizabeth A., Dana A. Weiser, Donald E. Lavigne, and R. Corby Kelly. "From Furious to Fearless: Faculty Action and Feminist Praxis in Response to Rape Culture on College Campuses." *Family Relations* 66, no. 1 (2017): 75–88.

CHAPTER TWO

"LAS DOCTORAS"
A Podcast for Community Empowerment

By Cristina Rose and Renee Lemus

We met in the play yard at a parent/toddler class with our children. Like destiny waiting to unfold, a chance meeting turned into a creative partnership. We quickly realized we were both *profesoras* with PhDs, teaching in Women and Gender Studies departments at California State Campuses. We had similar backgrounds and immediately connected. We began to work together through a community organization we were both a part of to integrate our m/othering with our career goals. From there, our relationship grew organically and the ideas started to flow. Now, two years in, we are celebrity podcasters who host hour long episodes twice a month marketed through our Instagram and Patreon and available through our website and "wherever you listen to your podcasts." We let intuition guide our topics and our guests are *comadres* in the field. Though we both love teaching and have a deep passion

Figure 2.1: *Las Doctoras*: Photography by Carolina Adame.

for our academic fields, we also feel very strongly we want to create a life that is conducive to centering our m/otherwork and our creativity in addition to our scholarly and pedagogical pursuits. It was from that perspective, that *Las Doctoras* Podcast and our creative partnership was born and now thrives. The podcast is our collaborative scholarship.

When we shared our work as professors with friends and community members, a comment we often received was, "I would love to sit in on your class." Additionally, we realized a traditional academic career trajectory did not feel right to us. We wanted the flexibility and freedom to be there for our children as much as possible, to play a central part in their education. We see our parenting work as activism and liberatory work. Thus, we wanted our creative work together to both serve as a bridge between the ivory tower of academia and the communities to which we belong as well as give us the space to do scholarly work in a non-academic setting. *Las Doctoras* podcast is the manifestation of our efforts to make accessible the feminism that we teach as *profesoras* in the university. Our goal is to create public accessibility, thus, empowering our communities, dismantling the ivory tower, and sharing our creative partnership as a means of personal and collective growth.

EMPOWERING OUR COMMUNITIES

Our communities, that is, communities of color rooted in Latinx ancestry, need more public feminisms. Evidence of this is obvious to us in the responses we receive to our work: the need for naming and the space for critical thinking. We have witnessed such a deep hunger in our communities, hunger and thirst for language, a language to name and articulate the experiences of our people. Be it fellow mothers or parents, or those in our Latinx/Filipinx communities, they know the familiar face of oppression, of sexism, racism, xenophobia, and heteronormativity. They know

Figure 2.2: *Las Doctoras* Logo: Another genius move of Renee. Logos are hard work to create an image that encapsulates our message! Branding for us is about owning our work. It is citing our work while questioning capitalism at the same time. We are very intentional with everything we do including creating this logo invoking the spirit of La Virgen.

how it lives and breathes in their lives. Yet, those feelings and knowledge are often gaslit, dismissed, shot down, or otherwise silenced in the face of white supremacist, patriarchal, and capitalist power.

As academics, we have been afforded time and space to philosophize, to theorize, to critically think about and analyze these power systems in addition to experiencing the pain of the weapons and abuse of these same power systems. Thus, we have learned the language to name these oppressions, to call them out, to fight back against those who seek to silence. This is not to say that academia is the only place this language of oppression is created because, of course, we understand that oppressive language is in the air we breathe within white-male culture; rather, we recognize the privilege in having the time to have had these nuanced conversations within academia. Furthermore, in a society founded in hierarchy, education allows us ground to stand on, gives us authority. Many people of privilege—white, male, class, educated privilege—see us and listen to us because of our doctorates. We become authority figures simply with a "PhD." Altogether, this education and authority are a privilege. And, so we take on these roles with a deep sense of responsibility. We have witnessed people in our communities seek validation for these experiences of white and male oppression, which we have been able to name, in part, with the language we learned in academia. Yes, that was sexist; yes, that was racist; yes, you experienced sexual harassment. It is through that validation and naming that we see our communities being fed and feeling empowered. This empowerment is evident when students find liberation in naming and distancing themselves from diet culture and white-male savior beliefs as well as simply asking the questions they always feared to ask, such as, "may I ask you about my period?"

We realized through our work as educators and as mothers who experienced home births and are surrounded by birth workers, nowhere is validation more needed than in conversations on shame and menstruation. In our "Flow Series" during our founding season, we addressed this shame directly. We spoke with educators in reproductive justice; we named, through the lens of feminism, the language of oppression, and we shared our own personal stories as well. The feedback we received confirmed for us how profoundly our communities needed these discussions; moreover, that the podcast was allowing our followers to speak out and up about their own stories of shame and menstruation. One comment we received on our podcast on Apple Podcasts, reads:

"Having cafecito ...
If you need to get woke about your flow, your body, your experiences, all of it listen to this! This podcast is a gift in my life."

Another follower commented:

La Cultura Cura
Las Doctoras is such a beautifully rich and heartwarming program. It's so inspiring to listen to these funny and visionary women, that with their interviews and stories, bring to life- my childhood, memories of my first teachers, mi mama y las abuelitas, nuestra cultura and everything I hold dear. Thank you Las Doctoras for your work, for naming patriarchal, misogynist "norms" and validating the experience of woc. Each episode weaves in collective struggles and resilience and I just think it's lovely medicina ♥♥♥

And, finally, another comment:

AmaZing & much needed conversations
Thank you both for these amazing episodes full of not only education. but giving us words to explain things that as a woman, a brown immigrant woman I have not been able to put Into context especially in the greater world outside my emotional experiences. I love listening & I wish I could sit there and have these conversations with you. Your episodes fill my mind & my heart.

Providing the podcast as a container for these themes, such as life-giving menstrual blood in our cultural context, gave this listener and continues to give all of us language for our collective experiences, at times, unnamed in our communities.

Because these conversations were held within a safe space to speak to collective trauma for Latinx women of color, quite naturally, we came into conversation about another theme made invisible in our community: colorism. Later on in our first season, we found ourselves in conversation with a community member tackling the issue of colorism within her own family history and structure. This *comadre* had written a piece and published it in the *New York Times.* Our discussion gave her the space to speak to past trauma and present grief as well as the work she was doing to celebrate darkness in her family. This episode gave us the space to name internalized racism as well as the generational wounds of colonization in our families' lives. It is because of this episode, perhaps, that we received the attention of Irina Gonzalez of *Oprah Magazine.* In her piece, "The Best Spanish and Latino Podcasts for Learning—and Laughing," Gonzalez writes, "Although fairly new, this podcast is definitely worth mentioning thanks to the host's frank conversations surrounding race, gender, sexuality, and reproductive justice ... In other words? They are seriously knowledgeable. Catch recent episodes on colorism and parenting as well as spirituality and social justice."[1] At this point in our podcast career, we were only one month into our work. This shout out really confirmed for us how much our conversations resonated with our communities. We had already been wondering about why academia was not serving everyone in our families; this public recognition of our feminist and decolonial podcast helped us understand that these conversations *should* and needed to be taken out of the ivory towers to empower ourselves and others to work toward ending all forms of oppression, that this was a part of our life work as *Las Doctoras*. Basically, our *chisme* (gossip) sessions recorded as podcast episodes created a bridge between our academic discourse and our families and friends outside of academia.

Figure 2.3: *Las Doctoras* and Tequila: The format we bring to the podcast is an invitation into a casual conversation with us. Images of us in our homes is important to us. We bring the spirit of our ancestors, the spirit of hospitality to our listeners and to our scholarship. Photograph credit: Carolina Adame.

DISMANTLING THE IVORY TOWER(S)

We recognize the ways in which academia perpetuates gatekeeping and a hierarchical approach to information. We believe to truly dismantle the ivory tower, academia cannot be the only space where these conversations on the dismantling of white supremacist, capitalist, cis-hetero-patriarchy take place. There needs to be spaces outside of the university where we can create dialogue, theorize, and conceptualize about our lived experiences. Thus, our podcast is such a space, a space to have critical conversations in a more accessible modality.

Feminism is our way of being. Asking questions is our job. We are both *profas* of gender studies in the CSU system, and we've spent our whole lives living into feminist principles such as equity for all, respect and celebration for femininity/the femme within all beings, relational ways of existing in the world, and sharing the wisdom of our femtors such as Ana Castillo, Cherrie Moraga, and, of course, Gloria Anzaldua. We are *Las Doctoras*, a feminist podcast advocating for the multiply oppressed. Yes, that's what we do. We complicate "normalized" conversations about race, gender, and class; it's our activism, our action. We bring these same complications to our teaching too by sharing the *Las Doctoras* podcast as well as the skills of questioning. Asking questions and creating space for questions are our way of processing our *feminista/activista* work in our classrooms. Each of these pieces implements our theories and studies and thoughts and hopes.

And, yet, we know the work of public feminisms goes deeper, we call for the deconstruction of the institutions that raised us. As professors and mothers, we situate our work in a critique of this country's borders and its history of colonization that perpetuated violence, slavery, and genocide on our ancestors.[2] We also engage in the reclamation of the borders our families occupy in spiritual and energetically divided spatialities, particularly in a pedagogical framework entrenched in systems of power meant to sustain a patriarchal, white supremacist, capitalist ideology in our children. Unlike our parents or grandparents, we have a choice; we can participate in all these steps of reclamation, paths of *conocimiento*. We may have the freedom to survive and thrive. We can resist, liberate, and celebrate. And, this means, in the words of Audre Lorde, no longer using the master's tools to dismantle the master's house.[3]

This growing level of understanding around what dismantling looks like brought in new waves of conversation on the podcast: Spirituality and Activism, Femtorship, and the centering of *Latinx Parenting* as well as *Chicana M/otherwork*. In one of our most popular episodes, we explore the topic of spirituality and social justice. We have witnessed that the conversation around spirituality is too often focused solely on positive thinking or the idea of love and light. We feel, as well as other scholars and thinkers, that this is a narrow focus and does not take into consideration the structural inequalities at play. Spiritual rhetoric often fails to acknowledge the barriers involved in accessing spiritual resources or modalities. We call out the apolitical and ahistorical grounding of particularly white spiritual spaces. We also recognize that we are not the first to be calling this out, and give credit to the other scholars and practitioners who are doing work in this area, including Rachel Ricketts. We dive deep into how we have been thinking about this topic for a long time and ultimately try to articulate the need for more complexity and nuance when discussing spirituality. In the episode, we bring the image of birth into the conversation, reflecting on how active labor involves rest. Altogether, we call for the need to have spirituality be grounded in social justice, and for social justice work to integrate spiritual practices as self-care.

Many followers also commented on our episode on Femtorship. In this episode, we interview Lucha Arevalo and Jovita Murillo Leon, two fellow academic *muxeres* doing amazing work in education, public policy, and public health respectively. In the interview with our guests, we talk about the importance of mentorship or as Lucha calls it "femtorship." We also discuss our intentions and investments in academia as grounded in our love for our communities, and in our feeling of responsibility to give back to those we can mentor. Jovita and Lucha each talk about the obstacles they had to overcome in navigating the, often toxic, space of academia, and how their research speaks to their own experiences in higher education.

Finally, in our episodes with *Latinx Parenting* and *Chicana M/otherwork*, we address the dismantling of binaries associated with parenting and activism as well as academia. In our interview with *Latinx Parenting*, we talk with Leslie Arreola Hillenbrand and Lizeth Toscano, the founders of *Latinx Parenting*. Our conversation brought up so many topics including generational trauma, mother wounds, gender roles, and more. We shared with our guests how their work has helped us to heal and create more conscious approaches with our children and our own parents that take into consideration our cultural values and the systemic power dynamics at play. Our main takeaway from our conversation: Parenting with nonviolence creates a modality by which we can begin to see children as full human beings that need our love, compassion and guidance to realize their full potential as individuals and equals. As Lizeth points out, parenting models rooted in domination and violence come from colonization,

> they don't come from the inherent goodness of our ancestry. Peaceful parenting was ours at one point. Because of slavery and racism our parents had to adapt to a cruel and hard world, and to make good children was to obey. [They thought] if I did not discipline my child, then the master was going to discipline my child.

In other words, domination was normalized through multiple colonial power constructs like racism, patriarchy, and gender binaries, as well as through the idea of the parent child relationship as hierarchical in nature. Domination is first normalized in the home between parent and child often using violence and abuse so that all other power dynamics rely on similar violent approaches in order to exhibit authority and maintain power. If we truly want to dismantle all structures of oppression, we must begin in the home by reimagining the parent/child dynamic outside a paradigm of domination.

SHARING OUR CREATIVE PARTNERSHIP

Shortly after meeting and recognizing our magic, our friendship grew and we realized in addition to having similar life goals in terms of our career trajectories and in our approaches to motherhood and family and in our passion for social justice, we desired to work together in a deeper capacity. A Creative Partnership. Founded on

Figure 2.4: *Las Doctoras*, Frida, and Chavela: Inspired by a photograph of Frida Kahlo and Chavela Vargas, we wanted to capture their playfulness, their connection, their freedom, their strength. Frida continues to inspire us to create our own reality. Photograph by Carolina Adame.

our joy of working together and energized by the friendship we have built; we are grounded in the present and able to visualize a future together. We check in regularly to keep the love of our conversation, and, of course, we can't help but talk about gender and race.

We hope the transparency of our creative partnership through our *Las Doctoras* platform serves as an innovative method to share all that we have learned in our academic and personal journeys. The rigors of academia, the challenges of parenting, and the profound work of relationship—these all contribute to our schooling. And, all of it is a daily investment of time and energy. Transparency like this takes raw vulnerability. In each episode of our podcast, sometimes with the help of some tequila, we dive into raw vulnerability as we talk about our own personal flow and birthing stories, in our discussions on body politics when it comes to fat shaming and diet culture, and finally, in our purpose as *semillas de nuestra abuelas.*

The episodes that particularly come from this powerful vulnerability, showcasing our partnership, are our flow and birth stories. In the episode "Dr. Renee's Flow and Birth Story," our episode description states, "we hear Dr. Renee tell the story of her journey with her flow and all the things she learned along the way that led her to having a home birth, and a birth center birth." She shares,

> In this journey the lesson I learned the most was how little I knew about my body and how much work it took for me to find comprehensive information about my body. This all tells me that this is a larger problem when other people who menstruate and birth do not have access to comprehensive information. Ultimately, I had two beautiful births and I am very grateful, but the entire journey had led me to want to work toward reproductive justice.

This empowered voice that details intimate moments around body and birth is only met with equal strength in the episode "Dr. Cristina's Flow and Birth Story." Our episode notes state:

> Her story is so powerful in that she is so vulnerable in telling us so much about what was going on in her life that was impacting her relationship to her flow. Her story culminates with the birth of her child, and concludes with Renee and Cristina discussing the importance of these stories. We reflect on wanting to normalize positive birth experiences, and how much this idea plays a part in the work we do. You will learn so much about Cristina and she should be applauded for her raw vulnerability in bringing her story to light.

Cristina speaks to this directly when she states,

> In reflecting on the story of my relationship with my body and my moon cycle (period), I realize that I can clearly see a distinction before and after I turned thirty. At thirty, I moved into a home and farm with other women; I was a part of women's circles regularly; I began a PhD program in Women's Spirituality. I believe that I can thank, in particular, the wisdom I gained from women of color birth community as well as in my own experience giving birth. It has been a long, labyrinthine journey to be real, and reflecting on the journey brought up a lot of sadness and anger for me. I know I am not alone, and I share my story in the hopes that it encourages our listeners. Body awareness and moon celebrations are a part of my life now, and my community inspires this in me!

These conversations only deepen as we move into topics around Body Politics and Birth Control as well as Fat Shaming and Diet Culture.

And, then, of course, we bring this creative partnership into our parenting. In our episode on "Semillas de las Abuelas," you hear us talking about the healing power of writing a book and how healing is a part of our intention in writing a book that brings together our collection of recipes, celebrations, songs, and stories of our grandmothers. But, it's also more than that. It's a book that is also about integrating a way of being, a way of living, and a way of knowing that honors the history and ways of our ancestors, our *Abuelas*, scarred by the wounds of colonization while giving us a way to heal those wounds. This is about grounding our everyday lives in a deep spiritual connection to our ancestors so that we may recognize the oppressive social dynamics by which we live, and allow ourselves and our children to survive and thrive in spite of them, and then push back on these forces as we work toward liberation.

CONCLUSION: "BRINGING YOU CONVERSATIONS ON RACE, GENDER, SEXUALITY, SPIRITUALITY, REPRODUCTIVE AND SOCIAL JUSTICE"

We are *Las Doctoras*. Two scholars/mothers/writers/*muxeres*, seeking to give voice to our communities, deconstruct the oppression in academia, and simply enjoy our friendship with all its joy and curiosity. Dr. Renee Lemus and Dr. Cristina Rose host a podcast in which we discuss issues of reproductive justice, social justice, motherhood, sexuality, race, and gender. We bridge our scholarship as academics with our experience as Latinas, mothers, daughters, partners, and women to speak to the nuances and complexities of those intersecting identities. This is us. Bringing you conversations on new, intersectional, and interdisciplinary perspectives on public feminisms through a popular podcast. Celebrating three years of us in 2021, we now have over 3500 Instagram followers, a Book Club featured on #fiercebymitu, and finally, have created a Writing to Our Ancestors online course.

Moving forward, our focus, guided by our ancestors, is to step further into spirituality and sexuality. Then too, we want to tackle toxic masculinity. As we do so, we think of our children and future ancestors. There is a lot of trauma and shame as well as joy and passion in the lives of those we teach and mentor and love. We hope to be able to eventually incorporate our students and own children into our work more directly. Maybe as guests on our podcast! Simply, we want to find a nice work, homelife balance that fulfills us and our vision for a more equitable future for our children, our students, and the next seven generations.

NOTES

1. Irina Gonzalez, "These Are the Best Spanish and Latino Podcasts for Learning and Laughing," *Oprah Magazine*, October 6, 2020, https://www.oprahmag.com/entertainment/g28834390/best-spanish-podcasts/.
2. Gloria Anzaldua, *Borderlands/La Frontera* (San Francisco: Aunt Lute Books, 1987).

3. Audre Lorde, "The Master's Tools Will Never Dismantle the Master's House," in *Sister Outsider: Essays and Speeches* (Trumansburg, NY: Crossing Press, 1996), 110–114.

WORKS CITED

Anzaldua, Gloria. *Borderlands/La Frontera: La Nueva Mestiza*. San Francisco: Aunt Lute Books, 1987.

Gonzalez, Irina. "These are the Best Spanish and Latino Podcasts for Learning- and Laughing." *Oprah Magazine*, October 6, 2020. https://www.oprahmag.com/entertainment/g28834390/best-spanish-podcasts/.

Lorde, Audre. "The Master's Tools Will Never Dismantle the Master's House." Essay. In *Sister Outsider: Essays and Speeches*, 110–114. Trumansburg, NY: Crossing Press, 1996.

CHAPTER THREE

FROM CLASSROOM TO PAVEMENT
Creating a Walking Tour of Calgary's Historic Sex Trade Industry

By Kimberly A. Williams

I confess: I love a good walking tour. I suppose this comes from having lived my entire life in or near several popular tourist-destination cities. Indeed, walking tours have long been integral to how I've absorbed the layered cultures and various histories of even my own many adopted hometowns over the years, so it makes perfect sense that each time I (re)visit a new city, I make it a point to include at least one walking tour in my adventures. I try to go beyond the surface, seeking out themed tours on, say, Newport's Black history, the working-class feminists of London's East End, the cemeteries of New Orleans, or even a haunted walk through Calgary's storied Inglewood neighborhood here in southern Alberta. I like to walk the streets and breathe the air while learning from an engaging guide about hidden histories, subversive politics, forgotten events—all the good stuff that the mainstream narratives tend to leave out. And I'd always had in the back of mind that, when I finally settled in the city that would be "home" in this vagabond academic life of mine, I'd create and offer a historical walking tour of my own. About what, I had no idea, but because my research and teaching interests have always been guided by where I live, or, more specifically, by what's missing in the *stories told about* where I live, I knew my feminist curiosity about that place (wherever it may be)—its rhythms, its people, its energies, its concerns, and engagements—would reveal itself in due course.

I was right, and this chapter will describe the process by which I, a white settler, a queer feminist killjoy,[1] and a WGSS professor trained in intersectional feminist praxis, critical masculinity studies, and transnational feminist activisms, transformed a single course-based field trip into a popular historical walking tour of Calgary's still-robust adult consensual sex trade industry.

CALGARY'S HIDDEN HERSTORY

One crucial story that's missing from our city's narrative about itself is that its premier tourist attraction, the one-hundred-year-old Calgary Stampede,[2] has long been a popular sex tourist destination.

From almost the moment I arrived here back in 2009, I began hearing from my students that the annual Stampede is the locus around which Calgary's still-robust adult consensual sex industry swirls. They told me that cis and trans women from all over western Canada come to Calgary to work during these (in)famous ten days every July, often making enough money to more than cover next year's university tuition.

But could I corroborate the anecdotal with actual evidence? And, assuming I could, for exactly how long had all this been going on?

I wanted to know more.

Figure 3.1: Highway signs link the city inextricably with its annual rodeo and western heritage. Photo by the author.

So, I began researching in earnest the history of Calgary's consensual adult sex industry. What I quickly learned was that although much research had been done on histories of the sex trade in other Canadian cities,[3] very little is known about Calgary's sex trade. Although historian David Bright skirts the topic, his central focus is on the early days of the Calgary Police Service (CPS).[4] The work of journalist James H. Gray (1971) and that of historian Judy Bedford (1981) are the only formally published histories of our city's sex industry to date. Branding Calgary "the booze, brothel, and gambling capital of the far western plains,"[5] Gray's chapter in a book about red light districts in Canada's prairie cities offers a snapshot of the relationship between alcohol consumption and prostitution in Calgary from the start of colonial settlement in the late nineteenth century through the 1920s. Bedford's article more narrowly focuses on the CPS's efforts between 1905 and 1914 to eradicate prostitution from the city.[6] If you know where and how to look, it is glaringly obvious that those efforts were wildly unsuccessful.

Research the world over demonstrates that wherever there are large groups of single, itinerant men, there is a thriving sex trade.[7] Research also indicates that, to use Gray's terms, where there is booze, there are brothels, because those industries have historically supported each other. As a settler colonial outpost established in the 1860s explicitly to facilitate the European settlement of the Canadian west, then, nineteenth-century Calgary seems to have had all the conditions to support a robust sex industry. The new city's population was comprised in those early days almost entirely of white settler men. First came members of the brand-new Northwest Mounted Police (NWMP),[8] sent by Canada's first prime minister, John A. MacDonald, to erect Fort Calgary on the banks of the Elbow and Bow Rivers. After the NWMP came ranchers and loggers and construction workers, followed by the railmen who connected the east and west branches of the Canadian Pacific Railway through Calgary in 1881. Then came the miners and quarrymen, followed a decade or so later by machinists and merchants, and lawyers and doctors, for a total population by 1900 of roughly 4000 people. Estimates suggest, however, that there were no more than five hundred white settler women living in or near Calgary during this time. In short, Calgary's rapid settlement in the late nineteenth century by largely "unattached young men in the prime of life,"[9] in combination with its wild whiskey trade,[10] would seem to have offered opportunities aplenty for the city's consensual adult sex industry to thrive.

Drawing on three main types of archival sources (private documents, municipal/provincial records, and historical newspapers), I discovered that there's been an erasure of the people, politics, and places of our city's consensual adult sex industry. This will likely come as no surprise to anyone reading this chapter. After all, the lives, experiences, and contributions of any people who are not white settler cismen are largely (still) erased from what passes as mainstream history.

His story.

And since early Calgary's adult consensual sex workers, always already stigmatized, were overwhelmingly white women,[11] any evidence of their important economic, political, and cultural contributions to a growing colonial outpost city have been doubly erased. This happened both discursively and literally. Discursively, their lives and experiences were disappeared in favor of a more positive narrative that ranks Calgary, Canada's fourth-largest city and the center of the country's multi-million dollar oil and gas extraction industry, as among the world's best places to live.[12] To facilitate this obliteration, the sex workers who helped settle and build this thriving urban center in this land where the vast Canadian prairies meet the Rocky Mountain foothills are reduced to jokes and wild stories, while all evidence of today's consensual adult sex industry is either ignored or rendered invisible. Most people whom I tell about my research claim to have no idea that there are sex workers still living in Calgary! And more broadly, in terms of legislation and policy, sex workers are (still) criminalized, marginalized, and vilified.[13]

This discursive erasure of Calgary's adult consensual sex industry has also been facilitated by a literal erasure with the goal of "urban renewal." Strolls (i.e., physical areas in a city where street-based sex workers sell their services by literally walking up and down a sidewalk[14]) have been moved from the city center to its outskirts. Nineteenth-century buildings, where sex workers used to live, have been mostly torn down or renovated. Entire city blocks, Calgary's historic strolls, have been paved over to create parking lots or build high-rise apartment buildings. These gentrification projects have been particularly obvious in the East Village and Victoria Park, two of Calgary's oldest residential neighborhoods that, for a whole host of reasons, fell into disrepair and disrepute in the mid-twentieth century.[15] But because they border Stampede Park, the 137 acres adjacent to Calgary's downtown core that has been home to Calgary's annual rodeo and western heritage festival since the 1890s, whipping these neighborhoods into "family friendly" shape has for some decades now been a linchpin of that influential organization's redevelopment plan, in partnership with the city-managed Calgary Municipal Land Corporation.

I teach at a small, undergraduate liberal arts university, so if I'm ever to produce scholarship, my courses must necessarily and explicitly inform my research, and vice versa. As such, I've chosen to use several of our "shell" courses (which enable faculty to teach one-off special topics without going through the cumbersome administrative process of proposing an entirely new course) to advance my research program. I used one of these, WGST 3309: *Contemporary Feminist Debates,* during Winter 2015 to investigate with my students the long history and complex politics of Calgary's thriving sex industry within the context of several local and trans/national conversations that were swirling around us at the time. These included:

- The problematic conflation of adult consensual sex work with sex trafficking[16] which became particularly salient here in Calgary in the mid-2010s when Operation Northern Spotlight attracted the attention of the local mainstream media.[17]
- The ongoing debates between criminalization, legalization, and decriminalization of sex work,[18] which were dragged front and center in Canadian politics in the mid-2010s when the Supreme Court of Canada deemed Canada's prostitution laws unconstitutional and asked the federal government to go back to the drawing board.[19]
- The poor social, economic, and political status of women in our city, largely as a consequence of Alberta's heavily male-dominated extractive economy.[20]

- And the long, celebratory ramp-up to what was in 2017 the forthcoming 150th anniversary of Canadian Confederation, which was not only ignorant of Canada's settler colonial past, but also largely devoid of women as historical actors.

Given the complexity and interrelatedness of these larger conversations and debates, my goals for the course were similarly nuanced. Through content, discussions, and activities, I hoped that, by the conclusion of the course, successful students would have learned the following about Calgary's robust sex industry:

- Its political, social, and economic dynamics.
- The role(s) of our city's first white settlers in creating and sustaining it.
- The different perspectives and approaches of the City of Calgary to its still-robust sex trade industry, the CPS, and relevant community-based service organizations.
- The locations (both historical and contemporary) of Calgary's major brothels and strolls, and how and why they came to be located in those parts of our city.
- The differences between criminalization, legalization, and decriminalization, and why Canadian sex workers generally advocate the latter.

This seminar-style course intended for advanced WGSS students met once each week for three hours. Most of our meetings were spent discussing whatever reading, watching, and/or listening we'd done in preparation for class that week. We had several guest speakers during the semester, including the head of the CPS Counter Exploitation (a.k.a. "Vice") Unit, feminist scholar Shawna Ferris, and a few people from the two community-based organizations here in Calgary, Shift Calgary and Reset Society, that offer services to sex workers.

But since this course was about our city, about what happens every day down the street from our campus, I wanted us to get out of our classroom and onto the pavement. I wanted us to go out and breathe the air, to walk the very streets we were talking about, to stand where factories and machine shops had once dominated the banks of Calgary's two working rivers. To see where buildings had once stood, where people had once lived, to understand when and why entire neighborhoods had been torn down in the service of neoliberal capitalism and gentrification and what—and who— had taken their place. So, I decided to create a walking tour and put it on the syllabus. From the beginning of the semester, I made sure that my students knew that we'd be meeting downtown one afternoon in March during our regular class time. They knew to clear their calendars and get out their warmest toques and coats and gloves, because we were going outside! When the day finally arrived, we walked around the city center for well over three hours, enjoying a rare warmish March day and stopping periodically to weave the threads of local history into a global present.

Toward the end of the semester, one of my students suggested that such a tour would offer an intriguing and refreshingly feminist counterpoint to the events typically on offer during Calgary's annual Stampede Week each July. So, two years later, during Canada's year-long national/ist celebration of the 150th anniversary of Confederation, I began offering it as "Booze, Broads & Brothels" to the general public.

ABOUT THE TOUR

Offered several times each spring and summer since 2017 (with forced time off in 2020 and 2021 as a result of the COVID-19 global health pandemic), the walking tour promotes awareness of the poor social, economic, and political status of women in our city and contravenes conventional popular and legal narratives by amplifying the voices of sex workers and highlighting their agency, as opposed to their victimization and/or criminality.[21] In Calgary, this has meant drawing attention to our city's past and present sex workers as laborers within an ongoing settler colonial project that revolves around resource extraction and, thus, favors white, cisgender men as wage earners. I offer the tour by pay-what-you-can donation, and all proceeds go to Shift Calgary, our city's only agency offering a harm-reduction and rights-based approach to support people in the sex industry.

Although the tour has changed quite a bit since I first offered it to my students (it's significantly shorter, for example), its bones have remained essentially the same in both content and concept. I lead participants along a three-kilometer circular route to relevant sites throughout Calgary's downtown core, past the corporate headquarters of some of the world's most recognizable energy companies, including Shell, Enbridge, Halliburton, Husky, and Kinder Morgan, along the banks of the Bow River, and through the East Village, only to end up almost where we started, about a block from Calgary City Hall.

MARKETING STRATEGIES

I first launched the walking tour in May 2017 with a website that I keep updated with links to Eventbrite and Facebook event pages announcing individual tour dates each year. I also designed a marketing postcard (see Figure 3.2) that I used some professional development funds to have reproduced in bulk.

I travel every day with a stack of postcards in my bag so that I can leave a few in strategic locations around town: in the lobbies of hotels, restaurants, and coffee shops along the route, at doctors' offices, at massage clinics, and so forth. I also always bring a stack with me when I attend local events. Calgary has lots of little neighborhood street fairs and festivals as well as bigger, citywide events like the annual Pride Parade, and all of these are great opportunities to distribute and/or leave stacks of postcards

Figure 3.2: Postcard for walking tour.

for likely tour-goers. Each year in early May, as people here are thinking ahead to what they'll do when it finally stops being cold, I make the rounds of feminist, queer, and other related social justice-oriented community organizations and ask permission to leave a stack of postcards in their public waiting areas.

I also use social media, particularly my Facebook and Twitter accounts, to publicize each upcoming tour date, which I link to an Eventbrite listing so that I can keep track of registrants and, so I don't have to handle cash on-site, collect the pay-what-you-can donations for Shift Calgary in advance. I allow a maximum of just twelve people on any given tour in order to keep each event small and personalized; too many people means that the group can easily get split up at traffic lights. A larger group makes it less feasible for me to customize the tour when attendees ask questions along the way.

In keeping with my professional and political goal of mobilizing the freedom and privilege of tenure to advocate for social justice outside my classrooms, in and for the community in which I live and work, I also give talks on this research at as many community events as possible. I've been invited to present for large groups at Calgary's monthly Nerd Night, the Chinook Country Historical Society, the Calgary Public Library, and even a local chapter of the Rotary Club, to name just a few. These events, to which I always bring a stack of postcards, have frequently led to requests for private tours for groups of friends or colleagues.

SUBVERSIVE FEMINISM

Broadly, my objective for the tour is to make visible the invisible—but still very salient—histories, people, and places of Calgary's early days of colonial settlement. I subversively deploy an anti-racist, intersectional feminist lens to, as this volume's call for papers described, "advance public knowledge and help maintain a vibrant cultural awareness of issues affecting" women and other gender and sexual minorities in Calgary. Our city's contemporary adult consensual sex trade industry is inextricable from its settler colonial history, and I weave into my tour narrative the many ways in which that past is still very much present in the lives and experiences of marginalized and oppressed people in our city.

Figure 3.3: Langevin Bridge, c. 1915; photo courtesy of the Glenbow Archives.

As we make our way to the various parking lots and street corners that comprise the tour stops, I use prints of archival photos from the local Glenbow Museum Archives to show tour-goers the relevant buildings and other structures that used to be on/near that geographical location and explain what happened there in connection to the sex industry. For example, when we stop on the paved path underneath what is now called Reconciliation Bridge, a modern steel structure across the Bow River that connects the East Village to the Bridgeland neighborhood, I show tour-goers an archival photo (see Figure 3.3) of its ancestor (from two bridges ago) to discuss how the racket of carriage wheels and horse hooves on the wooden platform was the cause of a 1906 municipal by-law that still makes it illegal for livery (and modern taxi) drivers to transport sex workers to their clients, and vice versa.[22]

Throughout the tour I deploy local author Aritha van Herk's understanding of Alberta's early white settlers as "mavericks"[23] to encourage tour-goers to question this celebratory designation by remembering that these much-lauded fur traders, railway workers, coal miners, loggers, NWMP and CPS officers, businessmen, ranchers, and, later, oil men were not only the primary instruments of Canada's settler colonial project, but also the clients of Calgary's sex workers. As I remind my audience: a thriving sex industry can never exist without demand! It follows, then, that it's unfair to focus only (and usually negatively) on the suppliers without also considering the crucial role of their clients.

This is why I challenge tour-goers to think about our city's early sex workers as "mavericks," too.[24] In a growing city full of (mostly) unattached working-class white settler men with nothing to do in their free time but gamble and drink, the services provided by Calgary's sex workers in the late nineteenth and early twentieth centuries were crucial to maintaining social cohesion and stability. In those early years of settlement, Calgary's annual population growth far outstripped the size of its fledgling police service,[25] and the CPS depended on the city's sex workers to keep morale high and crime low while also acting as informants; gleaned from gossip and pillow talk with their wide variety of clients from all echelons of Calgary society, they provided valuable intelligence about who was doing what, where, when, and why.

Our city's early sex workers also contributed mightily to the local economy. As employers in their own right, they hired construction workers, domestic servants, contractors, landscapers, and other laborers as needed—including other sex workers. They also ordered home furnishings, used laundries, and regularly purchased food, dry goods, and other supplies from local merchants. Like van Herk, whose chapter on the women who settled Alberta is called "Ladies, Women, and Broads,"[26] and in the tradition of feminist reclamation of words that are meant to be sexist insults, weaponized to devalue particular ways of being in the world, my tour names the sex workers who helped establish our city as "broads" in the unapologetically feminist sense of the word: courageous and savvy entrepreneurs who suffered no fools. Indeed, a stop at my favorite parking lot (Figure 3.4), likely the

Figure 3.4: Still from video [available in online edition] of the author leading a tour at the likely former home site of Pearl Miller, Calgary's longest-working madam. Photo courtesy of the author.

former site of the home of Pearl Miller, Calgary's longest-working madam,[27] enables me to make this point quite clearly.

Relatedly, I work throughout the tour to contravene popular and legal narratives by highlighting the agency of Calgary's early sex workers.[28] I help tour-goers to reframe our local debate in terms of socioeconomic status and economic migration in order to more accurately reflect the realities of sex workers' lives,[29] both then and now. In Calgary, this means drawing attention to our city's historic and contemporary sex workers as (mostly) poor and working-class laborers within an ongoing settler colonial project rooted in extractive industries that continue to heavily favor white, cisgender men as wage earners. It is here that I surprise most tour-goers with the publicly available but little-known fact that brings Calgary's past home to roost in its present: the political, social, and economic status of women in our city is abysmal. Calgary is consistently ranked among the worst urban areas in Canada for women to live based on several factors, including: high rates of men's violence against women, lack of political representation, poor sexuality education, and a massive gender wage gap resulting from occupational segregation that leads to the feminization of poverty.[30] Since women and other gender and sexual minorities in our city have long been able to make significantly more money selling sex than working in Alberta's male-dominated extraction-based industries of logging, mining, ranching, and, more recently, oil and gas, "Is it any wonder," I ask my audience, "that some would choose sex work?"

Because most of my information about the individual women I talk about on the tour comes from court proceedings and CPS arrest records, I am also careful to frequently remind my audience that criminality was socially constructed based on laws written by elite, white settler men.[31] Most of the women whose arrest records I've read in the CPS archive were apprehended not for selling sex, which was illegal in Victorian Calgary, but for "vagrancy."[32] This was a common offence levied against people who, in the opinion of the arresting officer, were unable to give an account of themselves and seemed to be in the wrong part of the city, at the wrong time, doing something they shouldn't be doing. In 1913, for example, a woman named Effie Brady was apprehended by a CPS constable because

> she was wandering around the streets of the city after dark in the company of a woman who had been convicted of being an inmate of a house of ill fame and she accosted and spoke to nine or ten different men in a period of twenty minutes.[33]

Was Effie Brady actually a sex worker? We'll never know for sure. But that's why my tour is also about how "proper" notions of Victorian femininity were policed in early Calgary. It's about how the settler women who lived here were disciplined for being (apparently, but not always) unmarried and for choosing to make a living in a way that gave them a measure of social and economic independence in a cisman-dominated city.

I point out, too that little seems to have changed in the way police and other arms of the justice system treat sexual assault survivors—especially when they are presumed to be sex workers. To illustrate this point, I recount the story of Della English, who was apprehended in 1910 by a Calgary police constable name Burt Fisher because he believed her to be walking where and when she shouldn't have been, without the companionship of a man, and in the company of another woman who was a known sex worker. Having no technical charges to lay against either woman in that moment, he escorted English's friend home and then attempted to rape English, reasoning (according to her later testimony) that it wasn't such a big deal because "others had been there before."[34]

Sixteen-year-old Della English fought Constable Fisher off that night, but he managed to succeed in his quest several nights later, after which she had the wherewithal and courage to report the incident. Transcripts of the subsequent magistrate-led inquiry, rife with slut-shaming and victim-blaming and imbued with racism, read as if they were typed up yesterday rather than more than one hundred years ago; thoroughly without evidence, most witnesses concurred with suggestions by Fisher's legal counsel not only that English's "general reputation" was as "a common street walker," but also that she at least associated, if not actually lived, with members of Calgary's Chinese community.[35] Although Constable Fisher was fired from the CPS, it was for punching his boss, Chief Thomas Mackie, during an argument about his treatment of English, not explicitly for raping her.

I also draw tour-goers' attention to the fact that because the identities of sex workers usually became known only *after* they encountered the criminal justice system, my knowledge of the women whose experiences I discuss as part of the tour is gleaned largely from CPS arrest records. As such, we will never know about the lives of the majority of Calgary's sex workers, past or present.

And because *buying* sex wasn't illegal in Victorian Calgary, clients are virtually impossible to identify with any certainty, as well. What this all means is that the white settler sex workers whom I talk about on my tour were by no means the only sex workers working in Calgary during the late nineteenth and early twentieth centuries; they were, however, among those who got arrested and/or were so well-known that they've become the subjects of animated myths and tall tales or,[36] in the case of Rosalie Newgrass, notorious as Calgary's first-ever murder victim.[37]

Newgrass is the only sex worker included on my tour who wasn't a white settler. I mention her during our first stop as part of my statement to tour-goers that Calgary's adult consensual sex industry is a settler colonial invention; it is a direct result of Ottawa's post-Confederation nation-building policies that encouraged white settlement in the hereditary and current homelands of the Niitsitapi (the Blackfoot Confederacy: Siksika, Piikani, and Kainai) and the Îyârhe Nakoda (Chiniki, Wesley, and Bearspaw) and Tsuut'ina Nations. As such, the white settler sex workers whose experiences are part of my tour were also participants in and beneficiaries of Canada's ongoing settler colonial project. To drive home this point, I come back to Newgrass about ninety minutes, or two and a half kilometers, later as the only racialized sex worker on the tour—and the only one to have been murdered while doing her job. This, I argue, was not a coincidence.

I discuss the circumstances of Newgrass's murder as well as the toxic combination of misogyny and white supremacy that undergirded the 1889 trial of her murderer, white settler William "Jumbo" Fiske, in light of the recent finding that Canada has committed a genocide against Indigenous women, girls, and Two Spirit people.[38] I ask tour-goers to think about what happened to Newgrass in light of the Final Report of the National Inquiry into Missing and Murdered Indigenous Women and Girls, which argues quite convincingly that, as part of this genocide, settler narratives here in Canada have for five hundred years devalued and dehumanized Indigenous women to the point that it has become socially acceptable to commit violence against them with impunity. As I tell my audience, Newgrass's experience is a perfect example of this discursive process that has had devastating material consequences. This Cree teenager was far from home (Calgary is not in Cree territory), and to this day, nothing is known about why or how she got here, or about what or who she may have left behind. Instead, all that is known about her is that she was Calgary's first murder victim. This maps what is known about Newgrass quite neatly onto the "D" for dead in what journalist Duncan McCue calls the "WD4 Rule." According to McCue, when Indigenous people appear in mainstream cultural narratives, it is as some combination of the four "Ds ": drumming, dancing, drunk and/or dead or, for Indigenous men, "W" for warrior.[39] As feminist scholars have long pointed out, though, Indigenous *women* must also contend with the settler colonial trope of the drunken, promiscuous "squaw,"[40] which, according to the gruesome logic of white supremacy, both proves their worthlessness and justifies white settler violence against them.[41] Newgrass was Indigenous and a sex worker in a time, place, and space in which both were the subject of fervent policing and surveillance with the goal of eradication. Lastly, even though Fiske turned himself into authorities and confessed to the murder, the first trial's jury acquitted him. Although the magistrate declared a mistrial, and Fiske was eventually retried, convicted, and sentenced to fourteen years hard labor, I explicitly link that first all-white, all-male jury's unwillingness to convict one of their own in the murder of a young Indigenous woman to the many more contemporary acquittals that have since occurred—most infamously of Raymond Cormier for the 2014 murder of Anishnaabe teenager Tina Fontaine[42] and Saskatchewan rancher Gerald Stanley for shooting Colten Boushie (Cree) in 2016.[43]

WHAT'S NEXT?

I began offering "Booze, Broads & Brothels" because I was looking for a way to get past my immediate post-tenure funk,[44] some way to use my position and privilege in the service of my community, some way to make my feminist scholarship matter in a more tangible way. I'm both surprised and delighted to report that since I began offering the walking tour in May 2017, several dozens of people have taken it, and some two hundred more have heard me talk about it and my research in various contexts around town—and even at the Canadian Embassy in London in 2017 as part of the annual conference of the British Association of Canadian Studies. Additionally, by offering the tour roughly once every three weeks from May through September since 2017—with forced time off during 2020 and 2021 as a result of the COVID-19 global health pandemic—I've raised just over $2,500 CAD (roughly $1870 USD) for Shift Calgary.

With an eye toward the future, my next step is to develop a GPS-enabled self-guided audio walking tour app so that interested audiences can take the tour on their own, using their smartphones. My hope/plan is that tour-goers will pay a small fee to download the app, and that fee would then be donated to Shift Calgary. Further, modelled after Laurie Bertram's work on the history of Toronto's sex industry, I'm also planning to build a permanent, internet-based public history archive for my research, thus providing scholars, students, service providers, policymakers, and the general public free online access to the information provided on the tour. It remains important for Calgarians to acknowledge and accept the robust history of our city's sex industry in order to understand the complex roots of its dogged longevity. Relatedly, my hope is to contribute a critical, self-reflexive approach to the ongoing revitalization of Victoria Park and the East Village by providing locals and tourists with a fun, engaging way to explore Calgary's oldest neighborhoods through the people who used to live, work, and play here.

NOTES

1. Sara Ahmed, *Living a Feminist Life* (Durham, NC: Duke University Press, 2017).
2. Kimberly A. Williams, *Stampede: Misogyny, White Supremacy, and Settler Colonialism* (Winnipeg: Fernwood Publishing, 2021).
3. For example, see Laurie Bertram, "Canada's Oldest Profession: Sex Work and Bawdy House Legislation," University of Toronto Libraries, exhibit, 2016, https://exhibits.library.utoronto.ca/exhibits/show/bawdy; Kerri Cull, *Rock Paper Sex: The Oldest Profession in Canada's Oldest City* (St. John's: Breakwater Books, 2017); Daniel Francis, *Red Light Neon: A History of Vancouver's Sex Trade* (Vancouver: Subway Books, 2006); Shawna Ferris, *Street Sex Work and Canadian Cities: Resisting a Dangerous Order* (Edmonton: The University of Alberta Press, 2015); Leslie Jeffrey, "Prostitution as a Public Nuisance: Prostitution Policy in Canada," in *The Politics of Prostitution: Women's Movements, Democratic States, and the Globalisation of Sex Commerce*, ed. Joyce Outshoorn (New York: Cambridge University Press, 2004), 83-102.
4. David Bright, "Loafers Are Not Going to Subsist Upon Public Credulence: Vagrancy and the Law in Calgary, 1900-1914," *Labour/Le Travail* 36 (Fall 1995): 37-58; David Bright, "The Cop, the Chief, the Hooker, and Her Life," *Alberta History* 45 (Autumn 1997): 16-26.
5. James Gray, *Red Lights on the Prairies* (Toronto: Macmillan of Canada, 1971), 150.
6. Judy Bedford, "Prostitution in Calgary 1905-1914," *Alberta History* 29, no. 2 (1981): 1-11.
7. Kamala Kempadoo, Jyoti Sanghera, and Bandana Pattanaik, *Trafficking and Prostitution Reconsidered: New Perspectives on Migration, Sex Work, and Human Rights* (New York: Routledge, 2015); Laura Augustin, *Sex at the Margins: Migration, Labour Markets and the Rescue Industry* (London: Zed Books, 2007); and Na Young Lee, "The Construction of Military Prostitution in South Korea during the US Military Rule, 1945-1948," *Feminist Studies* 33, no. 3 (2007): 453-481.
8. The NWMP are now known as the Royal Canadian Mounted Police (RCMP), or "Mounties."
9. Gray, *Red Lights*, x.
10. James Gray, *Booze: When Whiskey Ruled the West*, 2nd ed., Western Canadian Classics (Saskatoon: Fifth House, 1995).
11. According to Gray (*Red Lights*, 158), local officials contended that there were Black, East Asian, and white women working as sex workers in Calgary. Based on what I've unearthed so far from the arrest records in the CPS archives, however, Calgary's sex workers in the late nineteenth and early twentieth

centuries were overwhelmingly white settler women. For a wide variety of socio-cultural reasons, this demographic shifted gradually during the late-twentieth century so that in recent decades Calgary's visible sex workers are mostly racialized women. I say more below about the demographics of Calgary's early sex workers.

12. Sarah Rieger, "Calgary Ranked World's 5th Most Livable City by Economist Intelligence Unit," *CBC News*, September 3, 2019, https://www.cbc.ca/news/canada/calgary/calgary-livable-cities-index-1.5269432. I always ask, "For whom?" but that's a question I unpack in my forthcoming book on the Calgary Stampede.

13. Strictly speaking, selling sex for money, goods, or services is *not* illegal in Canada. However, all other related aspects of the sex trade industry are. These include: living off the avails of prostitution, advertising one's sexual services, operating a bawdy house, and buying sex. Sex worker rights advocates argue that the criminalization of these activities makes it essentially impossible for sex workers to do their jobs safely. For further info, see "Infosheet: Sex Work and Changes to the Criminal Code After Bill C-36: What Does the Evidence Say?," Canadian Alliance for Sex Work Law Reform, June 2015, https://sexworklawreform.com/infosheets-impacts-of-c-36/.

14. Susan McIntyre, "Strolling Away" (Department of Justice Canada, Research and Statistics Division, 2002). According to McIntyre's report, "[t]his constant movement was necessary historically because of the old Vagrancy charges," which, as I discuss below, the CPS used to apprehend anyone who was unable to provide a "satisfactory" account of where they were from, why they were in a given spot, and where they were headed (69).

15. Max Foran, "Coalitions and Demolitions: The Destruction of Calgary's East Victoria Park, 1960–1998," *Prairie Forum* 32, no. 1 (2007): 17–46.

16. Jo Doezema, *Sex Slaves and Discourse Masters: The Construction of Trafficking* (London: Zed Books Ltd., 2013) and Jyoti Sanghera, "Unpacking the Trafficking Discourse," in *Trafficking and Prostitution Reconsidered: New Perspectives on Migration, Sex Work, and Human Rights*, ed. Kamala Kempadoo, Jyoti Sanghera, and Bandana Pattanaik (New York: Routledge, 2015), 3–24.

17. This annual coordinated effort of law enforcement agencies working nationwide to quell sex trafficking continued despite the objections of sex worker rights groups across Canada that warned that the operation would infringe on the rights and safety of consensual adult sex workers. For more info, see: Saltwire Network, "RNC Defends Operation Northern Spotlight," *The Telegram*, October 18, 2017, http://www.thetelegram.com/news/rnc-defends-operation-northern-spotlight-156331/; Michelle Keep, "Police Need

to End Operation Northern Spotlight," *The Indy* (blog), November 2, 2017, https://theindependent.ca/2017/11/02/50527/; and "SWAN Vancouver | Operation Northern Spotlight," accessed September 30, 2020, https://www.swanvancouver.ca/northern-spotlight.

18. Chris Bruckert and Stacey Hannem, "Rethinking the Prostitution Debates: Transcending Structural Stigma in Systemic Responses to Sex Work," *Canadian Journal of Law & Society / Revue Canadienne Droit et Société* 28, no. 1 (2013): 43–63, https://doi.org/10.1017/cls.2012.2.

19. Sex workers and their allies argue that replacement legislation passed the next year, the Protection of Communities and Exploited Persons Act (PCEPA), is at least as restrictive as the old suite of laws, if not more so. See, for example, "Infosheet: Impacts of Sex Work Laws (PCEPA/C-36)," *Canadian Alliance for Sex Work Law Reform* (blog), May 12, 2017, https://sexworklawreform.com/infosheets-impacts-of-c-36/. See also Chris Bruckert, "Protection of Communities and Exploited Persons Act: Misogynistic Law Making in Action," *Canadian Journal of Law & Society / Revue Canadienne Droit et Société* 30, no. 1 (2015): 1–3, https://doi.org/10.1017/cls.2015.2.

20. Katherine Scott, "The Best and Worst Places to Be a Woman in Canada 2019" (Canadian Centre for Policy Alternatives), March 2019, accessed July 10, 2020, https://www.policyalternatives.ca/publications/reports/best-and-worst-places-be-woman-canada-2019.

21. Emily van der Meulen et al., *Selling Sex: Experience, Advocacy, and Research on Sex Work in Canada* (Vancouver: UBC Press, 2013); see also Ferris, *Street Sex Work and Canadian Cities*.

22. Bedford, "Prostitution in Calgary 1905–1914."

23. Aritha van Herk, *Mavericks: An Incorrigible History of Alberta* (Toronto: Penguin Canada, 2001).

24. Kimberly A. Williams, "Mavericks, Too," Sheri-D Wilson (blog), 2020, https://sheridwilson.com/yyc-pop/kimberly-a-williams/.

25. Bright, "Loafers," 40.

26. van Herk, *Mavericks*.

27. Gray, *Red Lights*, 181–182. See also Nancy Jo Cullen, *Pearl* (Calgary: Frontenac House, 2006).

28. van der Meulen et al., *Selling Sex* and Ferris, *Street Sex Work*.

29. Melissa Hope Ditmore et al., *Sex Work Matters: Exploring Money, Power, and Intimacy in the Sex Industry* (New York: Zed Books, 2010).

30. Scott, "The Best and Worst Places to Be a Woman in Canada 2019."

31. Joel Best, "The Constructionist Stance," in *Constructions of Deviance: Social Power, Context, and Interaction*, ed. Patricia A. Adler and Peter Adler (Belmont, CA: Wadsworth Cengage Learning, 2012), 105–8.
32. McIntyre, "Strolling Away." See also David Bright, "Loafers."
33. Quoted in David Bright, "Loafers," 49.
34. David Bright, "The Cop, the Chief, the Hooker, and Her Life," *Alberta History* 45 (Autumn 1997): 18.
35. Ibid., 20.
36. One of these was "Diamond Dolly," who earned her nickname and similarly sparkling reputation during the 1910s as a result of a unique advertising method that involved donning all her silks, feathers, and finery to parade a horse-drawn carriage back and forth along the east–west avenues of Calgary's central business district whilst shouting out to current and former clients by name. It should be noted, too, that the horse she borrowed to pull her rented carriage was widely rumored at the time to belong to Calgary's chief of police, Thomas English. Or perhaps it was the other way around? Gray, *Red Lights*, 165. See also "Diamond Dolly, 'Queen of Calgary's Fleshpots,'" *CBC. Ca.*, accessed January 17, 2021, https://www.cbc.ca/player/play/987142723901.
37. Lesley Erickson, *Westward Bound: Sex, Violence, the Law, and the Making of a Settler Society* (Vancouver: University of British Columbia Press for the Osgoode Society for Canadian Legal History, 2011).
38. National Inquiry, "Reclaiming Power and Place: The Final Report of the National Inquiry into Missing and Murdered Indigenous Women and Girls," National Inquiry into Murdered and Missing Women and Girls, June 2019, https://www.mmiwg-ffada.ca/final-report/.
39. Duncan McCue, "What Does It Take for Aboriginal People to Make the News?," CBC, January 29, 2014, https://www.cbc.ca/news/indigenous/what-it-takes-for-aboriginal-people-to-make-the-news-1.2514466.
40. For example, see Rayna Green, "The Pocahontas Perplex: The Image of Indian Women in American Culture," *The Massachusetts Review* 16, no. 4 (1975): 698–714; Rayna Green, "The Tribe Called Wannabee: Playing Indian in America and Europe," *Folklore* 99, no. 1 (1988): 30–55; Judith Logsdon, "The Princess and the Squaw: Images of American Indian Women in Cinema Rouge," *Feminist Collections* 13, no. 4 (1992): 13–17; Sarah Carter, *Capturing Women: The Manipulation of Cultural Imagery in Canada's Prairie West* (McGill-Queen's University Press, 1997); Elise M. Marubbio, *Killing the Indian Maiden: Images of Native American Women in Film* (Lexington: University Press of Kentucky, 2006); and Janice Acoose-Miswonigeesikokwe, *Iskwewak*

Kah' Ki Yaw Ni Wahkomakanak: Neither Indian Princesses nor Easy Squaws, 2nd edition (Canadian Scholars' Press, 2016).

41. The racist slur "squaw" is believed to be a settler mispronunciation of *esquao*, the Cree word for woman and has recently been reclaimed as empowering by some Indigenous women. Muriel Stanley Venne, "The 'S' Word: Reclaiming 'Esquao' for Aboriginal Women," in *Unsettled Pasts: Reconceiving the West through Women's History*, ed. Sarah Carter (Calgary: University of Calgary Press, 2005), 123–27.

42. Heather Conn, "Tina Fontaine," The Canadian Encyclopedia. Historica Canada, December 5, 2019, https://www.thecanadianencyclopedia.ca/en/article/tina-fontaine.

43. Joe Friesen, "Thousands Rally across Canada after Gerald Stanley Acquitted in Killing of Colten Boushie," *The Globe and Mail*, February 10, 2018, https://www.theglobeandmail.com/news/national/protests-across-canada-after-acquittal-in-boushie-death/article37931825/.

44. Kerry Ann Rockquemore, "I Got Tenure: Now What?," *Inside Higher Ed*, August 30, 2017, accessed September 28, 2020, https://www.insidehighered.com/advice/2017/08/30/introductory-advice-academics-who-have-just-become-tenured-essay; Nikole D. Patson, "How I Recovered from Tenure-Track Burnout," *Science | AAAS*, April 25, 2019, https://www.sciencemag.org/careers/2019/04/how-i-recovered-tenure-track-burnout.

WORKS CITED

Acoose-Miswonigeesikokwe, Janice. *Iskwewak Kah' Ki Yaw Ni Wahkomakanak: Neither Indian Princesses nor Easy Squaws*. Second Edition. Toronto: Canadian Scholars' Press, 2016.

Ahmed, Sara. *Living a Feminist Life*. Durham, NC: Duke University Press, 2017.

Augustin, Laura. *Sex at the Margins: Migration, Labour Markets and the Rescue Industry*. London: Zed Books, 2007.

Bedford, J. "Prostitution in Calgary 1905–1914." *Alberta History* 29, no. 2 (1981): 1–11.

Bertram, Laurie. "Canada's Oldest Profession: Sex Work and Bawdy House Legislation." University of Toronto Libraries, exhibit. 2016. https://exhibits.library.utoronto.ca/exhibits/show/bawdy.

Best, Joel. "The Constructionist Stance." In *Constructions of Deviance: Social Power, Context, and Interaction*, edited by Patricia A. Adler and Peter Adler, 105–8. Belmont, CA: Wadsworth Cengage Learning, 2012.

Bright, David. "Loafers Are Not Going to Subsist Upon Public Credulence: Vagrancy and the Law in Calgary, 1900–1914." *Labour/Le Travail* 36 (Fall 1995): 37–58.

——. "The Cop, the Chief, the Hooker, and Her Life." *Alberta History* 45 (Autumn 1997): 16–26.

Bruckert, Chris. "Protection of Communities and Exploited Persons Act: Misogynistic Law Making in Action." *Canadian Journal of Law & Society / Revue Canadienne Droit et Société* 30, no. 1 (2015): 1–3. https://doi.org/10.1017/cls.2015.2.

Bruckert, Chris and Stacey Hannem. "Rethinking the Prostitution Debates: Transcending Structural Stigma in Systemic Responses to Sex Work." *Canadian Journal of Law & Society / Revue Canadienne Droit et Société* 28, no. 1 (2013): 43–63. https://doi.org/10.1017/cls.2012.2.

Canadian Alliance for Sex Work Law Reform. "Infosheet: Impacts of Sex Work Laws (PCEPA/C-36)." May 12, 2017. https://sexworklawreform.com/infoshe ets-impacts-of-c-36/.

Canadian Alliance for Sex Work Law Reform. "Infosheets: Sex Work and Changes to the Criminal Code After Bill C-36: What Does the Evidence Say?" June 2015. https://sexworklawreform.com/infosheets-impacts-of-c-36/.

Carter, Sarah. *Capturing Women: The Manipulation of Cultural Imagery in Canada's Prairie West*. Montreal, Canada: McGill-Queen's University Press, 1997.

Conn, Heather. "Tina Fontaine." The Canadian Encyclopedia. Historica Canada, December 5, 2019. https://www.thecanadianencyclopedia.ca/en/article/tina-fontaine.

Cull, Kerri. *Rock Paper Sex: The Oldest Profession in Canada's Oldest City*. St. John's, NL: Breakwater Books, 2017.

Cullen, Nancy Jo. *Pearl*. Calgary: Frontenac House, 2006.

"Diamond Dolly, 'Queen of Calgary's Fleshpots'." CBC.Ca. Accessed January 17, 2021. https://www.cbc.ca/player/play/987142723901.

Ditmore, Melissa Hope, Antonia Levy, and Alys Willman. *Sex Work Matters: Exploring Money, Power, and Intimacy in the Sex Industry*. London: Zed Books, 2010.

Doezema, Jo. *Sex Slaves and Discourse Masters: The Construction of Trafficking*. London: Zed Books, 2013.

Erickson, Lesley. *Westward Bound: Sex, Violence, the Law, and the Making of a Settler Society*. Vancouver: University of British Columbia Press for the Osgoode Society for Canadian Legal History, 2011.

Ferris, Shawna. *Street Sex Work and Canadian Cities: Resisting a Dangerous Order*. Edmonton: The University of Alberta Press, 2015.

Foran, Max. "Coalitions and Demolitions: The Destruction of Calgary's East Victoria Park, 1960–1998." *Prairie Forum* 32, no. 1 (2007): 17–46.

Francis, Daniel. *Red Light Neon: A History of Vancouver's Sex Trade*. Vancouver: Subway Books, 2006.

Friesen, Joe. "Thousands Rally across Canada after Gerald Stanley Acquitted in Killing of Colten Boushie." *The Globe and Mail*, February 10, 2018. https://www.theglobeandmail.com/news/national/protests-across-canada-after-acquittal-in-boushie-death/article37931825/.

Gray, James. *Red Lights on the Prairies*. Toronto: Macmillan of Canada, 1971.

———. *Booze: When Whiskey Ruled the West*. Second edition. Western Canadian Classics. Saskatoon: Fifth House, 1995.

Green, Rayna. "The Pocahontas Perplex: The Image of Indian Women in American Culture." *The Massachusetts Review* 16, no. 4 (1975): 698–714.

———. "The Tribe Called Wannabee: Playing Indian in America and Europe." *Folklore* 99, no. 1 (1988): 30–55.

Herk, Aritha van. *Mavericks: An Incorrigible History of Alberta*. Toronto: Penguin Canada, 2001.

Jeffrey, Leslie. "Prostitution as a Public Nuisance: Prostitution Policy in Canada." In *The Politics of Prostitution: Women's Movements, Democratic States, and the Globalisation of Sex Commerce*, ed. Joyce Outshoorn, 83–102. New York: Cambridge University Press, 2004.

Keep, Michelle. "Police Need to End Operation Northern Spotlight." The Indy (blog), November 2, 2017. https://theindependent.ca/2017/11/02/50527/.

Kempadoo, Kamala, Jyoti Sanghera, and Bandana Pattanaik, eds. *Trafficking and Prostitution Reconsidered: New Perspectives on Migration, Sex Work, and Human Rights*. New York: Routledge, 2015.

Lee, Na Young. "The Construction of Military Prostitution in South Korea during the US Military Rule, 1945–1948." *Feminist Studies* 33, no. 3 (2007): 453–481.

Logsdon, Judith. "The Princess and the Squaw: Images of American Indian Women in Cinema Rouge." *Feminist Collections* 13, no. 4 (1992): 13–17.

Marubbio, Elise M. *Killing the Indian Maiden: Images of Native American Women in Film*. Lexington: University Press of Kentucky, 2006.

McCue, Duncan. "What Does It Take for Aboriginal People to Make the News?" *CBC*, January 29, 2014. https://www.cbc.ca/news/indigenous/what-it-takes-for-aboriginal-people-to-make-the-news-1.2514466.

McIntyre, Susan. "Strolling Away." Ottawa, ON, CAN: Department of Justice Canada, Research and Statistics Division, August 2002.

National Inquiry. "Reclaiming Power and Place: The Final Report of the National Inquiry into Missing and Murdered Indigenous Women and Girls." National Inquiry into Murdered and Missing Women and Girls, June 2019. https://www.mmiwg-ffada.ca/final-report/.

Patson, Nikole D. "How I Recovered from Tenure-Track Burnout." *Science | AAAS*, April 25, 2019. https://www.sciencemag.org/careers/2019/04/how-i-recove red-tenure-track-burnout.

Rieger, Sarah. "Calgary Ranked World's 5th Most Livable City by Economist Intelligence Unit." *CBC News*, September 3, 2019. https://www.cbc.ca/news/canada/calgary/calgary-livable-cities-index-1.5269432.

Rockquemore, Kerry Ann. "I Got Tenure: Now What?" *Inside Higher Ed.* August 30, 2017. Accessed September 28, 2020. https://www.insidehighered.com/adv ice/2017/08/30/introductory-advice-academics-who-have-just-become-tenu red-essay.

Saltwire Network. "RNC Defends Operation Northern Spotlight." *The Telegram*, October 18, 2017. http://www.thetelegram.com/news/rnc-defends-operation-northern-spotlight-156331/.

Sanghera, Jyoti. "Unpacking the Trafficking Discourse." In *Trafficking and Prostitution Reconsidered: New Perspectives on Migration, Sex Work, and Human Rights*, edited by Kamala Kempadoo, Jyoti Sanghera, and Bandana Pattanaik, 3–24. New York: Routledge, 2015.

Scott, Katherine. "The Best and Worst Places to Be a Woman in Canada 2019." Canadian Centre for Policy Alternatives. March, 2019. Accessed July 10, 2020. https://www.policyalternatives.ca/publications/reports/best-and-worst-pla ces-be-woman-canada-2019.

"SWAN Vancouver | Operation Northern Spotlight." Accessed September 30, 2020. https://www.swanvancouver.ca/northern-spotlight.

Van der Meulen, Emily, Elya M. Durisin, Victoria Love, and Collection Ebrary Perpetual Access. *Selling Sex: Experience, Advocacy, and Research on Sex Work in Canada*. Vancouver: University of British Columbia Press, 2013.

Venne, Muriel Stanley. "The 'S' Word: Reclaiming 'Esquao' for Aboriginal Women." In *Unsettled Pasts: Reconceiving the West through Women's History*, edited by Sarah Carter, 123–27. Calgary: University of Calgary Press, 2005.

Williams, Kimberly A. "Mavericks, Too." Sheri-D Wilson D.Litt, C.M. (blog), 2020. https://sheridwilson.com/yyc-pop/kimberly-a-williams/.

———. *Stampede: Misogyny, White Supremacy, and Settler Colonialism*. Winnipeg: Fernwood Publishing, 2021.

CHAPTER FOUR

THE DAY ANGELA DIED

Imagining Violence and Reclaiming Indigeneity through Collaborative Performance

By Zoë Eddy

BODY FOUND

When Sally Lautner slapped the manilla folder down on the table, conversation stopped. Billy, a local park ranger, looked up from his late-night coffee and nodded. "Something I can do for you, Mr. Lautner?"

"These are for you. Need a formal ID," Lautner growled. The man, moody on a good day, stomped out of Skip's Bar. Billy furrowed his brow and checked his watch: 11:32 pm, and he was most certainly off the clock. Billy sighed and read the post-it hung askew from the folder's corner: *Body found on road leading out of town.*

Billy put down his coffee and cleared his throat. He had been chatting with friends prior to Sally's interruption. "Excuse me, folks," he said. Folder in hand he walked to the bar's backroom—a well-known closet that almost every local had frequented for a phone call or confession. Billy opened the folder. He didn't gasp, but he did inhale too quickly.

The photos, close up and clinical, were of Angela Montgomery. Last Billy had seen her, she was speeding out of town. With a smile and a wink, she had made a dirty joke as a goodbye—in truth, she was off to a book tour, but the joke was a funnier alibi. Angela didn't like to brag about her success.

Billy looked back to the photos and shuffled through them a second and third time. He reread the note and realized his hands were shaking.

Billy sat down and realized what most people hate to realize: someone he knew was dead.

INTRODUCTION

For those familiar with Indigenous women and North American justice systems, this vignette is chillingly familiar. The vignette, however grounded in the real world, is nevertheless taken from a work of fiction. The originating story is about an Indigenous woman, Angela Montgomery, who is found dead in a trench; her death is reported to local authorities. However, in this story, Angela's death receives quick reconciliation—a far cry from how things work in the real world. In the story, Angela's body is found quickly, and her friends and community are immediately able to rally for resolution and justice. In Angela's story, #JusticeForAngela will never need to sweep Twitter or Facebook. Angela's killer will be found, and the woman will be laid to well-attended rest. She will be surrounded and mourned by her tribal community. She will have had a full enough life that, at her various memorials, people will read from her books and celebrate her interviews on local news. Her death, which was senseless and cruel, will nevertheless be witnessed and cherished.

This is not how this sort of thing usually happens. In North America, Indigenous women go missing for months, maybe years, before their remains are found. Generally, family members lead the search, tirelessly patrolling highways and woodsy outcrops—half of the families' battles revolve around convincing authorities to assist them. Friends take to social media, tagging the names of the missing and murdered. Vigils are held, red dresses hung, and endless phone calls made. Eventually, the fatigue of searching, mourning, and demanding justice wears on the living. They spend the rest of their lives repeating names and calling for action. They mark a day in the year to wear a certain color, rehearse a certain poem, or merely try to remember in silence. As a seemingly numb country looks on, they feel their own words fall like leaves. They keep the pictures of the missing and murdered in their houses, but accept the loneliness of no justice, no peace. No peace does not always mean protests and action: sometimes it simply means sleepless, haunted, and angry nights.

To return to Angela and the day she died: Angela's story has a final miraculous turn. Angela comes back to life; she is still saucy, ambitious, and loving. She shrugs off the term "victim" and continues on with her life. She remains a leader in her community and continues to be a role model for other Indigenous women. Her death has made her stronger, wiser, and braver. She's not reborn, but instead simply gets to pick up where she left off.

Of course, these miracles and happy endings make it clear that *The Day Angela Died* is fictitious. Specifically, it is a work of fiction I organized and led in a uniquely collaborative performance arena: larp, or live-action roleplaying.

Since its origins in the late 1970s, United States larping has branched into hundreds of different systems and event types; larping outside the US is similarly varied. For this reason, it is difficult to offer a singular definition of larp. Based on my experience, larping, at its core, is a form of improvisational performance[1] with systematized rules, participant roles, and collaborative narratives. In many ways, larping is a way for adults to access the spaces of play and fictional roleplaying that are often associated with childhood: larpers take on a role and, for a set amount of time, act out that role with other participants in a unified system; this collaborative play allows participants—larpers—to explore a fictitious world together.

The larps with which I am the most familiar are a combination of tabletop gaming, online roleplaying games, and competitive sport fighting. Participants' roles within this space are generally structured along two lines: a) "staff" and "non-players characters" (NPCs) and b) "player characters" (PCs). Staff produce and guide the majority of content while PCs engage in the content.[2] Within these larps, there are generally conflicts that require some sort of resolution; in the events in which I have participated, sport combat, puzzle solving, physical challenges, and roleplay are used equally to resolve conflict; other systems resolve conflict without simulated combat, relying entirely on roleplay and/or other conceits. In the last ten years, larp has expanded to include both in-person and online interaction: social media forums, messaging sites, and email provide spaces where participants can extend the boundaries of larp. Beyond and within this set of general definitions, larps take on endless forms.

The larps in which I have participated and organized follow the aforementioned rules; they also generally align with the "campaign boffer larp" model. "Campaign games" are games that last for a year or more with multiple events occurring during a year; these events span the duration of a single day (a "one day") to a weekend long event. "Boffer" indicates that these campaigns use sport combat systems to resolve conflict; in these systems, players use padded weapon props and rely on a rules system adjacent to popular tabletop roleplaying games. Players also engage in puzzle solving, landscape manipulation, and interpersonal interaction to reconcile the various challenges the world puts forward. The model of larp is "player versus world" wherein the world, written and performed by the staff, offers conflicts and enemies for the players to overcome. Larps happen at both public and private sites, including campsites which span multiple acres; larps are open to the general public and are advertised primarily across social media. The larps I run and attend happen exclusively at private camps rented from Friday through Saturday, the general length of a larp event.[3]

The genres of these larp range across a spectrum. Some are high fantasy games borrowing from Tolkienian and *Dungeons and Dragons* style worlds. Others are post-apocalyptic, modern, and cyberpunk games. More recently, a variety of BIPOC and LGBTQ creators have offered games that explore narratives outside the standard fantasy or sci-fi setting.[4] Within all of these games, staffers write a world, a system, and an outlined narrative that players pursue. Together, staff and players navigate the world: improvisational roleplay—from casual interactions to deeply emotional confrontations within a given story—lead to often cathartic and powerful communal narratives. While, in many mainstream spaces, larp is dismissed as a niche "geek" hobby, I view it as a space with significant potential for community expression and play.

As an Indigenous activist, scholar, educator, and artist, I seize on the collaborative creative potential of larp: I use larp as a space to foster community engagement and social justice activity. My scholastic training informs my larp experience in different ways. Firstly, as an ethnographer, I have developed skills to address the interests and needs of my larp community and the Indigenous community members therein: in my capacity outside of professional research, we identify individual and community-oriented goals; these are based on interviewing individual community members formally as well as participating in events, outside of my own, to observe the culture of various larps. I then collaborate with Indigenous community members to address places where they feel their own needs are not met: as a community anthropologist, I collaborate with them, on both individual and communal levels, to build spaces where they feel their culture and experiences are equally valued. We work on ways, based on the data I have synthesized, to create more narrative opportunities to facilitate Indigenous leadership; this includes, but is not limited to, anti-racism efforts in larp, creating financial opportunities so Indigenous larpers can run their own games, and collaborating on Indigenous-lead game events.

In an adjacent arena, my scholastic work turns to public education for non-Indigenous participants. In public education, I address cultural histories and academic theories in an accessible and engaging way. In the fictional world, I work to present topics relevant to the lives of Indigenous people, such as this narrative. However, I also use larp as a community foundation within which to create new activist and charity venues. These have involved charity events wherein participants learn about gender violence and MMIWG2S,[5] community feasts featuring Indigenous cooking, and pop-up artisan markets featuring Indigenous artists. I have also created podcasts and blogs that address racism in the gaming community and strategies to reconcile it. I am currently collaborating with other BIPOC larpers to develop anti-racism training for event runners. The communal nature of larp, and the intimate relationships that develop within it, serve as a multivalent space wherein multiple activist-artists can network to create intersectional support systems.

My work in larp also has a recursive relationship with my work in the classroom. While my students do not generally participate in larps, I use larp community building and activism to inform my work with students. I bring my research on larp into classrooms: it is instructive in terms of social science methods, while also a tool to generate reflexive models of community engagement. As a social scientist, the goals of larp—community building through collaborative expression—are goals that I have folded into my classroom praxis. I talk with students about the importance of play and collaborative creative expression. We work through models of collaborative creative play as ways to build trust and empathy within communities; we also explore how collaborative play might potentially dismantle the research hierarchies inherent to social science work.

Within this essay, specifically, I investigate how collaborative community performance provides Indigenous artists with the space to explore violence against Indigenous women, girls, and two-spirit people. I examine how these performance arenas function as places for complex, embodied storytelling about gender-based violence. I detail how, as an Indigenous academic and activist, I have used my training in feminist anthropology to open a space for collaborative performance about Indigenous rights; these spaces are outside of university settings but engage with the sort of work I do in my classrooms. I further investigate similar projects in adjacent spaces. I argue that collaborative performance, as mediated by ethnographic practices and community engagement models, provides a space for both a) community awareness and engagement, and b) feminist reclamation of violence against Indigenous communities. I offer a practical model to encourage performance art as a viable community-based and feminist method to counter gender violence.

A CRISIS OF VIOLENCE

As detailed in a report from the National Congress of American Indians, 84.3% American Indian/Alaskan Native (AI/AN) have experienced violence in their lifetime, and 56.1% of AI/AN women have experienced rape; in summary, AI/AN women are 1.7 times as likely to experience violence and 2 times as likely to experience sexual violence as compared to non-Hispanic white women.[6] Despite these statistics, however, wide scale policy reform moves at a staggering, slow pace. When I was beginning my research, in 2013, the issue of missing and murdered Indigenous women, girls, and two-spirit people (MMIWG2S) seemed specialized: only those of us directly impacted seemed to care—to quote a friend, it was an "Indian Problem." In the wake of Tarana Burke's #MeToo movement, I remember feeling a sense of space—a newly emerging openness in which to consider how sexual violence impacts Indigenous women.[7] The explosion of hashtag activism and advocacy campaigns for and by BIPOC have allowed Indigenous people to enter an arena where we may join with other communities to address the injustices that affect us.

The gaping holes in North American legal systems have created a vacuum: Indigenous communities must navigate policies and barriers meant to disenfranchise them.[8] In response, Indigenous communities, including urban groups disconnected from tribal leadership and support, have established their own forms of action and healing. These networks run a broad spectrum of community art and advocacy. A small survey of landmark works includes art and museum installations such as The REDress Project, The Jingle Dress Project, *Walking with Our Sisters*, and *Hearts of Our People*. The Sovereign Bodies Institute, the National Indigenous Women's Resource Center, and the Coalition to Stop Violence Against Native Women are but a handful of the grassroots organizations dedicated to addressing sexual and gender violence affecting Indigenous communities. Individual activists and artists—including Christi Belcourt, Jordan Marie Brings Three White Horses Daniel, Rosalie Fish, Ilona Verley, Tanya Tagaq, Lisa Brunner, and Émilie McKinney—have provided a number of recent groundbreaking interventions across policy and platforms.

These activities center around a singular issue, but they are more so connected by community participation: Indigenous activism is often collective in its healing—the individual connects with their own experience and that experience ties them to a larger group. This practice of both individual and communal healing emerges in approaches to Indigenous health care and community programming.[9] Community and creation are paired processes essential to many forms of Indigenous activism and healing. Considering these arenas, and their power for healing and reclamation, I will discuss my own activism within larping to develop another potential model for communal performance.

This process has helped me bridge academic and non-academic community divides: firstly, this has enabled me to expand educational spaces outside the university setting; larps are informal creative classrooms where a multitude of people both learn and teach. Moreover, as my research has progressed, more non-academic larpers have entered traditional university spaces: in my own classes, larpers have provided accounts and workshops on their own skills and experiences relative to academic topics. Currently, I am collaborating with a small group of academic and non-academic larpers on a research project designed to explore racism and anti-racist action in larp communities. While larping is a hobby grounded in "playing pretend," so too is a place for meaningful public engagement.

LARPING AS COLLABORATIVE ACTIVISM

While larping defies easy definition, the majority of larps—regardless of genre—have two commonalities: a) embodied performance of a persona not one's own, and b) collaborative narrative. Over a set amount of time, ranging from a few hours to multiple days, people engage within an agreed upon system of resolution and perform a character; at most events, larpers depend on interacting with other players in order to build a story.

The communal and embodied aspect of larp initially attracted me to it. I have had a lifelong involvement with the performing arts and public education involving expressive arts. One of my longtime struggles with performing arts has been its barriers to access: training, venues, and a general elitism surrounding performance create serious limitations in terms of participation. An interview[10] with a larper echoed my sentiments; this individual, who has been larping for about fifteen years, stated, "I like dressing up, learning a role, and that sort of thing, but I always felt like I was a background person. In larp, I can be a main character, but also a supporting character to the other people—it's so different, and I don't need special training for it. I just show up." Conversely, larping is an arena structured as a game based in creative play: it does not require expertise to join.

I have been participating in and running and writing larps for the last eleven years. Over time, I have come to find that larp is not only a place where adults are allowed to engage in creative play, but also a place that can serve as community-based education, advocacy, and therapeutic expression. My projects specifically attend to larps as an arena for feminist advocacy related to Indigenous issues and Indigenous cultural reclamation. This mirrors my own fieldwork: as an Indigenous ethnographer, my research focuses on how various Indigenous communities reclaim heritage through visual art and performance. I have used this training and experience to create arenas—based on collaborative research, community critical self-reflection, and progressive program building—outside of the university setting and instead within an accessible larp space. The establishment of these communities outside of traditional academia is particularly important to me: it has been essential for establishing spaces for groups under-represented in conventional academic discourse. Ultimately, as an educator, I attempt to expand the tools of academia without creating the boundaries enforced by privileged institutions.

Larping serves as a site for advocacy and reclamation across intersections. Larp provides places where non-experts get to participate in expressive modes—including character development, narrative writing, and public performance—usually limited to "experts" from elite institutions. One individual, who has been larping for roughly twenty years since he was a teenager, explained that, in his daily life, he has no ability to creatively express himself; within larp, despite his lack of professional training, he has become known for his talent in prop construction and painting. Larping communities serve as foundations from which amateur caterers, crafters, musicians, and performers can eventually move into professional careers. Larp, which is often safe and supportive, serves as an arena without significant barriers to entry.[11] Similarly, the vast majority of larps in which I participated offered narrative spaces that encouraged supportive exploration of gender and sexuality. Larping affords space where a diversity of individuals can explore previously guarded arenas.

As both a scholar and a larper, my work builds on the potential of larp: my scholarship prioritizes gender equity, Indigenous methodology, and feminist theory. Within larp, I mobilize this focus to explore how larp can facilitate sexual and gender violence awareness, education, and communal healing. I work with a small coalition of other Indigenous creators, including members of my family, to write and hold Indigenous-forward larp events. I offer this foundation as a model relevant to feminist engagement with community spaces.

A DIFFERENT KIND OF MISSING

Like many Indigenous women, I am a survivor of Intimate Partner Violence (IPV) and sexual violence. The details are unimportant, at least for this discussion. However, the trauma that resulted from IPV shaped my approach to larp narrative and my practice as an activist-artist. As Robert Alexander Innes and Kim Anderson have stated, IPV often feels like a different kind of missing: "The recent focus has been on the missing and murdered Indigenous women, and rightfully so; however, these are only two forms of violence experienced by Indigenous women. Indigenous women are much more likely to experience physical and sexual violence, a fact that has been overshadowed by the number of murders that have taken place."[12] This violence is not the same as being murdered, clearly, but it nevertheless constitutes a loss of self. It is also, in many situations, a precursor that leads to homicide by an abuser. The impact of abuse is undeniable: abuse of any kind results in a host of post-traumatic disorders, including lifelong issues with intimacy and sexuality.[13]

For Indigenous women and two-spirit people, IPV is but another rung on the ladder of structural violence. IPV is intertwined with sexual assault, abduction, and murder. Personally, this network of trauma, connected to my position as both a woman and an Indigenous person, contributed to my artistic process and advocacy. Larp has provided an arena wherein healing can occur on both personal and communal levels.

Case Study: The Day Angela Died

I looked into the screen of my phone's camera—it was in selfie mode, and my face, nearly unrecognizable in the makeup, was staring back at me. I had done a decent job, I calmly reflected, on the makeup: it wasn't gory or over-the-top, but it certainly made me seem paler, bruised, and frozen. I had had to redo it twice: the first two attempts were garish, making me look like a rotted, cartoon zombie. I had moved away from the green and brown Mehron face paint, focusing instead on blues and greys. I hadn't based "my look" on anything except for my passing familiarity with stage makeup, my forensics training, and own quiet experiences with bruising and exposure.

I nestled myself into the blue tarp that I had spread across my bedroom floor. Settling into the plastic, I hit my selfie timer, pressed "Shoot," and closed my eyes. A minute later, sitting up alive in my bedroom, I looked down at the picture I had taken: an image of myself which looked very much dead.

It felt surreal. Here she was, an image of myself not mine, but inspired by the things that kept me up at night—the crime scene photos of dead women, battered and frozen on a highway. My own reflection, after a very scary evening, bruised and windburned, in a bathroom mirror. I was embodying something

I was not—a murdered Indigenous woman—while celebrating something I was—an Indigenous woman who might have been murdered more than a few times.

I shuddered, though my apartment was unseasonably warm. Satisfied with the images, I walked to my bathroom mirror. As I wiped away the makeup, I reflected on a January night, the previous year, when a car drove up. "Hey bitch, get the fuck in," the passenger, a grinning male with a knife, had growled. As I had sprinted away, skittering on the ice, I had cursed myself for wearing high heels while traveling alone.

So, these pictures, which would be the basis for Angela's death, felt strangely uncomfortable yet distantly familiar. They weren't my fate yet.

The Day Angela Died is a narrative that took place in one of the larps that I co-run with a larger team. This larp, *After Dark*, takes place in contemporary New England: an ode to the New England Gothic, it explores New England's history through supernatural analogies and horror-based plotlines—a ghost story entrenched in New England's oft-ignored history of colonialism and violence. Indigenous stories, particularly those grounded in contemporary life, are central to our storytelling (Five people on our eight-person running team are Indigenous). The player base of *After Dark* is also, relative to the rest of New England, diverse: we have a number of players who play the game specifically because it makes space for Indigenous and other BIPOC stories.

As an artist and writer, I use *After Dark* as a space to explore my own identity as an Indigenous woman; as an activist and survivor, I specifically use it to advance my own MMIWG2S advocacy projects. Working with my team, I decided to run a short narrative referencing the movement and the larger issues of violence that impact Indigenous communities.

In *After Dark*, one of my lead non-player characters (NPCs) was Angela Montgomery, an Anishinaabe woman modeled after stories of my mother's life in the 1970s and stories of my partner's

Anishinaabe aunts: she is a heroine—free-spirited as well as a well-respected writer and activist. She is a fictional role model inspired by my own aspirations of Indigenous womanhood. Despite my intimate connection with this character, I decided to kill Angela Montgomery after a virulent stream of news related to missing and murdered Indigenous women. It seemed like a painful and purposeful way to engage with my own history and scholastic expertise: how could I combine my experience with violence as well as my research on gender violence affecting Indigenous women? Moreover, how could I support and lead a community exploration of these topics? In what ways could I create a space that fostered not only awareness but activism? Regardless of my own identity, an exercise in performing the violent death of an Indigenous woman risked being exploitative. I wanted larp-as-activism to engage in four areas: a) creative expression, b) community collaboration, c) public education, and d) charity and fundraising. I see these four tenants as essential to the unique arena that larp provides.

Fictional Narrative

Within the *After Dark* narrative, I had established Angela Montgomery as an important character in the world. Extensive larp materials—particularly prose[14] and audiovisual materials—had been provided to players through websites, social media, and emailing lists; physical copies of these same materials were available at the physical game. As mentioned, the character is an Indigenous activist invested in community revitalization and creative expression: the materials I produced communicated this part of her character. These materials, as well as Angela's participation in the in-person experiences of players, helped me establish her within the players' worlds, as well as within her own.

Angela's death involved a group of roughly twenty players of mixed intersections; five Indigenous players were involved in this group. These same players, guided by the eight-person plot staff, were participants in a plotline that spanned six months; while the actual events took place over subsequent Friday-Sunday events, participants had between-event times to collaborate with one another. The same twenty-eight participants, both players and staff, were involved throughout the entirety of this narrative. The happening of Angela's death took place over a single event, the event itself lasting three days. On the first evening of the game, the players received news that she was murdered—rather than have the players find my body, I wanted to create an object that made the death both a permanent piece of visual art and something to be studied. I wanted to create the abject experience of witnessing a corpse that was uncanny and graphic: players discovering my body in-game, as the audience might experience in a theatrical production, did not accomplish this. This was personal and political: personal in that it was a reclamation of violence that had been done to my body; political in that it was a statement about the epidemic of violence impacting Indigenous women.

On the second day of the event, the Angela plotline engaged the players in a series of investigations. Within the context of this plotline, players explored the physical landscape to look for clues connected to Angela's death. This functioned similarly to Escape Rooms: players found prop objects that indicated the possible perpetrator and the context of the death; as an anthropologist with some background in forensic anthropology, I (in various NPC roles) led the players in thinking through the science of a murdered persons case in the context of violence against Indigenous women. During these plots, players were presented with the hurdles Native communities face: systemic inequities in legal proceedings, racialized sexism in courts, and public disinterest in justice for Indigenous women. On their own and in sessions supported by staff, players talked through what they had found as well as how the death and process impacted members of the community (specifically, NPCs who served as key parts of the community). I ended the event with a simple action: I hung one of my red dresses from a tree—a nod to Jaimie Black's REDress Project.[15]

The following event, which happened roughly two months later, the same players continued their investigation. Players, who had worked with NPC officials to present their materials and reports, were presented with the likely murderer (As the staff, we made the decision to keep this character off-screen as we felt making this individual physically present distracted from the larger narrative). The resolution to the case was anticlimactic: a staff member served as the federal agent who revealed the information, and the case was transferred to the courts outside of player agency. I was insistent that the reasoning behind the murder be nothing beyond senseless, cruel, and random—even in a game with supernatural elements, I wanted the narrative focus to be on the loss of an Indigenous woman's life rather than a grand conspiracy. Angela and her death, rather than the narrative of her killer, were important to me. The players, who were both Indigenous and non-Indigenous, found themselves in a frustrated grief: they had worked to resolve the death, but there was no true resolution to be found.

Over the next month, I felt profoundly uneasy. I had essentially fridged[16] a character who meant something to me, as well as a character who meant something to other people. I talked with my team about possible resolutions: maybe I could bring the killer to justice. My team, majority Indigenous, were split. We had told the story we wanted to tell, and that story is a sad one mired in systemic racism. Beyond this, as Indigenous game runners, it was one that felt authentic to our experiences: we all knew and/or related to women who had died violent deaths with little resolution. The feelings of frustrated sadness perhaps indicated that Angela's story had had its impact.

Still, I felt that the narrative could be better served by returning to Angela. At the third event, six months after the introduction of this plotline, the involved players received a multimedia message: very simply, a spirit had brought Angela back to life, and she was now a teacher—a teacher grounded in my cultural spiritual practices. Superficially, this may seem to have run counter to my goals: how does a "fantastical" ending further awareness? Working with my staff, I decided that bringing Angela back to life furthered goals beyond acknowledging trauma: the return of life, to us, indicated the potential of justice—Angela was no longer a stand-in for murdered women magically brought back into life, but instead a metaphor for justice enacted and a broken system fixed. Angela was a celebration of life and potential—specifically the potential of Indigenous women. In line with this, I ended the event as myself, in my jingle dress regalia, leading the Indigenous players in a private, tearful memorial for missing and murdered Indigenous women, girls, and two-spirits. One of my partners left an offering of sage, cedar, sweetgrass, and tobacco.

The entire performance, which spanned months, was imperfect and flawed, but it was singular and powerful. Below, I detail the four tenets of this project to model how larp and other performance art might serve as spaces for Indigenous reclamation of violence.

1) Creative Expression

Firstly, I used larp to explore my own positionality as an Indigenous woman, gender violence survivor, and activist. The work was informed by my desire to take my personal experiences and work them into a collaborative performance art piece. This venue allowed me to assert control of my own narrative while offering a fiction that reclaimed it; it also allowed me, as someone from a community frequently silenced, to engage in larger community witnessing. I was able to hold space for this narrative with a diverse group which included BIPOC activists and artists pursuing adjacent goals. As a group, we were collaboratively exploring history and trauma relevant to not only my own experience but larger networks of systemic racism and sexism. This sort of creative venue, for survivors of various intersections, serves as a potential place for transformative self-representations in collaborative spaces.

2) Community Collaboration

Community collaboration was essential to this project. My collaborators, fellow writers and players alike, were impacted by both gender violence and Indigenous rights issues. While I originated the story idea, various creators contributed suggestions and ideas for the narrative: our dynamic was fluid, cooperative, and supportive. This opened the space, across levels of participation and engagement, for creative expression and personal investment with both the fictive scenario and real-world issues. This had several dynamic outcomes.

Firstly, other Indigenous creators were able to engage in a space designed to explore community trauma. This resulted in a cascade of other creators engaging in their own therapeutic storytelling. Secondly, community collaboration allowed for non-Indigenous participants to learn about and empathize with Indigenous civil rights issues. This not only allowed for expanded awareness and conversation, but also facilitated those individuals' ability to engage with their own intersections of oppression and trauma.

Larp facilitates this process as larp is by necessity collaborative. While other creative forms involve tight hierarchies with central performers and prioritized voice, larp as creative play creates structured space for multiple collaborators.

3) Public Education

It was important for me to use the creative space to foster awareness. Gameplay is fictive and draws inspiration from the real world but is only representative. Before and after the larp, I presented facts, figures, and public testimonies related to gender violence against Indigenous women and two-spirits. I offered content warning to players so that they could opt into (or out of) potentially triggering narratives. Throughout the game, I made small exhibits of media related to this epidemic of violence. I provided resources not only for further education, but also for assistance for individuals impacted by sexual abuse (These materials were limited to a single room given the diversity and adjacent trauma of our community).[17] After the game, I provided the relevant materials online. I also provided out-of-game debriefing spaces, mostly online, so that participants could reflect on their reactions to the narrative.

This allowed me to present tangible research and resources. I was sensitive to the potential dangers of escapism: exploiting the story of Indigenous women, however deeply personal to me, risked allowing people to fantasize a racialized crisis. Firmly "out-of-game" work and communication allowed for continued conversation and advocacy work. The game allowed people to become creatively exposed to and invested in an issue; various materials, presented at various levels of complexity, allowed people to further educate themselves.

4) Charity

Finally, charity and fundraising were an essential part of this project. My practice as an artist-activist is to use art for communal work. This is grounded in both engaged feminist practices[18] and my cultural values that prioritize "giving more than taking." For this project, I worked with staff members and players to source ideas for charitable causes related to the project. We decided to divide our efforts between a) a North American advocacy organization and b) a local shelter that serves battered women and prioritizes BIPOC and LGBTQ survivors.

Larping is community oriented. Larpers, particularly in online arenas, frequently circulate crowdfunding resources, established campaigns, and other forms of charity engagement based on monetary donation. I offered those who could afford to participate easy access to vetted groups. For those who wanted to participate, but could not donate, my team and I offered resources where they could train themselves in public advocacy efforts.

TOWARDS RECONCILIATION

Larping serves as an embodied space where I can empower and share my own cultural, academic, historical, and personal context. Furthermore, as an activity rooted in community and creativity, larp is a space that promotes public education through dynamic play and reflection. As someone who has existed in multiple spaces—both academic and/or creative—I see this as an arena that offers engaged feminists the space to not only educate others, but invite others into collective creative moments; moreover, larp, as a profoundly interactive artform, allows for engagement beyond moments and into longer activist trajectories. I see larp as something with a profound potential for Indigenous agency in intersectional feminist art and play. In moments viewed as "playing pretend," we are perhaps able to find facets of not only ourselves, but our unreconciled and shared histories.

NOTES

1. Larping is often referred to as a "game." In this essay, I sometimes use the term "game" to refer to individual events. This is common parlance in the community that stems from the influence tabletop gaming has had on larp. Some aspects of larp are gamified forms of play: players use a rules system, with definitive ways to lose and win, to reconcile challenges. However, I view larp as much closer to performance: rich, immersive interpersonal roleplay, personal costuming, and scene setting are more important to the experience than rules. Rules provide an overall structure to provide shape to the collaborative performance of a story. Nevertheless, while "game" is something of a relic of the tabletop lineage, it remains an important part of larp vernacular.
2. This is a simplification of less common but important forms of larp. Some larps have deconstructed the staff/PC divide in pursuit of more collaborative narratives. These larps move away from a rigid hierarchy of content producer and content creator.

3. It bears repeating that larps, in terms of their mechanics and structure, vary considerably. While I have offered the general structure with which I am familiar, other New England larps follow wildly different structures. Indeed, particularly in the wake of the COVID-19 pandemic and the cancelation of in-person events, entirely digital larps have become increasingly popular.
4. For a more detailed discussion of larp, embodiment, and race see: Zoë Antoinette Eddy, "Playing at the Margins: Colonizing Fictions in New England Larp," *Humanities* 9, no. 4 (2020): 143.
5. Missing and Murdered Indigenous Women, Girls, and Two-Spirits.
6. NCAI Policy Research Center, "Research Policy Update: Violence against American Indian Women and Girls," National Congress of American Indians, (February 2018).
7. Tarana Burke, "MeToo Was Started for Black and Brown Women and Girls. They're Still Being Ignored," *The Washington Post* 9 (2017).
8. Chris Cunnen, "Colonial Processes, Indigenous Peoples, and Criminal Justice Systems," in *The Oxford Handbook of Ethnicity, Crime, and Immigration* (New York: Oxford University Press, 2014), 386–407.
9. See: Brenda J. Child, *Holding Our World Together: Ojibwe Women and the Survival of Community* (Penguin, 2012); Joseph P. Gone, "The Red Road to Wellness: Cultural Reclamation in a Native First Nations Community Treatment Center," *American Journal of Community Psychology* 47, no. 1-2 (2011): 187–202; Paul E. Pedersen, "The Looking ahead Project: A Lesson in Community Engagement and Positive Change," *Journal of Community Safety and Well-Being* 4, no. 3 (2019): 58–62.
10. As I have been engaged in live-action role playing for eleven years, both structured and unstructured interviews have occurred in different venues and different times. While I have engaged in hundreds of events as a participant observer, the majority of my conversations and interviews have occurred outside of structured event spaces. Larping creates close bonds between people, and the friendships and professional relationships I have developed within larp have served as the foundation for my research; similarly, other researchers have asked me to serve as interlocutors. Since 2017, when I dedicated my research focus to issues of Indigeneity, roughly half of my conversations have occurred in person in various spaces outside of the active larp space and roughly half have occurred online in private chats on social media. The larping community uses social media extensively compared to the average social media user. All of my interlocutors are US nationals of varying ethnicities, genders, ages, and experience levels; I have indicated

these demographics when relevant. My interlocutors, both Indigenous and non-Indigenous, are anonymous by their own preference.

11. There are significant barriers to entry in larp. These barriers include, but are not limited to, issues of financial stability and disability. The aforementioned are most frequently cited among larpers.

12. Robert Alexander Innes and Kim Anderson, "The Moose in the Room: Indigenous Men and Violence against Women," in *Keetsahnak/Our Missing and Murdered Indigenous Sisters*, eds. Kim Anderson, Maria Campbell, and Christi Belcourt (University of Alberta, 2018).

13. Maria A. Pico-Alfonso, M. Isabel Garcia-Linares, Nuria Celda-Navarro, Concepción Blasco-Ros, Enrique Echeburúa, and Manuela Martinez, "The Impact of Physical, Psychological, and Sexual Intimate Male Partner Violence on Women's Mental Health: Depressive Symptoms, Posttraumatic Stress Disorder, State Anxiety, and Suicide," *Journal of Women's Health* 15, no. 5 (2006): 599–611.

14. There are roughly two-hundred pages of "world materials" that have been made available to players through free rulebooks. These rulebooks are provided prior to the game in order to prepare players to immerse in the world. In addition to these materials, players and staff alike produce prose, visual art, and performing art inspired by the game world. Much of this work has been professionally published. Specific to this essay, one of the poems I wrote and performed for Angela's plotline was reproduced in the *Yellow Medicine Review*. See: Zoe Eddy, "Speak Story," in *Yellow Medicine Review*, eds. Millissa Kingbird, Angela Trudell Vasquez, and Judy Wilson (Marshall, MN: Southwest Minnesota State University, 2019).

15. Jaimie Black, THE REDDRESS PROJECT, 2020. https://www.jaimeblackartist.com/exhibitions/

16. "Fridging" is a term that comes from feminist critiques of American comics: it refers to the death of a character, usually a woman, that motivates the protagonist, usually a man, to pursue the larger narrative; the "fridged" character is a plot device to evoke emotion and narrative progress. See: Hannah Starke, "The Degradation of Women to Plot Points in Superman and Classical Epics," in *Examining Lois Lane: The Scoop on Superman's Sweetheart*, ed. Nadine Farghaly (Scarecrow Press, 2013), 113–127.

17. Larp spaces include many people impacted by racism, sexism, and domestic violence. The general practice in New England larp prioritizes safe exploration of potentially triggering themes: these allow people to opt-in to plots that may be reminders of past trauma.

18. See: Amber Dean, Jennifer L. Johnson, and Susanne Luhmann, eds., *Feminist Praxis Revisited: Critical Reflections on University-Community Engagement* (Wilfrid Laurier University Press, 2019); LeeRay M. Costa and Karen J. Leong, "Introduction Critical Community Engagement: Feminist Pedagogy Meets Civic Engagement," *Feminist Teacher* 22, no. 3 (2012): 171-180.

WORKS CITED

Black, Jaimie. THE REDDRESS PROJECT. 2012. https://www.jaimeblackartist.com/exhibitions/

Burke, Tarana. "MeToo Was Started for Black and Brown Women and Girls. They're Still Being Ignored." *The Washington Post* 9 (2017).

Child, Brenda J. *Holding Our World Together: Ojibwe Women and the Survival of Community.* New York: Penguin, 2012.

Costa, Leeray M., and Karen J. Leong. "Introduction Critical Community Engagement: Feminist Pedagogy Meets Civic Engagement." *Feminist Teacher* 22, no. 3 (2012): 171-180.

Cunnen, Chris. "Colonial Processes, Indigenous Peoples, and Criminal Justice Systems." In *The Oxford Handbook of Ethnicity, Crime, and Immigration*, 386-407. New York: Oxford University Press, 2014.

Dean, Amber, Jennifer L. Johnson, and Susanne Luhmann, eds. *Feminist Praxis Revisited: Critical Reflections on University-Community Engagement.* Waterloo, ON: Wilfrid Laurier University Press, 2019.

Eddy, Zoë Antoinette. "Playing at the Margins: Colonizing Fictions in New England Larp." *Humanities* 9, no. 4 (2020): 143.

Eddy, Zoe. "Speak Story," In *Yellow Medicine Review*, edited by Millissa Kingbird, Angela Trudell Vasquez, and Judy Wilson, 49-50. Marshall, MN: Southwest Minnesota State University, 2019.

Gone, Joseph P. "The Red Road to Wellness: Cultural Reclamation in a Native First Nations Community Treatment Center." *American Journal of Community Psychology* 47, no. 1-2 (2011): 187-202.

Innes, Robert Alexander and Kim Anderson. "The Moose in the Room: Indigenous Men and Violence against Women." In *Keetsahnak/Our Missing and Murdered Indigenous Sisters*, edited by Kim Anderson, Maria Campbell, and Christi Belcourt, 175-192. Edmonton, AB: University of Alberta, 2018.

NCAI Policy Research Center. "Research Policy Update: Violence against American Indian Women and Girls." National Congress of American Indians. February 2018.

Pedersen, Paul E. "The Looking Ahead Project: A Lesson in Community Engagement and Positive Change." *Journal of Community Safety and Well-Being* 4, no. 3 (2019): 58–62.

Pico-Alfonso, Maria A., M. Isabel Garcia-Linares, Nuria Celda-Navarro, Concepción Blasco-Ros, Enrique Echeburúa, and Manuela Martinez. "The Impact of Physical, Psychological, and Sexual Intimate Male Partner Violence on Women's Mental Health: Depressive Symptoms, Posttraumatic Stress Disorder, State Anxiety, and Suicide." *Journal of Women's Health* 15, no. 5 (2006): 599–611.

Starke, Hannah. "The Degradation of Women to Plot Points in Superman and Classical Epics." *Examining Lois Lane: The Scoop on Superman's Sweetheart*, edited by Nadine Farghaly, 113–127. Laneham, MD: Scarecrow Press, 2013.

CHAPTER FIVE

THERE HAVE ALWAYS
BEEN APOCALYPSES

Queer Apocalypse Solutions for Liberation and Survival

By Helis Sikk, Lindsay Garcia, and José Roman

INTRODUCTION

Queer Apocalypse Solutions (Q.A.S.) grew out of a queer-romantic-academic-creative partnership in the rural Midwest. Helis grew up in a small town in Estonia, a country that was part of the Soviet Union. Lindsay is from a suburb of New York City, born on the same street where *The Stepford Wives* was filmed. In 2018/2019, we were teaching at a small liberal arts college in Indiana. The town of 10,000 people and the gown of about 2,200 students did not mingle well. Although we met queer and social justice-oriented people in town who were not affiliated with the college, the community off-campus was not welcoming to difference. A Muslim student wearing a hijab had a gun pointed at them, our Black queer students were profiled at the local Walmart, and racist and homophobic slurs were found written on campus buildings.[1] There was a sign on someone's lawn near our apartment that said "No Trespassing. Not responsible for accidents." We were one of the only visibly out queer couples in town, both on and off campus. Mostly we felt safe, but not always. Having lived in a myriad of places, we have seen how bias manifests differently depending on location. Some of those places include the hyper-heteronormative Williamsburg, Virginia, where we fell in love and completed our American Studies PhDs, St. Petersburg, Florida, where we witnessed a botched COVID response first-hand, and Laramie, Wyoming, where Helis got her Master's degree, and where ten years prior to that Matthew Shepherd was murdered for being gay. Although the Midwest is touted for its niceness, we witnessed outward racism and homophobia that we had not seen in the other places we lived. So, in the gray dead of winter of 2019, surrounded by moldy, flooded cornfields that caused severe allergies for some residents, *Queer Apocalypse Solutions* was born.

Q.A.S. is an art-life project that recognizes that some of us are already living in apocalypses due to the violence inflicted against various identity and life circumstances pertaining to sexuality, race, gender, class, geographical location, nationality, immigration status, and dis/ability. Our definition of "apocalypse" is purposefully "feral," following Mel Chen—a metaphorical archive that brings together experiences and moments that are individually apocalyptic for us or our participants.[2] These apocalypses are often caused by what the late Lauren Berlant saw as "slow death," or the "destruction of life, bodies, imaginaries, and environments by and under contemporary regimes of capital."[3] Similarly, Rob Nixon's concept of "slow violence" is also relevant to our project since it addresses the way environmental racism and classism are often uneven, invisible, and unspectacular to those who don't experience it.[4] Q.A.S. finds these daily, often unconsidered apocalypses to be acute and important to highlight. Q.A.S. began a year prior to the wide-spread emergence of COVID-19, a grand-scale apocalypse, which intensified the many apocalypses that queer people already felt. Through tactics ranging from satire to serious, we attempt to find the entire spectrum of experiences and emotions through our programs, boldly imagining a future where queer people are able to freely become their best selves.

Beyond these theorizations, the project comes out of our own personal, creative, and scholarly experiences. Helis is an Estonian immigrant to the U.S. who holds a green card through our marriage. She writes about anti-LGBTQ+ violence in media representation and also is trained as a vocalist and musician. Lindsay is a university administrator and a scholar of animality studies, researching dehumanization in visual culture along the axes of race, nationality, and sexuality, as well as a performance, video, and social practice artist. We met at a house party in Williamsburg, VA in 2014, when we were both graduate students in William & Mary's American Studies program. We have both taught gender and sexuality studies classes, and we believe that praxis is as important as theory. During the COVID-19 pandemic, we both earned jobs at Brown University and moved to Providence, Rhode Island—Lindsay is the assistant dean of the college for junior/senior studies and recovery/substance-free student initiatives, and Helis teaches gender and sexuality studies at the Pembroke Center for Teaching and Research on Women. This project combines our knowledges and skills as well as our desire to bring such things into the public and digital spheres outside of traditional academic environments. Our brainstorming sessions for the project take place over the dinner table, walking our dog in Spanish-moss laden forests in South Carolina, and driving from Florida to our "apocalypse bunker" at Lindsay's parent's house in wooded, coastal Maine, where we connect the theories of affect studies with concrete discussions of our collective mental health, the feminist musings of our group texts, anti-racist orientations to our day-to-day activities, and new materialist philosophies of nature and culture in our spiritual and adventure-laden lives.

We have since taken on a third member of the collective, José Roman, a former co-worker of Lindsay's at Mastering Diabetes, who manages our Instagram designs and has also lived through many intersecting apocalypses. A native of Venezuela, in 2018, due to acute political unrest and a humanitarian aid crisis, he was forced to drop out of college in Caracas and return to his hometown to take care of his family. In late 2019, since there was no end in sight, he and his boyfriend fled Venezuela in search of refugee status in Peru. Venezuela and Peru are the only two South American countries that don't recognize same-sex marriage. He states: "In Venezuela there is an LGBTQ+ movement, and there's pride and all that, but at a much smaller scale because it's mostly organized by common people or civilians. There's no real government support behind it. Peru is a lot more involved, but it's extremely homophobic and sexist, so there's a lot of conflict and debate. There's no LGBTQ+ rights whatsoever. It's a kind of 'pick your poison' situation. Venezuela kind of hates everyone equally, but Peru hates specifically women and any non-male, non-cis, non-straight person."[5] While José and his boyfriend say that Peru has given them a chance to breathe, stand still, and think what their next move should be, they have also had trouble finding long-term employment due to nativist prejudices and COVID-19, which he and his roommates contracted early on, even though they had been extremely careful. While José recognizes the privileges he has by working from home for an American company and having a landlady who has been very kind to them, he still suffers from PTSD and other effects of his challenging life experiences.

Bringing all these influences together, our work follows the spirit of what Alyson Campbell calls "'feral pedagogies': community engagement with teaching and learning in a spirit of generosity that is removed from the elitism of academic institutions and the professionalization of arts training."[6] As Campbell, we seek to "(queerly) de-domesticate [our] academic skills and let them run wild outside a system that is fundamentally unequal."[7] Our ethos acknowledges that queer people and other historically marginalized people have experienced overlapping apocalypses that foster resiliency. All of our principles remain grounded in the belief that we can create positive change in our communities when we start small. Since apocalypses continue to explode in the United States and abroad, our project remains nimble to address whatever specific actions need to take place. So far, Q.A.S. has engaged in one-on-one apocalypse consultations, educated queer youth on how to deal with daily zombie attacks, taught webinars for white people who desire to practice anti-racism in their work and lives, and built an online community of like-minded folks.

The novel coronavirus has impacted LGBTQ+ communities in many uneven ways. Approximately one-third of LGBTQ+ people work in industries that are in a high-risk category for contracting the virus.[8] The stresses that are part of LGBTQ+ people's lives put us at higher risk of chronic conditions, which have comorbidities with COVID-19.[9] Furthermore, the effects of social isolation can be heavier on queer and trans people who rely on networks outside their home pod for support. LGBTQ+ people, especially youth, have higher rates of suicide, addiction, and poor mental health that make isolation more deadly or harmful, especially if living with caregivers who reject their identities.[10] Lindsay, who has type 1 diabetes and is a person in long-term recovery, has additional risks due to the high rates of complications among diabetic people and also is at risk for a recurrence of substance use disorder, though thankfully, remains sober.[11] The Trump administration rolled back a number of recent gains for queer and trans people, especially involving government aid and discrimination in health care.[12] This has caused many disturbances for people who need hormone therapy, HIV-preventatives, or gender-affirming surgery, which is often labeled as non-essential. And all of the talks of "quarantines" and viral load are undoubtedly re-traumatizing for those queer people who survived and continue to survive the HIV/AIDS epidemic, for before the illness was understood, countless stigmas against gay people associated with pandemics were promoted in popular media that still have resonances today.

Below we have listed the twelve points from which our project emanates. We opted for twelve because the number signifies completion and wholeness: there are twelve months in a year; it takes twelve steps to complete a recovery program; there are twelve works of Hercules, twelve animals of the Chinese horoscope, and twelve main divinities in Greek mythology, among others.

#1: *Q.A.S.* BELIEVES THAT ALL APOCALYPSES ARE PERSONAL.

In April of 2019, *Queer Apocalypse Solutions* kicked off at the Gender, Bodies, and Technology conference, a small feminist science and technology conference led by scholars at Virginia Tech, on the lower level of The Hotel Roanoke & Conference Center in Virginia. We set up a staging area at the end of a hallway in which we hosted individualized apocalypse consultations that participants had signed up for in advance to focus on their "unique identity pressure points, including financial responsibilities, fears, and phobias, specific medical and physical needs, as well as geographic proximity to borders."[13] This practice of one-on-one care follows the second wave feminist slogan "the personal is political" which emerged with consciousness raising sessions that allowed women to articulate their intimate, personal experiences as political crises.

Wearing our matching *Q.A.S.* consultant uniforms, we began the sessions with the question, "What is your personal apocalypse?" We asked every individual we conversed with to situate themselves within their particular "end of the world." As such, we let go of all expectations as to where the conversation would lead and met people where they were instead of where mainstream society might position them. In this way, we were able to address the apocalypses that people experienced, both ones that were specific to them and the ones that were communal or shared by people

Figure 5.1: *Q.A.S.* at the Gender, Bodies, and Technology conference in Roanoke, VA.

with similar identity pressure points. Some of our participants included a former New York lawyer-turned-professor, a queer geographer based in Arizona, and the chair of a women's studies department in Virginia, each with vastly different worst-case scenarios in their lives.

#2: *Q.A.S.* BELIEVES IN ACTIVE LISTENING.

The framework of thinking of different kinds of hardships as apocalypses opened up the conversations with our participants, none of whom we knew personally prior to this experience, to talk about difficulties in their lives in new, queer ways. Based on our experiences in recovery and employing the improvisational comedy exercise of "Yes and … " the conversations' topics ranged from cyber bullying to the loneliness of moving to a new place; from being a queer cis-woman in a STEM field to the challenges of saying "no" due to feelings of worthlessness; from eco-anxieties to seven-hour commutes. We were students of our participants' lives as much as we offered an amicable ear. Based on these conversations, we developed a *Queer Apocalypse Solutions* plan for each participant that included one individualized suggestion—such as reading cultural texts like Octavia Butler's *Parable of the Sower* or doing a fifteen-minute cute cat video meditation each morning before rising from bed. We also included instructions for finding apocalypse buddies with shared apocalypse situatedness and building accountable communities with people who think differently. Ultimately, we found that people wanted someone who was non-judgmental to listen to them outside the medicalized therapeutic setting or a gossipy friend group. We were just some fellow queers who may "get it."

#3: *Q.A.S.* BELIEVES THAT CHANGE IS CREATED THROUGH INTENTIONAL CONVERSATION.

Through the *Q.A.S.* consultations as well as in our daily lives, we have found that a lot of the deeper work happens through pointed engagement with friends, mentors, mentees, teachers, students, family members, neighbors, and, even, people standing in the grocery line next to you.

This tends to be more obvious in the classroom, where, as teachers, we can curate the content in order to have radical conversations about social justice. However, most of our everyday interactions are less bound by the teacher-student power dynamic and structured learning environment. Much queer community-building and knowledge production happens in peer-to-peer dialogue, through texting, social media, spending time with friends, and even through wearing cultural signifiers that enable other queer people to identify you and send you a knowing glance. We learn from each other constantly. While Lindsay taught Helis some of the ways it was ok to be queer in public, Helis taught Lindsay the queer theory that queer experience is grounded within. It can be counter-productive to imagine change that creates a full generational paradigm shift, but, in small increments, we can change the lives of the people around us in impactful ways. By thinking about social justice action as not something that is reserved solely for "activists," we invite participation from a broader range of people.

#4 *Q.A.S.* BELIEVES IN THE VALUE OF TEACHING PRACTICAL SKILLS, SPECIFIC TO THE MOMENT AND TO ONE'S ENVIRONMENT.

Metro Inclusive Health invited *Q.A.S.* to give two workshops, entitled "Queer Skills for Surviving a Zombie Apocalypse," on queer survival for their 2020 youth summer camps. Metro Inclusive Health, headquartered in St. Petersburg, FL where we lived at the time, provides crucial services for LGBTQ+ people in the area, including anything from HIV testing and counseling, to substance use programs and social activities. Similar to the queer potentiality that Metro Inclusive Health provides in the Tampa Bay area, our workshops aimed to show participants ways to create space for themselves in the often-hostile environment.

Our workshops were built around an imaginary queer road trip during the COVID-19 apocalypse while also taking into account the unique ways in which the demanding physical and anti-LGBTQ+ cultural landscape of Florida coalesce. One of the primary skills we taught was how to make a mask out of an old T-shirt without sewing—something that can be done in the back of a car with a pair of scissors (ideally) or a sharp pocket knife. Additionally, we taught campers how to find "safer" bathrooms in the woods in order to avoid potential exposure to the virus in public restrooms. We also discussed how not to get stuck in a Floridian marsh or wetland (step only on the areas where you notice at least some vegetation such as glasswort), how to identify the key characteristics of local poisonous snakes (big heads, small necks, chunky bodies, and thick tails), and how to keep hydrated in the heat without having to make unnecessary restroom stops. In addition to these very specific life skills, we also shared recommendations for queer films (*The Adventures of Priscilla, Queen of the Desert; Boys on the Side; Carol*) that would provide a queer break in the hetero flow of time.

#5 *Q.A.S.* BELIEVES IN HUMOR AS A TOOL FOR SURVIVAL.

"We laugh, that we may not cry," critic Roger Ebert famously said. Historically, humor has been used by queer communities to deal with the (threat of) violence, death, and doom that can be part of our experiences. Laughter and playfulness are key components of Q.A.S. praxis, be it our apocalypse consultations or Instagram posts that provide suggestions for daily actions. Our entire workshop for LGBTQ+ youth was also framed through the lens of humor. Since zombies are an entertaining concept for many of us, we asked participants, "Who are the zombies in our lives?" We defined "zombies" as people who are trying to destroy queer joy by making them abide by the norm: a homophobic school counselor, a transphobic (and often drunk) relative, or your best friend who "outs" you in front of your crush. Expanding the metaphor of zombies allowed us to talk about very serious topics in a humorous way. Our positionality as a queer married couple actively fighting our own zombies added a layer of playfulness. We recognize that humor is not always the only or the best way to discuss all topics, but it is vital for queer survival, especially during the impending dooms of 2020 and 2021. Imagining transphobic culture as a zombie does not fix the many injustices it brings, but it can help us to deal with the world on a daily basis.

#6 Q.A.S. BELIEVES IN INTERGENERATIONAL LEARNING.

Millennial- and Generation Z-led environmental activism, anti-gun violence movements, and defund police protests have all demonstrated that young people are the change-makers that the rest of the society needs to take seriously. We believe that in order to build trust between young people and adults, we need to spend more time learning each other's languages when it comes to fighting for social justice issues that matter to us all. For us, feral pedagogies in practice mean that the roles of the student and teacher are fluid. We are both teachers and students at the same time. Metro Inclusive Health summer camps provided space for this kind of reciprocity. A number of the queer youth saw us as the future they could be. We received feedback from one of the camp leaders that quoted a camper saying: "i literally was in the queer survival workshop and watching the lesbian couple teaching it being like 'MAN ... I can be like that one day ... YO ... "[14] And we saw in them the future that will be—young people who are unabashedly themselves and unafraid to hold us accountable and share their emotions. This new generation has opportunities to be "out" that were not afforded to us, whether that was from growing up in a post-Soviet country, a Latin American country with few LGBTQ+ anti-discrimination laws, or a white suburb where heteronormativity was seemingly the only way.

#7: Q.A.S. BELIEVES IN DIRECT ANTI-RACIST ACTION REGARDLESS OF YOUR OWN IDENTITY.

After a resurgence of Black Lives Matter protests in the wake of the murders of George Floyd, Breonna Taylor, Ahmaud Arbery, and many others, several white friends of ours from different communities outside academia reached out to us about what they could do. June of 2020 had a similar feeling to the unexpected 2016 election of President Trump, causing grief, panic, and a desire to get out there and *do* something. Not knowing where to start when the issues seemed so vast was, for many, a block to just starting. Thus, we decided to use our academic training that centers social justice and critical race approaches to cultural studies to develop a four-part webinar series, which we titled *Four Lessons on Race for White People** (*all are welcome), that took place in July 2020, when the momentum of early June protests was already waning. This series was open to anyone who came across it but was targeted towards non-academics. It was advertised on our social media profiles and through emailing friends and colleagues. Of the thirty participants that joined us, it was a majority of people who were friends, friends-of-friends, or members of our communities spanning Maine, Virginia, D.C., Indiana, North Carolina, Florida, and Pennsylvania. We wanted to educate other white people to recognize their own complicity in white supremacy while also teaching them more about the ways in which Black people have fought for liberation in the United States during the past 500 years. To ensure not to re-create the violence that white feminists have done in the past, we centered the voices of Black people and grounded our workshop in Black feminist thought as much as possible at every level of our workshops—whether this was using definitions of "racist" and "anti-racist" by Ibram X. Kendi or showing Kerry Washington's rendition of Sojourner Truth's famous "Ain't I a woman?" speech in order to contextualize Kimberlé Crenshaw's concept of "intersectionality."[15]

#8: Q.A.S. BELIEVES THAT ACCOUNTABILITY IS ONE OF THE KEY TACTICS TO DISMANTLE WHITE SUPREMACY.

In addition to educating, we also wanted participants to leave the webinars with a set of actions they could take to combat racism in their own communities. This was not going to be another book club. Casual racism most commonly takes place in day-to-day conversations and actions, so we wanted to balance individual action with an understanding that racism is an issue of structural inequality that has to be combated with enormous force. As such, we structured each session similarly. Beginning with self-reflection, participants looked at how their own upbringing made them part of larger systems of white supremacy, often in ways that were invisible. The issues covered included: white fragility, privilege, positionality, and how racial biases develop generationally. From there, we defined certain terms, from the most basic, "What do we mean when we say we are talking about race?" to more complex ideas, such as "slow death."[16] Next, we gave history lectures pertaining to important current events. We started with situating the Black Lives Matter movement within genealogies of Black resistance. Other subjects included: voter suppression, the prison industrial complex, calls to defund the police, and medical racism in the context of COVID-19. All of these sections were designed to be a starting point for our participants to think about their own communities, their position within them, and why Black people are excluded from certain social spheres. Q.A.S. believes that white supremacy can be challenged by teaching white people how to be accountable members of their communities, which means standing up for racial injustice. Afterwards, all materials with additional resources, which we had created as part of the four lessons, were made available to the participants via Google Classroom.

#9: *Q.A.S.* BELIEVES IN THE STRENGTH OF DIFFERENT FORMS OF ACTIVISM SPECIFIC TO ONE'S SKILLS, COMMUNITY, AND ENVIRONMENTS.

We believe that activism is not limited to gathering in the street to protest. To be sure, these gatherings are essential for a number of reasons, but we also think that activism has to take place at many different levels and break with norms of civic engagement in order to create long-lasting change. Furthermore, many public imaginaries pertaining to ideas about what activism is block people from participating in social action. Therefore, as part of our *Four Lessons* webinar, we taught participants accountability by starting where they are and starting before they are ready. At the end of each lesson was a homework assignment. First, participants were asked to make a list of all of the communities that they are involved with, whether they are golf clubs, organizations formed around identity (LGBTQ+ or ethnic groups, for example), fitness centers, educational institutions, and so on. Then, following the personal reflection on privilege, participants looked at their position within each of those communities, to help identify where they had the loudest voice or which community was most in need of intervention. Following a series of prompts, participants researched one of their communities to identify where historic and present inequity meet. Then, they made a list of all of their skills. In the last session, we brought this all together by planning how they could use skills they already have to take action against racist policies/ideas/practices within their communities. A white kindergarten teacher in Virginia decided to bring more diverse adults to read books in her online class so that the students could see themselves represented by thoughtful grown-ups. A white woman who was part of a diversity committee in the public sector of suburban Philadelphia saw how certain issues were not being brought up. A queer student of color invited their white parents to the workshop and was able to have conversations about race that were less triggering and more productive for all parties. Our participants were able to come away with a new way of engaging the world, knowing that they have the power to bring impactful change at the local level, even if they didn't consider themselves activists or "progressive." In January 2021, we developed a workshop and zine centered around how to build an anti-racist New Year's Resolution for 2021, as part of "A Teachable Moment," an art exhibition at Stove Works in Chattanooga, Tennessee. This project focused on how new energy in anti-racist organizing has created the potential for sweeping change through community-based art.

#10 Q.A.S. BELIEVES IN THE IMPORTANCE OF ONLINE LIFE FOR QUEER SURVIVAL.

Since the early years of the internet, queer people have fiercely created communities in online spaces. Here, we do not mean community in the neoliberal kind of way that markets gender and sexual diversity as a shared, universal value. Instead, we mean "community" as something that is fractured into many subcultures and dispersed groups. The internet has allowed queer people to find their own queer people, not one "queer community." As part of our desire to be in the long game of activism, Q.A.S. has a public facing Instagram account. In November 2019, we launched the #QASYearofResistance, which answers the question many posed following the 2016 election: "What can I do?" This social media action brings together queer people and allies who believe in creating positive change in their everyday life through humor and small daily suggestions. Creating posts was a collaborative effort between Lindsay, Helis, and José, who was situated in Venezuela and, later, Peru. In these exchanges, Lindsay and Helis learned from José about South American queer cultures and what it was like to be a queer refugee while José got to tap into his creative side and learn from Lindsay and Helis about North American queer cultures. Lindsay and Helis came up with the daily actions, and José used his graphic design skills to create visually engaging posts with a coherent theme. Our audience varies from former students, to college friends in Estonia, to elderly people in the recovery community that we know in real life, to additional people we know only through this platform, and others. Our Instagram action became even more of a queer life source when COVID-19 brought the world to a standstill in March 2020. It was a nurturing space to practice feral pedagogy. We taught our audience, but also learned from them as they shared with us how they took action based on our daily suggestions. During the height of what was called "doom scrolling" in 2020, we asked our audience to share what they would do instead of scrolling Instagram late at night and received responses that prompted us to try new things.

#11 *Q.A.S.* BELIEVES IN THE POWER OF CULTURAL EXPRESSION.

Q.A.S. encourages the creation of new worlds through representation, while recognizing that representation is not the be-all and end-all of activism. Sara Ahmed writes in *Living a Feminist Life*

CLOSE YOUR EYES AND IMAGINE HOW YOUR PET SEES YOU. ARE YOU THIS AWESOME BEING WHO IS JUST THE BEST CREATURE ON EARTH? WELL, YES, YOU ARE.

#QASYEAROFRESISTANCE

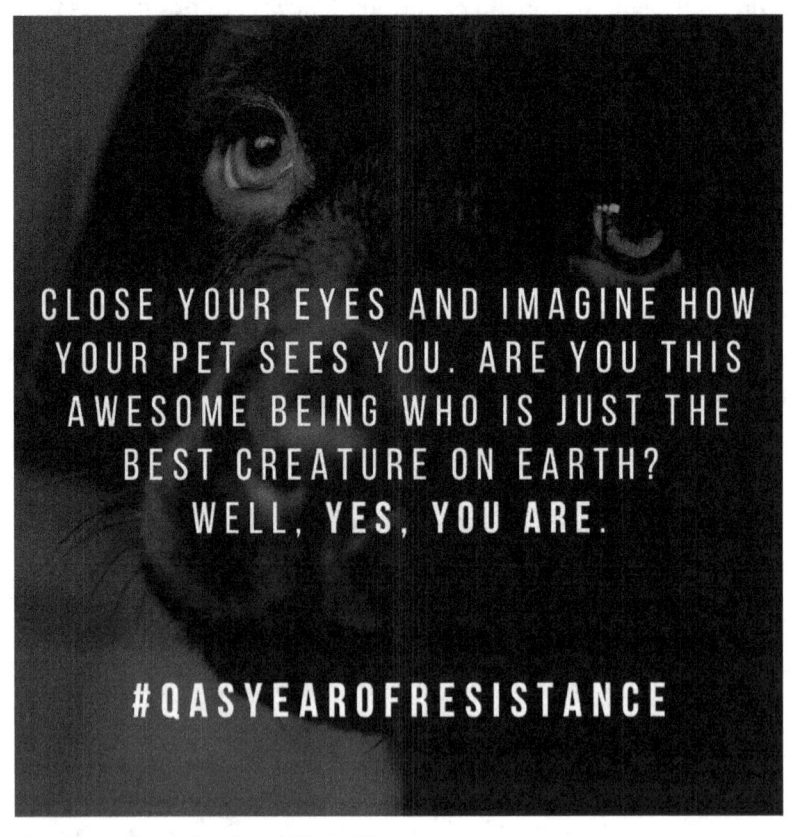

Figure 5.2: Example of #QASYearofResistance.

about the importance of feminist killjoy survival kit that consists of all kinds of tools that make our activism sustainable. Number one on her list are books.[17] Our Instagram account extends our survival kit to art, film, video, and performance recommendations that fuel our feminist souls. The recommendations range from the performative documentary *Maquilapolis* by Vicky Funari and Sergio De La Torre to turning up a Harry Styles song and dancing it out. The joy we get out of cultural productions is another part of our survival. Q.A.S. also suggests creative activities, since the act of creation directly adds queer representation to the universe. Additionally, nature and culture come together in our project. Q.A.S. firmly believes that queer people need to create an intimate relationship with the natural world for their survival and that inserting themselves into forests, oceans, and deserts is a radical act. All of these tactics, above all, help us to look inside and outside ourselves to imagine a less apocalyptic future.

#12 Q.A.S. BELIEVES IN SUSTAINABLE LIFE-BUILDING.

The many urgent social and environmental justice issues that 2020–2022 brought to the foreground are overwhelming, to say the least, even though they are not new problems. The gravity can be paralyzing. We have all felt at times that our actions cannot possibly be enough to dismantle the racist cis-hetero-patriarchy and anthropogenic climate change that dominate the globe. Q.A.S. believes that, in addition to vast cultural shifts played through mass media like the protests that came from the murder of George Floyd, we can make small, incremental, changes each day. However, in so doing, we need to make our activist lives sustainable. It is easy to run out of steam. The actions that our posts on Instagram encourage, follow the lineage of the radical self-care praxis originally articulated by Audre Lorde that is crucial for the survival of queer people who do social justice work.[18] We build each day around social justice praxis. We are in it for the long haul. And you can be too.

CONCLUSION

These twelve key points comprise the *Q.A.S.* manifesto at the moment. Having these core principles of our project enables us to consciously, slowly, and/or quickly react to large cultural changes in society. As a queer project, we recognize that the twelve points may shift and change as the apocalypses we live through evolve. In fall 2020, we avoided an apocalyptic re-election when Joe Biden and Kamala Harris won the U.S. Presidential Election. The Biden administration does not come with the daily dose of terror as Trump's, but it is far from the kind of radical queer liberation we continue to work towards. The state-level legislative attacks against LGBTQ+ and voting rights since the 2020 election confirms that we cannot remain complacent. The work of *Q.A.S.* is not done and must continue.

What is for *Q.A.S.* next? Teaching in the classroom and in our community continue to be crucial components of our work toward liberation. We advise students through radical feminist ethics of care, explain compulsory heterosexuality to parents' friends, bring American books on how to be a feminist in recovery to friends in Estonia, and do not hire contractors with Blue Lives Matter stickers on their cars. *Queer Apocalypse Solutions* is a daily embodied ethos that aims to build a more feminist, a more anti-racist, a more non-normative public sphere. In the next two years, we plan to strengthen and expand our current *Queer Apocalypse Solutions* network by developing this project into other realms, such as a syllabus-based podcast about masculinity and an art book for those who are willing to take small everyday actions to contribute to creating large-scale positive change.

In solidarity,

Queer Apocalypse Solutions

NOTES

1. Peter Nicieja, "Hate Is Rising: How Does DePauw React?," *The DePauw*, November 9, 2018, accessed August 31, 2020, https://thedepauw.com/hate-is-rising-how-does-depauw-react/; Maddy McTigue, "Racist Graffiti Found in Hogate Hall," *The DePauw*, January 18, 2019, accessed August 31, 2020, https://thedepauw.com/racist-graffiti-found-in-hogate-hall/; Kantaro Komiya, "President McCoy Answers to International Students on Bias Incidents," *The DePauw*, April 24, 2018, accessed August 31, 2020, https://thedepauw.com/president-mccoy-answers-to-international-students-on-bias-incidents/.
2. Mel Chen, *Animacies: Biopolitics and Racial Mattering and Queer Affect* (Durham, NC: Duke University Press, 2012).
3. Lauren Berlant, *Cruel Optimism* (Durham, NC: Duke University Press, 2011), 101.
4. Rob Nixon, *Slow Violence and the Environmentalism of the Poor* (Cambridge, MA: Harvard University Press, 2011).
5. José Roman, Instagram Direct Message, August 17, 2021.
6. Alyson Campbell and Dirk Gindt (eds.). *Viral Dramaturgies: HIV and AIDS in Performance in the Twenty-First Century* (Cham: Palgrave Macmillan, 2018), 62.
7. Ibid.
8. Michelle Samuels, "A Snapshot of How COVID-19 Is Impacting the LGBTQ Community," *BU Today*, June 12, 2020, accessed August 31, 2020, http://www.bu.edu/articles/2020/how-covid-19-is-impacting-the-lgbtq-community/.
9. Charlie Whittington, Katalina Hadfield, and Carina Calderón, "The Lives and Livelihoods of Many in the LGBTQ Community Are at Risk amidst COVID-19 Crisis," *Human Rights Campaign Foundation*, 2020, accessed December 28, 2020, https://www.hrc.org/resources/the-lives-and-livelihoods-of-many-in-the-lgbtq-community-are-at-risk-amidst-covid-19-crisis.
10. Amy E. Green, Myeshia Price-Feeney, and Samuel H. Dorison, "Implications of COVID-19 for LGBTQ Youth Mental Health and Suicide Prevention," *The Trevor Project*, 2020, accessed December 28, 2020, https://www.thetrevorproject.org/wp-content/uploads/2020/04/Implications-of-COVID-19-for-LGBTQ-Youth-Mental-Health-and-Suicide-Prevention.pdf.
11. American Diabetes Association, "COVID-19 and Diabetes," accessed August 12, 2021, https://www.diabetes.org/coronavirus-covid-19.
12. Sheila Kaplan, "Health Care Advocates Push Back against Trump's Erasure of Transgender Rights," *The New York Times*, June 13, 2020, accessed December 28, 2020, https://www.nytimes.com/2020/06/13/health/trump-health-care-transgender-rights.html.

13. Quoted based on the original sign-up form titled "Sign up for Queer Apocalypse Solutions at Gender, Bodies, Technologies 2019," accessed December 28, 2020, https://docs.google.com/forms/d/e/1FAIpQLSdkrETCaZ TwTionr-XNoByJUjmkgz-VnnJjX3fI5kGVCEQNRA/viewform?usp=sf_link.
14. Email from Emma Makdessi to queerapocalypsesolutions@gmail.com, August 5, 2020.
15. Ibram X. Kendi, *How to Be an Antiracist* (New York: One World, 2019); Kerry Washington, "Kerry Washington Reads Sojourner Truth's 1851 Speech, 'Ain't I a Woman?' during the Voices of a People's History of the United States," October 5, 2005, Los Angeles, CA, accessed August 31, 2020, 3:00 https://www.youtube.com/watch?v=yq3AYiRT4no; Kimberlé Crenshaw originally coined the term "intersectionality" in the paper Kimberlé Crenshaw, "Demarginalizing the Intersection of Race and Sex: Black Feminist Critique of Antidiscrimination Doctrine, Feminist Theory and Antiracist Politics," *University of Chicago Legal Forum* 1989, no. 1, Article 8. A more accessible article on intersectionality is available here: Jane Coaston, "The Intersectionality Wars," *Vox*, May 28, 2019, accessed August 31, 2020, https://www.vox.com/the-highlight/2019/5/20/18542843/intersectionality-conservatism-law-race-gender-discrimination.
16. Lauren Berlant, *Cruel Optimism* (Durham, NC: Duke University Press, 2011).
17. Sara Ahmed, *Living a Feminist Life* (Durham, NC: Duke University Press, 2017), 240.
18. Audre Lorde, *A Burst of Light* (Ithaca, New York: Firebrand Books, 1988). See also, adrienne maree brown, *Pleasure Activism: The Politics of Feeling Good* (Chico CA: AK Press, 2019); Dean Spade, *Mutual Aid: Building Solidarity During This Crisis (and the Next)* (Brooklyn, NY: Verso Books, 2020).

WORKS CITED

Ahmed, Sara. *Living a Feminist Life*. Durham, NC: Duke University Press, 2017.
American Diabetes Association. "COVID-19 and Diabetes." Accessed August 12, 2021. https://www.diabetes.org/coronavirus-covid-19.
Berlant, Lauren. *Cruel Optimism*. Durham, NC: Duke University Press, 2011.
brown, adrienne maree. *Pleasure Activism: The Politics of Feeling Good*. Chico, CA: AK Press, 2019.
Campbell, Alyson and Dirk Gindt, eds. *Viral Dramaturgies: HIV and AIDS in Performance in the Twenty-First Century*. Cham, Switzerland: Palgrave Macmillan, 2018.

Chen, Mel. *Animacies: Biopolitics and Racial Mattering and Queer Affect*. Durham, NC: Duke University Press, 2012.

Coaston, Jane. "The Intersectionality Wars." *Vox*, May 28, 2019. Accessed August 31, 2020. https://www.vox.com/the-highlight/2019/5/20/18542843/intersectionality-conservatism-law-race-gender-discrimination.

Crenshaw, Kimberlé. "Demarginalizing the Intersection of Race and Sex: Black Feminist Critique of Antidiscrimination Doctrine, Feminist Theory and Antiracist Politics," *University of Chicago Legal Forum* 1989, no. 1, Article 8.

Green, Amy E., Myeshia Price-Feeney, and Samuel H. Dorison, "Implications of COVID-19 for LGBTQ Youth Mental Health and Suicide Prevention." *The Trevor Project*, 2020. Accessed December 28, 2020. https://www.thetrevorproject.org/wp-content/uploads/2020/04/Implications-of-COVID-19-for-LGBTQ-Youth-Mental-Health-and-Suicide-Prevention.pdf.

Kaplan, Sheila. "Health Care Advocates Push Back against Trump's Erasure of Transgender Rights." *The New York Times*, June 13, 2020. Accessed December 28, 2020. https://www.nytimes.com/2020/06/13/health/trump-health-care-transgender-rights.html.

Kendi, Ibram X. *How to Be an Antiracist*. New York: One World, 2019.

Komiya, Kantaro. "President McCoy Answers to International Students on Bias Incidents." *The DePauw*, April 24, 2018. Accessed August 31, 2020. https://thedepauw.com/president-mccoy-answers-to-international-students-on-bias-incidents/.

Lorde, Audre. *A Burst of Light*. Ithaca, NY: Firebrand Books, 1988.

McTigue, Maddy. "Racist Graffiti Found in Hogate Hall." *The DePauw*, January 18, 2019. Accessed August 31, 2020. https://thedepauw.com/racist-graffiti-found-in-hogate-hall/.

Niciega, Peter. "Hate Is Rising: How Does DePauw React?" *The DePauw*, November 9, 2018. Accessed August 31, 2020. https://thedepauw.com/hate-is-rising-how-does-depauw-react/.

Nixon, Rob. *Slow Violence and the Environmentalism of the Poor*. Cambridge, MA: Harvard University Press, 2011.

Samuels, Michelle. "A Snapshot of How COVID-19 Is Impacting the LGBTQ Community." *BU Today*, June 12, 2020. Accessed August 31, 2020. http://www.bu.edu/articles/2020/how-covid-19-is-impacting-the-lgbtq-community/.

Spade, Dean. *Mutual Aid: Building Solidarity During This Crisis (and the Next)*. Brooklyn, NY: Verso Books, 2020.

Washington, Kerry. "Kerry Washington Reads Sojourner Truth's 1851 Speech, 'Ain't I a Woman?' during the Voices of a People's History of the United States."

October 5, 2005. Los Angeles, CA. Accessed August 31, 2020. 3:00 https://www.youtube.com/watch?v=yq3AYiRT4no.

Whittington, Charlie, Katalina Hadfield, and Carina Calderón. "The Lives and Livelihoods of Many in the LGBTQ Community Are at Risk amidst COVID-19 Crisis." *Human Rights Campaign Foundation*, 2020. Accessed December 28, 2020. https://www.hrc.org/resources/the-lives-and-livelihoods-of-many-in-the-lgbtq-community-are-at-risk-amidst-covid-19-crisis.

PART II

ACTIVISM AND PUBLIC EDUCATION

In this section, writers discuss how they share feminist scholarship and knowledge with broader audiences through public education. Sharon Barnes' "Take Back the Night: Feminism on the March" explores how the organization of a local offshoot of the international, grassroots Take Back the Night event was begun and has continued for twenty-five years in an Ohio community. In her essay "Public Feminism through Law and Policy Advocacy on Reproductive Rights," Carrie N. Baker discusses how she has used her background as a feminist scholar in her advocacy work for reproductive rights. In "Building Bridges: Researching with and not for Students on Diversity and Inclusion Policy," Gabrielle Rodriguez Gonzalez, Jack Kendrick, and Megan Nanney analyze the possibilities of "trickle-up diversity work" in order to create trans-inclusive diversity policies. Calla Evans uses her essay "Reflecting on Fat Activism as Research Methodology" to introduce her research on "infinifat" fashion that combines scholarship, photography, and social media in an ethnographic study. In their "'March into the Archives': Documenting Women's Protests," Jessica A. Rose and Lynée Lewis Gaillet offer a case study that demonstrates the vast possibilities of community archival work by looking at a local community's preservation of material from the 2017 Women's Marches. Lastly, in *"Maa Beti ka Rishta:* Desi Muslim Mothering Practices as an Archive of Public Feminism," Mariam Durrani, Zainab Shah, and Nazneen Patel provide an incisive analysis of their personal narratives and experiences of *desi* motherhood.

CHAPTER SIX

TAKE BACK THE NIGHT
Feminism on the March

By Sharon L. Barnes

Of the many ways that pervasive sexism prompts academic feminists to engage with communities, one persistent issue that has held the interest of feminists in virtually every community is violence against women and girls, especially domestic violence, sexual assault, and rape. Feminists both in and out of the academy have responded to violence against women and girls in a broad range of ways, including systemic approaches like demanding legal reforms (such as sexual harassment laws), community outreach and education programs, rape crisis and domestic violence shelters and hotlines, and the creation of SANE (Sexual Assault Nurse Examiners) nurses and victim advocate positions and insisting that survivors have access to them. Less formal approaches include spontaneous protests and picketing at sexist events and venues, feminist art in galleries, publications, and on the streets, boy- (or

Figure 6.1: Student Organizers from Woodward High School, TBTN 2006. All photos from the author's personal collection.

girl-) cotts, and, as Gloria Steinem famously titled an early book, many other *Outrageous Acts and Everyday Rebellions*.

Take Back the Night marches are a community response to violence against women and girls that have been ongoing in communities all over the world since the first such event in the 1970s, and they make an excellent case study for the relationship between feminist thought on paper and feminist activism "on the march." Take Back the Night is an international, grassroots effort to raise awareness about, protest, and end all forms of violence against women and girls. Depending on the local community's interests and organizing preferences, each event takes a variety of forms, though they usually include a literal march of women carrying signs and banners in the dark, chanting slogans about our right to walk freely and safely, "Wherever we go, however we dress ... " ("No means no; yes means yes!"). The event often includes an emotionally powerful "speak-out" by survivors, along with community resource tables, art exhibits, and other elements that organizers include to support survivors and raise awareness in their communities. These grassroots events have a broad range of participants and organizing structures that often include a relationship to local colleges and universities, and therefore, a range of relationships to academic feminism.

The Toledo, Ohio, area Take Back the Night, an event that has been an ongoing part of the local feminist calendar for 25 years, represents a dynamic model of mutual community-academy partnership, demonstrating the power of feminist organizing across a range of differences, not only of those between academe and community, but also of age, race, class, expertise, strategic approach, and feminist opinion. Toledo's TBTN Collective, which formed at the local feminist bookstore in the 1980s, has welcomed a diverse group of members, including feminist academics, activists, professionals in the violence prevention and treatment field, and sometimes religious and political leaders and other interested partners. This event, the largest anti-violence against women event in our community, has served as a venue for public feminism, a training ground for feminist activists, and a unique and revealing "Petri dish" in which ideas and issues fomenting in academic feminism meet community and cultural norms. The results have been educational in multiple directions. A close look at some of the Collective's decisions and choices, large and small, and especially the more challenging conflicts, including those surrounding our decision-making process, the role of men in the event, the content of the program, the impact of race and class on the event and the organizing process, and the role and response of the media, offers an opportunity to see feminist theory made "on the march" in dialogue with communities. This collaborative model of feminist thought reveals the positive, iterative power of feminist collective organizing that produces as much theory as it applies, a process we must continue to honor as we grow in our ability to enact public feminism more inclusively and effectively.

In Toledo, the local Take Back the Night event emerged out of the concern about violence against women and pornography shared by Gina Mercurio, who opened the feminist bookstore

Figure 6.2: T-Shirts from the Toledo/NW Ohio Clothesline Project, TBTN 2013, UAW Local 12.

People Called Women in West Toledo in December of 1993, and other local feminists, including several who were associated with the community's largest institution of higher education, the University of Toledo. One member, Nancy Jane Woodside, a law student who had long been a civil rights and labor activist, organized and hosted a conference entitled, "Violence, Intimidation and Harm" in 1994, which featured, among others, Andrea Dworkin, whose groundbreaking work with Catharine MacKinnon (who was teaching nearby at the University of Michigan in Ann Arbor at the time) against pornography was garnering attention around the world, and Jeanne Kilbourne, whose "Killing Me Softly" series of documentaries about the harm done by the sexualization of women in advertising, was equally compelling and popular among academic feminists and media scholars.[1] The university contingent also included Diane Docis, who was the coordinator of the Sexual Assault Education and Prevention Program at the University of Toledo at the time and who had organized a "Take Back the Path" march on the UT campus in response to three reported rapes in a remote area of campus. These women from the university, along with graduate students from the university's Department of English, convened with other local activists at the bookstore to organize Toledo's first Take Back the Night in the fall of 1994. The event included a rally on the steps of the University of Toledo's University Hall and a march to Ottawa Park, a local venue approximately a mile away, with a small rally there. From my role as a participant in the first Toledo TBTN, when I was a doctoral student in the university's Department of English, I eagerly committed to serving on the Collective the following year, and have been an organizer for every Toledo TBTN since. Perhaps because the organizing has had a consistent community home outside of the university, was created by seasoned organizers largely from the community, and the organizers working at the university had strong roots in other community organizations, or perhaps because as a young graduate student I did not have a significant background in academic feminist theory, initially I did not perceive myself as bringing academic feminism, nor did I bring my students, to the event. Over the years, however, I've invited students to participate in organizing for, volunteering at, and attending the event. I've brought samples of the Clothesline Project, a graphic installation bearing witness to violence against women in which each survivor, or her surviving loved ones, creates a T-shirt depicting her experience with violence,[2] to my and others' classes, and I've made sure that students had a way to participate, regardless of where and when the event took place. When I moved my faculty line to the Department of Women's & Gender Studies, our department's role became even more significant, with student involvement and other support of the event increasing. I have presented TBTN as a case study for a course we offer called "Feminist Solutions to Social Problems," and our "Research and Methods" course, which has a significant focus on violence against women, has used items from Toledo's TBTN in their materials as well.

From the beginning, the Toledo Take Back the Night Collective has organized the TBTN event at different venues around the city and in neighboring communities, including at churches, union halls, community centers, schools, colleges and universities, parks, and the courthouse steps. The Collective's intention in moving the event was to remind the community that violence against women is a problem in all communities and neighborhoods, rich and poor, Black, white, brown, and mixed, among all religions, et cetera. The Toledo TBTN usually includes a public rally, a women's march, a men's event, a community resource fair and a display of the local Clothesline and Silent Witness Projects, both of which are public art responses to violence against women The Toledo Clothesline Project consists of well over 400 T-shirts, and has been a long-time part of the Take Back the Night Event. The Clothesline Project has become a force in the community by itself, with organizations and other groups "checking out" part of the project to display during other events about violence against women, community violence, or other community problems. The Silent Witness Project was founded in Minnesota in 1990 as a way to remember twenty-six women who had been murdered in acts of intimate partner violence that year by creating a life-size red silhouette of each woman, with a plaque briefly explaining her story; the project now has collections in every state and many countries around the world.[3] The Toledo/Northwest Ohio Silent Witness Project has honored 115 women and girls who have been murdered in our community.[4] The Silent Witness Project is also displayed on its own in the community, in whole or in part, at violence awareness events. Countless hours of organizing Toledo's TBTN have yielded events as large as 400+ participants engaging in one or all of the event's activities.

The grassroots Toledo Take Back the Night Collective, like many others around the world, is comprised of volunteer members from a variety of contexts, backgrounds, and circumstances, who agree to a series of operating principles and goals and share the work of organizing the event. During its years of organizing, Toledo's Take Back the Night Collective has articulated mission statements that include calls for action, demands for accountability, and creating a safe space for survivors. Appendix A of this chapter contains the full text of the most recent version of the Toledo TBTN Vision Statement. During the countless hours of twenty-five years of organizing, the Collective has undergone many personnel changes and addressed a number of issues that were also topics of vibrant discussion in academic feminism, among them accessibility, childcare, racism, sexuality, communication, money, the vision, goals and location of the event, and the presence and role of men, of transwomen, of the police, of community service organizations, of media, and of politicians. The positions and actions taken by Toledo's TBTN Collective, rather than being driven by the academic feminists in the Collective, in fact demonstrate that feminist theory at its best is a recursive process, emerging not from academe and moving to the street, but rather, being driven by the lived experiences of women complemented, refined, challenged, and confirmed by feminist thought applied to those experiences.

One key organizing principle of the Toledo TBTN Collective that demonstrates the mutually constitutive nature of feminist action and analysis is the Collective's commitment to consensus decision making. The Collective agreed and re-commits every year to make decisions according to the principle of consensus, which requires mutual agreement, or at least a willingness to not block consensus, before acting on decisions. The practice of consensus decision making was foundational early in the Collective's life, and was motivated by a commitment to power sharing and valuing all voices equally. Gina Mercurio, the bookstore owner and longtime feminist activist, had been involved in the peace movement and feminist grassroots organizing for many years on both coasts, including at the Pacific Women's Resource Center in Seattle, which had experimented with non-hierarchical, non-patriarchal models of leadership, including attributing 50 percent of the voting power in their organization to women of color (who were numerically underrepresented) and voting by majority and consensus. The practice of consensus decision making, of course, has a long history, particularly in matriarchal cultures, and has been significantly influential on some American feminists who had contact with the Gantowisas, Haudenosaunee (Iroquois) women elders, who were the drivers of their culture's economic and political decision making.[5] Given the volunteer corps of organizers in Toledo's Collective, all with complex and busy lives, the challenges of consensus decision making are magnified by race and ethnicity, age, number of years in the Collective (or perceived "experience" as an organizer), sexuality, class, personality, gender identity, and other factors, including the individual organizer's understanding of feminist values.

Of the many consensus decisions and positions taken by the Toledo TBTN Collective over the years that are deeply informed by feminist thought, a large number were not controversial, even if they weren't always obvious to all Collective members when first agreed in a given year. Eventually, an explanation of the consensus process became part of a "welcome packet" distributed to new members to help them understand that, yes, even if this is your first meeting, you are invited and expected to speak, and your opinion will matter. You could, in fact, hold up a decision for several meetings in a row, if need be, until you understood and were comfortable with an issue under consideration. While American feminist use of consensus was born of the model from matriarchal cultures and from intellectual critiques of patriarchal institutions, its application in the Toledo Collective was forged largely from feminist activist experience. The organizing experience of Mercurio and Woodside drove the Collective's choices in organizational decision-making structure, although one year, when the Collective was struggling with a strong divergence of opinion on a strategy forward, I consulted with Dr. Barbara Alice

Mann, an Iroquois scholar, who is my friend and colleague at the University of Toledo, for advice on how indigenous communities navigated consensus on trying topics.

The consensus decision-making process was often a rich and rewarding space to learn from each other, and sometimes a site of frustration and even silencing. Newer Collective members, especially younger members or students, frequently remarked that the experience of joining a collective of "experienced" feminists was both intimidating and thrilling, as they entered the group of strong, opinionated, committed women, found their voices, became comfortable, and embraced the power and joy embedded in the process of feminist organizing. Two sisters, Sarah and Gina Vidal, who became long-term organizers, commented often over the years about the process of "finding their voices" in the Collective, learning to trust that their opinions would be valued, and appreciating how that process helped them grow in confidence. Having their voices respectfully listened to may have been exciting and empowering, but some also reported that being given "feminist explanations" of why their ideas were not acceptable in the Collective meetings was also painful and inhibiting. Even as the practice of consensus promoted the power of every single voice, certainly the long-time members and experienced feminists often "held sway," not only because they were able to articulate survivor-centered reasons for their positions, but also because they could explain why certain other ideas were ineffective or politically problematic, often because they had tried or at least considered the ideas in previous years.[6]

The feminist consensus-building process, while sometimes uncomfortable for Collective members newer to feminist analysis and sometimes tedious for longer-term members who had been through the topic a time or ten, was an opportunity to develop feminist critical thinking, to explore new paths of resolution for recurring issues, and ultimately to establish a positive and productive site of growth into more sophisticated feminist thinking for many Collective members, both new and long-term, both academic and community members. Collective member Gaby Davis notes, "It's a great theory—but many people found it more than just a little difficult. You say that it could be "uncomfortable" and "tedious"—but it was way more than that. It was soul-searching—value crunching—bias breaking. There were real make-or-break moments where people had to confront who they were at their core. It is where academic ideas pushed up against community norms and values."[7] The process, which emerged from early activists' experiences in other feminist contexts, became infused with the knowledge and experience of each member, including our awareness of the process's long history. Similarly, foundational feminist concepts such as sexism and victim-blaming, and later, the social construction of gender, were deployed in deliberations among collective members whose exposure to feminist thought varied widely. Those who were there as survivors, or in one member's case, as an organizer who was there because her daughter had been murdered, confronted notions of womanhood, access, and structural sexism, classism, and racism through the deliberations about inclusion, diversity, and access that emerged in the organizing. As the only traditional "academic" in the Collective, I did not "bring feminist theory to the community"; rather, like all members, I shared observations gleaned from what I knew not only from my exposure to feminist theory, but also from my experience and observations. For example, my knowledge of feminist critiques of Catholicism, from Mary Daly and Elizabeth Schussler Fiorenza to the contemporary (specifically SNAP's[8]) analysis of sexual abuse by priests, helped me articulate why it might be problematic to hold the event at a Catholic high school, based on some women's (and children of all sexes') experiences of abuse by the church, structural sexism in the church, and the church's positions on reproductive justice and lesbian rights. Mercurio's class consciousness often prompted the Collective to filter a decision through the lens of how it would impact women with few resources or access to support. A hallmark of Toledo's Take Back the Night organizing has been how much we have taught and learned from each other over the years.

Collective decisions frequently emerged from feminist commitments to equity of access, with special attention to the impact of decisions on minoritized women, especially around issues of race and class. Decisions such as providing free, professionally supervised childcare at events and organizing meetings, sign language interpretation, an accessible bus for women with mobility concerns, and transportation for university students, as well as efforts to foster diverse representation of race, age, ethnicity, and experience in the program, and in the Collective itself, all emerged from an intersectional feminist understanding of access. The intellectual root of these considerations did not emerge from the academy's influence on the Collective; in fact, most of these decisions emerged from feminist activists who had experience in other feminist organizations addressing similar concerns. For example, the feminist bookstore was the book vendor at the Michigan Womyn's Music Festival, which had a history of having sign language interpreters at all events; Mercurio and other members' experience there motivated the Collective to engage interpreters for TBTN. Ensuring the participation—in the Collective and in the event's programs—of women with visible disabilities and diverse age, race, ethnicity, gender expression, and sexuality continued to be a value, even as academic feminism challenged our understanding of concepts like "access," "diversity," and "inclusion." All considerations were aired at meetings, discussed, analyzed, and if questions emerged, evaluated through our collective feminist lens for justice and access. In another example, after years of the Collective providing volunteer childcare to ensure that mothers could attend the event, a newer member of the Collective, who was also a new mother, inquired about the qualifications and security in our childcare setup. The Collective's commitment to providing childcare had emerged from an awareness of how survivors who were mothers, especially mothers and families who experienced poverty, would find it very difficult if not impossible to pay for childcare for an entire evening, for an event that lasted sometimes up to five and even six hours, and who would thus be "expensed out" of participating if we didn't provide it. The conversation about qualifications raised the Collective's awareness not only about security and the need for high-quality professional supervision of our childcare volunteers, but also about legal responsibilities, for the Collective and the hosting venue. Additionally, as a part of the Collective's attention to class issues, we felt that it was important to pay the professional childcare workers, who we recognized worked long hours and had to basically do an "overtime shift" to take on the responsibility of supervising our volunteer childcare workers. Providing professionally supervised and compensated childcare and snacks and activities for the children was, in the eyes of the Collective, supporting a feminist commitment to access and inclusion of poor women and women with children. A similar commitment sparked the accessible bus and transportation centered from the university, primarily for students, but also for women who could use the city bus to get to the university and then take the university-accessible bus to the venue, which would make the event available to women who did not have their own transportation and to women who had mobility issues and could not physically "march." Often such insights about improving access, whether brought by newer members or long-timers, university or community members, were met with nods of agreement and admiration as we developed a multi-directional common commitment to the women who attended the event, sometimes year after year as part of their healing process.

The decision to host the event at different venues around the city and surrounding suburbs was primarily motivated by the Collective's feminist analysis of the ubiquity of violence against women, and to counter racist and classist stereotypes about what neighborhoods or groups of people were more likely to experience (or perpetrate) violence against women. While it is true that mainstream academic feminism in the 1990s was being challenged to analyze its racism by another generation of women of color feminists, the impetus for this decision came not from academics in the Collective, but from the feminist knowledge of the activists, who had long been involved in working-class feminist initiatives that paid special attention to race and access, Gina Mercurio in particular, who, in addition to her work in inclusive organizations in Seattle, had worked with 9 to 5, an organization devoted to equity in access and pay for working women, in Cleveland. Mercurio often cites the work of Andrea Dworkin, in particular *Letters from a War Zone*, in which Dworkin reprints many essays that began as speeches at Take Back the Night events, as influential to her intersectional understanding of violence against women.[9] Dworkin's analysis of class and race in pornography and prostitution, especially in the documentary, *On Pornography: The Feminism of Andrea Dworkin*, also influenced the Collective's understanding of the importance of addressing how women in different communities experienced violence and institutional responses to it in different ways.[10] Gaby Davis, who founded the Domestic Violence Clinic at the University of Toledo College of Law in response to what she heard from women at the "speak out" portion of our TBTN, brought insights from legal scholar Kimberlé Crenshaw, while Diane Docis, the Sexual Assault Education and Prevention coordinator at the university, brought a wealth of knowledge of survivor-centric practices to our deliberations. The professionals in the field from the community also had much to contribute about the ubiquity of violence against women across socioeconomic, ethnic, and religious communities.

An early march was held in the rather blighted downtown Toledo, on the steps of the courthouse; as we marched through the empty downtown, stopping at various locations for speeches and survivor stories, we wondered about who our event was targeting in the empty evening streets. In other years, however, we were able to connect with community centers or neighborhood organizations

Figure 6.3: TBTN 2004, University of Toledo College of Law.

in order to share a venue and bring the event's message to new groups of people. Sometimes we chose a venue because it was near a site of a femicide—or because we wanted to draw attention to an institutional failure, whether that be police or prosecutorial mishandling of a case or biased coverage in the local newspaper. In one memorable year, 2006, we held the event at Woodward High School, in whose neighborhood a neo-Nazi rally the previous summer had provoked rioting and violence. We were warned by our police partners, who regularly encouraged us to "just walk on the sidewalk" so as to avoid disrupting traffic and angering people (and thereby also negate the need for a police escort to stop traffic), that they could not guarantee our safety if we chose to march in the neighborhood. To be fair, we also had a long-term commitment to the event from the Toledo Police Department's Domestic Violence (DV) Office dedicated officer, Mary Jo Jaggers, who attended and provided volunteer officers to stop traffic for the march, and one of the university's officers, Tressa Johnson, who made it a point to keep an old university police van in commission so we would be able to transport the sadly rapidly growing number of Silent Witnesses, based on the number of murders of women locally, from their home in Bowling Green, Ohio. That year, we also had a vibrant and active group of high school women and a fantastic and committed teacher who helped us raise awareness among the students. We had also already developed a "community letter" that we distributed along the march route, informing the neighborhood of the march, our intentions, and our meeting times, and inviting them to help organize and march, or at least turn on their porch lights in support of the cause. That chilly night in October, with tensions somewhat high, we set out with our banner, flashlights, signs, and chants, and the number of people who came outside to clap, flash their porch lights, or even stroll down the sidewalk to join in, was higher than ever. We heard from the Woodward High School staff that the students and families reported that that year's march was an especially healing experience for a lot of community members. While the Collective was not free of racial tensions, the presence of women of color in the Collective and in the program and the vibrant presence of young women of color from Woodward High School figured significantly in the community's perception of the event.

Decisions about partnerships, such as with the public schools, unions, churches, and police, came with Collective analysis of the partnering organization's relationship to our understanding of feminist values: about their commitment to women's leadership, reproductive rights, fair treatment of LGBTQA+ people, racial justice, pay equity, and women's access to leadership, among other things. The UAW Local 12 Women's Committee hosted us twice at their union hall, sent organizers to the Collective for years after, and paid for the creation of a Silent Witness to remember a member's daughter who had been murdered by her husband. Many good relationships and much mutual education about issues facing our groups came

Figure 6.4: Participant in community rally, University of Toledo Health Science Campus, TBTN 2012.

from these partnerships. The Collective engaged in significant discussions about the role of police at the event, particularly in light of growing public awareness about state violence against people of color. If we wanted to march in the street, we were required to have a permit and officers to handle traffic, so debates about whether it was worth making the liaison included discussions about the role of state violence in the lives of minoritized women. In early years, women of color at the speak out had talked about police ignoring their needs and called for help in holding police accountable. The Collective responded by involving the dedicated DV officer in the organizing, the program, and in training the volunteer officers. When Officer Tressa Johnson, a woman of color, joined the Collective, the positive role of police at the event became a mainstay. As the work of Beth Ritchie,[11] Kimberle' Crenshaw,[12] INCITE! Radical Women of Color,[13] the feminists of color in the abolitionist movement, and, later, the Black Lives Matter Movement, challenged women in the Collective to think more critically about how the presence of police impacted women of color's participation in the event, the Collective decided to continue to work with the police based on our longstanding relationship with women of color officers and the strong sense of empowerment participants reported from marching in the street and stopping traffic. Undoubtedly, the discussion about the role of police and the experiences of women of color with state violence will continue to impact future Collective decisions about how the march will be organized.

Other issues that created significant and sometimes intractable debates and sources of conflict in the Collective included the role of men, and—to a lesser extent in number of years, but not in intensity—the presence of transwomen, vendors (especially selling self-defense items), and politicians, but the content of the program remained a perennial source of ongoing deliberation. Depending on the year, the issues over programming might emerge on their own or as part of another debate; for example, one organizer who was also a survivor and a worker in the field of violence against women was deeply committed to the idea that, because we will never end violence against women without bringing men on board, we must involve men in all aspects of the event. Long-time organizers, who had made a commitment long before to feature women public figures, speakers, artists, and singers as a feminist commitment to women who do this work often without proper recognition and compensation, objected to her push for her father, and more men in general, to participate in the program, believing that his presence, while supportive and positive, contradicted the commitment to featuring women in significant positions at the event. The presence of men in the march was even more fiercely debated along similar lines. Organizers who wanted to emphasize men's positive support in healing and in challenging other men's violence wanted men in the march as a demonstration of their importance and significance as allies, while others, committed to the notion that the entire founding principle of the event was about women's right to walk alone at night without men (as protectors or harassers), felt that the presence of men at the women's march would be a violation of that principle and defeat the purpose of the event. They argued that creating the simultaneous "men's event" with a well-respected man in the field helping the men in attendance work on what they could do to be better allies in ending violence against women was enough. While all of the Collective members recognized the importance of involving men in the movement to end violence against women, members' different individual experiences, understandings of the issue of separatism in feminism, and commitments to various feminist principles and agendas drove their positions and caused friction in the Collective's attempts to move forward on the question. Interestingly, a new generation of organizers in the post-pandemic era have made different choices about the role of men and police in the event, without a discernable impact on the size of the event or effect on participants.

Another challenge to the Collective's feminist principles regularly emerged in the writing of the program for the "rally" part of the event. The rally, open to the entire community and featuring a mix of performers and speakers, usually occurred about an hour

Figure 6.5: Toledo TBTN 2017, (the new) Woodward High School.

after the opening of the "resource fair," tables organized by local agencies and organizations that worked directly with survivors or otherwise supported women. The rally typically lasted around an hour and was followed by the men's event/women's march and "speak out." The rally program, like the location, varied every year depending on the focus decided by the Collective, and it regularly featured performances by singers, poets, drummers, and occasionally theater troupes, politicians, and public officials; it frequently highlighted survivors as featured speakers. The challenge for the Collective was to facilitate content for the program that met the Collective's demand that it not participate in victim-blaming or contradict the Collective's principles. Responsibility for the rally's welcome and other parts contributed by collective members were reviewed, edited, and collaboratively created in ways that met the Collective's shared understandings of our message and agenda. The program often responded to situations in the community, such as a particularly disturbing femicide, or to debates going on at the national level. The difficulty came when women politicians and public officials, who were hard-pressed to produce a script ahead of time and have it reviewed, not to mention stay on schedule, were part of the program. Reviewing lyrics of songs by women singers who were volunteering to perform at the event to ensure that they met the Collective's shared feminist values also created challenges as the Collective sought to find language that reflected an understanding of violence against women, did not engage in victim-blaming, and hopefully encouraged and supported survivors in their healing process and/or demanded justice in some other way, while also respecting the singers' artistic autonomy. One year, when the Collective partnered with Start High School to put on the event, the school's anti-dating violence group wanted to do a skit that featured a dramatized sexual assault and its aftermath. Collective members worked with the students and their school advisor to negotiate the meaning of the skit, their artistic integrity, and their understanding of how the enactment of an assault might impact a room full of survivors.

Similarly, another difficulty in the program was about how to honor the experience and interpretation of a survivor's experience if the survivor herself had internalized self-blame. One year, I worked for a very long time with a survivor from that year's partnering organization for the event discussing statements in her prepared remarks about how she had "gotten herself into trouble." After a long and open conversation about how I perceived the implications of the phrase to place the responsibility on her, rather than on the perpetrator of her assault, she insisted that removing the phrase would mean that she was not taking responsibility for her role in the incident, in effect, denying her power at the time and her agency in interpreting her own story later. As we talked through her thinking and mine, we negotiated our understandings of agency and victim-blaming, and our sense of how the message would be received, and we ended up with the phrase, "I got myself into the situation, and I could get myself out." Members of the Collective felt that the script was still troublingly victim-blaming, but the survivor felt that it was not only empowering, because she *did* get herself out, but that it was also true to her experience. In this situation, she and I compromised as much as we felt comfortable, while still being true to our values, and the result, I think, really pleased no one, although the Collective hesitatingly agreed not to remove her talk from the rally's program.

Most of the difficult negotiations routinely involved divergent understandings of feminist principles, and sometimes, as in the cases described above, different understandings of what constituted the most significant feminist value in operation. When such conflicts emerged, the Collective often returned to a central question that guided a lot of our decisions: "Who is this event for?" Often, the part of our mission focusing on Take Back the Night as a "healing event for survivors" became the top feminist priority, followed by "A call to action for the community."

In the twenty-five years in which I have participated in Toledo's Take Back the Night, sitting in the circle with young women, old women, survivors, mothers of survivors, mothers of women who did not survive, workers in the field, academic and activist feminists, and women representing nearly every race, color, and creed, my experience of feminist solidarity around a commitment to ending violence against women has remained strong and affirmed by the iterative process of collaboratively making decisions about the event with the multiple and sometimes contradictory experiences of diverse survivors in mind. My role as an academic did not often emerge as the most significant aspect of my voice on the Collective. In fact, the largest contribution my relationship to the university brought to the Collective's organizing was my capacity to engage the institution's resources on behalf of the event, such as securing a location, funding from our women's center to sponsor the accessible bus and generating resources from departments and offices around campus to support the creation and distribution of the event's publicity materials. Many friendships were made and a few were broken over conflicts between members' understandings of feminism or feminist priorities in the Collective. While some have argued that a "free for all" definition of feminism means ultimately that we stand for nothing, such as bell hooks' claim that, "This 'anything goes' approach to the definition of [feminism] has rendered it practically meaningless,"[14] what has been true for our Collective is that feminist principles are what we forge in solidarity with each other, repeatedly, resolutely, and hopefully revolutionarily, through collective consensus, difficult decisions and dialogues, and in consideration of our diverse experiences. Academic feminism at its best is both responsive to and engaged in this broad and lively public conversation.

NOTES

1. Jeanne Kilbourne, *Killing Me Softly: Advertising's Image of Women*. Dir. Margaret Lazarus, Renner Wunderlich, Patricia Stallone, and Joseph Vitagliano. Cambridge Documentary Films, 1979; *Still Killing Us Softly*. Dir. Jeanne Kilbourne, Margaret Lazarus, and Renner Wunderlich. Cambridge Documentary Films, 1987; *Killing Us Softly 3*. Dir. Sut Jhally. Media Education Foundation, 1999; and *Killing Us Softly 4*. Dir. Sut Jhally. Media Education Foundation, 2010.
2. The Clothesline Project, "Home," accessed August 15, 2021, http://theclotheslineproject.org/.
3. The Silent Witness National Initiative, "About Us," accessed December 18, 2020, https://www.silentwitness.net/about-us.html.
4. Bethany House, "The Silent Witness Project," accessed December 18, 2020, https://www.bethanyhousetoledo.org/silent-witness-project/.
5. See Barbara A. Mann, *Iroquoian Women: The Gantowisas* (New York: Peter Lang, 2000) and Sally Roesch Wagner, *Sisters in Spirit: Haudenosaunee (Iroquois) Influence on Early American Feminists* (Summertown, TN: Native Voices, 2001). Iroquois culture's power-sharing model of governance also influenced Benjamin Franklin's understanding of balance of power and served as a model for the American three branches of government.
6. Feminist critiques of the consensus model follow these and other lines. See the work of Anna Snyder on consensus at the UN 4th World Conference on Women for discussion; Anna Snyder, *Setting the Agenda for Global Peace: Conflict and Consensus Building* (New York: Routledge, 2003).
7. Gabrielle Davis, interview by author, Toledo, OH, July, 2020.
8. SNAP, the Survivors Network of those Abused by Priests, was founded in 1988 by Barbara Blaine, of Toledo; it is now a transnational network with over 25,000 members, accessed December 29, 2020, https://www.snapnetwork.org/about.
9. See Andrea Dworkin, *Letters from a War Zone* (New York: Lawrence Hill, 1989).
10. See Andrea Dworkin, *On Pornography: The Feminism of Andrea Dworkin*. Omnibus, 1991. Documentary. Available on YouTube at https://www.youtube.com/watch?v=L9j7-zZks08.
11. Beth Ritchie, "Battered Black Women: A Challenge for the Black Community," in *Words of Fire: An Anthology of African-American Feminist Thought*, ed. Beverly Guy-Sheftall (New York: The New Press; originally *Black Scholar* 16, 1995).
12. Specifically, for her work on violence against women of color, see Kimberlé Crenshaw, "Mapping the Margins: Intersectionality, Identity Politics and

Violence against Women of Color," in *The Feminist Philosophy Reader*, eds. Alison Bailey and Chris Cuomo (New York: McGraw-Hill, 2008), 279–309. For her ongoing work on the importance of intersectional analysis in addressing social justice issues generally, see Kimberlé Crenshaw, *On Intersectionality* (New York: The New Press, 2017) and Kimberlé Crenshaw, Luke Charles Harris, Daniel Martinez HoSang, and George Lipsitz, eds. *Seeing Race Again: Countering Colorblindness across the Disciplines* (Berkeley, CA: University of California Press, 2019).

13. Especially, INCITE! Women of Color Against Violence, ed. *Color of Violence: The INCITE Anthology* (Durham, NC: Duke University Press, 2016).

14. bell hooks, *Feminist Theory: From Margin to Center* (Boston: South End, 1984), 23.

WORKS CITED

Bethany House. "The Silent Witness Project." https://www.bethanyhousetoledo.org/silent-witness-project/.

Clothesline Project. "Home." Accessed August 15, 2021. http://theclotheslineproject.org/.

Crenshaw, Kimberle. "Mapping the Margins: Intersectionality, Identity Politics and Violence against Women of Color." In *The Feminist Philosophy Reader*, edited by Alison Bailey and Chris Cuomo, 279–309. New York: McGraw-Hill, 2008.

———. *On Intersectionality*. New York: The New Press, 2017.

Crenshaw, Kimberle, Luke Charles Harris, Daniel Martinez HoSang, and George Lipsitz, eds. *Seeing Race Again: Countering Colorblindness across the Disciplines*. Berkeley, CA: University of California Press, 2019.

Davis, Gabrielle. Interview by the author, Toledo, OH. July, 2020.

Dworkin, Andrea. *Letters from a War Zone*. New York: Lawrence Hill, 1989.

———. *On Pornography: The Feminism of Andrea Dworkin*. Omnibus, 1991. Documentary. Available on YouTube at https://www.youtube.com/watch?v=L9j7-zZks08.

hooks, bell. *Feminist Theory: From Margin to Center*. Boston: South End, 1984.

INCITE! Women of Color Against Violence, ed. *Color of Violence: The INCITE Anthology*. Durham, NC: Duke University Press, 2016.

Kilbourne, Jeanne. *Killing Me Softly: Advertising's Image of Women*. Dir. Margaret Lazarus, Renner Wunderlich, Patricia Stallone, and Joseph Vitagliano. Cambridge Documentary Films, 1979.

———. *Still Killing Us Softly*. Dir. Jeanne Kilbourne, Margaret Lazarus, and Renner Wunderlich. Cambridge Documentary Films, 1987.

———. *Killing Us Softly 3*. Dir. Sut Jhally. Media Education Foundation, 1999.
———. *Killing Us Softly 4*. Dir. Sut Jhally. Media Education Foundation, 2010.
MacKinnon, Catharine A. *Sexual Harassment of Working Women: A Case of Sex Discrimination*. New Haven, CT: Yale UP, 1979.
———. *Feminism Unmodified: Discourses on Life and Law*. Cambridge, MA: Harvard University Press, 1987.
MacKinnon, Catharine A., and Andrea Dworkin. *Pornography and Civil Rights: A New Day for Women's Equality*. Minneapolis, MN: Organizing Against Pornography, 1988.
Mann, Barbara A. *Iroquoian Women: The Gantowisas*. New York: Peter Lang, 2000.
Ritchie, Beth. "Battered Black Women: A Challenge for the Black Community." In *Words of Fire: An Anthology of African-American Feminist Thought*, edited by Beverly Guy-Sheftall. New York: The New Press, 1995; originally published in *Black Scholar* 16 (1985).
Silent Witness National Initiative. "About Us." https://www.silentwitness.net/about-us.html.
Snyder, Anna. "Critiquing Consensus: An Analysis of Processes Designed for Non-governmental Collaboration." In *Consensus Decision Making, Northern Ireland and Indigenous Movements*. (Research in Social Movements, Conflicts and Change, Vol. 24), edited by Patrick G. Coy, 31–60. Bingley, UK: Emerald Group Publishing Limited, 2002.
Survivors Network of those Abused by Priests (SNAP). "About." https://www.snapnetwork.org/about.
Wagner, Sally Roesch. *Sisters in Spirit: Haudenosaunee (Iroquois) Influence on Early American Feminists*. Summertown, TN: Native Voices, 2001.

APPENDIX A: TOLEDO TAKE BACK THE NIGHT'S VISION STATEMENT

Take Back the Night: Our Vision

Toledo's Take Back the Night event is held annually to:

- Call for action to end all forms of violence against women including sexual assault, intimate partner violence, stalking, sexual harassment, and child sexual abuse.
- Demand women's right to live without violence and the threat of violence.
- Remind the community that violence against women is a serious problem.
- Call for effective community action to promote women's safety and freedom from all forms of violence.
- Symbolically reclaim the streets and the night for women.
- Empower women with the presence and support of other women.
- Create a space where women feel safe to speak out about the violence in their lives, mourn those who have suffered from violence, support those who are living with violence, and honor those who have survived.
- Recognize the struggle of all women who fight for an end to violence against women and honor the commitment of those who have been holding Take Back the Night marches since the 1970s.

CHAPTER SEVEN

PUBLIC FEMINISM THROUGH LAW AND POLICY ADVOCACY ON REPRODUCTIVE RIGHTS

By Carrie N. Baker

Feminist scholars have knowledge and skills that are useful for passing better laws and public policies. A background in the history and current status of women's rights as well as feminist social movements, combined with feminist intersectional perspectives, can provide a strong foundation for feminist scholars to engage in law and policy advocacy—including work on legislation, regulatory change, and policy implementation, as well as in community organizing for legal change.[1] These activities can include community-based research, media work, testifying at legislative hearings, submitting public comments on proposals for regulatory change, public awareness campaigns to mobilize people to support legal change or pressure businesses to follow the law, and public writing.

In this essay, I will describe how I have used my academic background to advocate for reproductive rights over the last fifteen years. I offer my story as a case study to illustrate some ways scholars can engage with the public on social justice issues. With a law degree and a Ph.D. in women's studies, I study and research the history of women's rights in the United States and women's social movements to expand legal rights.[2] I stay up-to-date on legal developments for my classes, so I understand current law and advocates' strategies to expand and enforce women's rights. Using this knowledge, over the years I have engaged in activism to expand women's rights in the communities where I have lived. I will here offer a case study of feminist community engagement with two examples. In part one of this essay, I will focus on a 2006 campaign to get pharmacies to sell Plan B emergency contraception (EC) after the FDA made it available over the counter. In part two, I will focus on a recent statewide campaign to pass abortion rights legislation in Massachusetts. In these campaigns, I used my feminist academic knowledge and teaching skills to conduct research to support these efforts, engage in public writing and speaking to advance these issues, and to organize in my community. In these ways, I acted on issues that I explored in my scholarship and teaching out in the world, and then brought what I learned back into my teaching and scholarship. The benefit goes both ways. On the one hand, scholarship is strengthened when informed by community engagement, avoiding ivory tower abstraction and irrelevance to the broader world. On the other hand, the women's movement is strengthened when rooted in feminist historical and intersectional scholarship. Just as the field of women's and gender studies grew out of the women's movement, a continuing connection to that movement keeps the field relevant, dynamic, and impactful.

SPEAKING OUT ABOUT PLAN B EMERGENCY CONTRACEPTION ACCESS

In the reproductive rights section of my gender, law, and policy course, I teach a class on contraception. In the early 2000s,

I closely followed and taught about the political fights at the FDA for over-the-counter approval of Plan B emergency contraception (EC). On August 24, 2006, after years of conservative obstruction, the FDA finally approved Plan B for over-the-counter sales, but only for individuals age 18 and older. Because Plan B remained a prescription product for women 17 and younger, it was sold only in retail pharmacy outlets from behind the pharmacy counter and under the supervision of a pharmacist, which meant that all adult women had to show proof of age to a pharmacist in order to obtain Plan B.

Under the FDA approval, Plan B became available over the counter in November of 2006. On December 16, I was shopping at my local Kroger grocery store in Rome, Georgia, where I had been a loyal customer for over a decade. While I was grocery shopping, I remembered that emergency contraception was now available over the counter so I thought I would see if I could buy a box. It was not an emergency, but I thought it would be nice to have a back-up method of contraception on hand. I walked up to the pharmacy counter and asked if I could buy Plan B. The woman on duty told me that they didn't carry it. She said she had no problem with it but that the head pharmacist would not allow them to sell it. She didn't tell me where else I might go to get it. I then went to the service counter and requested that Kroger order it. The grocery store manager called me a couple of days later and said he would look into it and get back to me. A month later, when I had heard nothing at all from Kroger, I called back and spoke to the manager again. He said that the pharmacist refused to carry emergency contraception and that Kroger policy allows pharmacists to decide whether to carry it or not. He said that Kroger also requires that if they refuse to sell Plan B, they must tell the patient where they can go to get it. He acknowledged that they had not followed their own policy in my case. I asked him why they wouldn't carry it and he said that he did not know. He gave me the name of the pharmacist and told me to ask her myself.

At this point, I emailed friends of mine in Rome to tell them what had happened, and I received enraged support. An employee at our local sexual assault center told me that two on-call ER doctors at the local public hospital had recently refused to give EC to a rape victim because of "moral reasons." Another woman who worked at the local teen health clinic told horror stories of pharmacists refusing to give her young clients back their prescriptions after they tried to get emergency contraception. A third woman told me of her own experience with a broken condom a few years before and about how it had taken her days and conversations with multiple medical professionals to find out about EC and get it. I met with a group of women in the community, and we strategized about how to handle the situation locally.

In the meantime, I contacted Georgians for Choice (our state pro-choice coalition) and NARAL (the National Abortion and Reproductive Rights Action League). Georgians for Choice asked me to join their EC Task Force and invited me to speak about my experiences at their annual March for Women's Lives in late March, which I agreed to do. At first, national NARAL said that they couldn't help me because they were targeting five major retailers, not including Kroger, to get them to change their policies, and they didn't have the resources to work with smaller retailers. But they did ask if they could record my story and refer the press to me if necessary, and I agreed. They then put me in touch with the local NARAL office in Georgia. The local NARAL invited me to participate in a press conference on the issue. In the heat of the moment, before I thought about how challenging it would be to speak about something as personal as contraception in front of a bank of microphones at the Georgia State Capitol, I agreed.

A week before the press conference was scheduled, I finally mustered the nerve to return to Kroger to confront the pharmacist. When I asked her why she would not sell emergency contraception, she said she had religious objections to it. I asked her what her religious objections were. She said she didn't believe in abortion. I told her that emergency contraception did not cause abortion.

She had no response. I then asked her if she distributed Viagra and she said yes, to anyone who asked for it. To prepare for the press conference, I wanted to get a sense of how widespread this problem was. At the time, I was teaching a senior seminar in women's studies, so I asked some of the students to help me out by contacting all the local pharmacies and finding out who carried EC and who refused. Many of them did not stock EC.

The press conference was on the Georgia State Capitol steps on March 9, 2007. Throngs of reporters were there, before whom I told my very personal story of being refused emergency contraception at Kroger in Rome, Georgia. The story got picked up by Associated Press and went national and international. The local NARAL office negotiated on my behalf with Kroger, who were very difficult and at times hostile to our concerns. In the press, Kroger said they would "make accommodations" for customers requesting EC if pharmacists refused to provide it, but Kroger's official policy still did not require pharmacists to ensure that customers received EC when they asked for it.[3] Georgians for Choice developed a campaign in which we encouraged people to keep their Kroger receipts and write on the back asking Kroger to carry EC; we then collected the receipts and turned them in to Kroger to pressure them to carry EC. At the march, we collected an enormous number of receipts and sent them to Kroger.

More generally, I worked with all of these groups to conduct a public education campaign, because so much of the resistance to EC was due to confusion about what exactly it was. I participated on a local TV program with a pharmacist and a nurse, talking about EC—what it was and was not, and how to use it. I wrote a letter to the editor of my local paper to explain my position after being criticized by the editorial page editor. As a result of the local NARAL referrals, I was regularly interviewed by newspaper reporters asking about my experience.

The publicity finally piqued national NARAL's interest, and they stepped in and began to negotiate on my behalf with Kroger. National NARAL conducted their own survey of Kroger stores around the country and found out that 27 percent were refusing to distribute EC. As part of a public awareness campaign, NARAL developed a mailer featuring my story. On one side of the mailer was a picture of a male pharmacist saying to a man, "Sorry, Sir— no Viagra for you. I DON'T BELIEVE IN IT." On the other side was a picture of me with the following text: "It's hard to imagine a man being denied Viagra. But pharmacists across America are refusing to sell birth control to women. I know—it happened to me" (see Figures 7.1 and 7.2).

NARAL was asking people to imagine men being treated the same way women are treated—being denied pharmaceuticals necessary to have a full and satisfying sexual life.

In June of 2006, national NARAL invited me to Washington, D.C., to speak at a press conference called by New York Representative Carolyn Maloney for the introduction of a bill, the Access to Birth Control Act ("ABC"), which would ensure that women have timely access to birth control, including emergency contraception, at the pharmacy counter. Interns at NARAL filmed an interview with me, which was placed on YouTube, where I discussed my experience and why I was speaking out on the issue.[4]

Figure 7.1 and 7.2: NARAL 2007 Publicity for Plan B Campaign. Source: NARAL.

160   PUBLIC FEMINISMS

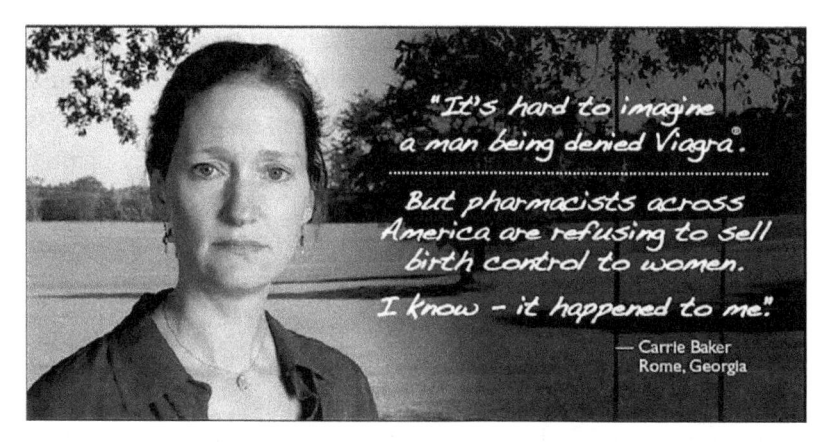

Figure 7.2

Close to a year after Kroger's initial denial of my request for EC, the grocery chain finally adopted an official policy that required the distribution of EC at their stores. If a pharmacist did not want to sell EC, then they needed to hand the request over to another pharmacist or technician. If no one in the pharmacy would sell EC, then they had to find a Kroger employee outside of the pharmacy to sell it. Kroger also established a 1-800 hotline for customers to report if they were refused EC.

I was able to do this community work because I had studied the history of birth control in the United States. I knew what emergency contraception was and that it was not an abortifacient, despite what the scolding pharmacist told me. I had followed the political and regulatory battles that led to over-the-counter availability of the medication, and I knew that I had a legal right to access it. This led me to trying to buy it and to knowing that they should not have blocked my access to the drug. But more importantly, my scholarship on social movements gave me ideas of how I might fight Kroger's refusal to sell the medication to me. I knew what organizations to reach out to because I had studied the reproductive rights movement, and I knew what strategies might be effective in combatting the suppression of emergency contraception, like surveying the pharmacies to see how widespread the denial of emergency contraception was and framing the issue as discriminatory treatment. This background gave me the confidence to pursue the campaign to raise awareness about emergency contraception and demand that Kroger change their policy. Afterward, I brought this community work back into my scholarship and the classroom. Using the campaign as a case study, I wrote an academic article examining how public discourses on emergency contraception imagine women's bodies and sexuality.[5] To this day, when I tell the story of the Plan B campaign to my students and share the article with them, they love the story, especially the idea of their professor getting turned away at the pharmacy counter but then fighting back, and it's fun to tell because it was quite harrowing at the time but humorous in retrospect.

This community engagement experience piqued my interest in taking what I knew from my academic studies out into the community to fight for social change. In the years since, I have deepened and widened my community engagement on reproductive rights issues, eventually including public writing, testifying before the Massachusetts legislature, and leading a community organization. In the latter capacity, I was tested to put the theories I taught in the classroom into practice in the community. The lofty and idealistic principles we discussed in the classroom were often challenging to translate and apply to on-the-ground work in my community. In the next section, I'll describe some of these challenges and the rewards, both for myself and my scholarship, as well as my students.

DEEPENING COMMUNITY ENGAGEMENT ON REPRODUCTIVE JUSTICE

Over the years, my interest in reproductive rights grew. After arriving at Smith College in the fall of 2011, I became part of a reproductive politics faculty seminar in the Five College

Consortium (Smith, Amherst, Mount Holyoke, Hampshire, and University of Massachusetts, Amherst). In the fall of 2012, I began teaching a course on reproductive justice. In 2014, I joined with other faculty members to develop a Five College certificate in reproductive health, rights, and justice, which had a community engagement component. In this way, I became more aware and connected to organizations working on these issues in western Massachusetts, including our local Title X clinic Tapestry Health, the nearby Planned Parenthood in Springfield, and the Abortion Rights Fund of Western Massachusetts (ARFWM). In 2016, I joined the board of the ARFWM and became its president in 2018. In this capacity, I have been integrally involved in a range of community activities relating to abortion rights, including public writing and speaking, legislative advocacy for state-level abortion rights legislation, and research on maternal health. In this work, I have drawn extensively on my scholarly knowledge of history, social movements, law, and policy, and I have leveraged academic resources to which I have access to support this work. I have also engaged my students in this community work in various ways, and I've brought the knowledge I have learned through this work back into the classroom.

But first I had to develop skills to do this publicly engaged work, including public writing and speaking as well as working with policymakers. I turned to a number of organizations that provide training and networking opportunities for public engagement, including the *Ms.* Committee of Scholars, the Women's Media Center, the Scholars Strategy Network, and the Op Ed Project. The *Ms.* Committee of Scholars advises the magazine on content and recruits and trains feminist academics to write for popular media. In 2010, I completed the *Ms.* Writers Workshop for Feminist Scholars to learn how to translate academic scholarship for a public audience.[6] Women's Media Center's (WMC) SheSource is an online database of media-experienced women experts, whom they connect to journalists, bookers, and producers. I completed

WMC's Progressive Women's Voices program, which provides media and leadership training. The Scholars Strategy Network guides and supports faculty members not only on how to translate scholarship for the public but also on how to connect to and influence policymakers in particular. And the Op Ed Project trains people from underrepresented groups "to take thought leadership positions in their fields" through public writing and speaking.[7] All of these organizations connect scholars with mentors to guide and support them in developing public writing and speaking skills. They also help scholars interested in public engagement to connect with journalists, editors, and policymakers.

Combining my academic background with skills developed through these trainings, and using the connections that resulted from them, I have been able to work for reproductive rights through my own public writing and at the local, national, and international levels as a source for journalists and as a community activist. Journalists find me through the Women's Media Center (WMC) SheSource and through Smith College's Community Relations Office. I have developed relationships with people at local television and radio stations,[8] as well as with newspaper and magazine journalists. I am a regular writer for *Ms.* magazine, both the print edition and online, writing on abortion law, abortion pills, telemedicine abortion, self-managed abortion, books and films on abortion, abortion politics, contraception, pregnancy discrimination in employment, and the criminalization of pregnancy.[9] I also have a column in the local paper in my hometown, where I address state and national reproductive health and rights issues.[10] As a member of the Scholars Strategy Network, I have written a policy paper on telemedicine abortion and made a podcast on the issue.[11] And I have written articles on the history of birth control and abortion for the women's health collective *Our Bodies, Our Selves*.[12]

In this media work, I use my knowledge of history, law, and policy, as well as feminist intersectional theory, to provide the public with an accessible but deep and nuanced understanding of what's at stake in contemporary controversies related to reproduction. I place current issues in historical context and explain the impact of proposed laws or court cases. For example, in the fall 2019 issue of *Ms.* magazine, I published a story on the Trump administration's "domestic gag rule" that barred reproductive health clinics from referring patients to abortion providers.[13] I explained the history of family planning funding in the U.S. from the passage of Title X in 1970, to the Reagan and Bush administrations' efforts to restrict Title X providers from talking to patients about abortion, to the Supreme Court decision on the issue in 1992, to the Clinton administration's regulations protecting patients' right to accurate, comprehensive reproductive health care information. I highlighted the disproportionate impact of the domestic gag rule on low-income people, young women, and people of color. My academic background helped me to understand and expose the history and power dynamics of the domestic gag rule.

My public writing has often enabled me to connect activists with each other to further their work. For example, in August of 2019, I wrote an article about an activist, Kat Sullivan, who used billboards to raise awareness about child sex abuse and pressure policymakers in New York to pass a law allowing survivors to sue perpetrators.[14] Afterward, I stayed in touch with Kat. When recently I was writing a *Ms.* article on medication abortion, I interviewed activists at the National Women's Health Network, which was running a campaign to lobby the FDA to remove restrictions on the abortion pill. Around this time, Kat emailed me and said she had access to some billboards and asked if I knew anyone who might be interested in using them for free. I immediately thought of the NWHN. I put them in touch with each other, and they collaborated on creating billboards in Albany, New York, encouraging viewers to contact the FDA to request removal of the abortion pill restrictions (see Figures 7.3 and 7.4). I then covered the billboards in a *Ms.* article on feminist activism to remove the FDA restriction on the

Figures 7.3 and 7.4: NWHN 2020 billboard campaign to remove FDA restrictions on the abortion pill in Albany, New York.

Figure 7.4

abortion pill.[15] Getting to know these amazing activists, connecting them, and amplifying their work through public writing has been extremely meaningful to me. And bringing these stories back into the classroom has been an effective way to engage and inspire my students.

In addition to public writing, I have also engaged in legislative advocacy. As ARFWM president, I have organized in my community to pass state-level legislation—called the ROE Act—to make abortion more accessible in Massachusetts. The ROE Act created an affirmative right to abortion in the state of Massachusetts, as well as eliminated a 24-hour waiting period and parental consent and allowed abortion after 24 weeks in cases of fatal fetal anomaly. As part of a ROE Act Coalition, I worked closely with activists across the state to coordinate support for the legislation. As part of this effort, I wrote several opinion editorials for the local newspaper,[16] appeared on a local radio show,[17] and testified before the Joint Judiciary Committees of the Massachusetts Legislature on June 17, 2019, on the harm that parental consent laws impose on young people in the state. I worked with others in the community to organize city council resolutions in support of the ROE Act in Northampton, Amherst, Easthampton, and Greenfield. I covered the Northampton hearing for *Ms.* magazine.[18]

The COVID-19 pandemic created a new set of challenges for access to reproductive health care, including barriers to contraception and abortion as well as maternal health equity. I spoke out in multiple ways. In addition to publishing numerous *Ms.* magazine articles on abortion access during COVID-19, I participated on several virtual panel discussions on this issue, one sponsored by NARAL and another by Massachusetts Rep. Mindy Domb. And Massachusetts Rep. Lindsay Sabadosa invited me to speak at a town hall on telemedicine abortion access during COVID-19. I know both of these legislators because they serve on the ARFWM advisory board. In my writing, I focused particularly on telemedicine abortion and self-managed abortion. I wrote a policy paper on telemedicine abortion with Scholars Strategy Network,[19] and I did an Instagram takeover @MsMagazine on telemedicine abortion access during COVID-19. I also worked closely with the MA COVID-19 Maternal Equity Coalition to produce a report for the legislature about how to address maternal health and equity during the pandemic[20] and publicized it with an op-ed in the local paper.[21]

I have invited my students to join in this activism so they can learn firsthand about social change. Some attended the ROE Act hearings as well as the Maternal Health Equity Town Hall. Some interned for the ARFWM and for other movement organizations, including NARAL and Planned Parenthood in Massachusetts. Two students in Smith's Statistical and Data Sciences program did data analysis of the ARFWM's client base, producing a report used in strategic planning and fundraising. My student research assistants regularly assist me with my public writing—transcribing interviews, conducting research, and editing pieces. Many are now doing public writing themselves.[22] I have worked closely with the reproductive justice student group on campus, connecting them to community activists that they have brought to campus and providing them with updated information about the status of the ROE Act and community events.

Students have also benefited from this community work because I bring what I learn through community engaged activities back into the classroom. I share my op-eds, news stories, and policy reports with my students, and I update them about recent legal and legislative developments. I often develop ideas for new articles in my discussions of these developments with students. For example, when the Trump administration proposed vast religious and "moral" exemptions to the Affordable Care Act contraception mandate, my students' questions inspired me to read the entire 200-plus pages of the proposals so that I could explain it to them. Based on that work, I wrote a story for *Ms.*—"The 10 Most

Egregious Things about Trump's New Rules on Birth Control Coverage."[23] I also explained how my students could submit public comments on the proposals and encouraged them to do so (always emphasizing that they don't have to agree with me and that they should come to their own positions).

Finally, this public engagement is informing my scholarly research agenda. I'm now working on a book project focused on analyzing the rollback of reproductive rights as a form of systemic reproductive coercion and gendered violence. My public writing has led to my scholarly research in the past, in the case of my second book, *Fighting the US Youth Sex Trade: Gender, Race, and Politics*—which grew out of a *Ms.* magazine feature article I wrote in 2010, "Jailing Girls for Men's Crimes."[24] The interviews with front-line activists that I do for my public writing often lead to questions that I then pursue in my scholarship.

CONCLUSION

This case study of community engagement illustrates a range of ways faculty and students can apply their academic knowledge in their communities to further feminist social change, including with community-based research and public writing, by joining activist organizations and participating in educational programs, and through public speaking. From my early engagement with the Plan B campaign in Georgia to this recent work on the ROE Act in Massachusetts, public engagement has made my scholarship and teaching more impactful and meaningful. I have learned so much from the people I encounter in my public work—especially the activists and lawmakers that I interview for my public writing and with whom I work on legislation and public policy. This community-engaged work has deepened my knowledge about reproductive rights and fueled my scholarship and teaching. This work has also enabled me to forge deeper, more meaningful connections with my students as they learn, grow, and engage themselves in the world around them. Through this work, I am able to move across existing boundaries by challenging the divisions between colleges and the communities in which they exist.

This work answers the call of bell hooks for feminist scholars to make their work accessible to broader publics.[25] The field of women's and gender studies grew out of the women's movement. My experience is a case study of how faculty and students in the field continue to be deeply connected with this social movement today and how we are still working to further the feminist fight for social justice.

NOTES

1. M. V. Lee Badgett, *The Public Professor: How to Use Your Research to Change the World* (New York: New York University Press, 2017).
2. My first two books, *The Women's Movement against Sexual Harassment* (New York: Cambridge University Press, 2008) and *Fighting the US Youth Sex Trade: Gender, Race, and Politics* (New York: Cambridge University Press, 2018), explore how women have organized to influence public policy.
3. "Kroger To Staff: Plan B Is OK," CBS News, March 9, 2007, at https://www.cbsnews.com/news/kroger-to-staff-plan-b-is-ok/.
4. "Carrie Baker—Refused Birth Control at Her Pharmacy," YouTube at http://www.youtube.com/watch?v=J5iicsr_19g.
5. "Women's Bodies and Sexuality in the Public Sphere." In *Imagination and the Public Sphere*, edited by Susan Cumings, 84–99 (Newcastle Upon Tyne, UK: Cambridge Scholars Press, 2012).
6. Carrie N. Baker, Michele Berger, Aviva Dove-Viebahn, Karon Jolna, and Carmen Rios, "Amplifying the Voices of Feminist Scholars in the Press," *Feminist Formations* 32, no. 2 (Summer 2020): 29–51.
7. "Mission," Op Ed Project, at https://www.theopedproject.org/mission.
8. "An Ill Wind Blows," *The Bill Newman Show*, WHMP, June 20, 2019 (radio), discussion of abortion rights at 30:30 min; "Massachusetts Pregnancy Workers Fairness Act," *Connecting Point with Carrie Saldo*, WGBY Public Television, April 11, 2018.
9. See "Carrie N. Baker, Author at Ms. Magazine," *Ms.*, https://msmagazine.com/author/carriebaker/.
10. See "Byline: By Carrie N. Baker," *Daily Hampshire Gazette*, https://www.gazettenet.com/Byline?byline=By%20Carrie%20N.%20Baker.

11. Carrie N. Baker, "Increase Access to Abortion Pills Via Telemedicine Abortion," *Scholars Strategy Network*, May 6, 2020; Carrie N. Baker, "No Jargon: The Future of Abortion Care?" *Scholars Strategy Network*, June 11, 2020.
12. Carrie N. Baker and Kirsten Thompson, "A Brief History of Birth Control in the US," *Our Bodies, Ourselves* (July 2020), at https://www.ourbodiesourselves.org/book-excerpts/health-article/a-brief-history-of-birth-control/; Carrie N. Baker, "History of Abortion Law in the United States," *Our Bodies, Ourselves* (August 2020), at https://www.ourbodiesourselves.org/book-excerpts/health-article/u-s-abortion-history/.
13. Carrie N. Baker, "The Gag is in Place," *Ms.*, September 19, 2019.
14. Carrie N. Baker, "Three Billboards Outside Her Abuser's Workplace," *Ms.*, September 3, 2019.
15. "Feminist Multi-Front Battle to End FDA's Abortion Pill Restriction," *Ms.*, May 21, 2020.
16. See "Byline: By Carrie N. Baker," *Daily Hampshire Gazette*, https://www.gazettenet.com/byline?byline=By%20Carrie%20N.%20Baker.
17. "An Ill Wind Blows," *The Bill Newman Show*, WHMP, June 20, 2019 (radio), discussion of abortion rights at 30:30 min.
18. Carrie N. Baker, "How Local Activists Are Organizing for Reproductive Rights," *Ms.*, June 14, 2019
19. Carrie N. Baker, "Increase Access to Abortion Pills Via Telemedicine Abortion," *Scholars Strategy Network*, May 6, 2020.
20. Carrie N. Baker, "Giving Birth in a Pandemic: Policy Recommendations to Improve Maternal Equity During COVID-19," MA COVID-19 Maternal Equity Coalition, July 2020.
21. Carrie N. Baker, "Maternal Health in Massachusetts During the Pandemic," *Daily Hampshire Gazette*, July 23, 2020, A6, at https://www.gazettenet.com/Columnist-Carrie-N-Baker-35315361f.
22. See "Smith Public Voices: Sophia Smith," https://sophia.smith.edu/smithpublicvoices/authors/. List includes my students who have written for *Ms.* magazine and other publications.
23. Carrie N. Baker, "The 10 Most Egregious Things about Trump's New Rules on Birth Control Coverage," *Ms.*, October 23, 2017.
24. Carrie N. Baker, "Jailing Girls for Men's Crimes." *Ms.* (Summer 2010): 26–31, at https://msmagazine.com/2010/12/08/jailing-girls-for-mens-crimes/.
25. bell hooks, *Feminism Is for Everybody: Passionate Politics* (Pluto Press, 2000): 112–113.

WORKS CITED

Badgett, M. V. Lee. *The Public Professor: How to Use Your Research to Change the World.* New York: New York University Press, 2017.

Baker, Carrie N. *The Women's Movement against Sexual Harassment.* New York: Cambridge University Press, 2008.

———. "Women's Bodies and Sexuality in the Public Sphere." In *Imagination and the Public Sphere*, edited by Susan Cumings, 84–99. Newcastle Upon Tyne, UK: Cambridge Scholars Press, 2012.

———. *Fighting the US Youth Sex Trade: Gender, Race, and Politics.* New York: Cambridge University Press, 2018.

Baker, Carrie N., Michele Berger, Aviva Dove-Viebahn, Karon Jolna, and Carmen Rios. "Amplifying the Voices of Feminist Scholars in the Press." *Feminist Formations* 32, no. 2 (Summer 2020): 29–51.

hooks, bell. *Feminism Is for Everybody: Passionate Politics.* London: Pluto Press, 2000.

CHAPTER EIGHT

BUILDING BRIDGES
Researching with, and Not for, Students on Diversity and Inclusion Policy

By Gabrielle Rodriguez Gonzalez, Jack Kendrick, and Megan Nanney

INTRODUCTION

While nearly 87% of trans people have at least some college education,[1] trans students experience significant rates of violence, isolation, and harassment, on the basis of their sex/gender throughout matriculation.[2] Research has pointed to institutional policy interventions being needed to redress these inequities. Recent indexes have documented that 1,072 colleges and universities include gender identity and expression language in their non-discrimination policies; 272 colleges have gender-inclusive dormitories or floors; 265 institutions allow for name changes on official registrars; 200 have at least one gender neutral or inclusive restroom; 89 include gender affirming care in student insurance plans; and 43 allow for pronouns to be listed on class rosters.[3] Other recommended policies and resources for trans inclusion address athletics, gender affirming campus health care or referral programs, LGBTQIA2+ centers and organizations, and workshops for faculty, staff, and incoming students.[4]

Despite widespread policy adoptions, critical trans and feminist scholars have noted a troubling trend: practitioners are spending more time writing diversity-related policies than enacting them.[5] Through what Sara Ahmed defines as the *non-performativity* of diversity,[6] institutions of higher education create empty commitments to diversity and inclusion, wherein symbolic solidarity with marginalized students stands in for the action of supporting these communities, thereby perpetuating the inequalities that diversity policies purport to address. Scholars such as Z Nicolazzo have described trans inclusion policies that "trickle down" as symbolic in nature, akin to "caution tape," meaning such policies can be easily pushed away, torn down, or otherwise disregarded, thus doing little, if anything, to actually improve students' quality of life on campus.[7] For instance, the emergence of trans-inclusive housing or restrooms—albeit a best practice that proliferates the options where trans students may exist on campus in a comfortable and safe environment—overlooks the fact that having one stall, floor, or building dedicated to the practice of trans inclusion marks the *rest* of campus as *un*safe and *exclusive*. Allow us to be clear: these policies are certainly necessary and are better than nothing. The issue, however, is that diversity and inclusion work often ends there—with the adoption of a policy or the creation of a space—suggesting that there is a singular point of arrival wherein institutions *are* inclusive and diversity work is no longer necessary.[8] As a result, current trickle-down diversity and inclusion policies mark these campuses as safe and inclusive, consequently treating students as the problem in need of fixing or accommodation in order to fit within the pre-existing institutional structure.

In this chapter, we explore the impacts of trickle-down diversity work and imagine the possibilities of trickle-*up* diversity work as an alternative through our shared experiences as trans and non-binary students, alumni, and faculty at three historically women's colleges (HWC).[9] HWCs have been a central site for discussing transgender diversity, inclusion, and policy particularly after Smith College, an HWC in Massachusetts, denied the admission of Calliope Wong in 2013.[10] Such debates, which have continued on these campuses, center around the institutional purpose of these colleges as well as ask for whom these colleges are for and how they determine womanhood—by sex or by gender. As a result of trans student-led activism, over half of all HWCs have since adopted formal admission policies that allow for the admissions of trans women, men, and non-binary applicants, though these policies vary widely across institutions regarding the various criteria of who is considered admissible.[11]

But what happens once students are admitted under these policies? Ideally, because these colleges publicly commit to including trans students as part of the student body, they would be welcomed and supported on campus. Yet, recent research has begun to uncover a different reality.[12] For example, trans participants in one study spoke at length about hostile climates on their campuses, with some feeling merely tolerated and others detailing experiences of being bullied, harassed, and targeted by peers and employees, describing the campus as volatile and unwelcoming to all forms of gender diversity. One participant noted: "I was constantly asked, 'Why do you go here?' and 'If you're a male, why did you apply to go to an all-women's university?' ... And even though I would ask the staff for help with this bullying problem, they would do absolutely nothing. I talked, personally, to the president of the university about this issue ... she told me that neither she nor the school board have any intention of changing the trans policy anytime soon."[13] In the extreme, another study shared the experiences of two trans masculine students who were forcibly institutionalized after being misgendered, verbally harassed, and physically assaulted by campus police because the students' gender presentation did not match the image or name listed on their student IDs.[14] Such examples show that merely accepting trans students does not equate to fostering a welcoming environment on campus. Again, while certainly such policies are necessary, they do little to actually *include* trans students if students' presence is tenuous at best.

One intervention to remedy such a disconnect between policy and practice is *trickle-up policy-building*.[15] This feminist practice alters how those invested in equity come to know, make, and implement policies, understanding diversity work as something that is organized, led, and for the primary benefit of those who have historically been cast aside and silenced within these institutions. In other words, a trickle-up approach "prioritizes building leadership and membership on a 'most vulnerable first' basis, centering the *belief that social justice trickles up, not down.*"[16] As a result, any rights would invariably "trickle-up" to those groups who historically face lesser amounts of vulnerability and violence, recognizing that gender mediates everyone's lives.[17] In this way, institutional policies can not only accommodate trans people, but center these populations in order to determine what best benefits us all.

In what follows, we engage in an ethnographic dialogue to theorize key considerations for practicing trickle-up policy work as a public feminist method with, and just not for, trans students. Specifically, we draw on our experiences as trans and non-binary students, alum, and faculty across three HWCs. Gabrielle Rodriguez Gonzalez is a non-binary Puerto Rican-Dominican Mount Holyoke student majoring in English. As an aspiring writer and filmmaker, Gabrielle's work is invested in creating new worlds that critique the cemented choices of a racist, transphobic, and homophobic society. A recent graduate of Smith College, Jack Kendrick is a white trans man and international student. Jack joined our team through his interest in improving the college experience for future trans students. Megan Nanney, a white non-binary femme, also graduated from Smith and has been a research fellow at Mount Holyoke and held faculty status at Smith and Hollins University. Megan comes to this work through their academic and applied research, which centers around how communities and institutions grapple with in/exclusion through the frame of diversity and exclusion. The authors are also three of the founding members of *Trans @ HWCs*,[18] a trans-led research organization and resource site dedicated to shifting the conversation from *admitting* trans students to *supporting* trans students at HWCs through education, advocacy, and empowerment. As we discuss below, our shared investment in this project is to re-envision what it means to *do*—rather than just espouse—diversity and inclusion work as an interactive process that can be driven by the students whom policies affect.

DUOETHNOGRAPHIC METHODS

To explore key strategies for navigating diversity with, and just not for, trans students, we employed a duoethnographic method. Duoethnography is a method where two or more researchers engage in a multi-step dialogue to interrogate and re-conceptualize beliefs of a single, fixed, and absolute reality.[19] What distinguishes duoethnography from autoethnography or mere conversation is that it provides multiple collective perspectives on phenomena to collaboratively develop critical tensions, insights, and perspectives of a shared experience. Through this dialogue, the reflections become ethnographic data, allowing the researchers to juxtapose their experiences to collaboratively discover and explore the shared, overlapping, and divergent areas between their perspectives and understandings with the desire to challenge dominant and universalizing narratives and effect positive social change.

Because duoethnography centers each author's perspective and voice, we found it a particularly fitting tool to explore the enactment of trickle-up policy work. Therefore, in developing our approach, we decided to engage in "dialogue" over a ten-week period. This method allowed us to invest fully in the process of making space for one another's perspectives, respond to one another, and generate new meanings of our experiences while permitting readers to witness the authors both in conversation.[20] To address a set of questions regarding our personal investments and experiences in diversity work, we first reflected and wrote our thoughts individually. Then, together, we met virtually and discussed our reflections, upon which we offered feedback, asked additional questions, and identified primary themes and differences in our experiences emergent in the data, which we further explored over the remaining weeks, resulting in nearly forty pages of dialogue.

We began our dialogue by focusing on a photograph relating to our shared investment in trans inclusion at HWCs. According to Richard Sawyer and Joe Norris, beginning with an artifact adds "contexture," or texture of the context, to the duoethnographic dialogue to enhance the effectiveness of the text.[21] The photograph we chose was from the Instagram profile @historicallywomens.com, a popular meme profile for students and alumni of HWCs.

We chose this image due to a heated debate in the profile's comments and "stories" feature after a HWC student reposted the image but edited it by crossing out the word "historically." As commenters noted, the use of "historically" is a student-led effort intended to acknowledge the school's past of exclusively accepting female applicants, while emphasizing the fact that its present and future student body is gender diverse, particularly including transgender, non-binary, and gender non-conforming students. By covering up "historically," this signaled to trans students that they neither belonged nor are welcomed on campus. In the segment of the dialogue reproduced below, we start with the question at

Figure 8.1: Two frames of men yelling at each other, the first stating "You go to that all-girls school, right?" and in the second frame, the other man replies "It's actually a historically women's [sic] college."

the heart of the debate surrounding this image: does what we call these colleges matter?

THE DIALOGUE

    Jack: Thinking of when the student reposted that meme on her story and covered up the "historically" in "historically women's college," of course there was instant uproar in the

BUILDING BRIDGES   179

community. She was called a TERF[22] because of her "erasure" (both literally and metaphorically) of trans people, but it wasn't the removing of the "historically" that made her a TERF. I don't use the "HWC" label and clearly, I am not a TERF. I think this is an example of when labeling becomes the main focus of the issue, it actually becomes harmful and unproductive, because it caused quite a big rift in the community and so much energy was spent debating whether we should call it a HWC, when clearly not everyone will ever agree on the correct label for these institutions. In my opinion, if we just improved the experiences of marginalized groups on campus, it wouldn't actually matter whether the college was called a women's college or a historically women's college, because the root of the issue would be solved instead of just being repackaged.

Gabrielle: It's interesting now because that event seems to show the name is a call to arms/trigger word. I can understand why these labels may be important, but at the end of the day I'd much rather be actively cared for in secret than be traumatized but publicly proclaimed.

Jack: Also, now that I'm thinking about labels and such, the whole labeling thing seems to be a technique of division as well, from the institution itself and also from within student communities.

Gabrielle: Yes! A way to calm the real issues that trans folks are bringing up. They (students and the institution) can do their monthly "We care about trans people!!" charade and leave us to die. This seems to be the way institutions fix things: change language and then stop there.

Jack: Labels really do seem to be the be-all and end-all. I think this is probably because language is the most public facing aspect of these institutions and so "woke" labels are used to mask the issues to the community at large, including to students in the community. Seeing as we're talking about "public feminisms," I might argue that these colleges view labelling and language as their most important and necessary public feminist projects, whereas in reality I think we can all agree that they are largely virtue-signaling vanity projects that have no real impact on the experiences of marginalized groups on campus.[23]

Megan: That brings up a great point. There is debate about who should do the work of diversity. Some say that the majority should do the work, but that leads to a "trickle-down" effect. Others say to center those at the margins, creating a "trickle-up" effect, but this also puts an onus of labor on marginalized communities.

Jack: I don't believe that the onus for creating a just and equitable environment should completely fall on those that are in marginalized groups, but these voices should be centered and elevated in conversations around their own inclusion. With a "trickle-up" structure, the danger is forcing those at the margins to relive and rehash their trauma and experiences over and over again in order to educate the masses, which is obviously counterproductive. However, with a "trickle-down" scenario, we risk the majority speaking over those at the margins or using their re-education and "activism" as a kind of self-improvement exercise. So much of diversity "work" seems (non)performative (e.g., calling these schools "historically women's colleges") instead of actually creating any sort of meaningful change on campus. At Smith, for example, trans students created a list of demands of changes they'd like to see—these are changes that start with and center trans students—like hiring trans counselors or faculty, actively recruiting trans women to apply, or, even at the bare minimum, requiring all people on campus to attend training on gender and sexuality and paying the workshop leaders. That would actually improve the trans experience at the college.

Gabrielle: Yes! Pay those that are part of this community, with training and experience in the area, to do the work. It's that simple! It's critical to remember that those at the top are usually there because they are working within and for the majority system. This would imply a trickle-up effect, but I would say that paying the folks who have experience in these spaces speaking directly to those at the top will have a better outcome. Those at the bottom are (usually) already familiar with the work and don't need to be told what needs to be done.

Jack: The college experience can be pretty traumatic for the most marginalized people, and once they graduate it is understandable that they might want to distance themselves from the college. Yet, it is also true that things only ever seem to get done when alumni hound administrators. It seems the most active alumni have always felt they belonged to their HWC; they don't strike me as the kind of people that will really hold the college accountable.

Gabrielle: Marginalized students have to deal with classism, racism, ableism and any other "isms" on top of transphobia. Understandably, they're trying to survive rather than focusing on organizing. The problem boils down to the isolation of students from each other. While it sounds paradoxical, there needs to be some sort of institutional support for students to hear the grassroots work done by generations before so those interested can continue the work. This is where the real support comes from. It's all well and good for there to be "commitments to diversity and inclusion" but if student-led efforts that transform the institution are ignored, erased, or forgotten, then what's the point?

The barriers that exist to add things into Mount Holyoke's archives are just one example of how little they value public feminism and just how much they make hollow promises of inclusion. One of my friends, a Frances Perkins scholar[24] and immigrant, tried to submit a documentary to the archives on the experiences of various marginalized students and their lives on campus during the COVID pandemic. She found that she had to give up all creative rights for it to be added. Giving up all your rights as a creator so you can document students' histories during a historic time is just not something that reflects an institution's care to actually center students. The institution *needs* to value grassroots work enough to cement it into their historical canon, making it accessible to future generations of students to foster community and center diverse experiences on campus.

Megan: That makes me think of these oral histories of trans students and alumni that were part of the first trans history archive at one of the colleges in my research. I originally went into my fieldwork thinking that trans students were going to be central to campus life after the admission policy was adopted, but it turned out to be nearly the opposite—many of the students were isolated from one another and the campus community as a whole. Part of the reason was because students were unaware of the student activism that occurred even five years prior—a lot of trans history has been lost, either due to mistrust of students providing it to the institution, or it was kept from students due to institutional gatekeeping. For example, I wanted to look at the Board of Trustee minutes to know how the policies were decided at the schools in my dissertation, but those are restricted from being viewed for fifty years! So, like the oral histories, a lot of the history that we have uncovered and continue to collect in our work together has come from alternative sources outside of institutional reach—online, interviews, and documents laying around in people's personal files. That's also why our resource site is so important. It's one way that knowledge and history become shared within the community, linking applicants and students and alumni to resources they might not otherwise know about or have access to.

Jack: This is hard because it goes back to who should do this work. It shouldn't be our job to improve our campus because of the institution's neglect or apathy to our situation when they promised to support us—that's the administrators' jobs. Our job is to be students. It is really easy to engage people that are already on either side of the issue with you and really difficult to engage people that don't have an opinion. Scholars can try and engage people with community-based learning, but you can't make people actually care enough to partake.

Gabrielle: Reminds me of the diversity conference at my school, which many complain is not attended by those who need to listen and instead those who already are interested/know about it.

Jack: I agree with you, but I do think that in a larger context it is still important to mobilize more people towards trans inclusion. The most at-risk trans people are outside of the liberal women's college bubble, and we need to be working towards liberation for them, too.

Gabrielle: Oh absolutely! It's critical for this work to be included in the plans for the larger movement but in the context of colleges, the majority of resources should be allocated to caring for these marginalized folks directly! I know that one of your goals, Megan, was to not only work with an all-trans team, but to also give trans people training in research and policy work, so we can continue supporting marginalized communities with these skills. Trickle-up work is not leeching from community members and getting all the credit. Trickle-up work is looking to the folks who have already been doing the work and uplifting them in their liberation.

BUILDING BRIDGES

Trans admission policies at HWCs are an imperative first step for trans inclusion on campus. But there is more to diversity work than just opening the gates. Gates are barriers. Even when they are opened just a slight bit, say, for transgender students, they can still be shut for others: "Even an open gate is not accessible for everyone."[25] Building bridges on the other hand, provides an accessible path over barriers, allowing all to enter. In this paper we position trickle-up methods as one such bridge that extends diversity work beyond traditional scholarly publications and institutional policy documents. Rather, trickle-up policy-building *transforms* how diversity and inclusion is created so that diversity work is done *with,* and not for, the students whom these interventions are meant to assist.

Using duoethnography, a method of collaborative ethnographic dialogue, we grapple with the challenges and benefits of trickle-up work through our individual and collective experiences as trans students, alum, and faculty at three HWCs. As we discuss, trickle-up methods are uniquely positioned as a public feminist approach toward trans justice at HWCs because they engage with and center the histories, experiences, and knowledges of trans students, which have been historically left out of the decision-making process at these colleges despite public commitments to including them. We also note the unique challenges that trickle-up methods present, placing the onus of diversity work on students in environments that isolate trans community from forming in the first place. As Jack stated, "It shouldn't be our job to improve our campus ... Our job is to be students." Indeed, we acknowledge that it is important to mobilize *all* people, cis and trans, to work towards trans justice. But through this dialogue, we come to the collective conclusion that trans liberation can only be possible when diversity work shifts from the top ("trickle-down") to centering those at the margins ("trickle-up").

For example, we have recently used trickle-up methods to create *Trans @ HWCs*, a trans-led and student-centered organization and resource site dedicated to shifting the conversation from *admitting* trans students to *supporting* trans students at HWCs. As discussed in the dialogue, we have found that organizing work at our own institutions has been difficult for trans students because they are often isolated from one another and the work of prior students, causing students to have to reinvent the wheel every few years and advocate for the same changes with little to no progress. Therefore, we formed *Trans @ HWCs* to build that bridge—connecting trans students to accessible and transparent information, support services, and community-building platforms. The site features a "college search", where students can look up resources, articles, videos, websites, and student stories about each HWC in the United States. Unlike other popular college resource websites or indexes, however, all *Trans @ HWCs* resources are produced and gathered by trans students at these colleges themselves. This prevents institutions from hiding behind the mere presence of a policy or resource and it provides first-hand accounts of what it is actually like for trans students on campus. Additionally, by connecting students not only with resources at their own institution, but also with students across institutions, students are able to share ideas and strategies in order to support one another in trans justice work.

While our chapter focuses on trans students at HWCs, we contend that the implications of trickle-up policy as a public feminist method are far-reaching, extending to both other gender-segregated as well as gender-expansive spaces. As feminist scholars and activists, instructors and researchers, policymakers and implementers, our emphasis must be on institutional transformation on our campuses and any effort must prioritize the issues of trans people to lead in our mutual liberation. In many ways, these colleges are already well equipped with the tools that they need to not only support trans students, but to help them thrive on campus. Perhaps more important than the content of new policies, the key to supporting students is the students themselves. As Gabrielle stated, "[look] to the folks who have already been doing the work and [uplift] them in their liberation." To this end, we envision a future in which our institutions can become gender-affirming colleges, actively supporting and advancing gender justice for all community members.

NOTES

1. Jaime M. Grant et al., *Injustice at Every Turn: A Report of the National Transgender Discrimination Survey* (Washington DC: National Transgender Center for Equality and National Gay and Lesbian Task Force, 2011).
2. Z Nicolazzo, *Trans* in College: Transgender Students' Strategies for Navigating Campus Life and the Institutional Politics of Inclusion* (Sterling: Stylus Publishing, 2017).
3. "Campus Pride Trans Policy Clearinghouse," *Campus Pride*, accessed August 6, 2021, https://www.campuspride.org/tpc/; Alexander K. Davis, "Toward Exclusion through Inclusion: Engendering Reputation with Gender-Inclusive Facilities at Colleges and Universities in the United States, 2001–2013," *Gender & Society* 32, no. 3 (2018): 321–347.
4. "Campus Pride Trans Policy Clearinghouse."
5. Nicolazzo, *Trans* in College*; Sara Ahmed, *On Being Included: Racism and Diversity in Institutional Life* (Durham, NC: Duke University Press, 2012).
6. Ahmed, *On Being Included*.
7. Nicolazzo, *Trans* in College*.
8. Nicolazzo, *Trans* in College*.
9. As we discuss, there is debate regarding what we should call these colleges. Some terms proposed have included "Single-Sex", "All Women's", "Predominantly Women's", "Women-Centered", "Gender-Inclusive", "Gender Diverse", "Gender Selective", and as used in this chapter, "Historically Women's Colleges." We use the latter term to acknowledge the historical mission of these colleges for women while highlighting that not all students are "women", akin to Historically Black Colleges and Universities (HBCU), and due to the term's favorability amongst current students at these colleges.

10. Following this internationally publicized event, Calliope Wong changed her name for privacy purposes. We choose to use the name associated with the event here, rather than her chosen name, in order to respect her confidentiality. Megan Nanney, "Transgender Student Experiences in Single-Sex Colleges," *Sociology Compass* 14, no. 8 (2020): 1–14.
11. Nanney, "Transgender Student Experiences."
12. Nanney, "Transgender Student Experiences"; Megan Nanney, "Open Gates, Broken Promises: Inclusion Policies and Transgender Student Experiences at Gender-Selective Women's Colleges," (PhD Dissertation, Virginia Polytechnic Institute and State University, 2020); Annie Freitas, "Beyond Acceptance: Serving the Needs of Transgender Students at Women's Colleges," *Humboldt Journal of Social Relations* 39 (2017): 294–314; Laura Boyd Farmer, Claire K. Robbins, Jennifer L. Keith, and Challen J. Mabry. "Transgender and Gender-Expansive Students' Experiences of Genderism at Women's Colleges and Universities," *Journal of Diversity in Higher Education* 13, no. 2 (2020): 146–157.
13. Farmer et al., "Transgender and Gender-Expansive Students' Experiences of Genderism," 151.
14. Nanney, "Open Gates, Broken Promises."
15. Kari Dockendorff, Megan Nanney, and Z Nicolazzo, "Trickle-Up Policy-Building: Envisioning Possibilities for Trans*formative Change in Postsecondary Education," in *Rethinking LGBTQIA Students and Collegiate Contexts: Identity, Policies, and Campus Climate*, eds. Eboni M. Zamani-Gallaher, Devika Dibya Chouduri, and Jason L. Taylor (New York: Routledge, 2019), 153–168.
16. Dean Spade, *Normal Life: Administrative Violence, Critical Trans Politics, and the Limits of Law* (Durham, NC: Duke University Press, 2015), 137 (emphasis added).
17. Nicolazzo, *Trans* in College*.
18. transhwcs.org, to be released Fall 2023.
19. Richard D. Sawyer and Joe Norris, *Duoethnography* (Oxford: Oxford University Press, 2020).
20. Sawyer and Norris, *Duoethnography*.
21. Sawyer and Norris, *Duoethnography*.
22. Trans-exclusionary radical feminist.
23. Ahmed, *On Being Included*; Davis, "Toward Exclusion through Inclusion."
24. The Frances Perkins program at Mount Holyoke is for students of a non-traditional age who have not yet earned an undergraduate degree.
25. Nanney, "Open Gates, Broken Promises," 247.

WORKS CITED

Ahmed, Sara. *On Being Included: Racism and Diversity in Institutional Life*. Durham, NC: Duke University Press, 2012.

Campus Pride. "Campus Pride Trans Policy Clearinghouse." Accessed August 6, 2021, https://www.campuspride.org/tpc/.

Davis, Alexander K. "Toward Exclusion through Inclusion: Engendering Reputation with Gender-Inclusive Facilities at Colleges and Universities in the United States, 2001–2013." *Gender & Society* 32, no. 3 (June 2018): 321–347. https://doi.org/10.1177/0891243218763056.

Dockendorff, Kari, Megan Nanney, and Z Nicolazzo. "Trickle-Up Policy-Building: Envisioning Possibilities for Trans*formative Change in Postsecondary Education." In *Rethinking LGBTQIA Students and Collegiate Contexts: Identity, Policies, and Campus Climate*, edited by Eboni M. Zamani-Gallaher, Devika Dibya Chouduri, and Jason L. Taylor, 153–168. New York: Routledge, 2019.

Farmer, Laura Boyd, Claire K. Robbins, Jennifer L. Keith, and Challen J. Mabry. "Transgender and Gender-Expansive Students' Experiences of Genderism at Women's Colleges and Universities." *Journal of Diversity in Higher Education* 13, no. 2 (2020): 146–157. https://doi.org/10.1037/dhe0000129.

Freitas, Annie. "Beyond Acceptance: Serving the Needs of Transgender Students at Women's Colleges." *Humboldt Journal of Social Relations*, no. 39 (2017): 294–314.

Grant, Jaime M., Lisa A. Mottet, Justin Tanis, Jack Harrison, Jody L. Herman, and Mara Keisling. *Injustice at Every Turn: A Report of the National Transgender Discrimination Survey*. Washington DC: National Center for Transgender Equality and National Gay and Lesbian Task Force, 2011.

Nanney, Megan. "Open Gates, Broken Promises: Inclusion Policies and Transgender Student Experiences at Gender-Selective Women's Colleges." PhD Dissertation. Virginia Polytechnic Institute and State University, 2020.

Nanney, Megan. "Transgender Student Experiences in Single-Sex Colleges." *Sociology Compass* 14, no. 8 (2020): 1–14. https://doi.org/10.1111/soc4.12817.

Nicolazzo, Z. *Trans* in College: Transgender Students' Strategies for Navigating Campus Life and the Institutional Politics of Inclusion*. Sterling, VA: Stylus Publishing, 2017.

Sawyer, Richard D. and Joe Norris. *Duoethnography*. Oxford: Oxford University Press, 2020.

Spade, Dean. *Normal Life: Administrative Violence, Critical Trans Politics, and the Limits of Law*. Durham, NC: Duke University Press, 2015.

CHAPTER NINE

REFLECTING ON FAT ACTIVISM
AS RESEARCH METHODOLOGY

By Calla Evans

INTRODUCTION

In her 2016 book *Fat Activism*, Charlotte Cooper calls for increased, sustained, and meaningful engagement by fat studies scholars with fat activists. She sees these types of engagements as key to undoing and unravelling assumed knowledge of fatness, fat activism, and the lived fat experience. Cooper presents her own lifelong engagement with fat activism and fat activists in support of her argument that developing fat activist research methodologies is key to "generating other kinds of community-based knowledge that puts fat people at the centre of its production."[1] But what can a fat activist research methodology look like in practice? Answering Cooper's call, this chapter will attempt to answer this question through an exploration of my own experience with fat activism as a methodological foundation.

In 2019, I completed a research project titled *Inviting the Infinifat Voice to the Fatshion Conversation: An Exploration into Infinifat Identity Construction, Performance and Activism*. This project explored how those at the largest end of the fat spectrum (self-identified "infinifats") experience the mainstream fashion industry and the ways in which they are "hacking" a system that largely ignores them, redirecting social currency and building towards an infinifat-inclusive fashion future. The project also explored the infinifat relationship to fashion and dress through a social justice lens, drawing attention to how contemporary framings of superfatness are reinscribed through a lack of mainstream clothing options and how the lack of accessible fashion disproportionately impacts those who embody other marginalized identity markers. Throughout the entire research design, execution, and presentation of the *Inviting the Infinifat Voice* project, I kept Cooper's call for a fat activist research methodology front of heart and mind. In this chapter I will further her definition of what a fat activist research methodology is and reflect on what it can look like in practice at three defined points in the project's life: initial research impetus, research design and data collection, and final project dissemination and next steps. My hope is this chapter will encourage thought and discussion around the possibilities of activist-engaged research design and execution, particularly for fat studies aligned scholars.

ACADEMIC CONTEXT AND AUTHOR POSITIONALITY

The academic field of fat studies is built upon a foundation of fat liberation and fat activism. According to Katariina Kyrölä and Hannele Harjunen, fat studies stands in contrast to academic fields which pathologize fatness and frame fat as an "epidemic" that must be "eradicated."[2] Fat studies instead "focuses on fat as a gendered, culturally produced and variable category and experience."[3] Accordingly, feminist fat studies are committed to unravelling embodied normativities and challenging boundaries of identity construction and performance, operating in concert with other academic fields such as gender, ethnicity (or race), disability, and queer studies. Fat is a fluid, often socially constructed identity marker that can intersect with all of the identities mentioned above in complicated and complicating ways.

One of the key objectives of fat studies is epistemological justice: a reframing of who is able to claim knowledge and expertise about the lived fat experience. Much of early fat studies work is what Cooper calls "oppositional literature," meaning scholarly output and research that challenges dominant framings of fatness and establishes fat people as important knowledge producers about fat and fatness.[4] This stands in opposition to "obesity" experts who are often far removed from fat embodiment and whose knowledge of fatness is frequently weaponized against fat people as a marginalized group. Cooper returns to the concept of a shift in power around who should be constructing knowledge of fatness in *Fat Activism*. Reflecting on her own desire to amplify the voices of fat activists within the academy, Cooper states that it is "imperative that epistemology derived from fat people's own experience must be taken seriously in order to know about fat and change how knowledge and power are currently used against fat people."[5] Yet how do fat studies scholars engage with and elevate fat knowledge? Cooper answers this question by describing her "scavenging" of qualitative methods in which she primarily *does* the activity she is interested in researching: fat activism. Additionally, she interviews other fat activists from her personal network and engages with fat activism archives in the United States, United Kingdom and Germany, but what I was, and still am, primarily interested in is how Cooper locates and works outwards from her own fat activist practice *as* a research method. As an emerging scholar, this concept of activism as research method seems counter to much of what I have learned about the ways in which research methods and methodologies stand to legitimize knowledge. However, as Ben Agger states, "[Research] methods make the reader believe that she is reading science and not fiction, but it is all fiction anyway."[6] For me, this quote reminds us that there are numerous, if not infinite, ways of knowing, including those that would not normally appear in a mainstream research methodologies textbook. Using my own fat activist practice as a starting point and then engaging with other fat activists felt, to me, as an important way to counter many of the fictions about fatness that permeate mainstream research.

To this end, it is important for me to locate myself and my activist practice in this research. I am a mid-fat[7], white, Queer, able-bodied, cis-woman settler living in the colonial project known as Canada. I have been fat since childhood; I cannot remember a time in which my body was not read as fat. Before returning to academia as an older graduate student, I would not have considered myself a fat activist. It was through engagement with fat studies scholars such as Charlotte Cooper that I now consider many of my day-to-day activities as part of my fat activist practice. Indeed, simply existing unapologetically as a fat person in the world, be it in online spaces or physical, "real life" situations, can be considered a form of fat activism. I actively cultivate fat community, engage in large-scale and small-scale fat activism projects and am positioned as a "fat expert" in many contexts within my academic institution. As a white, mid-fat person I do not struggle to see myself reflected in mainstream fat activism spaces. However, I am involved in an ongoing personal reflection on who is missing from fat activism and how I can leverage my relative privilege to support and amplify their voices and activism work.

INVITING THE INFINIFAT VOICE IMPETUS

The initial idea for the *Inviting the Infinifat Voice* project came while I was taking a graduate class on (re)fashioning the body. Each week we would engage with a series of readings on different experiences with fashion and dress: one week on trans dressing experiences, another week on racialized folks and their experience with clothing and fashion. When we got to the week on fat and plus-size dressing, I was excited. As a newer graduate student, it is always an unexpectedly pleasant experience to start from a place of personal knowledge and experience as opposed to grasping for an entry point into texts, theories, and concepts which can feel foreign and overwhelming. However, I was, to put it lightly, disappointed in the selected readings. The majority of research at the intersection of fat studies and fashion studies is focused on the fashion and dressing experiences of primarily cis-women who fit the conventional definition of "plus-size." The readings assigned in my class were no different. I found myself furiously highlighting and annotating: while it is true that plus-size women have fewer options than their thinner, "straight-sized" sistren, what about those who are "too large" for mainstream, commercially available plus-size fashion? What about those who are both "too large" and also embody other historically marginalized identities? To me this seemed like an obvious misstep: while much of the existing research on plus-size dressing claims to illuminate the plight of the plus-size dresser, the real plight, at least in my mind, is felt by those who are ignored by the plus-size industry entirely. If approaching fashion and dress through a social justice lens, as many of the assigned articles from that class claimed to do, would it not make sense to start with the most ignored, the most marginalized, and work outwards from there?

At the same time as I was taking the (re)fashioning course, I had stumbled upon a podcast called *The Fat Lip* and the associated Instagram account run by the host, Ash. Ash is a superfat activist who has coined the term "infinifat". On her blog, also titled *The Fat Lip*, Ash explains the origin of the term infinifat:

> So, if [US dress size] 12 is small fat, 20 is midfat, and 26 is superfat, what exactly does that make a size beyond-36? Because the reality is that my body is as similar to a size 26 as that 26's is to a size 12—that is: not really similar at all. My experiences and struggles are completely different than a 300-pound person's. I weigh an

entire fat person more than that. How can we be in the same fat spectrum category?

Honestly, I don't know if this is a question that ever gets asked because my feeling is that a lot of fats don't even know that beyond-36s exist. But we do. And we need fat positivity too.

But what should we fats on the very very very fat end of the fat spectrum be called? I humbly propose "infinifat." Because what size am I? I really have no fucking idea. A size greater than any assignable size number. Infinity? [8]

While this chapter isn't necessarily about the infinifat community specifically, what I would like to draw attention to here is my engagement with Ash and her activism practice as presented on *The Fat Lip* as a way of responding to the research gap I was coming up against. While fashion studies scholars have been lacking in their attention towards the superfat and infinifat fashion experience, Ash (and others like her) have been doing important activist work to amplify the voices of those at the largest end of the fat spectrum, particularly as they are ignored by the mainstream plus-size fashion community. I saw my job, as a fat activist and fat studies scholar, as simply amplifying Ash's voice, and the voices of those in her infinifat community, to a volume loud enough to reach academia.

RESEARCH DESIGN AND DATA COLLECTION

The first step, for me, towards the amplification of the infinifat experience was scavenging my own activist-aligned research methods, to borrow from Cooper. I merged photo elicitation and semi-structured interview methods in an effort to create a space in which the project's participants could establish their own representational voice and present their own unique infinifat epistemologies. I initially reached out to Ash from *The Fat Lip* podcast and she was the first participant in the project. Through her "infinifat" community, four other participants were recruited and participated in the project. I had an open and direct conversation with Ash that I was specifically seeking a diverse group of infinifat voices beyond the white, heteronormative, able-bodied fat body that is often the most heard in fat activism spaces. Demographic data was collected as an optional question at the conclusion of our interviews with the preamble that this data was being used primarily to establish the demographic makeup of the participants as a group and to address how intersecting identities and lived experiences may interact with dressing practices. The question was purposefully phrased in an open-ended manner, allowing participants to work from their own definition of what "demographic" information to include. To this end, two participants identified as non-white (one as African American, the other as Hispanic), one participant identified as disabled, and one participant identified as gender non-binary. Mentions of class and socio-economic status happened throughout the interviews. For example, one participant who described themselves as white and middle-class, mentioned the relative financial privilege they have in being able to "buy up" a large quantity of a specific type of pants that is available in their size, motivated by the fear of that specific type of pants being discontinued, while another participant, who described themselves as African American and growing up in poverty, spoke about growing up as a fat child wearing adult women's garments purchased from a thrift store as children's or girl's clothing was not available, or affordable, in their size. I am grateful to Ash for "opening the gate" to her infinifat community, and while I want to acknowledge her role in selecting participants for this specific project, it's also important to recognize the ways in which she impacted participant recruitment and selection.

In designing this critical ethnographic study, I followed Marisol Clark-Ibáñez's example of mobilizing self-identification and auto-image production to complicate the lines between subject and object of study.[9] The qualitative methodological approach of critical ethnography moves beyond the classic ethnographic method of a "neutral" researcher recording, contesting the often assumed position of knowledge holder and expert—and the corollary mirror image of the passive object of study—by centering the question of how knowledge is constructed by dominant powers, and how that knowledge maintains or reinforces unequal power dynamics, including within and through the study itself.[10] Critical ethnography provides the tools to investigate the power dynamics at play in the research process itself, and in the lived experiences being described by research participants, while mitigating imbalances by foregrounding the research subject voice. In other words, the participant is centered as the knowledge expert as opposed to the researcher-as-expert. Historically, much of the scholarly work around fatness and fat identity has focused on quantitative ways of articulating the fat experience. However, as Lauren Downing Peters explains, "fatness can be best understood as a dual construct: as both biological truth and as a personal and social experience."[11] Through the design of this project, I attempt to amplify the voices of self-identified infinifat subjects and center them as the experts of their own lived infinifat experience.

My semi-structured interview approach draws from social anthropologist Sophie Woodward's ethnographic research method of merging formal interviews with casual conversations about dress, also known as "wardrobe interviews," and combines it with aspects of photo elicitation interviewing (PEI) in which participants often take images after receiving prompts from a researcher and the resulting photographs are analyzed alongside semi-structured interviews. Woodward describes her wardrobe interview approach as akin to "hanging out" with women in their bedrooms and closets as they navigated the process of selecting what to wear for the day.[12] This process allows her to "arrive at an in-depth understanding of the multiple and often contradictory issues and identities that are articulated through the material culture of clothing."[13] Woodward is less interested in the specific garments selected by her participants and more concerned with the ways in which they respond to normative beauty ideals and wider societal expectations through their sartorial choices. These interviews can more clearly illuminate how participants make sense of their identity in the world through clothing than traditional interview techniques alone.

When applying Woodward's wardrobe interview technique to my own study I was most interested in the conversational, casual tone she references: this approach of "hanging out" with my participants and talking about their clothing challenges and successes. However, in-person wardrobe interview sessions were not possible in my study due to the geographic distance between myself and my participants. Thus, I attempted to recreate important aspects of the wardrobe interview process through photo elicitation. I asked my participants to send me digital photographs of themselves in outfits that brought them joy and outfits that caused them to feel frustration. These images provided an invaluable entry point for our semi-structured interviews that I framed as casual conversations around their experiences with dressing.

Describing her own use of photo elicitation interviews (PEIs), Marisol Clark-Ibáñez states, "Photographs elicit extended personal narratives that illuminate the viewers' lives and experiences."[14] She later goes on to explain that photographs, especially in her use of the photo elicitation interview methodology, act as a communication medium between researcher and participant, stating "Researchers can use photographs as a tool to expand on questions and simultaneously, participants can use photographs to provide a unique way to communicate dimensions of their lives."[15] This was true of my experience with photo elicitation. Take, for example, this image from Kelly:

This image provided a starting point for a conversation about the pattern grading challenges faced by infinifat people when they are able to find clothing in larger sizes. Pattern grading is the process of adapting a standard pattern for additional clothing

Figure 9.1: An image from participant Kelly of them taking a picture of themselves with their phone while wearing a yellow cardigan, pink tank top, and flowered pants.

sizes. Kelly stated during our interview that they[16] included this image specifically as an illustration of poor pattern grading and went on to describe, in detail, how various aspects of the image (the folded sleeve cuffs, gaping arm holes, etc.) speak to this issue. By emailing this image to me prior to our interview, Kelly was able to establish that this was an issue that they wished to discuss during our interview, further disrupting the traditional researcher-subject power dynamic. The use of photo elicitation overall helped to build rapport between myself and the participants. Clark-Ibáñez speaks to this in her use of PEIs, stating "Photos can lessen some of the awkwardness of interviews because there is something to focus on, especially if the photographs are taken by the interviewee and they are therefore familiar with the material."[17] My intention here was that through the submission of personal photographs, project participants could feel secure in the knowledge that we would be able to address their specific concerns around clothing and dress as

I myself am not an infinifat or superfat person. My positionality in this regard did come up in multiple interviews. I currently consider myself to be mid-fat, although my body size has ranged between mid- and superfat throughout the years. I spoke honestly with interview participants about how I came to the project and that as a not superfat or infinifat person myself, my desire was to allow their voices and experiences be heard without restriction. I am also a white, middle-class, able-bodied, cis-woman and when speaking to participants whose identities differ from my own, I made a concerted effort to create space for them to speak about their own lived experience in as much detail as they were comfortable sharing with me. When disseminating the project findings, be it in written or presentation format, I opted to include large, intact quotes from the participant interviews in an effort to afford participants greater epistemological agency over their own experiences and knowledge. This goes hand-in-hand with a semi-structured, creative interview methodology in establishing the research subjects as experts in knowing what it is to be infinifat and the impact a lack of clothing options has on the lived infinifat experience, particularly for those participants who embody identities outside of those most often heard in fat activism spaces.

I must address one of the main drawbacks of photo elicitation in the context of this project. Despite the fact I included a statement that the photo elicitation aspect of the interview was not a requirement for participation, potential participants without the ability or desire to contribute images may have felt that this project was not accessible to them. One potential participant expressed they did not have access to a camera or smartphone and that was a barrier for their participation. In future situations where I would be able to interview participants in-person this objection could be overcome by me photographing the participants or by simply talking about their clothing while looking at the garments; this is outlined by Woodward in a more traditional "wardrobe interview."[18] This barrier to access, whether explicit or implied, is a potential drawback of any research methodology that asks participants to contribute resources to the interview experience and is often felt most acutely by those at the margins of an already marginalized group.

DISSEMINATION AND NEXT STEPS

I have presented the findings from the *Inviting the Infinifat Voice* project in a great variety of settings both inside and outside of academia. I attend an academic institution that houses one of the most prestigious fashion schools in Canada and I have spoken about this project and the importance of working towards an infinifat-inclusive fashion future with both faculty and design students in settings ranging from intimate graduate seminar classes to large undergraduate lectures. I believe it is important for students to be exposed to this type of activist-grounded academic work. In my own teaching I have designed assignments where students not only engage with activist organizations within their communities, but also consider what they can offer those organizations in terms of

Figure 9.2: Image of Calla Evans speaking to a large gathering of Ryerson undergraduate fashion students.

skills and resources, in order to encourage critical thought around what a reciprocal relationship can look like between community and academia. I have been interviewed in mainstream publications about this topic, such as *Elle* magazine and *Style Democracy*. The main findings of the project have been published in an open access academic journal. Through social media I engage with small-scale fashion designers and companies, particularly those in Canada, to encourage them to increase their size ranges, sharing with them my findings through the links noted above. I am part of a loosely organized network of fat activists working towards greater fashion inclusivity for super- and infinifat folks.

I am acutely aware of how my relative privilege as a mid-fat, white, able-bodied, cis-woman impacts the reception of this work. The reception would arguably be different if I myself was a superfat or infinifat person. However, with each and every presentation I strive to center the voices of the project participants through including their images (shared with consent) and sharing large, intact quotations from our interviews. In many ways, I see the use of the participant-provided images in the dissemination of the project findings as a form of activism: the participant-provided images challenge many of the overwhelmingly negative depictions of superfat folks in popular culture. That being said, I also consider myself a caretaker of these images and I am both conscious and careful of where they are shared and in what contexts.

Presenting this work to current and future fashion industry gatekeepers, such as undergraduate and graduate fashion students at Ryerson University, is one way that I see this project connecting back to Cooper's fat activism as research methodology argument. Deliverance to an infinifat-inclusive fashion future will not eliminate the intersecting axes of oppression faced by those at the largest end of the fat spectrum, but it is an important step towards addressing many of the systemic barriers infinifat and superfat people face. My own fat activism practice has been greatly influenced and expanded through this project. Not only did many of the participants challenge my own assumptions about the lived superfat experience but the questions and critiques I have faced when presenting this work to greater academic and public audiences have forced me to publicly situate and name my fat activism as centering the experiences of the fattest among us. Specifically, participants' statements of feeling "left out of" and "too much for" mainstream fat activism underscore the importance of this work for me personally. For audiences who struggle with the concept of fat liberation and fat acceptance for those at the largest end of the fat spectrum, this project offers an important and necessary entry point into the super- and infinifat liberation conversation: it is difficult to argue with the idea that everyone deserves access to clothing that allows them to fully live their lives, even when (or perhaps especially when) you believe that fully-lived life should include a focus on weight loss. As Ash stated during our interview, after reflecting on the lack of workout clothes for infinifat people, "that's so crazy and counter-intuitive, because all the thin world wants from fat people is for them to lose weight and to exercise and go to the gym. But there are no clothes to do that." I strongly believe in the importance of more non-superfat or infinifat fat activists doing just as I have, by participating in the ongoing process of critiquing and challenging their own perceptions of "acceptable" fatness and fat identities.

While publicly presenting this work to fashion gatekeepers and others can be seen as a form of fat activism, it does not go far enough. When sharing the final work with project participants the most common comment I received was "So now what? What are you going to do to help fix this problem?" While I had achieved the main objective of the *Inviting the Infinifat Voice* project through the inclusion of infinifat voices at the fashion, or fatshion, table, it became glaringly obvious that I needed to take this work from the academic realm into the public sphere and directly engage with those who are excluding superfat and infinifat bodies with their fashion offerings. To this end, I am currently working on a collaborative, open-access toolkit for inclusive fashion sizing. This toolkit project asks three main research questions: 1) What are the main challenges facing small-scale fashion designers in terms of offering more size inclusive garment options from both a design and business perspective? 2) What knowledge of inclusive design practices can be gained from companies that offer more size inclusive garment options? 3) How can this knowledge be mobilized in a way that cultivates community knowledge building and is rooted in activist practices? These questions are being answered through a qualitative, needs assessment-oriented project design and will ultimately culminate in a community-based open access online toolkit that is being supported by the Centre for Fashion and Systemic Change at Ryerson University. I am working closely with the infinifat and plus-size fashion community, mainly through social media platforms such as Instagram, to identify small-scale fashion designers that are "doing it right" in terms of size inclusive practices as well as those designers and companies that the communities wish would adopt similar practices. The project works to identify the challenges small-scale designers face when expanding their size offerings, both from a design perspective as well as a business perspective and addresses these challenges with knowledge gained from those who are already reaching the communities involved.

From my experience considering the "what now?" question from the *Inviting the Infinifat Voice* project participants and working on the inclusive fashion sizing toolkit, I would like to suggest that it is impossible to consider a fat activist research methodological design that doesn't incorporate some aspect of public dissemination and engagement. It's not enough merely to consider what a fat activist research methodology looks like from the perspective of how knowledge is being constructed and whose knowledge we are building from, we also need to consider how that knowledge is being disseminated. For Cooper her work lives on in her book, *Fat Activism*, which she wrote with attention towards an accessible written voice. She describes her work as a "para-academic" project, stating "although this study reflects scholarly conversations to some extent, I speak and write with a voice that I hope is accessible to many and I avoid or explain jargon where possible"[19]. It is not a large leap to argue that for Cooper, this para-academic approach can be seen as an integral part of a fat activism research methodology. In the same way I consider the *Inviting the Infinifat Voice* and the inclusive fashion sizing toolkit to be para-academic projects. While the initial objective was to expand scholarly conversations around plus-size dressing and fat fashion, both projects have become much more through activist and public engagement. Prioritizing accessibility, not only in writing style and voice but also in other aspects of research dissemination, is an important tool in breaking down barriers that exist between activist and academic work.

CONCLUSIONS

Returning to the question of what a fat activism methodology could look like in practice, I hope that the reflections contained within this chapter can further discussions around the very definition. While Cooper's description of "scavenging methods" to construct her fat activism methodology could imply a haphazard process, I argue that, in fact, Cooper illuminates an intentional and thoughtful approach towards a working definition of what a fat activism methodology can and should contain. My own experience supports this argument. *Inviting the Infinifat Voice* is a project that firmly straddled the activist/academic border at every step. From idea impetus, and research design, to dissemination and next steps, this was, and continues to be, a project deeply connected with activist objectives and ways of knowing. *Inviting the Infinifat Voice* uniquely positioned participants as knowledge experts and research collaborators in consideration of the emancipatory and activist underpinnings of fat studies. The research design worked to actively challenge the inherently unbalanced researcher/ participant power dynamic and provide participants with the tools they needed to establish their own representational voice and present their own unique infinifat epistemologies. The ways in which *Inviting the Infinifat Voice* has been taken up within and outside of the academy also points towards the possibilities offered by a fat activist research methodology. I hope that you are similarly inspired as I was when I came across Cooper's first-steps of defining what a fat activism research methodology looks like for her and I hope that these reflections encourage thought and discussion around what activist-engaged research design and execution can look like in practice.

NOTES

1. Charlotte Cooper, *Fat Activism*, (Bristol: HammerOn Press, 2016): 32.
2. Katariina Kyrölä and Hannele Harjunen, "Phantom/Liminal Fat and Feminist Theories of the Body," *Feminist Theory* 18, no. 2 (2017): 99–117
3. Ibid.
4. Charlotte Cooper, "Fat Studies: Mapping the Field," *Sociology Compass* 4, no. 12 (2010): 1020–1034.
5. Charlotte Cooper, *Fat Activism*, 33.
6. Ben Agger, *Public Sociology: From Social Facts to Literary Acts*, 2nd Ed., (Rowman & Littlefield Publishers, 2007).
7. For background on the activist origins of the fat spectrum and its impact on theorizing fatness through a social justice lens See: http://thefatlip.com/2016/12/20/beyond-superfat-rethinking-the-farthest-end-of-the-fat-spectrum/; https://ravishly.com/ash-fat-lip-podcast; https://fluffykittenparty.com/2019/10/05/fategories-understanding-smallfat-fragility-the-fat-spectrum/; https://fatpositivecooperative.com/2019/01/03/exact-numbers-and-levels-of-fatness/.
8. Ash, "Beyond Superfat: Rethinking the Farthest End of the Fat Spectrum," *The Fat Lip*, December 20, 2016, Retrieved March 23, 2018, from http://thefatlip.com/2016/12/20/beyond-superfat-rethinking-the-farthest-end-of-the-fat-spectrum/.
9. Marisol Clark-Ibáñez, "Framing the Social World with Photo-Elicitation Interviews," *The American Behavioral Scientist (Beverly Hills)* 47, no. 12 (2004;): 1507–1527.

10. Carol Grbich, *Qualitative Data Analysis: An Introduction*, (SAGE Publications, 2007).
11. Lauren Downing Peters, "You Are What You Wear: How Plus-Size Fashion Figures in Fat Identity Formation," *Fashion Theory* 18, no. 1 (2014): 46.
12. Sophie Woodward, *Why Women Wear What They Wear*, (Oxford: Berg, 2007).
13. Ibid., 31.
14. Marisol Clark-Ibáñez, "Framing the Social World with Photo-Elicitation Interviews," *The American Behavioral Scientist (Beverly Hills)* 47, no. 12 (2004): 1511
15. Ibid., 1512.
16. Kelly is gender non-binary and uses they/them pronouns.
17. Marisol Clark-Ibáñez, "Framing the Social World with Photo-Elicitation Interviews," 1512.
18. Sophie Woodward, *Why Women Wear What They Wear*.
19. Charlotte Cooper, *Fat Activism*, 8.

WORKS CITED

Agger, Ben. *Public Sociology: From Social Facts to Literary Acts*, 2nd ed. Washington DC: Rowman & Littlefield Publishers, 2007.

Ash. "Beyond Superfat: Rethinking the Farthest End of the Fat Spectrum." *The Fat Lip*, December 20, 2016. Retrieved March 23, 2018, from http://thefatlip.com/2016/12/20/beyond-superfat-rethinking-the-farthest-end-of-the-fat-spectrum/.

Clark-Ibáñez, Marisol. "Framing the Social World with Photo-Elicitation Interviews." *The American Behavioral Scientist (Beverly Hills)* 47, no. 12 (2004): 1507–1527.

Cooper, Charlotte. "Fat Studies: Mapping the Field." *Sociology Compass* 4, no. 12 (2010): 1020–1034.

Cooper, Charlotte. *Fat Activism*. Bristol: HammerOn Press, 2016.

Downing Peters, Lauren. "You Are What You Wear: How Plus-Size Fashion Figures in Fat Identity Formation." *Fashion Theory* 18, no. 1 (2014): 46.

Grbich, Carol. *Qualitative Data Analysis: An Introduction*. London: SAGE Publications, 2007.

Kyrölä, Katariina and Hannele Harjunen. "Phantom/Liminal Fat and Feminist Theories of the Body." *Feminist Theory* 18, no. 2 (2017): 99–117.

Woodward, Sophie. *Why Women Wear What They Wear*. Oxford: Berg, 2007.

CHAPTER TEN

"MARCH INTO THE ARCHIVES"
Documenting Women's Protests[1]

By Jessica A. Rose and Lynée Lewis Gaillet

Without knowledge of women in history as actual history, dead women are sheer ghosts to living women

—*and to men (Mary Ritter Beard, 1944)*

To combat erasure and silencing of women's public work, feminist researchers must harness the interdisciplinary power of archival crowdsourcing to capture, accurately portray, and sustain women's rhetorical activism. Those who are currently working to shift public and historical narratives—including Black Lives Matter, LGBTQ+, and intersectional feminist activists—must ensure that their community stories are accurately recorded and preserved as a fundamental part of their work. This call for in-community archiving is not new. Mary Ritter Beard, early twentieth-century organizer of the short-lived World Center for Women's

Archives (WCWA), attempted to document nineteenth- and twentieth- century women's work and activism by collaborating with organized groups and private donors to collect and collate materials attesting to women's achievements. Though the WCWA effort ultimately stalled, Beard's vision persists as contemporary archivists encourage us to capture acts of twenty-first-century women's activism, recognizing the need to counteract "the archival silence that has assisted with the historical delegitimation of women's interaction with the state and women as political actors."[2] In part, earlier attempts like Beard's failed because a project of this magnitude requires interdisciplinary collaboration among archivists, scholars, community members, and collectors, as well as patrons. However, the time is right to revisit Beard's strategic archival plan given current methods of digital collection and availability of online finding aids, a twenty-first-century emphasis on interdisciplinary research, and increased collaborations among researchers, community archivists, and special collection librarians. This essay revisits Beard's efforts and profiles one local example from the 2017 Women's Marches as a model for how communities might establish accurate, ground up collections that contribute to archives that are publicly and globally accessible to activists, students, and scholars.

Developing a material historical record of feminist work and activism represents an important first step in creating a more complete chronicle, but bringing that historical record to its most relevant constituents is necessary in order to sustain movements and collections through symbiotic growth. Beard understood this important act; it served as an impetus for her expansive collection efforts (described below). Like current feminist archivists, Beard insisted that scholars, teachers, and citizens must learn from historical silencing, erasure, and the disruption of public memory. We must continue devising collation strategies and searchable databases to capture, house, and connect the work of women, while also sharing these materials publicly. Consider, for example, the

New York Historical Society Museum and Library's commitment to foregrounding the legacy of women's rhetorical actions. The Center for Women's History (located within the museum) explores women's work across race, class, and sexuality through permanent and visiting installations, topical lectures and programming, and galvanizing features such as the history of women's political advocacy film *We Rise*, narrated by Meryl Streep and including original music by Alicia Keys. The Center's initiatives, like many others across the country and world, further Beard's mission: to keep women's historical accomplishments, writ large, in the public eye. In this essay, we ask how local communities can build ground up archives, making their work accessible by linking collecting and collation efforts with other like-minded projects.

MARY RITTER BEARD

In the early 1930s, Beard collaborated with Hungarian pacifist and feminist Rosika Schwimmer to organize the WCWA. Adopting French historian Fustel de Coulanges' motto "No documents, no history," Beard envisioned an archive of women's papers and organizational records that would provide a foundation for women's history as an academic field and serve the public good.[3] She raised funds, founded a board of directors, and collected documents from Schwimmer and a broad network of women activists, including suffragist leaders, club and university women, the New York Public Library, private patrons, and President Franklin Roosevelt's WPA women's initiatives. Headquartered in New York with strong ties to Washington D.C., the WCWA was well-publicized; supporters came from a range of national special interest women's organizations (Business and Professional Women, the National Council of Negro Women, Jewish Women Leaders, etc.). While the collection reflected Beard's specialized interests (the pacifist movement, women's suffrage), she diligently worked to realize a collection representing the breadth of women's activities, including artifacts from unknown women. However, despite all best intentions, by the early 1940s, factionalism among WCWA supporters, shaky financial support, and an increasingly militaristic atmosphere in the United States and abroad led to Beard's resignation and forced the dissolution of the WCWA.[4]

Beard recommended Smith College archivist Margaret Grierson as her successor, leading to the creation of the Sophia Smith Collection, one of the world's largest women's history manuscript collections, founded in 1942. Both women worked with Harvard historians to create what would become the Schlesinger Library at Radcliffe, in an effort to preserve social history and celebrate women's accomplishments. These two institutions received many of the WCWA documents and together carried on the WCWA mission, at least partly due to Beard's influence, while also creating programming and public announcements to encourage those outside the academy to engage with the materials. This collection is currently collated in the Five College Archives and Manuscript Collection finding aid.

FEMINIST PRAXIS IN THE ARCHIVES

Current feminist approaches to archiving, by both archivists and scholars, parallel established feminist approaches to theory by shifting towards a praxis that includes participation in movements and the design of activist pedagogies meant to recover and accurately portray the lives of women. Former Schlesinger curator Eva Steiner Moseley asserted in 1973 that the disregard of women's public and private contributions "has not only meant little or no space given to them in historical writings, but it has also meant little or no space given to women's papers in manuscript repositories and little or no effort to acquire these materials."[5] In response to a tradition of neglect and collecting processes with "discriminatory overtones," she raised the possibility of separate collections dedicated to women, while contemplating whether women's repositories are enough to sustain public memory and history.[6]

Calls by Moseley and others for archiving an increased number of women's materials were followed by a proliferation of women's collections in the United States and a distinct feminist presence emerging in methods of archival work. Archivists Marika Cifor and Stacy Wood contend that, though not yet fully integrated into archival work, a feminist praxis "is aimed at more than attaining better representation of women in archives" and that through intersectional feminist theory, archives have "transformational potential."[7] To address these possibilities, Cifor and archivist Michelle Caswell advocate for the inclusion of feminist ethics in archiving, especially where community stories might serve as witness statements. Citing human rights archives, Caswell and Cifor urge fellow archivists to collect from the ground up, using an "approach marked by radical empathy" where "implicated communities [are] not just a target group of users, but central focal points in all aspects of the archival endeavour, from appraisal to description to provision of access."[8] Additionally, they investigate how adopting feminist ethics might shift relationships between archivists and stakeholders in order to address social justice concerns, positing the nature of archivists as more than keepers, "sentinels" or "accomplices" and shifting their roles to that of "caregivers, bound to records, creators, subjects, users, and communities through a web of mutual responsibility."[9]

Modeling the feminist approaches suggested by Moseley, Caswell, Cifor, and Wood, the archives at Smith College engaged in the two-year *Steinem Initiative* that aimed to teach women's and gender activists how to learn from, contribute to, and use their own histories. The project organizers contend that activist histories can do more than serve as a historical record, and that women's and gender history can be harnessed and mobilized as "an organizing tool to advance movements of social justice."[10] *Steinem Initiative* co-founder Joyce Follet stresses that historical materials and ephemera can be critically important for activist communities who "risk losing their stories" because they so often work in the moment but have little time to document, reflect, and preserve, resulting in half-written records, lost voices, and motives.[11] The project devised curricula to put "historical knowledge, archival evidence, and documentation methods in the hands of organizers" for their everyday use and included an Activist-in-Residence position, public history and scholarship programming, and The Gloria & Wilma School for Organizers.[12]

Feminist responses to archives and activist materials, like those of Caswell and Cifor, and the Smith archives, address the possible expansion of archivist roles, moving the work from passive to active, but they also expand on the work of humanities' scholars whose critique of archival methodologies has helped shape scholarly conversations for the last two decades. Specifically, scholars and activists in women's and gender studies have extensively assessed archival responsibilities and contributions to the erasure or minimization of marginalized communities and cultures; see, for example, Anjali Arondekar's work on erasure and colonial archives[13] and Saidiya Hartman's critical fabulations responding to the widespread historical erasure of Black life and experiences.[14] Likewise, feminist research in archives reflects back to Moseley's 1973 question: are women's repositories enough to sustain public memory and history? History has proven that the answer is no. So, now we ask: how can feminist research that links community and institutional archives support broad, ground up collecting? How can stakeholders collaborate to increase awareness/access and move towards generating a more equitable record? What are the consequences of failing to recognize the activist potential of archival work and research—of passing on opportunities to actively collect, record, and research marginalized voices, or of obscuring these voices?

Archivist and activist Lae'l Hughes-Watkins, borrowing a phrase from James Baldwin, notes that mainstream and institutional archives have long furthered "institutional practices that have permitted sexism, racism, classism, discriminatory application against the differently abled, religious minorities, LGBTQ+ persons, and others, [so that] community archives have shouldered the brunt of charting a course that bears the truth of America's 'bloody catalogue of oppression.'"[15] She also highlights the promise of course-correction via "engaging in social justice through reparative archival work in the form of the diversification of archives, advocacy/promotion, and then utilization within an academic archive has set a process in motion that has shown early signs of creating feelings of inclusivity."[16] Her proposal echoes other calls for activism in archival work, including those of archivists who both collectively and individually recognized an exigence for collection during the Women's Marches held January 21, 2017.

"MARCH INTO THE ARCHIVES"

The 2017 Women's March, prompted by the election of Donald Trump and his treatment of women, minorities, immigrants, and the disabled while on the campaign trail, gained steam as organizers both planned a national protest in Washington D.C. and encouraged sister marches across the country. Echoing fractures within other historical women's marches, these efforts too faced in-fighting and criticism and were criticized specifically for lack of intersectionality and diminished trans inclusion.[17] Simultaneously, feminist archivists were discussing how best to account for the pace and momentum of unfolding history. Given their intimate knowledge of how women and minority political voices are preserved, feminist archivists saw a specific need to capture events as they unfolded. Repositories, archives, and libraries independently expressed an interest in gathering march organizational documents, posters, images, ephemera, and oral histories—and collecting projects quickly emerged.

Figure 10.1: ["We the People" Young Activists at the Women's March]. January 21, 2017, photograph, courtesy of Angela Christie.[18]

Consider, for example, Georgia State University's (GSU) 2017 Women's Marches collection, developed and spearheaded by Women's and Gender and Sexuality archivist Morna Gerrard. Over the span of a year and a half, Gerrard engaged March participants and local women's activists in collection and preservation. Volunteers donated hats, buttons, flyers, and other ephemera, as well as training to take oral histories, travelling all over the state to do so. Composed of ephemera, recorded protest chants, and oral histories with 2017 March organizers and participants (gathered from different socio-political communities), this project illustrates ways to build ground-up regional collections that both document women's rhetorical activities and link to national collating projects[19]. While mirroring the goals of national March archiving efforts, such as the *Women's March on Washington Archive* project (a March archival project conceived in partnership with of one of the event's major spin-off non-profit's, *March On*), the GSU March collection also highlights local organizers and regional discussions to specifically "chronicle women's activism and advocacy in Georgia and the Southeast."[20]

The March materials were featured in the library's annual Georgia Women's Movement Spring Event, designed to highlight and publicize the standing collections in the library and to celebrate Georgia women. The 2018 event profiled organizers of three state protest marches: Janel Green (Executive Director of the Georgia Alliance for Social Justice), Amanda Hollowell (Communications Director for Georgia's WIN List and Education Specialist for LifeLink of Georgia), and Kate Van Cantfort (non-profit professional and small business owner), who organized protest activities held in Atlanta, Savannah, and Athens. In a featured panel discussion, the organizers discussed how their individual experiences and training, specific locales, and city ordinances influenced the way events were scheduled and executed. This organized discussion of activists (open to the public) drew "on feminist epistemologies that place value in lived experience" and relied upon the participants' "personal experiences as humans, archivists, and archival studies scholars."[21] But the event also benefited those budding activists seeking shared knowledge about how to further their own work.

GSU's Gerrard, who attended the D.C. march and identifies as an activist-archivist, notes that the Women's March is particularly significant for archival studies because, for the first time, archivists nationally organized *en masse* to collect and preserve alongside unfolding events. Archivists watched as the March grew from a nebulous idea to an international movement, recognizing the potential of its oral histories, records, and ephemera to have broad "historical value in the context of women's rights, social movements and the current political climate."[22] Gerrard calls this process of collecting-in-the-moment "active collection" and found the year she spent documenting the Women's Marches to be profoundly connected to her identity as an archivist and as an activist.[23] During the 2016 election cycle, she expected to document local efforts to

Figure 10.2: [GSU Special Collections "March into the Archives" event program], paper, 8.5"x11", 2018, courtesy of Lynée Gaillet.[24]

help elect the first female U.S. president; but, the results of the election shifted her focus to preserve and document multiple sites of current women's social and political activism.

These materials became the foundation of GSU's Women's Marches 2017 collection. Donated artifacts include protest posters, stickers, postcards, and wearables. Traditionally, such ephemera, if not discarded immediately or left at the scene as evidence of dissent, are cast off over the course of a lifetime through relocation, clean-up projects, and in estate settling. These losses, in which worth is assigned or measured, translate to losses of rhetorical nuance in historical conversations, making acts like those of Gerrard and other archivists particularly significant. In examining GSU's ephemera and listening to the oral histories, one is immediately struck by how intersectional participant voices are and just how connected conversations of dissent were before,

Figure 10.3: Kristina Graves. "Knitted Pussy Hat with Five (5) Buttons," ca. 2017, knit yarn, metal, and plastic, 4"x 7", GSU Women's Marches 2017 collection. Courtesy of Morna Gerrard. For Graves' oral history, see https://digitalcollecti ons.library.gsu.edu/digital/collection/marches/id/409/rec/338.[25]

during, and after the original marches. Evidence includes stickers of Rosie the Riveter wearing a hijab, posters connecting feminism and Black Lives Matter, as well as materials that advocate for trans and LGBTQIA+ rights, all of which identify different conversations happening among members of the two key organizing non-profits that emerged out of the original march: *The Womens March* and *March On*. Buttons, t-shirts, flyers, photographs, etc. amplify the voices of activists across movements.

The goals of GSU's Women's Collections, and the March collection specifically, respond to feminist archival efforts; they also echo the archival scholarship of queer theorists and activists, like Jack Halberstam, and collection efforts profiled in Alana Kumbier's *Ephemeral Material: Queering the Archive* (addressing queer zines, disabilities, photography, filmology, and drag communities). Halberstam contends that for some subcultures the archive "is not simply a repository; it is also a theory of cultural relevance, a construction of collective memory" that actively requires "users, interpreters, and cultural historians."[26] Kumbier showcases examples of such construction where the aim is to produce collections "by including genres and materials that catalyze cultural formation, political action, and help cultures represent and transmit historical and emotional information" in both a scholarly and public setting.[27] Archiving women's marches is comparable, particularly given the reliance on ephemera to document events. Women's March archives and archivists may "lack financial and labor resources, [but] they possess an important resource that conventional archives often don't have—that of community knowledge," often processed by those who have lived experience, memory of particular events, and interest in passing down documented cultural history.[28]

Grassroots archivists have dual purposes: to add local activism to the public record and to correct or sustain community/political activities within public memory. For example, Gerrard's collections are all community-driven and located within sites of protest and social justice; she actively engages with the communities she documents, sharing her process and the materials publicly and with community members: "The act of documenting my communities actually [ensures] their histories are documented and available," not just for future scholars or historians, but also for those looking to understand the foundations of their movements, the legacies they have inherited, and potential strategies they might employ.[29] Gerrard regularly receives requests to speak to community groups about her documentation; she notes that only a few are interested in archives—most want to learn more about their own histories and activism, and see how fairly they are being officially remembered.

APPLYING LESSONS TO CREATING INFRASTRUCTURE

We now ask: how can we create a national archive of local March knowledge and experience, one that reflects community stakeholders' interests, is easily searchable, freely accessed, and available to public activists? Obstacles to maintaining a vibrant collection of March artifacts and ephemera, oral histories, and ethnographies include not only finding, capturing, collecting, and collating often fragile materials and elusive memories but also connecting the various regional lived experiences in a sustainable storehouse. One current model for connecting women's march collections is Danielle Russell and Katrina Vandeven's project; they partnered with the *March On* organization to form the *Women's March on Washington Archive* project (WMWA), now housed at the University of Florida.[30] The WMWA's goal is to "document the evolution and intersection of organizers' identities, daily lives, political activism and roles in the March On movement [and record] the scope of the movement and the range of reasons individuals are organizing so that the beginnings and continuation of this diverse, women-centric political resistance may be documented in their own words and through their own lens."[31]

National digital repositories like the WMWA, dedicated to preserving women's history, serves as a model for beginning to build a national infrastructure for accessing, studying, and teaching with feminist archives. In recognition of the anniversary of the 2018 marches, Russell and Vandeven expanded the project to include artifacts from the "Me Too" movement as well. The organizers, heeding the warnings of prior efforts, try to ensure that current events and participants don't suffer the same fate and that materials are available for scholarly investigation, classroom study, and future activists. The Five College Archives & Manuscript Collections provides another model for how a world collection archive might be integrated. This project provides access to finding aids representing collections of historic records held by the Five Colleges (Amherst, Hampshire, Mount Holyoke, and Smith Colleges and the University of Massachusetts Amherst) and is funded by The Andrew W. Mellon Foundation. The collections are particularly strong in the areas of women's history, social history and activism, African American studies, business and labor history, regional history, the sciences, politics and diplomacy, religion and missionary work, the arts, and education—making it an ideal repository for Women's March collections. The site includes over 1000 finding aids from seven repositories, and organizers plan to add research guides as they become available.

CONCLUSIONS

While limited, the Five Colleges example offers some ideas for safeguarding the integrity of politically and socially-charged collections. Specifically, it demonstrates that collective archiving—linking individual archives that share similar foci—may be the best way to fulfill Beard's vision. Collective archiving provides stability, continuity, and checks on the works of others. The importance of these efforts is abundantly clear given the alarming National Archives' scandal of January 2020 in which copies of images of the Women's March were altered to minimize anti-Trump protest rhetoric for a public exhibition. In response to the resulting public backlash, the

National Archives corrected the images and tweeted, "We made a mistake. As the National Archives of the United States, we are and have always been completely committed to preserving our archival holdings, without alteration."[32] Despite these corrections, the situation identifies frictions that can arise between administrations, funders, archivists, stakeholders, and scholar-activists while hinting at the long-term consequences of failing to remain ethically focused on the communities and events being preserved.

Collective and collaborative archiving, as seen in the Five Colleges collections and among archivists co-preserving March documents, ephemera, and oral histories, provides one way to develop a body of records. Archivists, themselves, have actively engaged in conversations about how to develop such collaborations in the current moment. Radcliffe's 2018 workshop on technology and archival processing focused on "deepening the diversity of our collections to help researchers create a more complete and nuanced historical record," a goal that Schlesigner's Pforzheimer Foundation Director Jane Kamensky cited as "an imperative that will bring a form of reparation to the historical record in higher ed."[33] The keynote conversation between Dr. Beverly Guy-Sheftall (Spelman College) and Dr. Craig Wilder (MIT), focused on stakeholders in developing collaborative initiatives, identifying the roles that students and researchers play in developing more complete archives and highlighting the significance of collaboration— among archivists, archives, collections, and scholars. Guy-Sheftall personally spearheaded two collaborative initiatives for Spelman, one with Wayne State and another with Radcliffe. Collaborations like these, whether they are successful or they ultimately dissolve (as in the case of the Spelman-Wayne State collaboration), help to preserve multiple conversations occurring across multiple fields, industries, and locations. When successful, such collaborations have the potential to meet the goals of recovery and to develop more complete records by connecting marginalized experiences to other relevant collections.

Success and sustainability require long-term commitment of collaborators and funding in order to build an infrastructure where people can plug in and connect. Generating a database of co-relevant archives and special collections and then sharing digitized holdings represent the logical next steps in building collaborative archives. Beard's original vision was to create a space that recorded and preserved women's work, universally. She contended that there should be a place for everybody, a repository focused on subjects whose stories are no longer minimized or told without a full account. Archivists preserving the Women's March share these goals. In connecting individual collections, like GSU's Women's March Collection, with the national Women's March collection, individual threads of conversation become a chorus of evidence that fortifies against the historically diminished presence of those who shout from history's margins and connects conversations among generations of activists.

NOTES

1. We take our title, "March into the Archives," from Georgia State University's 2018 spring archival event, which documented the 2017 women's marches in three Georgia cities.
2. *Women's March on Washington Archive*, University of Florida, https://ufdc.ufl.edu/womensmarch.
3. Anka Voss-Hubbard, "'No Documents—No History': Mary Ritter Beard and the Early History of Women's Archives," *American Archivists* 58 (1995): 16–30.
4. Nancy F. Cott, ed., *A Woman Making History: Mary Ritter Beard Through Her Letters* (New Haven: Yale University Press, 1991). See Cott for a fuller description of Beard's life and work.
5. Eva Moseley, "Women in Archives: Documenting the History of Women in America," *The American Archivist* 36, no. 2 (1973): 215.
6. Moseley, 221.
7. Marika Cifor and Stacy Wood, "Critical Feminism in the Archives," *Critical Archival Studies*, special issue of *Journal of Critical Library and Information Studies* 1, no. 2 (2017): 2.
8. Michelle Caswell and Marika Cifor, "From Human Rights to Feminist Ethics: Radical Empathy in the Archives," *Archivaria* 81 (2016): 24.

9. Caswell and Cifor, 25.
10. "The Steinem Initiative," Grécourt Gate, Accessed 20 October, 2020. https://www.smith.edu/academics/jandon-center/steinem-initiative.
11. "Putting History into Action: Gloria & Wilma School Links Activists and Archives," Grécourt Gate. https://www.smith.edu/news/gloria-wilma-school.
12. Joyce Follet and Sarah Gould. "Steinem Initiative Final Report," Accessed 20 October, 2020. https://www.smith.edu/sites/default/files/media/Documents/Jandon-Center/Steinem_Initiative_finalreport.pdf.
13. See Anjali Arondekar, "Without a Trace: Sexuality and the Colonial Archive," *Journal of the History of Sexuality* 14, no. 1/2 (2005): 10–27.
14. Sarah Haley, "Intimate Historical Practice," *Black Perspectives*, African American Intellectual History Society, (18 May 2020).
15. L'ael Hughes-Watkins, "Moving Toward a Reparative Archive: A Roadmap for a Holistic Approach to Disrupting Homogenous Histories in Academic Repositories and Creating Inclusive Spaces for Marginalized Voices," *Journal of Contemporary Archival Studies* 5, no. 6 (2018): 16.
16. Hughes-Watkins, 16.
17. Evan Greer, "The Women's March Left Trans Women Behind," *The Advocate*, January 25, 2017, https://theadvocate.com.
18. ["We the People" Young Activists at the Women's March]. January 21, 2017, photograph, courtesy of Angela Christie.
19. See https://digitalcollections.library.gsu.edu/digital/collection/marches for the digitized collection.
20. "Women's Collections," Georgia State University, finding aid, https://library.gsu.edu/special-collections/collections/.
21. Caswell and Cifor, "From Human Rights to Feminist Ethics," 25.
22. Gina Watts, "Applying Radical Empathy to Women's March Documentation Efforts: A Reflection Exercise," *Archives and Manuscripts* 45, no. 3 (2017): 191–201.
23. Morna Gerrard, personal interview in discussion with Jessica Rose and Lynée Gaillet. Atlanta, GA, October 15, 2020.
24. ["March into the Archives" event program], 2018, paper, 8.5"x11", courtesy of Lynée Gaillet.
25. Kristina Graves, "Knitted 'pussy hat' with five (5) buttons," 2017, knit yarn, metal, and plastic, 4"x 7", GSU Women's Marches 2017 Collection, Atlanta, Courtesy of Morna Gerrard. Hat not digitized; for more, see https://digitalcollections.library.gsu.edu/digital/collection/marches/id/269/rec/337.
26. J. Jack Halberstam, *In a Queer Time and Place: Transgender Bodies, Subcultural Lives* (New York: NYU Press, 2005), 169.

27. Alana Kumbier, *Ephemeral Material: Queering the Archive* (Sacramento: Litwin Books, 2014), 15.
28. Kumbier, 26.
29. Morna Gerrard, October 15, 2020.
30. *Women's March on Washington Archive*, University of Florida, https://ufdc.ufl.edu/WOMENSMARCH.
31. *Women's March on Washington Archive*, University of Florida, https://ufdc.ufl.edu/womensmarch.
32. Suzanne Rowan Kelleher, "Update: The National Archives Says 'We Made a Mistake' After Erasing Criticism of Trump from Photo," *Forbes*, January 18, 2020, https://forbes.com/sites/suzannerowankelleher/2020/01/18/the-national-archives-gets-slammed-for-rewriting-history-to-erase-criticism-of-trump/#4aff6aa52680.
33. "A More Complete Record: The Case for Archival Partnerships," (Introductory remarks and keynote conversation, Knafel Center, Radcliffe Institute, April 12, 2018).

BIBLIOGRAPHY

Arondekar, Anjali. "Without a Trace: Sexuality and the Colonial Archive." *Journal of the History of Sexuality* 14, no. 1/2 (2005): 10–27. Accessed June 20, 2020. https://jstor.org/stable/3704707.

Beard, Mary Ritter. "The Historical Approach to Learning About Women." Speech given at Radcliffe College, May 22, 1944. "Mary Ritter Beard Papers (A-9)," Schlesinger Library, Radcliffe College, Cambridge, MA.

Caswell, Michelle, and Marika Cifor. "From Human Rights to Feminist Ethics: Radical Empathy in the Archives." *Archivaria* 81 (2016): 23–43.

Cifor, Marika, and Stacy Wood. "Critical Feminism in the Archives." *Critical Archival Studies*, special issue of *Journal of Critical Library and Information Studies* 1, no. 2 (2017): 1–27. https://doi.org10.24242/jclis.v1i2.27.

Cott, Nancy F., ed. *A Woman Making History: Mary Ritter Beard Through Her Letters*. New Haven: Yale University Press, 1991.

Follett, Joyce and Sarah Gould. "Steinem Initiative Final Report." Accessed 20 October 2020. https://www.smith.edu/sites/default/files/media/Documents/Jandon-Center/Steinem_Initiative_finalreport.pdf.

Gerrard, Morna. Personal Interview in discussion with Jessica Rose. Atlanta, GA, July 31, 2020.

———. Personal Interview in discussion with Jessica Rose and Lynée Gaillet. Atlanta, GA, October 15, 2020.

Greer, Evan. "The Women's March Left Trans Women Behind." *The Advocate*, January 25, 2017. https://www.advocate.com/commentary/2017/1/25/womens-march-left-trans-women-behind.

Guy-Sheftall, Beverly, Craig Wilder, and Sarah Thomas. "A More Complete Record: The Case for Archival Partnerships." Introductory remarks and keynote conversation at Radcliffe Workshop on Technology & Archival Processing, Knafel Center, Cambridge, MA, April 12, 2018. https://projects.iq.harvard.edu/radworkshop2018/summaries-and-transcripts.

Haley, Sarah. "Intimate Historical Practice." *Black Perspectives. African American Intellectual History Society*, May 18, 2020. https://www.aaihs.org/intimate-historical-practice/.

Halberstam, J. Jack. *In a Queer Time and Place: Transgender Bodies, Subcultural Lives*. New York: NYU Press, 2005, 169.

Hughes-Watkins, Lae'l. "Moving Toward a Reparative Archive: A Roadmap for a Holistic Approach to Disrupting Homogenous Histories in Academic Repositories and Creating Inclusive Spaces for Marginalized Voices." *Journal of Contemporary Archival Studies* 5, no. 6 (2018). https://elischolar.library.yale.edu/jcas/vol5/iss1/6.

Kelleher, Suzanne Rowan. "Update: The National Archives Says 'We Made a Mistake' After Erasing Criticism of Trump from Photo." *Forbes*. January 18, 2020. www.forbes.com/sites/suzannerowankelleher/2020/01/18/the-national-archives-gets-slammed-for-rewriting-history-to-erase-criticism-of-trump/#26ede8b12680).

Kumbier, Alana. *Ephemeral Material: Queering the Archive*. Sacramento: Litwin Books, 2014.

Moseley, Eva. "Women in Archives: Documenting the History of Women in America." *The American Archivist* 36, no. 2 (1973): 215–222. https://doi.org/10.17723/aarc.36.2.36744h4q226234j7.

The Andrew W. Mellon Foundation. "Five College Archives & Manuscript Collections." Updated April 2008. https://asteria.fivecolleges.edu/.

Voss-Hubbard, Anka. "'No Documents—No History': Mary Ritter Beard and the Early History of Women's Archives." *American Archivists* 58 (1995): 16–30.

Watts, Gina. "Applying Radical Empathy to Women's March Documentation Efforts: A Reflection Exercise." *Archives and Manuscripts*, 45, no. 3 (2017): 191–201. https://doi.org/10.1080/01576895.2017.1373361.

"Women's Collections." *Georgia State University Library*. Atlanta. Accessed July 30, 2020. https://library.gsu.edu/special-collections/collections/.

Women's March on Washington Archive. Co-founders Danielle Russell and Katrina Vandeve. University of Florida. Accessed 4 August 2020. https://ufdc.ufl.edu/womensmarch.

CHAPTER ELEVEN

MA BETI KA RISHTA
Mother-Daughter Relationships as
Public Feminist Archives

By Mariam Durrani, Nazneen Patel, and Zainab Shah

INTRODUCTION

This chapter draws on three narratives of desi[1] Muslim mother-daughter relationships as an intimate and treasured feminist archive through which we publicly meditate on how the *ma beti ka rishta*[2] shaped our ways of living a feminist life.[3] Through the juxtaposition of our memories, the individual narratives converge into a form of collective knowledge production, illustrating how reflexive, narrative-driven conversations about both differences and similarities can transform how we understand individual experiences as part of a generative, public feminist archive. Each narrative and its descriptions index how socioeconomic class, educational background, religious community, heritage, and racialization (based on US migration) engenders specific understandings of feminism through storytelling as modality. By framing in relation to each other, we reflected on how sharing intimate details about our relationships with mothers/as mothers transforms personal connections into a public meditation on desi Muslim feminisms, community care, and solidarity work.[4] As Pakistani Shia Muslim girls and women in Lahore (like Zainab and her mother), for Indian Gujarati Muslim girls and women in the US diaspora (like Nazneen and her mother), for single Pakistani Muslim mothers in the US academic workplace (like Mariam and her queer desi mother-scholar colleague), we know what it feels like to be seen through myopias of Western, liberal feminism and its inevitable failure to perceive our lived experiences as Pakistani and Indian, Shia and Sunni, desi and brown cisgendered immigrant women. Experientially we know that these categories can be further split again and again, revealing ever deeper ways of being women, of being mothers, of being daughters, and of being feminist. Although the *ma beti ka rishta*, or mother-daughter relationship is often framed as fraught with tension about intergenerational differences, this chapter presents it as a rich archive for thinking collaboratively about vulnerability as a condition and source for feminist expressions of empathy, solidarity, and activism. For desi Muslim transnational immigrant families, there are real and important differences between what daughters see for themselves and what mothers imagine for their daughters, which can be and remain as sources of tension. However, as our narratives illustrate, these relationships simultaneously offer possibilities for vulnerability, wisdom, and commitments to empathy within and beyond the home. That is to say, we learned that by attending to dynamics within mother-daughter relationships, we uncovered different forms of willful world-traveling and connection that acknowledged and affirmed plurality in and among women.[5]

This chapter began as informal conversations in a Zoom-based book club during 2020; over time, Mariam, one academic in the group, proposed transforming our conversations into a collaborative writing project about the *ma beti ka rishta* as a kind of desi Muslim feminist archive. Through the writing process, we developed a generative exercise where our similarities and differences of being desi *and* Muslim women could breathe with and against each other. By bringing them together, we engage in a public act of feminist knowledge production where the particularities of desi Muslim mother-daughter relationships are foundational to archives of brown maternal knowledges and possibilities for solidarity arise across differences within these archives.[6] Thus, our personal memories come together as a public feminist archive to think with, to theorize about, and to love desi Muslim mothers and daughters. Our approach draws from Naveen Minai and Sara Shroff's queer feminist framework of *yaariyan* (or friendships) as modes of survival, pleasure, and accountability, organized by *gupshup* (or everyday conversations between friends) and *baithak* (or modalities of creating and holding space).[7] Inspired by Minai and Shroff's imaginative framework, we offer our stories as a publicly archived *gupshup* about desi Muslim mother-daughter relationships as a site of brown feminist knowledges.[8] Together we explored the incommensurability of being Shia in Sunni-dominant worlds, of being a desi Muslim in the racist United States and the casteist Hindu-dominant diaspora worlds, and of being a single mother in patriarchal academic worlds. Collectively the stories demonstrate why desi Muslim feminists and their lived experiences are irreducible to simplistic renderings of the "Muslim woman" subject in so many limited Western imaginings and related fictions. In this way, these acts of everyday *gupshup* offer much more than ephemeral, personal connections, but rather our private *gupshups* arranged as a feminist archive offers citations for each of us to push understandings of difference and a practice of thick solidarity that extends beyond the *ma beti ka rishta*.

LAHORE, 1997, ZAINAB

It's Muharram[9] again. Like other Pakistani Shia children, I am wearing my black shalwar kameez[10] reserved for this time, but also worn occasionally throughout the year to look very cool. Ama and I go to majlis[11] and, as per usual, we carpool afterwards with whoever needs a ride. This time it's Fizza, and I am filled with awe as our knees touch in the backseat of our white Mitsubishi Lancer. Fizza, a legendary marsiya singer, lives in Chauburji, a part of Lahore I rarely get to visit so I am excited. Over the forty-five-minute ride as the streets narrow with the traffic of street vendors, tongas, pedestrians, rickshaws, and bicycles, Ama and I learn about Fizza's life. She lives alone. Never married, doesn't plan on it. And has dedicated her life to her craft.

"Your voice is beautiful mashallah." I've been wanting to say this since I first heard her sing many years ago; my face hot from the effort. She responds with a comfortable appreciative laugh and tells me that mine can be too. I don't believe her, even as I briefly imagine myself in the middle of the crowded room at Ahmed House, leading a moment of collective grief, surrounded by my Shia sisters, aunties, and mothers. Ama nudges me playfully and encourages me to consider reciting a marsiya or noha[12] this Muharram. I want to please them both so I say yes, and immediately regret it. We settle on a Seraiki[13] noha and later as I learn the words, and Ama translates, I suddenly have access to the language of my ancestors and the language of a major separatist movement. I practice with Ama every night. Her appreciation keeps me going. On the sixth night, the last night of practice, she senses my fear and my hesitation. "I know you can do this," she tells me, and in that moment, I believe her.

When we arrive at Ahmed House the next morning, Ama smiles at the two policewomen stationed at the entrance, opens her bag and prepares for a pat down. Targeted Shia killings and sectarian violence have been up this year. Although our ancestors are from Multan, still a Shia stronghold, we are migrants in the largely

Sunni city of Lahore, and my family understands the necessity for this level of security. We take off our shoes, making a mental note of where we left them, and enter.

The space is expansive, and the ceilings are high. It is clear Aunty Samina had it constructed precisely for majlis. Sunlight filters in through the large windows all around. Women with very young children make their way up the stairs to a balcony that wraps around the hall, where tiny hands grip the railing and wide eyes peer over. Up on the second floor is also where they keep the alams,[14] and once in a while the light bounces off a gold or silver hand of Fatima, reminding me that it is her shadow we hope to be seated in.

We are early because that's how Ama is. I try not to think of the *noha* I have agreed to recite later. The salaams, waves, big smiles, nods, and handshakes continue as the aunties greet each other, stretching and spreading their bodies as much as they can without actually getting up off the floor. There is an excited but contained chatter. The majlis commences with Kisa[15] and an hour of marsias; histories sung in melancholic dirges in ancestral languages, and Karbala told in notes held high by women I am connected to through these moments of collective grieving for a past injustice. We are in the hundreds by now, and I don't need to look back to know there's a sea of women behind me. My knees touching thighs, ankles, backs; moving as an individual becomes impossible.

I am lucky today. The aalima, a skilled storyteller, leaves me in awe. The first orators I ever encountered were desi Shia women like her, governing the power of an oral tradition passed down by our foremothers. Her tone varies with the mood of the moment that she's describing; her pauses are measured. She has carried this crowd through an understanding of theory, ethics, and morality that provides the appropriate context for the significance of Karbala, the sacrifices made, the reasons we remember and mourn this historic loss, and how it connects the injustices of the past to the present moment and Pakistan's militarized government.

I know why we remember history; I know how it helps us move forward. She captivates me, and the stillness in the room tells me I am not alone. It ends with the recounting of the battle of Karbala, our heaviness leaving us in tears and sweat.

And then it dawns on me. I got swept away by the story, but now it's almost time to recite the noha I've been practicing. The room is loud with wails, and as women start to stand up, clear the center and form a circle. A few others vie for the mic and start reciting competing nohas. The matam[16] sounds like a drum beat and everyone is on the same page. My body feels small and I'm not so sure I'll be able to take the mic or compete. Ama taps me on my shoulder and I turn. Our eyes lock and she nods her encouragement. She senses my distress and holds my hand, leading me to the microphone. The noha ends; she pushes my body into the middle of the circle and shoves the mic in my face. The drum beat keeps going, and I know I have only a second to take control.

I start with the first line of the noha I've been practicing and my voice comes out shrill and all wrong. I can feel the matam slowing down as the crowd tries to listen to the words I'm reciting, jogging their memories for access points, to join in. I keep going and one verse later a group of women have started their own noha. They are loud and practiced and I cede territory. Ama hugs me from behind. I turn to look at her and she is beaming. I know I did well, however brief this triumph was. Afterwards there is plenty of food for everyone and as we eat my aunties tell me how proud they are, how I was able to command everyone's attention, and was I sure I was only thirteen? It felt good to have used my body and my voice in this way, and to be loved for taking up space.

NEW JERSEY, 2003, NAZNEEN

Saturday afternoons are for groceries. The morning is filled with dusting and vacuuming the house, scrubbing the bathroom floors, changing bed sheets, and opening doors to fill rooms with air freshener, taking breaks every now and then to watch Bollywood favorites interviewed on AVS TV (paid weekly programming on a public access channel). We shower, self-satisfied, rinsing the morning's grime off, and the weekend officially commences. At 1PM, we head out. The ritual is always the same: Pathmark (also known as "regular groceries"), followed by Patel Brothers for "Indian groceries".

At Pathmark, I follow behind my mother quietly, careful not to interrupt her concentration. She has a prescribed path she follows from the moment she walks in. Her list of items is ordered accordingly, so as to avoid any extra passes through a single aisle. She is not distracted by brightly colored signs announcing sales and deals because she has already studied the week's circular and has plotted to earn more in savings than the store advertises. Held tightly behind her neatly written list (complete with category sub-headers) is a worn, stained white envelope full of coupons. She delicately thumbs through the wisps of cut paper with precision. She locates the ones that match items in her cart and methodically slips them to the front of the stack.

Over the years, I've learned that my role in this ritual is to follow and to listen attentively, to imbibe the scripture being wordlessly passed down to me like an inheritance. I am the stocker, obediently pulling items off the shelves as they are announced and stacking them sensibly in the cart (I've been publicly reprimanded for flattening the toilet paper rolls under heavy jugs of laundry detergent, requiring a second pass at an aisle and, thus, demonstrating my ineptitude. But I do apply feedback effectively and immediately). I am careful to read and re-read labels because it's important that we get the 32 oz. shampoo bottle and not the 24 oz, or else the coupon does not apply.

I am taught about prudence and practicality (always Frosty Flakes, never Frosted Flakes). I learn about the discipline needed to resist temptation. I learn that this American world is full of excess, things we don't need, a place in which we must be vigilant.

Without careful navigation, it is too easy to get lost, to lose sight of who we really are, what we really value. We must approach it with caution, well-armed and prepared to take from it what we need and leave the rest, because "the rest" is not for us. Not for me: a good, obedient, desi daughter. I know I should be noting the process and its rules; committing the steps to memory for future use is implied. As with everything, my mother is the teacher and I, the student.

Occasionally, on the rare days when we've chatted or laughed together on the drive over, I skip alongside her, playfully presenting items not on her list for approval. Lucky Charms? A pack of Bubblicious? It is thrilling when she begrudgingly mutters, "*Rakh le*" ["keep it" in Gujarati]. There is a rhythm to her (our) life. *Adhaan*,[17] and hijabs, and lists and coupons and routes through the grocery store, set up deliberately to protect us from the perils of life in an unfamiliar place, from the cursed gaze. The ritual is an exercise in agency.

In the twenty or so minutes it takes to reach Patel Brothers, we transform into different versions of ourselves. I chat excitedly about grabbing a kebab roll to snack on. We pull into the chaotic parking lot—negotiations begin before we ever enter the store. My mother jumps out almost instinctively, having a lifetime of experience back home of the quickness required to get anywhere or anything in the bustling city of Mumbai. I join her a few minutes later, pushing a cart I had to rescue from the middle of the lot and clean out. At Patel Brothers, my mother is an artist. No lists, no coupons, just the masterful evaluation of sabzis, the memorized staples (tomatoes, onions, green chili, ginger), the ancestral knowledge of each *mirch, daal, aata* (common words for spice, lentils, flour). She reaches for a handful of bitter gourd and bumps into a small aunty. They laugh and immediately begin chatting as they fill plastic bags with their sifted-for selections. I am always amazed by desi mothers' *andaaza* (or estimation), filling the bag with the just-right amount for their planned menu. At Patel Brothers, my mother does something different from Pathmark; here she lingers. She notices when a particular vegetable has become available or when, "This week's *methi* [or fenugreek leaves] looks fresh!" She luxuriates and imagines and fantasizes. She is open to and even expecting detours and the awkward-but-necessary doubling-back for fresh yogurt she caught the stocker replenishing.

In each space, we shrink or expand accordingly. At Pathmark, I sense her compulsions, her desire for control, her disdain for inefficiency, her efforts to wrangle every stray thought into submission. I can hear her running through a script, one developed and revised over decades, designed to render a foreign world coherent. At Patel Brothers, she seems at "home", at ease, legible. An Indian woman, happily making small-talk, slipping between Hindi and Gujarati, both mother-tongues. And yet ...

At the register, after every item has been accounted for, the cashier announces the total: $56.23. My mother hands her the credit card while pointing out the tamarind candy to me. *"Chaiyye?"* ("Want it?" in Urdu) she asks invitingly so I lean down to grab some when I hear the cashier's chirpy voice begin a conversation. *"Tame Patel cho?"* ("Are you a Patel?"), she asks my mother in Gujarati. A curiosity, no doubt, aroused by seeing the Hindu name on the credit card and then seeing my mother's hijab.

"Haan!" ("Yes!"), my mother replied. *"Oh, tamaro husband tamaru* religion follow *karva* allow *kareche?"* ("Oh, your husband allows you to practice your religion?" in Gujarati), the cashier inquires, fascinated and wide-eyed. *"Eh sukam mane naa paarse?"* ("Why would he stop me?" in Gujarati), my mother replies, confused and not understanding why her Muslim husband would stop his Muslim wife from practicing their shared religion, slower to the understanding that was more immediately obvious to me. I see a flash across her eyes. It lands. A smirk creeps across her face but I know it is really exasperation. *"Na, na, eyvu kai nathin,"* ("No, no, it's nothing like that" in Gujarati), she says dismissively, finally computing the anti-Muslim sentiment embedded in the line

of questioning and having no interest in further explication. She signs and we leave. In the car, my mother and I laugh because that's the only expression that seems to fit. In trying to understand the world, in the world trying to understand us, we realize that we only make sense to each other.

CAMBRIDGE, 2017, MARIAM

He was late. I had a feeling that something would come up, and as usual, it did. I had already packed my daughter's overnight bag, making sure I packed her favorite doll and hoodie, before getting dressed myself. Black sweater, dark denim, chunky necklace, and blow-dried hair so it looks like the requisite attention has been paid. The undergraduate Pakistani student group had invited me to speak about my research on the politics of gender in Pakistani higher education. I was admittedly a little nervous about my talk, but more so because I know my daughter's father might get late. That meant that our 2nd grader might be in the audience while I lectured, not an ideal situation for research talks.

I was well aware that the academic profession is not the most hospitable to mothers in general, but especially not for single mothers. Ever since I gave birth four months before starting graduate school, I tried to make it work the best that I could. Some days were better than others. Sometimes it meant bringing her to class, to a meeting, and today, maybe this conference. On the bus to campus, she promised to do her best to be patient until her baba showed up. I did my best to sound like it was all under control. That's what moms are supposed to do, right?

We walked into the building and the undergraduate in charge of welcoming the speakers led us to one of the conference rooms. Inside I saw my co-panelist reviewing her notes quietly on a tall wingback chair, before looking up to see me, my daughter, the overnight bag, and her doll. I froze. I felt exposed, visible, vulnerable. *Ugh. How unprofessional do I look right now? It must be* *obvious that I'm a single mom. Who else brings their kid to a Saturday conference. She probably thinks I'm divorced too. Well, she's right about that. *sigh* But still does it have to be the first thing people know about me? Where is he??*

I introduced myself. "Hi, so nice to meet you. Yes, yes, this is my daughter. Her father was supposed to pick her up at home but he's going to meet us here instead. He lives in NYC. Yeah, it's hard. Oh sorry, he just texted. I'll be right back."

After dropping my child with her father, I must have walked in with the "look" I had given her dad still on my face. The other speaker must have seen my frustration and stress because she simply said, "You're incredible. That must have been really hard but you did great." I was surprised that somehow, she was also a divorced Pakistani mother-scholar. What are the odds, seriously? And so, I chose to believe her when she said I did well that day. Turns out, I needed her affirmation.

Over the next two hours, we got to know each other as scholars during the panel and the lively Q and A session, followed by cocktails and lunch at a nearby restaurant. As a newly minted PhD, this was my first time meeting a professional colleague with whom I could be both mother and scholar, with whom neither detracted from the other. My new friend and teacher was someone who could celebrate both at the same time. Our desi queer friendship began with this simple act of recognition, with the feelings of being *seen* and appreciated as single mothers and feminist scholars from Pakistan. On that day, she held space for me, for my daughter, for my scholarship, and for my fears of doing it all in public.

*****

Across these three stories, everyday moments as daughters and as mothers serve as a rich archive to study the possibilities created by loving attention to brown maternal knowledge.[18] Each story illustrates how the quotidian of the *ma beti ka rishta* offered insights about desi Muslim mother-daughter relationships that became accessible through close friendship, collaborative writing, and community-based knowledge production. Each storyteller narrated her experience of mother-daughter relationships in historically situated public spaces: Zainab's story of Shia women singing noha at majlis in Lahore, Nazneen's mother's refusal to respond to stereotypes at Pathmark and Patel Brothers in New Jersey, or Mariam's handling of childcare and professional responsibilities simultaneously in US academia. By juxtaposing these narratives into a public archive, our *gupshup* can be read as a challenge to situated systems of patriarchal and racializing authority in each respective context. Together these stories ask: how do we, as feminists of the global majority, situate ourselves within *and against* contemporary forms of oppression, discrimination, and violence in our everyday lives? How do we sustain practices of thick solidarity through the public archives of feminist storytelling?

For Zainab, as a Shia girl growing up in a Sunni supremacist context, her mother connected her to Shia women collectives organized for collective grief, remembrance, and learning. In the feminist collective space of majlis, Zainab shared space with and learned from women outside of her otherwise limited class socialization, planting seeds for politics that do not gloss over difference. Zainab's mother facilitated her daughter's performance at majlis, where she could take space more freely, by encouraging her to sing loudly. These moments laid the groundwork for Zainab to take up space later in life, including and especially in ways that her mother had not imagined or might not immediately approve. Over the years, Zainab always wondered what it was about this space that made her feel her most comfortable and supported in her body, in her skin. Writing her piece became an exercise in parsing that out. The majlis space was remarkable in that it was organized by women, where they took on varied, powerful roles, and supported each other in an environment that, outside of the majlis, was otherwise often hostile to her growth and development as a feminist. Later when she moved to the United States, she encountered more such hostile environments, especially in New York where she was often told quite pointedly by Americans that women were "liberated here". The painful absence of this particular space motivated her to create supportive, caregiving environments for her (and our collective) continued survival in the West. Without realizing it, this blueprint given by her Shia foremothers was the one she returned to when she began actively organizing and participating in women-run, women-first writer collectives in NYC, including The Unpublished Reading Series, and Two Truths and a Lie writing workshops.[19] More recently, she co-organized a book club with Mariam and Nazneen during the first eight months of the coronavirus pandemic. She continues to draw strength from and recreate the supportive feminist dynamics she encountered at majlis.

In her story, Nazneen narrated her experience of a desi Muslim mother-daughter relationship as a "constant birthing" through everyday rituals like Saturday grocery runs. We related to her chronicling of the seemingly banal rituals and skills that we were instructed to learn as traditions to one day pass on to our future desi Muslim daughters. Recognizing and celebrating the quiet composure that Nazneen's mother claimed for herself and her daughter facilitates a practice of thick solidarity within the mother-daughter relationship, where expectations, desires and possibilities for each woman's life may remain vastly different. It is through sharing these experiences in the store and later a brief *gupshup* in the car that each woman becomes reconstituted through the *ma beti ka rishta* as shared, gendered, and embodied knowledge. Saturday grocery runs and other domestic rituals provided a language for their mother-daughter relationship, helping Nazneen connect to her mother even as a tension persists in how connected her mother is to Nazneen's daily life as a feminist, activist educator, coach, partner, and friend. At the same time, Nazneen acknowledges that one day she may understand these mother-daughter rituals anew should she decide to become a mother herself. In this way, the *ma beti ka rishta* offered us a shared feminist archive whose meaning and significance, similar to other archives, changes as material conditions and realities change and shift over time.

In Mariam's story, she explores how bringing her child to a conference facilitated a collision of her multiple life-worlds in intellectually and emotionally capacious ways. She recounts the unexpected support she received from another divorced queer feminist mother at the conference. Based on this chance encounter, Mariam realized how building a shared archive with her new friend shifted her own understandings about divorce and related misogynistic, racist narratives about "broken homes." She remembers the questions people would ask in the early divorced years: "Was it really *that* bad?", "What will happen to your daughter now?" Getting divorced during graduate school presented a difference set of expectations, assumptions, and "concerns" from academic colleagues about how her career would weather that moment. Across these layered rubrics of normalized patriarchal culture, single motherhood becomes either invisibilized or perceived as deficient. But single mothers often do the work because they have to, whether or not this labor is seen or appreciated. Mariam managed the challenges and joys of single motherhood while conducting multi-sited fieldwork, writing her dissertation, applying for jobs, and moving four times in five years as a brown Muslim family. Throughout Mariam recognized that empathy and solidarity from feminist collectives and feminist theory fortified her resolve to deal with work, motherhood, and chronic illness slowly, carefully, and intentionally. Her evolving understanding of feminist friendships and *ma beti ka rishta*, as a mother and as a daughter, through public and private *gupshups* was life-sustaining and life-affirming.

In *Living a Feminist Life*, Sara Ahmed states that feminism needs feminists to survive and feminists need feminism to survive. This chapter extends this maxim through our curated public feminist archive reflecting on desi Muslim mother-daughter relationships as a source of knowledge and wisdom, essential for our feminist killjoy toolkits.[20] Our collective rumination on the *ma beti ka rishta* presents generative possibilities to think about thick solidarity by appreciating the incommensurabilities across our three stories and between the mothers and daughters in each. By weaving our narratives together, we thought generatively and collaboratively about how the rifts/connections between daughters and their mothers, between daughters, and between mothers hold knowledges that society conditions us to overlook and undervalue. Each story, each meeting, each draft, each revision formed the foundational *gupshups* that grew into a public feminist archive, facilitating discussion about our role and responsibilities within systemic racism, (neo)colonialism, neoliberal capitalism, and patriarchal worlds. The collaborative writing process revealed what we can learn when we start conversations that embrace difference as central to feminist praxis and politics. As 2020 wore on, conversations that began about intimacies of the mother-daughter relationship became the bridge to discussions about urgent political movements and our responsibilities in this moment. Even as we narrate what is commensurable and remains incommensurable between us, curating a public *gupshup*-based archive provided the creative language to imagine feminist world-traveling and worldmaking that is inclusive of *all* mothers, daughters, and their communities.

NOTES

1. We use desi here as an identity descriptor for people from South Asia or its diasporas. The term circulates in everyday usage by speakers of South Asian languages and others living within the subcontinent and beyond. In the United States, community activist organizations like Desis Rising Up and Moving (DRUM) who work with South Asian and Indo-Caribbean low-wage immigrants in New York City draw on this identity term to build working class solidarity. It is also used frequently on social media to reference South Asian culture and practices. Etymologically desi is based on the Sanskrit stem

word, *des*—translated as "country" or "homeland" broadly speaking. As such, desi is used primarily by speakers of Sanskrit-based South Asian languages.
2. In Urdu, *ma beti ka rishta* translates to "mother daughter relationship".
3. Sara Ahmed, *Living a Feminist Life* (Durham, NC: Duke University Press, 2017).
4. Our understanding of feminist solidarity draws on *thick solidarity* as a conceptual framework for building relations of solidarity that mobilize "empathy in ways that do not gloss over difference, but rather pushes into the specificity, irreducibility, and incommensurability" of experiences. Roseann Liu and Savannah Shange, "Toward Thick Solidarity: Theorizing Empathy in Social Justice Movements," *Radical History Review* 132 (2018): 190.
5. Maria Lugones, "Playfulness, 'World'-Travelling, and Loving Perception," *Hypatia* 2, no. 2 (1987): 3–19.
6. For more on mother-daughter relationships as a site of brown maternal knowledges, see Moon Charania, "Making Way for Ghosts and Mothers: Storied Socialities, Sexual Violence, and the Figure of the Furtive Migrant," *Meridians* 18, no. 1 (2019): 206–226; and Sara Shroff "Between mother and daughter: Brown erotics and sacred note," *Journal of Lesbian Studies* 26, no. 1 (2021).
7. Naveen Minai and Sara Shroff, "Yaariyan, Baithak, Gupshup: Queer Feminist Formations and the Global South," *Kohl: A Journal for Body and Gender Research* 5, no. 1 (2019). https://kohljournal.press/yaariyan?fbclid=IwAR2Kn2sgkpe2m_Pvs7a6__Od1SgaJcSsmrjyWvF2_f3raRni3OZ8EV_6Prc.
8. Minai and Shroff.
9. Muharram, the first month of the Islamic lunar calendar, begins with ten days of mourning for the martyrdom of Hazrat Hussein ibn Ali (Prophet Mohammed's grandson). Hazrat Hussein and seventy-two of his family and followers were killed on the tenth day of Muharram in 680 A.D. at Karbala in modern-day Iraq.
10. *Shalwar kameez* is the two-piece outfit worn in Pakistan. The *shalwar* are typically loose-fitting trousers worn with a *kameez* or long tunic. Black clothing is symbolic of mourning and is preferred by Shia Muslims during Muharram.
11. Majlis refers to a special gathering or meeting. During Muharram, Shia Muslims gather at all-women or all-men majlis events to collectively mourn the martyrdom of Hussein and his family by reciting *marsiyas*, or elegiac poems remembering the martyrs.
12. Noha refers to a lament about the tragedy of Karbala.
13. Seraiki is the language spoken by 25.9 million people in Pakistan, concentrated in southern Punjab but with a large diaspora across the subcontinent and around the world. The Seraiki linguistic community has a rich literary and

political community across South Asia, and has led a separatist movement, demanding equal rights and justice.
14. Alam in Arabic means flag or standard. Where Karbala and the events of Ashura are concerned, the alam represents the banner held aloft by Hazrat Abbas bin Ali, the alamdar or standard-bearer of Imam Hussain.
15. *Kisa* refers to foundational oral history for Shia Muslims.
16. *Matam* refers to the acts or gestures of lamentation. At Shia *majlis* events, *matam* includes ceremonial chest thumping.
17. *Adhaan* is the Islamic call to prayer which occurs five times a day. At Nazneen's mother's house, they have a special clock that fills the home with the sound of the call.
18. Charania; Shroff.
19. In 2014–2016, Zainab co-founded and ran the Unpublished Reading Series, a salon for writers who are or have been underrepresented in mainstream media. In 2013 Zainab joined Two Truths and a Lie, a writer's workshop run by Bushra Rehman; she continues to be an active participant today.
20. Ahmed.

WORKS CITED

Ahmed, Sara. *Living a Feminist Life*. Durham, NC: Duke University Press, 2017.

Charania, Moon. "Making Way for Ghosts and Mothers: Storied Socialities, Sexual Violence, and the Figure of the Furtive Migrant." *Meridians* 18, no. 1 (2019): 206–226.

Liu, Roseann and Savannah Shange. "Toward Thick Solidarity: Theorizing Empathy in Social Justice Movements." *Radical History Review* 132 (2018): 189–198.

Lugones, Maria. "Playfulness, 'World'-Travelling, and Loving Perception." *Hypatia* 2, no. 2 (1987): 3–19.

Minai, Naveen and Sara Shroff. "Yaariyan, Baithak, Gupshup: Queer Feminist Formations and the Global South." *Kohl: A Journal for Body and Gender Research* 5, no. 1 (2019). https://kohljournal.press/yaariyan?fbclid=IwAR2Kn2sgkpe2m_Pvs7a6__Od1SgaJcSsmrjyWvF2_f3raRni3OZ8EV_6Prc.

Shroff, Sara. "Between mother and daughter: Brown erotics and sacred notes." *Journal of Lesbian Studies* 26, no. 1 (2021): 45-52. DOI: 10.1080/10894160.2021.1960617.

PART III

PUBLIC WRITING AND SCHOLARSHIP

Chapters in this section primarily articulate approaches to community engagement that tie feminist scholarship into public writing. Aviva Dove-Viebahn's "A 'Feminist Lens' on Activism and Inclusion in the Film and Television Industry" chronicles the intersection of her research, pedagogy, and public writing through a series of online interviews with women working behind the scenes in the film and television industry. In "Feminism, Faith, and Public Scholarship," Susan Shaw explores how her work bridges the gaps between feminism and Christianity in order to increase accessibility and understanding in both communities. Alex Ketchum's essay, "University Media Relations, Public Scholarship, and Online Harassment," assesses how universities respond to the online harassment of their scholars, providing policy information and practical guidance alongside this analysis. Begüm Acar, Nefise Kahraman, and Senem Kaptan's "Translation as Feminist Activism: Amplifying Diverse Voices through *Amargi Feminist Review*" takes on as a case study the translation and outreach work of a Turkish journal via a feminist collaborative. "Love and

Marriage and the World's Best Editor" serves as both a memorial to and a story of scholar Audrey Bilger's varied work with editor Michele Kort through several public-facing publications. Lastly, Julie R. Enszer's multifaceted career as a writer, scholar, publisher, and editor of the long-running lesbian feminist journal *Sinister Wisdom*, takes center stage in her essay "Scholar, Writer, Editor, Publisher: Multifaceted Engagements in Feminist Public Writing."

CHAPTER TWELVE

A "FEMINIST LENS" ON ACTIVISM
AND INCLUSION IN THE FILM
AND TELEVISION INDUSTRY

By Aviva Dove-Viebahn

In April 2015, as part of my freelance work with *Ms.* magazine, I had the unique opportunity to interview writer and director Joey Soloway (then creator and showrunner of the Amazon series *Transparent*, 2014-2019) for a short sidebar as part of a longer piece on women showrunners in Hollywood.[1] I had interviewed other filmmakers, mediamakers, and industry creatives for a few articles in the past, but something about this particular interview stuck with me.[2] For one, it segued surprisingly well with a course I had taught the year prior (Fall 2014) entitled "Media, Community and Identity Politics;" I would go on to teach a similar course in Spring 2017 and another relevant course, "Looking for Love: Sexuality and the Politics of Representation," in Spring 2018. For another, Soloway's assertion during the interview that "There are so many ways in which we're kept away from our voices and from power that nobody's even conscious of," sparked for me a wider interest in considering how women and non-binary creators in television and film were addressing not just sexism, racism, homophobia, and/or transphobia in their careers, but also how they were finding ways to address the challenges inherent to working in a male-dominated industry while engaging with feminist ideologies in their work.

In 2017, I began interviewing industry creatives, not quite knowing where it would lead. For a while, I was unsure where to publish these interviews or how to use them in my own research, only aware that each conversation vibrantly elucidated the complex and also similar experiences of women working in diverse parts of the film and television industry, from production design and editing, to writing and directing. Other interviews,[3] conducted mainly for *Ms.*, as well as my own personal experiences as I began a tentative foray into screenwriting, convinced me of the continued value of this interview series despite the then-years that had passed since its inception. Finally, in August 2019, these conversations coalesced into the *Feminist Lens* project, an online series of interviews housed on *Ms.*'s online platform.[4] This essay chronicles the rationale for the interview series, what I learned and continue to learn from it, how conducting these interviews has impacted my pedagogy and research, and how my scholarly background informs my own nascent industry involvement as an emerging screenwriter. All told, these intersecting experiences challenge the belief, still prevalent in many disciplines, that academia, industry, and popular culture are separate and distinct spheres of influence.

The *Feminist Lens* interview series (henceforth *FL*) is by no means unique, and I do not mean to suggest that it is making a one-of-a-kind intervention in the film and television industry. Rather, I want to emphasize the opposite: it is only one of many such platforms that focus on women in media. As such, it offers a glimpse into the industry from the perspectives of those I have interviewed, rather than an all-inclusive overview, making it both individualized and specific; other platforms that give an all-inclusive overview, many of which are well-established, include *Women and Hollywood,* the *Women's Media Center, Film Fatales,* and *Women of Color Unite/The JTC List* (which I discuss further below), to name a few. There have also been a number of academic books published collecting interviews with women filmmakers; however, the focus of these collections has been primarily well-known or established directors and producers, whereas I have spent most of my time talking to those creatives whom one might consider emerging or mid-career. Moreover, an online platform lends itself to an immediacy not possible with print books.[5] Through *FL,* I demonstrate how even a relatively small or burgeoning platform can help establish a bridge between academia, industry, and the arts that aims to be mutually productive, reflective, and fulfilling. My involvement with *FL* also serves as a case study for the way scholarship, pedagogy, public writing, and art/media activism can have a reciprocal impact on various facets of one's career and work, underscoring the value of cultivating and maintaining ties to art and media communities beyond academia.

On a March 2017 trip to Los Angeles, I arranged interviews with women with whom I connected through mutual friends and industry networks, including screenwriter Linda Burstyn, writer and director Nia Malika Dixon (founder of the #BlackMuslimGirlFly Film Festival), actor and filmmaker Kamala Lopez (founder of Equal Means Equal), writer and director Destri Martino (founder of The Director List), comedian and writer Dani Klein Modisett (founder of Laughter on Call), and then script supervisor Rena Sternfeld-Allon (now also a director). In November of the same year, I spoke again to documentary filmmaker Therese Shechter, whom I had interviewed previously for an online piece, in New York City. While I found these interviews enlightening and enlivening, I had not yet found a good home for them, imagining at the time that they might become part of a book project. In 2018, I began a new position as an assistant professor of film and media studies at Arizona State University, which renewed my interest in finding a home for the wise words of these intrepid creatives, as I imagined how useful they might be to my students, many of whom were aspiring mediamakers themselves.

Around the same time, I had begun co-writing a screenplay, with Brittany K. Fonte, an endeavor that felt both adjacent to my scholarly writing and thrillingly new. While writing, I began to realize how much of its conception stemmed not only from the conversations I had been having with other filmmakers and writers for years, but also my own scholarly research on representations of race, gender, and sexuality in media. My writing partner and I were dedicated to writing a queer romantic comedy that featured two women of color and treated both sexuality and race as integrated lived experiences of the characters rather than merely tokenistic signposts. We eventually entered the screenplay in several film festivals, were named finalists, and had the opportunity to travel to Los Angeles, Austin, and other cities, where we began to make connections with more writers and filmmakers. Coming full circle, I was newly emboldened to channel these connections into *FL*.

To date, I have published interviews with fellow academic and filmmaker, Michele Meek, to whose anthology, *Independent Female Filmmakers*, I contributed an essay; actress, writer, and director Tess Paras, whom I met at the Broad Humor Film Festival in Venice, CA; Nia Malika Dixon, one of my 2017 interviewees; and the founder of Women of Color Unite, Cheryl L. Bedford, who is now also the producer developing my script. My two most recent interviews were with directors Zahra Rasool and Naima Ramos-Chapman, who created a collaborative virtual reality project about incarcerated women, *Still Here*, and filmmaker Patricia Vidal Delgado, regarding her feature debut *La Leyenda Negra*—these latter projects were ones I had the opportunity to see at the Sundance Film Festival, largely due to my academic work. I list these interviewees and their respective geneses here in order to emphasize how the roles of public scholar, industry neophyte, and academic all intersect and mutually inform the larger project.

One of the essential realizations I made through my work with FL alongside my scholarship and teaching, is that there are an abundance of women working in film, television, and digital media, contrary to mainstream discourse and the common (mis) representation of the media industry/ies as very male and very white. And yet, many of these women, especially women of color, have a difficult time making significant headway in both Hollywood and independent media.[6] The issue is not a dearth of women interested in and qualified to work on a film or television production, but rather that they are not as likely to be hired. Alternatively, while there are always a few women working on any given production, many times it is the same select few who receive the majority of the work. One interviewee revealed to me what she had observed as a common practice on many television shows: hiring a certain number of women directors each season (to meet a bare minimum quota), but only drawing those hires from a sanctioned "list" of known directors, making it nearly impossible for new directors to find an inroad.[7] Tokenism and exceptionalism are high on the list of problems facing women and members of other marginalized communities in the media industry. Those tasked with hiring often hire people they have worked with before or know, and successful women and people of color tend to be branded as exceptional. The latter means that those preferential "exceptions" may be frequently hired and become tokens for the overall diversity of a production, when, in fact, they are only a select few. Some recent television and film productions have pushed back, working hard to diversify their writing rooms in terms of race and gender or even having all-female writing rooms, but these are still far from the norm.[8]

FL and the knowledge of the people I have interviewed has enlightened me to aspects of the film, television, and media industry I may not have had opportunities to experience through my research, scholarship, or pedagogy. Most striking, perhaps, was

Cheryl Bedford's comment that her twenty-years-plus career has changed her perspective on what the ultimate goal of inclusivity in the media industry should look like. Instead of women of color needing to work "twice as hard for half as much," as the old adage goes, Bedford wants women of color to only need to be as good as "a mediocre white man":

> Women of color hold themselves to a higher standard when applying for jobs—and that's how places are hiring, too. So, when I say that I want women of color to be able to be like mediocre white boys, I'm not saying that they should be mediocre at their jobs. What I'm saying is "mediocre" is the median; there are people who are better and people who are worse. I want women of color to be able to be in the middle and still get hired. We shouldn't be competing with the white men who apply even when they're not as qualified.[9]

This reframing offers a compelling intervention in the discourse around race, gender, skill, and labor. Whereas white men, Bedford explains, frequently are hired due to nepotism or networking, whether or not they are more than basically competent at their craft, women of color struggle to even get their foot in the door no matter their skill, education, or talent. Bedford's nonprofit Women of Color Unite and her JTC List, which acts as a clearinghouse for women of color working in the industry, were essentially created so no one could claim that they could not find women of color to hire in any given position on a film or television set. Taking things a step further, in the summer of 2020, Bedford and Thuc Nguyen, founder of The Bitch Pack, masterminded what has quickly become the largest and fastest growing diversity and inclusion program in Hollywood, #StartWith8Hollywood, which challenged established industry producers, writers, directors, agents, and others to commit to mentoring at least eight women of color and guide them in their careers.[10] While what mentoring looks like for each mentor-mentee pairing varies—some mentors and mentees have one general meeting where the mentee may glean a bit of advice; other mentors dedicate themselves to sustained interaction with their mentees over the course of weeks or months—the program offers a valuable networking experience for women of color.

Some women have pursued another tactic as they make a place for themselves in the industry, enacting models for involvement that buck the business-as-usual trends in media production. Tess Paras explains why she began writing and directing in addition to her acting career: "So many people right now are multi-creatives. Economically, it's a way to sustain yourself in this business if you have something to say. Gone are the days of the Hollywood studio system where people say, you're going to be an actor and you're going to be in every single movie. It doesn't work that way in the current landscape."[11] In fact, two of her early written and produced shorts, "What if Catcalls Were Cheeseburgers?" and the music video "Typecast," reflect on her experiences as a woman and as a Filipina in Hollywood, merging her acting and comedy writing skills to critically examine how women, particularly women of color, are treated.

Creatives like Nia Malika Dixon, Zahra Rasool and Naima Ramos-Chapman, and Patricia Vidal Delgado push back against conventional narratives surrounding female characters. Dixon writes and directs projects representing Black and/or Muslim women and girls who do not necessarily conform to society's expectations. "I like to challenge authority," Dixon explains. "That's been my angle my whole life, so I'm pretty much like this unicorn out here, this Black Muslim woman who doesn't cover, who's independent." She later elaborates how much of the impetus behind her work has to do with representation: "Representation matters. Growing up watching movies, I never saw myself."[12] Similarly, Delgado's *La Leyenda Negra* reimagines a queer coming of age narrative through the lens of immigration politics, using primarily amateur actors to portray the high school students she centers on. The films which most interest her are "exercises in empathy," and so she prefers watching and making media "that give [her] a window into someone else's lived experience, into someone else's truth."[13]

While approaching inclusive representation from another angle, via documentary and docudrama in augmented and virtual reality, Ramos-Chapman similarly reflects on the value of finding new modes for creating and collaborating:

> I think the structure [of producing *Still Here*] itself is counter to the way that we're told traditionally to make films, which I think is in and of itself powerful because that structure is something inherited from military-like practices. You know, they say "shooting" for a reason, and there's a director and there's this very strict hierarchy. That's how you make a film. But I think allowing space to let different people lead and not being afraid to challenge each other and say, you know, this doesn't feel quite right to the experience even though it might sound good.[14]

Gleaned from these interviews, considerations of how to approach the production and the reception of film, television, and other media in ways that are mindful of the need for inclusive representation both behind and in front of the camera continue to inform my pedagogy, scholarly research, public writing, and screenwriting.

To wit, my conversation with Dr. Michele Meek, both an assistant professor at Bridgewater State University and filmmaker, reminded me about the important roles the syllabi we write and how we teach media play in how our students learn and how they think of themselves as potential mediamakers post-graduation:

> I think it's really important when we use the word "marginalized," we realize that someone has been marginalizing them. There's a subject to that sentence. Often, many of us as scholars think we're not the ones marginalizing [women filmmakers] because we're for equality. But when you really start to reflect on what you're

teaching and what you're writing about, you might be shocked to discover that you're more part of the problem than the solution.[15]

As such, I have made a greater effort to incorporate women and people of color throughout all my syllabi, not just in special topics courses on identity politics or gender or core courses like Arizona State University's "Race, Gender and American Media," but also in broader courses like the required "Television and Cultural Studies." While I include specific weeks devoted to issues surrounding representations of race, sexuality, femininity, and masculinity in that course, I also weave programs by and featuring women and people of color throughout the entire semester.

Furthermore, in my scholarly research, I am working on a monograph exploring gendered exceptionalism in the representation of women in contemporary serial narratives, assessing the way producers, writers, and directors portray women's knowledge and power through their characters. My work with *FL* has shifted the scope of my research away from pure content analysis in order to also consider how and when gender and race parity on the production side influences these representations. Perhaps the presence of more women and people of color in a writers' room or otherwise behind the scenes on a television or film set correlates positively with an increase in diverse representation of women *on the screen*, including various characters of differing backgrounds and perspectives. In a related vein, these scholarly questions gleaned from *FL* and my pedagogy have also filtered into my own screenwriting, where throughout the process of revising, workshopping, and developing our script, my writing partner and I increasingly emphasize the political and cultural necessity of realistic and varied forms of representation even in what, on the surface, may seem to be a fairly mainstream (albeit queer) romantic comedy. These intersections between *FL*, my other public writing, the screenplay, my scholarship, and my pedagogy emphasize the vibrant possibilities of making connections between public and academic, between art and politics, and between entertainment and ideology.

In this chapter, I have discussed how underrepresented mediamakers speaking about their work in Hollywood and other parts of the film, television, and media industry can serve multiple purposes—scholarly, academic, and professional. I have also included examples of ways anecdotal, personal narratives (provided by the film and TV creatives I have interviewed) are broadly applicable to feminist activism and speak to wide audiences. These discussions are especially timely due to the growing attention in mainstream and independent filmmaking and television to the representation of women and other marginalized people both in front of and behind the camera. These concerns further influence how we conceptualize media literacy and issues of representation in media for viewers, broadly writ, as well as academics and students. While some scholars may want to write off mainstream film and television as mere entertainment, media scholars are all too aware of the way media representation informs and reflects on the complex lived experiences of women, people of color, and LGBTQIA+ individuals. By channeling that knowledge into public writing and engagement, we can increase awareness of and advocate for both those underrepresented individuals working in the industry and those who are conscientious, eager viewers in search of thoughtful and multifaceted representation.

NOTES

1. Dani Klein Modisett, "The Women Who Steal the Show," *Ms.* magazine, Spring 2015: 20–25.
2. At the time, Soloway went by a different first name, which is the name used in my published interview with them. Aviva Dove-Viebahn, "What Does the Female Gaze Look Like," *Ms.* magazine, Spring 2015: 24–25. Previously, I had published two other print articles, and several online pieces, that included interviews with filmmakers: "Pockets of Resistance: A New Documentary Tells the Story of the New Jersey 4," *Ms.* magazine, Fall 2014: 48–49, and "Living History: Two Recent Documentaries by Women Filmmakers Illuminate Icons Angela Davis and Alice Walker," *Ms. Magazine*, Summer 2013: 42–45.

3. For example, with *The Handmaid's Tale* (2017–present) costume designer Ane Crabtree and with *The Glorias* (2020) director Julie Taymor. See "Shouting in Silence: The Ms. Q&A with Former 'Handmaid's Tale' Costume Designer Ane Crabtree," *Ms.* magazine (online), August 12, 2019, https://msmagazine.com/2019/08/12/shouting-in-silence-the-ms-qa-with-former-handmaids-tale-costume-designer-ane-crabtree/ and "'The Glorias' Film Explores the Many Faces of Gloria Steinem," *Ms.* magazine (online), September 5, 2020, https://msmagazine.com/2020/09/05/the-glorias-film-explores-the-many-faces-of-gloria-steinem/.
4. All interviews from the Feminist Lens project can be found here: https://msmagazine.com/tag/the-feminist-lens/.
5. See Jacqueline Levitin, Judith Plessis, and Valerie Raoul, *Women Filmmakers: Refocusing* (New York: Routledge, 2003); Michele Meek, *Independent Female Filmmakers: A Chronicle through Interviews, Profiles, and Manifestos* (New York: Routledge, 2019); and Melissa Silverstein, *In Her Voice: Women Directors Talk Directing (Volume 1)* (Women & Hollywood, 2013). Several other academic books specifically examine the role of women filmmakers in U.S. media production, including Christine Gledhill, Julia Knight, Jane M. Gaines, and Monica Dall'asta's edited anthology *Doing Women's Film History: Reframing Cinemas, Past and Future* (Champaign, IL: University of Illinois Press, 2015) and Katarzyna Paszkiewicz's *Genre, Authorship and Contemporary Women Filmmakers* (Edinburgh, UK: Edinburgh University Press, 2017).
6. See the Women's Media Center 2019 report, "The Status of Women in the U.S. Media," https://www.womensmediacenter.com/reports/the-status-of-women-in-u-s-media-2019.
7. The interviewee asked to remain anonymous in relation to this particular comment, but several industry sites have published reports regarding the difficulty women directors face. See Maureen Ryan, "TV Directors and Diversity: The Helmers Speak Out," *Variety,* November 10, 2015, https://variety.com/2015/tv/features/tv-directors-diversity-1201633554/; Lexi Alexander, "No More Excuses: Hollywood Needs to Hire More Female Directors," *IndieWire,* January 15, 2014, https://www.indiewire.com/2014/01/no-more-excuses-hollywood-needs-to-hire-more-female-directors-31286/; and Andrew Wiseman, "'Women Directors are not Allowed To Fail': 'American Psycho' Director Mary Harron—Venice Gender Equality Seminar," *Deadline,* September 3, 2019, https://deadline.com/2019/09/women-directors-are-not-allowed-to-fail-says-american-psycho-director-mary-harron-venice-gender-equality-seminar-1202709682/.

8. See Radhika Seth, "How more inclusive writers' rooms are redefining TV," *Vogue Australia* (online), August 5, 2019, https://www.vogue.com.au/culture/features/how-more-inclusive-writers-rooms-are-redefining-tv/news-story/e6fc3fe2d749ec860b76beb48c2399ee; and Lacy Rose, "'Empire': Meet the Writers Behind Broadcast's Biggest Hit," *The Hollywood Reporter,* September 17, 2015, https://www.hollywoodreporter.com/live-feed/empire-meet-writers-behind-broadcasts-824097.
9. Dove-Viebahn, "Feminist Lens: Cheryl L. Bedford's Vision for a Diverse and Inclusive Hollywood," *Ms.* magazine (online), June 18, 2020, https://msmagazine.com/2020/06/18/feminist-lens-cheryl-l-bedfords-vision-for-a-diverse-and-inclusive-hollywood/.
10. See https://www.startwith8hollywood.com/ for the program's website and, for press about the program, see Drury, Sharareh, "#StartWith8 Hollywood Program Offers New Hope for Women of Color in Hollywood," *The Hollywood Reporter,* August 27, 2020. https://www.hollywoodreporter.com/news/startwith8hollywood-program-offers-new-hope-for-women-of-color-in-hollywood.
11. Dove-Viebahn, "The Feminist Lens: Tess Paras Talks #MeToo Movies and Inclusive Casting," *Ms.* magazine (online), September 18, 2019, https://msmagazine.com/2019/09/18/the-feminist-lens-tess-paras-talks-metoo-movies-and-inclusive-casting/.
12. Dove-Viebahn, "The Feminist Lens: Nia Malika Dixon Tells Stories for Black, Muslim Women," *Ms.* magazine (online), October 16, 2019, https://msmagazine.com/2019/10/16/the-feminist-lens-nia-malika-dixon-tells-stories-for-black-muslim-women/.
13. Dove Viebahn, "Feminist Lens: Patricia Vidal Delgado's Insightful First Feature Confronts Imperialism, Past and Present," *Ms.* magazine (online), December 11, 2020, https://msmagazine.com/2020/12/11/la-leyenda-negra-feminist-lens-patricia-vidal-delgados-insightful-first-feature-confronts-imperialism-past-and-present/.
14. Dove-Viebahn, "Feminist Lens: Zahra Rasool, Naima Ramos-Chapman and Immersive AR/VR Installation 'Still Here'" *Ms.* magazine (online), July 31, 2020, https://msmagazine.com/2020/07/31/feminist-lens-zahra-rasool-naima-ramos-chapman-and-immersive-ar-vr-installation-still-here/.
15. Dove-Viebahn, "The Feminist Lens: Why Michele Meek Celebrates a Diversity of Icons in Film," *Ms.* magazine (online), August 28, 2019, https://msmagazine.com/2019/08/28/the-feminist-lens-why-michele-meek-celebrates-a-diversity-of-icons-in-film/.

WORKS CITED

Alexander, Lexi. "No More Excuses: Hollywood Needs to Hire More Female Directors." *IndieWire*, January 15, 2014. https://www.indiewire.com/2014/01/no-more-excuses-hollywood-needs-to-hire-more-female-directors-31286/.

Dove-Viebahn, Aviva. "Living History: Two Recent Documentaries by Women Filmmakers Illuminate Icons Angela Davis and Alice Walker." *Ms.* magazine, Summer 2013: 42–45.

———. "Feminist Lens: Patricia Vidal Delgado's Insightful First Feature Confronts Imperialism, Past and Present." *Ms.* magazine (online), December 11, 2020. https://msmagazine.com/2020/12/11/la-leyenda-negra-feminist-lens-patricia-vidal-delgados-insightful-first-feature-confronts-imperialism-past-and-present/.

———. "Feminist Lens: Zahra Rasool, Naima Ramos-Chapman and Immersive AR/VR Installation 'Still Here.'" *Ms.* magazine (online), July 31, 2020. https://msmagazine.com/2020/07/31/feminist-lens-zahra-rasool-naima-ramos-chapman-and-immersive-ar-vr-installation-still-here/.

———. "Feminist Lens: Cheryl L. Bedford's Vision for a Diverse and Inclusive Hollywood." *Ms.* magazine (online), June 18, 2020. https://msmagazine.com/2020/06/18/feminist-lens-cheryl-l-bedfords-vision-for-a-diverse-and-inclusive-hollywood/.

———. "The Feminist Lens: Nia Malika Dixon Tells Stories for Black, Muslim Women." *Ms.* magazine (online), October 16, 2019. https://msmagazine.com/2019/10/16/the-feminist-lens-nia-malika-dixon-tells-stories-for-black-muslim-women/.

———. "The Feminist Lens: Tess Paras Talks #MeToo Movies and Inclusive Casting." *Ms.* magazine (online), September 18, 2019. https://msmagazine.com/2019/09/18/the-feminist-lens-tess-paras-talks-metoo-movies-and-inclusive-casting/.

———. "The Feminist Lens: Why Michele Meek Celebrates a Diversity of Icons in Film." *Ms.* magazine (online), August 28, 2019. https://msmagazine.com/2019/08/28/the-feminist-lens-why-michele-meek-celebrates-a-diversity-of-icons-in-film/.

———. "'The Glorias' Film Explores the Many Faces of Gloria Steinem." *Ms.* magazine (online), September 5, 2020. https://msmagazine.com/2020/09/05/the-glorias-film-explores-the-many-faces-of-gloria-steinem/.

———. "Pockets of Resistance: A New Documentary Tells the Story of the New Jersey 4." *Ms.* magazine, Fall 2014: 48–49.

———. "Shouting in Silence: The Ms. Q&A with Former "Handmaid's Tale" Costume Designer Ane Crabtree." *Ms.* magazine (online), August 12, 2019. https://msmagazine.com/2019/08/12/shouting-in-silence-the-ms-qa-with-former-handmaids-tale-costume-designer-ane-crabtree/.

———. "What Does the Female Gaze Look Like." *Ms.* magazine, Spring 2015: 24–25.

Drury, Sharareh. "#StartWith8 Hollywood Program Offers New Hope for Women of Color in Hollywood." *The Hollywood Reporter*, August 27, 2020. https://www.hollywoodreporter.com/news/startwith8hollywood-program-offers-new-hope-for-women-of-color-in-hollywood.

Gledhill, Christine, Julia Knight, Jane M. Gaines, and Monica Dall'asta eds. *Doing Women's Film History: Reframing Cinemas, Past and Future*. Champaign, IL: University of Illinois Press, 2015.

Levitin, Jacqueline, Judith Plessis, and Valerie Raoul. *Women Filmmakers: Refocusing*. New York: Routledge, 2003.

Meek, Michele. *Independent Female Filmmakers: A Chronicle through Interviews, Profiles, and Manifestos*. New York: Routledge, 2019.

Modisett, Dani Klein. "The Women Who Steal the Show." *Ms.* magazine, Spring 2015: 20–25.

Paszkiewicz, Katarzyna. *Genre, Authorship and Contemporary Women Filmmakers*. Edinburgh: Edinburgh University Press, 2017.

Rose, Lacy. "'Empire': Meet the Writers Behind Broadcast's Biggest Hit." *The Hollywood Reporter*, September 17, 2015. https://www.hollywoodreporter.com/live-feed/empire-meet-writers-behind-broadcasts-824097.

Ryan, Maureen. "TV Directors and Diversity: The Helmers Speak Out." *Variety*, November 10, 2015. https://variety.com/2015/tv/features/tv-directors-diversity-1201633554/.

Seth, Radhika. "How More Inclusive Writers' Rooms Are Redefining TV." *Vogue Australia* (online), August 5, 2019. https://www.vogue.com.au/culture/features/how-more-inclusive-writers-rooms-are-redefining-tv/news-story/e6fc3fe2d749ec860b76beb48c2399ee.

Silverstein, Melissa. *In Her Voice: Women Directors Talk Directing (Volume 1)*. Women & Hollywood, 2013.

Wiseman, Andrew. "'Women Directors Are Not Allowed to Fail': 'American Psycho' Director Mary Harron—Venice Gender Equality Seminar." *Deadline*, September 3, 2019. https://deadline.com/2019/09/women-directors-are-not-allowed-to-fail-says-american-psycho-director-mary-harron-venice-gender-equality-seminar-1202709682/.

Women's Media Center, "The Status of Women in the U.S. Media." https://www.womensmediacenter.com/reports/the-status-of-women-in-u-s-media-2019.

CHAPTER THIRTEEN

FEMINISM, FAITH, AND
PUBLIC SCHOLARSHIP

By Susan M. Shaw

The first piece of public scholarship I ever wrote, "Christian Fragility," was published on *Huffington Post* as my attempt to explain the Christian Right's opposition to marriage equality. I realized that as a feminist scholar who was raised in fundamentalist Southern Baptist Christianity, I had a unique perspective to offer to help the Left understand—and perhaps engage—evangelical Christians and their impact on US politics. In 2018, I began to write for *Ms. Magazine* online, starting with an effort to explain how Southern Baptist theology created a culture ripe for sexual abuse. That year, I also began to write for *Baptist News Global*, a progressive Baptist news web site, to offer an intersectional feminist lens on issues of religion to a progressive Christian audience. My inaugural piece explored how the first woman president of a cooperative Baptist seminary was pushed over the "glass cliff."

As a public scholar, I work at the crossroads of feminism and Christianity. My research has focused on Southern Baptist women and on feminist theologies. In writing for the public, I bring what I've learned from my research to bear on how I think about contemporary issues, ranging from the death of Sandra Bland to the Southern Baptist Convention's mishandling of clergy sexual abuse. My public writing has also led to a recent invitation by a progressive Christian press to write a book of essays with similar themes and approaches.

My work seeks to make Christian, particularly evangelical, issues, attitudes, and behaviors intelligible for a feminist audience and to bring feminist perspectives to contemporary faith issues for Christian audiences. While these two groups are not necessarily exclusive, they often seem to be at odds. Frequently, conservative Christians act as if they speak for all Christians, while more moderate and progressive Christian voices are drowned out by the predominance of highly visible conservatives, like Franklin Graham. Many feminists, then, may assume all Christians are anti-feminists. Many Christians also may only know feminist thought as it is filtered (and caricatured) through conservative media so they assume all feminists are anti-Christian. Christian feminists, then, have an opportunity to intervene at the intersections of feminism and Christianity to highlight convergences, overlapping concerns, and opportunities for collaborative activism.

As a professor, I also bring these concerns and approaches to the classroom. I teach courses on "Global Feminist Theologies," "Feminist Theologies in the U.S.," and "Feminism and the Bible" at a public university. In these classes, we work at the intersection of religion and feminism, drawing on many of the ideas that run through my public scholarship, and occasionally reading one of these pieces as a part of the class. My students tend to be either people who have grown up in a religious tradition that no longer works for them and who are looking for alternatives or people with no religious background whatsoever but who are curious about religion. Our conversations also often spark ideas for me for public pieces as I see places where greater clarity or deeper questions may be helpful in the public discourse.

This essay offers a personal perspective on doing public scholarship at the intersection of faith and feminism. My hope is that my experiences and reflections may help readers imagine how to find their own niches and navigate the complex and tricky terrains of speaking to diverse public audiences in ways that engage people in feminist dialogue about important contemporary social and political issues.

THE URGENCY OF THE PRESENT MOMENT

While I have always tried to write for a broad audience (including in my university press books[1]), the candidacy and then election of Donald Trump created for me an urgency to bridge faith and feminism for both Christian and feminist audiences. In this moment of "fake news," the dismissal of expertise, fabrications, and lies, making arguments from verifiable facts, reliable evidence, and truthful reasoning is more important than ever and, to me, makes public scholarship more needed and urgent as a counter to the misinformation and falsehoods purveyed on social media, right-wing "news," White House press briefings, and many white evangelical pulpits.

In early 2017, I wrote "Dear White, Christian Trump Supporters: We Need to Talk" for *Huffington Post*. In that piece, I spoke specifically to evangelical Christians. I started with my own commonalities with them as a white working-class kid who made her way up through higher education and into the middle class. Then, based on the very things I'd learned in my fundamentalist Southern Baptist church, I explained how I was baffled by their support for Trump. I questioned how his racism, xenophobia, white nationalism, and ethnocentrism squared with the God of love they claim to worship. I wrote:

> You say you want a Christian nation, but our founders were clear that was never their goal. In fact, the Constitution goes to great

lengths to protect the government from religion and religion from government. I also get the sense that you think people are not Christians if they aren't Christian in the same way as you. But can't we find some common ground? Can't we agree that all people should be free to practice their religion or practice no religion and should be safe from coercion based on religion? Can't we agree that we share values of love, kindness, respect, and community and then try to live those with each other? Do you really think a Christian, especially a biblical literalist, can want a wall built?

This is still my most shared piece. People got in touch with me via email. Most thanked me. Some were ugly. A few evangelical Christians engaged me in authentic dialogue.

As the years of the Trump presidency wore on, I wrote again and again about white evangelical support for Trump, the costs of Trump's divisiveness, and the impact of Trump's policies and practices that are unthinkingly applauded by most white evangelical Christians.

Because of evangelical Christianity's influence on US politics, feminists and progressive Christians need to be able to speak to conservative Christians, informed by accurate history, theology, science, and feminist theories. Writing public scholarship at this intersection of faith and feminism provides a way to consider the thorny issues of religion and politics to offer intellectual tools for readers to support their activist engagement with the politics of evangelical Christianity.

CHRISTIAN INFLUENCE IN THE PUBLIC SQUARE

People of faith have been engaged in US politics from the earliest days of the colonies when Puritans set sail from England to escape religious persecution, only to set up their own persecutions of dissenters in New England. In the religious wars of Europe,

Baptists saw the dangers of intertwining church and state, and so, in the US, beginning with Roger Williams' founding of Providence, Rhode Island, Baptists advocated for complete religious liberty and separation of church and state. At various times, adherents of different religious traditions have tried to sway public policy, from Quaker anti-slavery work, to Protestant women's involvement in the prohibition movement, to Catholic opposition to the death penalty.[2]

Evangelical and fundamentalist[3] Christians became especially politically involved with the election of Ronald Reagan and the rise of what would become known as the Christian Right (this coincided with the fundamentalist takeover of the Southern Baptist Convention and included some of the same key players). In 1981, no less than Billy Graham himself worried about the marriage of the religious and political Right. He told *Parade Magazine*, "It would disturb me if there was a wedding between the religious fundamentalists and the political right. The hard right has no interest in religion except to manipulate it."[4] Nonetheless, the Christian Right saw in Reagan someone who would work for their religious-political agenda, and so the identification of the Republican Party with evangelical Christianity began in earnest.[5]

Scholars have hypothesized that a number of converging issues played a role in the prominence of the Christian Right. With the successes of the Civil Rights Movement, white men (particularly in the South) felt a loss of power in the 1960s and 70s that was also threatened by the Women's Movement, the Gay Rights Movement, and the Antiwar Movement. These social movements disrupted traditional hierarchies of power and threatened social institutions that propped up white masculinity and the patriarchal social order. The political rise of evangelicalism and fundamentalism, then, in many ways was a backlash to social progress and an attempt to maintain white supremacist heteropatriarchy.

The impact on public policy, especially as it affects marginalized people, has been profound. Many evangelicals became single-issue voters, focusing their efforts on rolling back abortion rights and supporting presidential candidates who would appoint anti-choice justices to the Supreme Court.[6] In recent years, many have come to embrace a "full-quiver" theology that teaches married heterosexual couples should not use birth control but have as many children as God gives them. This thinking is to a great extent behind opposition to the Affordable Care Act's mandate for employers to provide contraception coverage[7]. Conservative Christians have also opposed marriage equality and employment protections and laws that assure equal treatment and access for LGBTQ+ people. They tend to be unquestioning supporters of the Israeli government because of their belief that Jews (which they often conflate with the nation of Israel) are God's chosen people and play a significant role in their apocalyptic vision of end times.

That particular belief begins in the story of Sarah and Hagar in the Bible, a narrative that also shows us the extent to which religion, politics, and gender have always mixed. It also shows how conservative Christian readings of the biblical text affect US foreign policy. Written around 950 BCE at the height of Jewish empire, the story reflects the author's contemporary grappling with questions of the kingdom's founding, success, and sustainability. In the story, Abraham is married to Sarah, and Hagar is Sarah's enslaved handmaid. God has promised Abraham and Sarah a son, but they get impatient, and Sarah offers Hagar to Abraham. Hagar gets pregnant, and Sarah becomes jealous and mistreats her. Hagar runs away, but God sends her back to Sarah and promises her son will become the father of a great multitude. She gives birth, and eventually Sarah becomes pregnant and gives birth to a son. Sarah doesn't want to see Hagar's son growing up with hers, and so she convinces Abraham to throw Hagar out of their family. God protects Hagar and Ishmael in the wilderness, and he grows up to be the patriarch of the Arab people. Sarah's son Isaac becomes the father of Israel.

Not surprisingly, the narrative becomes one of fathers and sons (as the women fade into the background) and continues to reverberate in the geopolitics of the Middle East today. Based on the biblical narrative's identification of Isaac as the son through which God's promises will be fulfilled, contemporary conservative Christians believe US foreign policy should privilege the nation of Israel. And so, to play to his base of evangelical Christians, Donald Trump moved the United States embassy to Jerusalem.[8]

This, of course, is but one example of how a conservative Christian reading of a biblical story with issues of gender, ethnicity, and religion at its core becomes a significant influencer of modern politics. Understanding these histories and intersections is important for people working for social justice as they seek to disrupt dominant narratives and oppressive political, economic, social, and religious policies and practices. Public scholarship that exposes and explains the workings of conservative Christian influence on contemporary politics can challenge unexamined assumptions about religion (on both the Left and the Right) and suggest paths forward for constructive engagement and activism that takes seriously the beliefs and practices of conservative Christians.

For example, womanist biblical scholar Delores Williams uses the story of Hagar to explore intersections of sexism, racism, poverty, and violence in the lives of Black women and argues that as God responded to the needs of Hagar, God responds to the needs of Black women. My co-author, Grace Ji-Sun Kim, and I use Williams' reading of Hagar in our book, *Intersectional Theology: An Introductory Guide*, to help make the case for an intersectional reading of the biblical text as a way to disrupt dominant and oppressive readings and to reimagine ways of reading the biblical text toward justice.

PERSONAL HISTORY AND PUBLIC SCHOLARSHIP

My analysis of current issues from the lenses of feminism and progressive Christianity is intertwined with my biography, and my personal stories often show up in my public pieces as a way to create connections with readers, build credibility, and personalize the impact of my analysis. I grew up a fundamentalist Southern Baptist in Georgia. When I enrolled in The Southern Baptist Theological Seminary in Louisville, Kentucky (before fundamentalists took it over in the mid-1990s), I encountered progressive Baptists, and I began to read liberation theologies that would profoundly shape my understandings of social justice. I became a feminist at Southern Seminary, although I had to seek out feminist theologies on my own after seminary. I started my teaching career in the religion departments of Christian liberal arts colleges, but I soon realized that my feminism, antiracism, and growing sense of self as queer were not a good fit. So, I went back to school to earn a graduate degree in women's studies, and then I joined the faculty of the Women's Studies (now Women, Gender, & Sexuality Studies) Program at Oregon State University where I began to teach courses on feminist theologies and feminism and the Bible. I also began in earnest my scholarship at the intersection of religion and feminism. As one who had grown up in fundamentalism, I am able to bring an insider/outsider perspective to my research and writing. While my first publications were university press books, as a feminist, I was committed to accessible scholarship, and so I wrote for a broad general audience when I published (with the University Press of Kentucky) *God Speaks to Us, too: Southern Baptist Women on Church, Home, and Society*, my findings based on interviews with more than 150 current and former Southern Baptist women across the country. I also wrote a book and workbook for a moderate Baptist press that made feminist biblical criticism and theology accessible for a lay audience, *Reflective Faith: A Theological Toolbox for Women*.[9]

When I began to write for online sites, I found an opportunity to publish more immediately in response to current events. Books, for me, are generally three-to-four-year projects, but I can write a 1,000-word piece in response to something in today's news and have it published tomorrow. The transition to writing public scholarship was in most ways easy for me since I was already writing accessibly in my books. The most difficult change was learning to say what I wanted to say in under 2,000 words instead of in 300 pages!

I still find myself amazed at the reach of public scholarship. My university press books reached audiences of hundreds across several years. A single piece in *Ms. Magazine* online or *Baptist News Global* can reach thousands in just a few days. Given the cacophony of online bloggers who do not utilize the tools of research, evidence, and citation, public scholars have the opportunity to bring the reasoned and supported scholarship of their disciplines to offer a counter to the bluster and misinformation that have come to characterize much online writing. For me, writing from the perspective of feminist Christianity has allowed me to add my distinctive experiences and expertise to important conversations about social justice issues.

Of course, speaking out comes with a price. After one piece was picked up by Campus Reform and Breitbart, I was trolled for about a week. I received vile, misogynistic, homophobic emails, and people contacted my dean and other university administrators to complain about me. I was fortunate that my university handled my case very well, although I know that is not the experience of many other academics, but the trolling still took an emotional toll, even as it strengthened my resolve to continue my public scholarship.

SPEAKING TO FEMINIST AUDIENCES

Again, I acknowledge an overlap among feminists and Christians. Progressivism has a long and important history within Christianity, and some of the earliest feminist academics to challenge their disciplines were Christian women theologians and biblical critics.

Nonetheless, many feminists may not have much if any background in Christianity, and, with good reason, a lot of feminists are hostile to Christianity because of many of its adherents' history of unjust, unethical, and oppressive actions towards women, people of color, and LGBTQ+ people. Yet, particularly in the United States, Christianity plays a large role in politics and public policy. While progressive Christians work toward social justice, many conservative Christians engage in the politics of the Religious Right, opposing reproductive justice, Black Lives Matter, ethical immigration policies, and LGBTQ+ rights, making feminist understanding of conservative Christianity an essential tool for engaging in resistance to the Right's oppressing influence in public policy, social relationships, and law.

As a public scholar, I try to interpret Christianity, particularly conservative Christianity, for a non-Christian audience. I am able to bring the scholarship of religion and Christian feminism to analysis of contemporary issues such as White evangelical support for Donald Trump, conservative Christian opposition to transgender rights, purity culture, and the problem of sex abuse in Southern Baptist churches. I'm also able to make progressive Christian thinking visible and suggest possibilities for coalitions of feminist activists and progressive faith groups. For example, I interviewed Quaker singer/songwriter Carrie Newcomer for *Ms.* In that piece, Carrie talks about how her spirituality inspires her activism and offers hope in this time of chaos. In another *Ms.* piece, I drew from United States and Baptist history to explain how the Trump administration's "Commission on Unalienable Rights" is actually a threat to religious liberty. Yet another piece explores how conservative Christian theology and biblical interpretation rooted in gender hierarchies underpin transphobia.

The feedback I receive from feminist readers suggests that they appreciate a deeper understanding of why conservative Christians believe and behave as they do. They often comment that my pieces help them have conversations with evangelical friends and family whom they do not understand (and who do not understand them). These personal conversations are important forms of activism that all feminists can do to reach people within their spheres of influence, and having timely, accurate information can help feminists feel well-informed and empowered to engage in difficult dialogues.

SPEAKING TO PROGRESSIVE CHRISTIAN AUDIENCES

Progressive Christian audiences often support social justice but may not know feminist theories, history, and research, and so I am able to utilize the tools of feminist scholarship to explore contemporary issues and events. For example, a piece for *Baptist News Global* suggested that Christians could come together to reduce the need for abortion by supporting practices research shows to be effective—access to contraception, accurate sex education, and empowerment of women. Another piece used a reproductive justice framework to argue against six-week abortion bans.

By far, my Christian reading audiences are predominantly white, and so I can use my public scholarship to encourage utilization of an intersectional lens in faith matters. An essay following the killing of George Floyd by police in Minneapolis drew from Black and Womanist theologies to invite readers to see the deaths of Floyd, Breonna Taylor, and others, through a theology of the cross, as a critique of White power and a call to dismantle structures of White supremacy. Another piece, arguing for an intersectional, multi-issue approach to social justice, offered this observation:

> If we take Jesus out of the stained-glass window for a moment, we realize that he was a working-class Jew living under empire who in his brief ministry confronted issues of disability, poverty, gender, sexuality, colonization and religious intolerance, to the extent he became enough of a threat to the state that the Roman Empire executed him.

Bringing together feminist theologies and feminist theories allows me to offer readers different perspectives on traditional religious beliefs and practices and to encourage readers to examine and challenge beliefs and practices that maintain discrimination, injustice, and oppression. For example, in one piece, I drew on the Jewish concept of *tikkun olam* (repair of the world) to suggest steps to take in transforming systems of power and privilege.

As a Baptist. I am deeply committed to full religious liberty and separation of church and state. I also recognize that faith is an important element in political participation. Many of my pieces ask readers to be mindful of the tensions inherent in belief in both religious liberty and separation of church and state, even as I encourage them to engage in progressive political action. I also critique the ways the Right has obliterated the clear line between church and state and has become an advocate for a narrow conception of religious liberty that favors their particular version of Christianity while violating the religious liberty of others, including other Christians. For example, I have written about the problems of federal funding for religious organizations and the troubling practice of public prayer at government events.

I do also keep in mind the possibility of conservative readers as I write to Christian audiences. In this moment of deep division, however, speaking across religious and political lines has become much more difficult. When we cannot agree that facts matter, that claims need verifiable data and reliable evidence, and that issues are more complex and nuanced than Facebook memes, we may not find much common ground. Still, I try to use insider language and my own understanding and experiences from within conservative Christianity to build bridges to new ideas and to draw from positive concepts in conservative Christianity—such as loving neighbors, doing good works, being kind, and listening for God's voice in unexpected places—to offer alternative readings of the Bible and different theological interpretations that may challenge and disrupt traditional oppressive beliefs and practices.

CONCLUSION

Whether I'm writing for a feminist or Christian audience, I always try to model doing good scholarship at the intersections of diverse disciplines, ideas, and traditions. I am careful to be as accurate as I can, to offer nuance, to cite reliable sources, and provide credible evidence. I don't pretend to be neutral. As a feminist, I always write, as Vivian May says, with a bias toward justice.[10] I try to say something in a way that it hasn't been said before, to add something new to the conversation, rather than simply adding to the cacophony. I look for the unexpected intersections of faith and feminism and invite my readers into a conversation with me, the scholarship, and these diverse communities. Often, I write things I need to hear and simply hope that others will overhear my conversation with myself and will find themselves in what I have to say. Based on responses I receive from readers who take the time to track down my email on my university's web site, I think my work does indeed offer benefit. I may most often be "preaching to the choir," as the saying goes, but, as I always say, "The choir needs preaching to as well."

NOTES

1. Susan M. Shaw, *God Speaks to Us, too: Southern Baptist Women on Church, Home, and Society* (Lexington: University Press of Kentucky, 2008); Mina Carson, Tisa Lewis, and Susan M. Shaw, *Girls Rock: Fifty Years of Women Making Music* (Lexington: University Press of Kentucky, 2004).
2. For more on Baptist history, see: McBeth, Leon. *The Baptist Heritage: Four Centuries of Baptist Witness* (Nashville, Broadman, 1987); Leonard, Bill J. *Baptists in America* (New York, Columbia University Press, 2005).
3. Not all evangelicals are fundamentalists, though almost all fundamentalists are evangelicals. Evangelicals are Christians who believe that sharing the Gospel of Jesus to convert people is a central requirement of their faith. Fundamentalists believe that the Bible is without error and is to be read literally (as well as other "fundamental" doctrines of faith).
4. Billy Graham qtd in Dargan Thompson, "6 Lessons from the Life of Billy Graham," *Relevant Magazine*, Accessed July 21, 2021, https://relevantmagazine.com/faith/what-billy-graham-can-teach-us/.

5. Daniel K. William, "Reagan's Religious Right: The Unlikely Alliance between Southern Evangelicals and a California Conservative," in *Ronald Reagan and the 1980s: Perceptions, Policies, Legacies*, eds. Cheryl Hudson and Gareth Davie (New York: Palgrave, 2008).
6. Ted G. Jelen and Clyde Wilcox, "Causes and Consequences of Public Attitudes Toward Abortion: A Review and Research Agenda," *Political Research Quarterly* 56, no. 4 (2003): 489–500; Andrew R. Lewis, *The Rights Turn in Conservative Christian Politics: How Abortion Transformed the Culture Wars* (New York: Cambridge University Press, 2017).
7. Lisa M. Corrigan, "So, You've Heard of the Duggars? Bodily Autonomy, Religious Exemption, and the American South," *QED: A Journal in GLBTQ Worldmaking* 3, no. 1 (Spring 2016): 138–147.
8. Stephen Spector, "This Year in Jerusalem: Prophecy, Politics, and the U.S. Embassy in Israel," *Journal of Church & State* 61, no. 4 (2019): 551–571.
9. Susan M. Shaw, *Reflective Faith: A Theological Toolbox for Women* (Macon, GA: Smyth & Helwys Publishing, 2014).
10. Vivian May, *Pursuing Intersectionality, Unsettling Dominant Imaginaries* (New York: Routledge, 2015).

WORKS CITED

Carson, Mina, Tisa Lewis, and Susan M. Shaw. *Girls Rock: Fifty Years of Women Making Music*. Lexington, KY: University Press of Kentucky, 2004.

Corrigan, Lisa M. "So, You've Heard of the Duggars? Bodily Autonomy, Religious Exemption, and the American South." *QED: A Journal in GLBTQ Worldmaking* 3, no. 1 (2016): 138–147.

Jelen, Ted G. and Clyde Wilcox. "Causes and Consequences of Public Attitudes Toward Abortion: A Review and Research Agenda." *Political Research Quarterly* 56, no. 4 (2003): 489–500.

Lewis, Andrew R. *The Rights Turn in Conservative Christian Politics: How Abortion Transformed the Culture Wars*. New York: Cambridge University Press, 2017.

May, Vivian. *Pursuing Intersectionality, Unsettling Dominant Imaginaries*. New York: Routledge, 2015.

Shaw, Susan M. *God Speaks to Us, too: Southern Baptist Women on Church, Home, and Society*. Lexington, KY: University Press of Kentucky, 2008.

———. *Reflective Faith: A Theological Toolbox for Women*. Macon, GA: Smyth & Helwys Publishing, 2014.

Spector, Stephen. "This Year in Jerusalem: Prophecy, Politics, and the U.S. Embassy in Israel," *Journal of Church & State* 61, no. 4 (2019): 551–571.

Thompson, Dargan. "6 Lessons from the Life of Billy Graham." *Relevant Magazine* (November 7, 2014). Accessed July 21, 2021. https://relevantmagazine.com/faith/what-billy-graham-can-teach-us/.

William, Daniel K. "Reagan's Religious Right: The Unlikely Alliance between Southern Evangelicals and a California Conservative." In *Ronald Reagan and the 1980s: Perceptions, Policies, Legacies*, edited by Cheryl Hudson and Gareth Davie, 135–150. New York: Palgrave, 2008.

CHAPTER FOURTEEN

UNIVERSITY MEDIA RELATIONS, PUBLIC SCHOLARSHIP, AND ONLINE HARASSMENT

By Alex D. Ketchum

You are being attacked by a network you cannot outmaneuver, in a system that does not value you enough to defend you. Some of the most vitriolic incidents of internet outrage against supposed liberal professors have picked off women, African Americans and other members of racial minorities: The internet outrage industrialists know we're easy targets, because the very university that pushed us to be public scholars won't do much to defend us when we're targeted.

Tressie McMillan Cottom [1]

INTRODUCTION

Universities often claim that they are committed to community engagement via publicly engaged scholarship and media work. Radio, television, podcast, and newspaper interviews are options for communicating one's research to the public, yet they are not without drawbacks. Professor of Publishing, Juan Pablo Alperin has established the ways in which universities espouse the importance of public scholarship yet do not actually value it in tenure decisions.[2] There is a cost to doing work in public spheres that disproportionately is paid by marginalized scholars.[3] In the above quote, sociologist Tressie McMillan Cottom recounts the experience of facing online harassment after doing public work.[4] It is not rare for women academics, Black and Indigenous scholars, and other scholars of color to face harassment online. Especially for scholars, such as myself, who engage with the public through media work, a writer's ideas are not the only thing attacked; threats of death and sexual violence can fill a scholar's inbox.[5] Racist trolls and gendertrolling[6] can intimidate scholars and dissuade them from doing this work.[7] Doxing, the act of broadcasting private or identifying information about an individual for the purpose of harassment—particularly racial- and gender-based harassment— has been well documented.[8] Women, gender non-binary people, queer people, and racialized people are more likely to not just have their ideas attacked, but their identities attacked. As journalist Amanda Hess explains:

> "Ignore the barrage of violent threats and harassing messages that confront you online every day." That's what women are told. But these relentless messages are an assault on women's careers, their psychological bandwidth, and their freedom to live online. We have been thinking about Internet harassment all wrong.[9]

Online harassment curtails the free speech of women and racialized scholars.[10] This kind of harassment diminishes the desire to participate in public-facing work, especially with the media.

Furthermore, even when harassment has not yet occurred, the fear of harassment can lead to self-silencing. In "Gender and the 'Impact' Agenda: The Costs of Public Engagement to Female

Academics," gender studies professor Heather Savigny notes how many female academics that she has interviewed have talked of how they made a conscious decision not to engage with the media for fear of abuse.[11] She argues that this silencing "becomes a form of symbolic violence; an expression of underlying relations of oppression and domination, which as Bourdieu suggests, becomes so normalized and routine that it occurs almost with the subordinate's own complicity," and thus, "women then are structurally positioned to be complicit in their own silencing" even when this can affect their career trajectories.[12] I personally have turned down opportunities to speak about my research on lesbian and feminist businesses with certain media outlets as past experience has shown me that I will experience an uptick in trolling, harassment, and sometimes threats afterward. While I still participate in publicly engaged scholarship and media work, this fear does lead me to turn down some opportunities that might benefit my career in the long run but could impact my psychological well-being in the short term. Online harassment also comes with increased anxiety and long-term health effects.[13]

Universities are often not equipped to assist scholars who experience these kinds of attacks, and public scholars are often left to languish with these problems on their own. During the summer of 2020, my research team and I sought to understand the kind of resources Canadian universities actually provide to support scholars doing public-facing media work. We wanted to know: What information do universities make available to scholars for dealing with trolling, doxing, and harassment when they do public-facing scholarship and media work? What is the availability of that information online (on the media relations offices' websites)? And what information do media relations offices/newsrooms[14] make available to scholars that might not be on their website (plans, policies, advice)? The goal of that research is to establish what practices already exist, what information and resources are missing, and to encourage all universities' media relations offices in Canada and beyond to develop a best practices plan. I focused our study on the Canadian context, as it was possible to feasibly contact every university and understand plans from a broad range of types of universities, from large research universities to small, rural universities.

This research does not exist in order to shame any specific institutions. Rather, this project seeks to encourage universities to create policies and protocols in order to support their scholars who are doing media work and who may experience harassment. It is our wish that media relations offices, which serve as a university's central point of contact with the media, across Canada and elsewhere will establish a set of guidelines, resources, and policies that can be customized on the needs of each university and scholar.

METHODS

Between May 1 and June 24, 2020, my research team began looking at the websites of the media relations offices of every Canadian university, including satellite campuses. We wanted to see what information, resources, and materials the media relations offices had on the topics of trolling, doxing, and harassment. The team of six research assistants divided the list of Canadian universities and searched the media relations offices' websites for any information related to what scholars should do in case they are trolled, doxed, or harassed. The search terms used included "trolling" "doxing/doxxing" (as it can be spelled both ways), and "harassment." For the Francophone universities, the search terms were "trolleur/trolleuse," "doxing/doxxing" (because even though you can translate it to "traçage de document," the term doxing is used as an anglicism), "harcèlement sur les médias sociaux," and "harcèlement par internet." As slight variation in search terms and different preferences of how one navigates a webpage could reveal different information, the team of research assistants double-checked all of the websites. Within the spreadsheet that we used to keep track of results; the research assistants indicated which universities they looked at. For the second round, which concluded on July 10, 2020, the research assistants had to look at universities that they did not look at the first time. We then went through the information and checked for inconsistencies. We considered that documents may be circulated internally. Media relations offices may host workshops. Even if information regarding trolling, doxing, or harassment was not available on the university websites, we wanted to know if university media relations offices had internal materials, protocols, or plans.

From May to mid-July 2020, the research team contacted every Canadian university's media relations office via email, using the same English or French script explaining the research project and asking what materials the office had for scholars regarding what to do about, the risks of, or the protocols to address the trolling, doxxing, or harassment that a scholar might encounter while doing public-facing scholarship. If offices did not respond within a few weeks of the first contact, they were contacted a second time. If emails bounced back or email addresses were no longer in use, we tried another email address.

RESULTS

After the first round of checking the websites, the research team found *no information* directly related to the topic of trolling, doxing, or harassment on the media relations offices websites of any Canadian universities. The closest example that the research team found was that Acadia University does have a Public Relations Guide on their website. In their "Social Media Primer," on pages 10 and 11, there is a section on "not lowering your standards" when people are "inappropriate."[15] However, it does not specifically address trolling and doxing. It also does not mention harassment based on gender, race, or sexual orientation. After the second round of searching media relations offices' webpages, *only one other example* was found, apart from the earlier example from Acadia University. In the Social Media Guide from the University of Fraser Valley, in the section entitled "Reply to messages and posts," there is the note that states, "If you receive a comment you feel could be harmful, you may wish to connect with the UFV Communications team before responding. They can assess the possible impact and help you come up with an appropriate response." [16] This was the most explicit example the research team found of information relating to harassment on a media relations office website or affiliated website. This is not to say that no resources or policies exist from the universities at all—rather that the research team looking particularly for search terms related to "trolling" "doxing" and "harassment" could not find any documents, statements, resources, policies, or procedures. This led us to the second step: directly contacting the universities' media relations offices.

We received responses from forty universities out of the ninety-eight universities that we contacted. We therefore had a 41% response rate. Of the forty media relations offices that responded, we learned that the University of Calgary was the only institution to have an explicit document dedicated to the topic of trolling, doxing, or harassment, although the document does not use those exact words to describe an attack. The document provides scholars with a list of resources including campus security, the local police, and the media relations office, as well as resources on campus such as Staff Wellness, Sexual Violence Support, the Women's Resource Centre, and Employee Assistance. In addition to the document from Acadia University discussed earlier, the Concordia University, OCAD, UBC, UBC Okanagan, and McGill University media relations offices have information related to social media best practices that recommend engaging with comments, particularly rude comments, respectfully, and the University of Manitoba asks for scholars to be respectful and dignified.[17] While these documents do provide practical tips for engaging on social media, they do not address racist, sexist, homophobic, or ableist comments or what to do about ongoing harassment. Furthermore, the emphasis of many of these documents, such as the ones produced by Algoma University, Brescia, and University of Ottawa, is on scholars or employees using official university social media accounts.[18] Those documents do not address what to do about trolling or doxing attacks that can occur on a scholar's personal social media accounts after doing public media work. These documents focus on maintaining the university's reputation more than on protecting faculty members from online harassment. None of the media relations offices that responded had any explicit policies. Most of the media relations offices who had protocols indicated that they would deal with harassment on a case-by-case basis.

It is important to make clear that the kinds of policies we are discussing are not the same as the occupational health and safety workplace laws that require employers to have policies against harassment within the workplace. University human rights offices will often deal with those cases of internal harassment. For this report, we are looking explicitly at the kinds of protocols, policies, documents, and workshops media relations offices within Canadian universities have to support their scholars who are doing public media work and who are trolled, doxed, or harassed while engaging in this work. So, unless harassers are from inside their university, the occupational health and safety workplace protocols do not apply.

While a few media relations office representatives did not think trolling, doxing, or harassment were things to be concerned about or thought that these were not issues that affected their university's scholars, several representatives said that they had heard concerns from their scholars and have had to deal with cases of harassment. Two media relations offices already incorporate these discussions in workshops and three expressed that they want to begin to include this material in future workshops.

DISCUSSION

It is significant that there is/was not any information regarding trolling, doxing, or harassment of scholars on media relations offices' websites through July 10, 2020. Universities are places of constant flux. Each semester university campuses welcome visiting scholars, graduate students, and new hires. In addition, even long-time faculty may become interested in doing public-facing scholarship. Even if the media relations office at your university has held a workshop in the past, the present group of scholars doing media work might not know about it. Having readily available information about what to do in case a scholar is trolled, doxed, or harassed while doing public-facing media work is important. As a scholar doing public-facing work, it is important to know that one's institution has a plan in case harassment occurs. Scholars may feel more confident in doing media work if they already know that their institution has clear protocols in order to give support and guidance if harassment occurs.

In addition, if scholars do experience harassment, they will already be under emotional duress. It is important that materials be readily available to support them during this difficult time, and that they do not have to spend time searching for assistance, likely without finding any information. It is understandable that for various strategic and legal reasons a media relations office does not want to post their documents or their entire plan for supporting scholars in case of harassment online—especially as individual cases may require individualized responses. However, having a notice on the media relations office website that acknowledges the risk of trolling, doxing, and harassment is useful. The office should, of course, not just say this, but actually have a plan in place that they can explain to their scholars when asked. If other offices at the university, such as faculty development offices, teaching centers, and/or campus security offices, develop protocols in case of external harassment, media relations office websites should direct scholars to those resources. It is helpful to include information about things scholars, including new graduate students, can consider ahead of time before beginning media work.

It is also helpful to include general information about the procedures. Telling scholars to ignore trolls is not a sufficient plan. A single mean comment can be ignored. A deluge of insults, death threats, threats of sexual violence, and similar forms of harassment cannot be ignored. Trolling, doxing, and online harassment can have serious implications for the person being harassed, including but not limited to: lowered self-esteem, lowered productivity, feeling unsafe, and more.[19] If universities are truly committed to community engagement via publicly engaged scholarship and media work, there is large room for improvement. In July 2020, with the exception of the two sentences from UFV, we could find no materials available on any Canadian media relations offices' websites regarding policies, procedures, or protocols that exist to explicitly support scholars who are trolled, doxed, or harassed. Of the university media relations offices who responded to our inquiries, few had materials readily available to support scholars. While working with scholars on a case-by-case basis can be useful for the individual receiving support, other scholars may not know what kind of support is available to them. Without adequate institutional support, scholars may be less likely to engage the public with their work and as a result get fewer citations, which then could impact their tenure, funding, and promotion prospects. As this harassment also disproportionately happens to marginalized scholars and people doing feminist and anti-racist scholarship, failing to address online harassment raises questions around labor equity.

The most optimistic findings from our research are that since this project began in May 2020 and since circulating our findings with the Canadian media relations offices we studied and on Twitter, several universities have already begun to work on creating protocols, documents, or workshops related to these topics. Several representatives from within and outside of Canada said that our research has made them interested in developing policies within their institutions. On May 5, 2021, University of Massachusetts Amherst professor Jennifer Lundquist co-organized an event with Ed Blaguszewski of her media relations office to discuss the strategies that faculty and administrators may use to prevent and respond to public harassment and to support faculty if and when it occurs.[20] I invited Jennifer Lundquist to speak at McGill University about the process of developing these policies in November 2021. Media relations officers were also invited and the event was recorded and made readily available in order to inspire others to develop these policies.[21] The effort to develop better policies can be a collaborative effort across universities. I strongly encourage universities to put information regarding a university's protocols for supporting scholars who are harassed while doing media work in a readily accessible place on the media relations office's website, even if the protocol is that the harassment will be dealt with on a case-by-case basis. Providing tips and resources for scholars beginning this work can also help guide the media work scholars do in the first place. No scholar deserves trolling or doxing for deciding to do public media work, and scholars who experience this harassment are not to blame. However, knowing in advance what to do in case a troll storm descends (such as immediately making all social media accounts private) can help a scholar avoid some suffering. Media relations offices can offer to deal with large waves of attacking tweets and posts for their employees. Communications officers can also document the harassment by taking screenshots if legal action becomes necessary. Furthermore, scholars may enter into media work with more confidence and enthusiasm if they know that resources exist to support them if something goes wrong.

BEST PRACTICES SHARED ACROSS INSTITUTIONS

I am not alone in suggesting that it is vital that universities "have a responsibility in the prevention and protection of harm." In addition, Emma Kavanagh, and Lorraine Brown argue that "there is a need to equip individuals with the skills and strategies to self-protect and tackle the harm they may be exposed to while actively engaging in online scholarship."[22] Similarly, in their Ethical Research Guidelines, the Association of Internet Researchers argue that "another essential measure is that institutions develop policy detailing support procedures for researchers experiencing online threats or harassment related to their work."[23] Tressie McMillan Cottom, professor at UNC Chapel Hill, has been calling on universities to develop protocols since 2015.[24] It is because of these reasons that I have assembled the list of resources and suggestions below.

Media relations offices should have dedicated space on their web pages devoted to the topic of online harassment, trolling, and doxing. They can include a statement of how the institution will support their scholars doing public-facing scholarship and media work. In addition, they can provide information for who scholars should contact in case they are harassed, trolled, or doxed while doing this work. On their websites, they can provide a list of resources that include tips scholars can take ahead of time, such as how to lock down your digital identity.[25] The offices can also provide a list of resources for scholars to use in case they are experiencing harassment, trolling, or doxing related to their media work. On their websites and during workshops, they can explain, or at least state, that they have policies to support their scholars in documenting the harassment (and actually develop those policies). The offices also need to include information about harassment, trolling, and doxing during workshops that the offices hold on public media work and hold specific workshops, at least once a semester since universities are states of constant flux, about harassment, trolling, and doxing.

Resources exist already outside of the academy that can assist scholars:

Femtechnet (https://femtechnet.org/csov/) provides resources for both survivors of this violence and employers who aim to support them.

Geek Feminism (https://geekfeminism.wikia.org/wiki/Miti gating_internet_trollstorms) provides advice to survivors of trolling.[26]

Crash Override (https://crashoverridenetwork.tumblr.com/ post/108387569412/preventing-doxing) provides additional support.

Cyberbullying.org (https://cyberbullying.org) offers lists and suggestions.

Cyber Civil Rights Initiative (https://www.cybercivilrights. org/online-removal/) provides information about online removal of offensive images, including nonconsensual pornography.[27]

Although most advice is targeted at individuals, universities can assist scholars in undertaking necessary steps to mitigate these situations. When this information is readily available on universities' media relations offices websites, scholars can more readily access it if or when they need it. While historically most scholars have faced this harassment alone, or with the help of a few peers, universities must assist their employees. Each university's media relations office can tailor this information for their scholars.

CONCLUSION

While this study focused particularly on Canada, these findings are applicable elsewhere. There are many challenges to public scholarship and media work already—a lack of sufficient institutional support against harassment should not be one of them. The Canadian Centre for Occupational Health and Safety (CCOHS) instructs employers that they should pay attention to online harassment.[28] Unfortunately, scholars often face cyberbullying and harassment alone. Researchers deserve to have institutional support from their institutions' media relations offices.

If universities and grant agencies are going to encourage their researchers to engage with public scholarship, there must be support for scholars doing this work in the form of detailing support procedures for researchers experiencing online threats or harassment related to their work. Furthermore, grant agencies, such as the Canadian Tri-Council which encourages scholars to do public scholarship and connect with the public, including via media work, should address this issue. I encourage the Tri-Council to create a dedicated document for guidelines related to online harassment, trolling, and doxing on their SSHRC, CIHR, and NSERC guidelines pages.[29]

At the moment, women and non-binary scholars, Indigenous scholars, scholars of color, queer scholars, scholars with disabilities, and other marginalized scholars are underrepresented in media work, which impacts public conceptions of expertise and the content and focus of media stories.[30] Creating workshops, developing protocols, and providing information to scholars about harassment, trolling, and doxing can empower scholars, especially scholars with marginalized identities, at your universities to actually want to do public scholarship and media work. Knowing that resources exist to support them, scholars will not have to worry about facing harassment alone. I hope to encourage universities, particularly media relations offices, to support this work.

ACKNOWLEDGMENTS

Thank you to my amazing team of research assistants: Kari Kuo, Dominique Grégoire, Mohammed Odusanya, Thai Hwang, Amy Edward, and Astrid Mohr. Thank you to Stefanie Duguay, PhD, and Hannah McGregor, PhD, for your feedback on an earlier draft of the report. Thank you to Juan Pablo Alperin, PhD, for your advice. Thank you to Carrie Baker and Aviva Dove-Viebahn for your constructive comments. Thank you to all of the folks at media relations offices in Canada who responded to our research team. We hope that these findings and this chapter will be useful resources for your work.

More information is available at the project website: https://publicscholarshipandmediawork.blogspot.com

Funding: This research is supported by Alex Ketchum's multi-year SSHRC Insight Grant: Disrupting Disruptions: The Challenge of Feminist and Accessible Publishing and Communications Technologies 1965–present.

The Canadian media relations offices spreadsheet https://docs.google.com/spreadsheets/d/16rBnfl9twd78-W_X88T35hYOj5FZ2sOJV59TDewNic4/edit#gid=0 shows the list of every Canadian university studied for this report. The name of their media relations office or newsroom is included, as there is some variability in how these offices are named or situated within each university. Please note that some universities listed are part of a university system that shares a single media relations office. This chart indicates whether or not the media relations office website includes information related to trolling, doxing, or harassment.

NOTES

1. Tressie McMillan Cottom, "The Real Threat to Campuses Isn't 'PC Culture.' It's Racism," *Huffington Post*, February 19, 2018, https://www.huffpost.com/entry/opinion-cottom-campus-racism_n_5a8afb80e4b00bc49f471b41.
2. Juan Alperin, Carol Muñoz Nieves, Lesley A. Schimanski, Gustavo E. Fischman, Meredith T. Niles and Erin C. McKiernan, "Meta-Research: How Significant Are the Public Dimensions of Faculty Work in Review, Promotion and Tenure Documents?," *Elife* 8, no. 1 (2019): e42254, Doi: https://elifesciences.org/articles/42254.
3. For the purposes of this research, we include tenure-track faculty, non-tenure track faculty, adjunct/sessional professors/instructors, and graduate

students. While these individuals are affiliated with the university, they deserve support from the university in their public-facing work.

4. Cottom, "The Real Threat to Campuses Isn't 'PC Culture.'"
5. Clare Mulcahy, Hannah McGregor, and Marcelle Kosman, "'WHOOPS I AM A LADY ON THE INTERNET': Digital Feminist Counter-Publics," *Atlantis: Critical Studies in Gender, Culture & Social Justice* 38, no. 2 (2017): 134–136; Jessica Megarry, "Online Incivility or Sexual Harassment? Conceptualising Women's Experiences in the Digital Age," *Women's Studies International Forum* 47 (2014): 46–55.
6. Trolling is an act of harassment, which primarily occurs online. It is a form of cyber bullying that can include posting rumors, threats, sexual remarks, violent comments, or hate speech.
7. Karla Mantilla, "Gendertrolling: Misogyny Adapts to New Media," *Feminist Studies* 39, no. 2 (2013): 563–570; George Veletsianos, et al., "Women Scholars' Experiences with Online Harassment and Abuse: Self-Protection, Resistance, Acceptance, and Self-Blame," *New Media & Society* 20, no. 12 (2018): 4689–4708; Nancy Worth, "Public Geographies and the Gendered Experience of Saying 'Yes' to the Media," *The Professional Geographer* 72, no. 4 (2020): 1–9.
8. Emily Harmer and Karen Lumsden, "Experiences of Online Abuse: Gendered Othering, Sexism and Misogyny," *Online Othering: Exploring Digital Violence and Discrimination on the Web* (2019): 117.
9. Amanda Hess, "Why Women Aren't Welcome on the Internet," *Pacific Standard* 6 (2014): https://psmag.com/social-justice/women-arent-welcome-internet-72170.
10. Jessica West, *Cyber-Violence against Women*, Battered Women's Support Services, 2014.
11. Heather Savigny, "Gender and the 'Impact' Agenda: The Costs of Public Engagement to Female Academics," LSE, 2019, https://blogs.lse.ac.uk/politicsandpolicy/gender-and-impact-in-academia/?fbclid=IwAR0JFtjVIC_RbsEOYk-DdErONwEEDOkxNsYXvF5gxFE-acVhbq4Ko9iFag8.
12. Savigny, "Gender and the 'Impact' Agenda."
13. Jerry Finn, "A Survey of Online Harassment at a University Campus," *Journal of Interpersonal Violence* 19, no. 4 (2004): 468–483.
14. These offices have a variety of names: Media Relations, Newsroom, Institutional Communications, and Communications. However, despite the variety of names, they all serve a similar function. The offices are a university's central point of contact with the media. Representatives from the media can contact these offices to connect with a university's scholars. The office

will also often work with journalists to promote newsworthy stories about a university's research discoveries and events, serving as a public relations office. It is not uncommon that the media relations office will also produce its own materials. For example, the McGill University media relations office, The Newsroom, will manage and promote, news, events, and announcements via the McGill Reporter, McGill Dans la Ville, What's New e-newsletters, as well as via their social media channels (https://www.mcgill.ca/newsroom/contacts).

15. "Public Relations Guide," Acadia University, https://www2.acadiau.ca/PubliCrelationsGuide.html.

16. "Social Media Guidelines," University of the Fraser Valley, https://www.ufv.ca/university-relations/marcom/social-media-guidelines/.

17. "Public Relations Guide," Acadia University, https://www2.acadiau.ca/PubliCrelationsGuide.html; "Handbook," Concordia University, http://www.concordia.ca/social/handbook.html; "OCAD University's Social Media Terms of Use," Ontario College of Art and Design University, https://www.ocadu.ca/about/socialmedia; "Social Media Moderation Guidelines," The University of British Columbia, http://assets.brand.ubc.ca/downloads/ubc_social_moderation_and_response.pdf; "Social Media Guidelines for UBC Okanagan Employees," University of British Columbia Okanagan, https://communications.ok.ubc.ca/socialmedia/; "Social Media Guidelines," McGill University Newsroom Institutional Communications, https://www.mcgill.ca/newsroom/socialmedia/guidelines; "Social Media at the University of Manitoba," University of Manitoba, https://umanitoba.ca/admin/vp_admin/ofp/fippa/media/Social_Media_Guidelines.pdf.

18. "Social Media Policy," Algoma University, https://www.algomau.ca/wp-content/uploads/2018/10/Social-Media-Policy.pdf; "Social Medias," University of Ottawa, https://arts.uottawa.ca/en/marketing/social-medias.

19. Veletsianos, et al., "Women Scholars' Experiences with Online Harassment and Abuse".

20. UMass Amherst, "When Public Engagement Comes with Public Harassment: How to Prevent, Respond, and Support Faculty," May 5, 2021, https://www.umass.edu/sbs/calendar/event/when-public-engagement-comes-public-harassment-how-prevent-respond-and-support?fbclid=IwAR2Bvwo96hsoFsrLIBouQHl43MVZ-_eLmMVj_-nAijkJcJ2aTP76ii2ekxs.

21. Jennifer Lundquist and Alex Ketchum, "Addressing the Digital Harassment of Scholars," video, November 17, 2021, https://www.feministandaccessiblepublishingandtechnology.com/p/videos.html.

22. Emma Kavanagh and Lorraine Brown, "Towards a Research Agenda for Examining Online Gender-Based Violence against Women Academics," *Journal of Further and Higher Education* 44, no. 10 (2019): 1–9.
23. Association of Internet Researchers, "Internet Research: Ethical Guidelines 3.0 Association of Internet Researchers," aoir.org, October 16, 2019, https://aoir.org/reports/ethics3.pdf.
24. Tressie McMillan Cottom, "Everything but the Burden: Publics, Public Scholarship, and Institutions," tressiemc.com, https://tressiemc.com/uncategorized/everything-but-the-burden-publics-public-scholarship-and-institutions/.
25. "Locking Down Your Digital Identity," Femtechnet, http://femtechnet.org/csov/lock-down-your-digital-identity/.
26. "Mitigating Internet Trollstorms," Geek Feminism Wiki, https://geekfeminism.wikia.org/wiki/Mitigating_internet_trollstorms.
27. "Online Removal Guide," Cyber Civil Rights Initiative, https://www.cybercivilrights.org/online-removal/.
28. "Internet Harassment or Cyberbullying," Canadian Centre for Occupational Health and Safety, last updated July 12, 2017, https://www.ccohs.ca/oshanswers/psychosocial/cyberbullying.html.
29. Government of Canada, Social Sciences and Humanities Research Council, "Policies Regulations and Guidelines," last modified February 7, 2020, https://www.sshrc-crsh.gc.ca/about-au_sujet/policies-politiques/index-eng.aspx.
30. Worth, "Public Geographies and the Gendered Experience of Saying 'Yes' to the Media," 1–9.

BIBLIOGRAPHY

Alperin, Juan, Carol Muñoz Nieves, Lesley A. Schimanski, Gustavo E. Fischman, Meredith T. Niles, and Erin C. McKiernan. "Meta-Research: How Significant Are the Public Dimensions of Faculty Work in Review, Promotion and Tenure Documents?" *Elife* 8, no. 1 (2019): e42254. Doi: https://elifesciences.org/articles/42254.

Association of Internet Researchers (AoIR). "Internet Research: Ethical Guidelines 3.0." aoir.org, October 19, 2019. https://aoir.org/reports/ethics3.pdf.

Cassidy, Wanda, Chantal Faucher, and Margaret Jackson. "The Dark Side of the Ivory Tower: Cyberbullying of University Faculty and Teaching Personnel." *Alberta Journal of Educational Research* 60, no. 2 (2014): 279–299.

Cottom, Tressie McMillan. "Everything but the Burden: Publics, Public Scholarship, And Institutions." tressiemc.com, 2019. https://tressiemc.com/uncategorized/everything-but-the-burden-publics-public-scholarship-and-institutions/#.

Cottom, Tressie McMillan. "The Real Threat to Campuses Isn't 'PC Culture.' It's Racism." *Huffington Post*, February 19, 2018. https://www.huffpost.com/entry/opinion-cottom-campus-racism_n_5a8afb80e4b00bc49f471b41.

Daniels, Jessie and Arlene Stein. "Protect Scholars Against Attacks from the Right." *Inside Higher Ed*, June 26, 2017. https://www.insidehighered.com/views/2017/06/26/why-institutions-should-shield-academics-who-are-being-attacked-conservative-groups.

Finn, Jerry. "A Survey of Online Harassment at a University Campus." *Journal of Interpersonal violence* 19, no. 4 (2004): 468–483.

Harmer, Emily, and Karen Lumsden. "Experiences of Online Abuse: Gendered Othering, Sexism and Misogyny." In *Online Othering: Exploring Digital Violence and Discrimination on the Web*, edited by Karen Lumsden and Emily Harmer, 117. New York: Palgrave Macmillan, 2019.

Hess, Amanda. "Why Women Aren't Welcome on the Internet." *Pacific Standard* 6 (2014). https://psmag.com/social-justice/women-arent-welcome-internet-72170.

Hodson, Jaigris, et al. "I Get By with a Little Help from My Friends: The Ecological Model and Support for Women Scholars Experiencing Online Harassment." *First Monday*, 2018.

Kavanagh, Emma, and Lorraine Brown. "Towards a Research Agenda for Examining Online Gender-Based Violence against Women Academics." *Journal of Further and Higher Education* 44, no. 10 (2019): 1–9.

Mantilla, Karla. "Gendertrolling: Misogyny Adapts to New Media." *Feminist Studies* 39, no. 2 (2013): 563–570.

Megarry, Jessica. "Online Incivility or Sexual Harassment? Conceptualising Women's Experiences in the Digital Age." *Women's Studies International Forum* 47 (2014): 46–55.

Mulcahy, Clare, Hannah McGregor, and Marcelle Kosman. "'WHOOPS I AM A LADY ON THE INTERNET': Digital Feminist Counter-Publics." *Atlantis: Critical Studies in Gender, Culture & Social Justice* 38, no. 2 (2017): 134–136.

Savigny, Heather "Gender and the 'Impact' Agenda: The Costs of Public Engagement to Female Academics," LSE, June 14, 2019. https://blogs.lse.ac.uk/politicsandpolicy/gender-and-impact-in-academia/?fbclid=IwAR0JFtjVIC_RbsEOYk-DdErONwEEDOkxNsYXvF5gxFE-acVhbq4Ko9iFaG8.

Veletsianos, George, et al. "Women Scholars' Experiences with Online Harassment and Abuse: Self-Protection, Resistance, Acceptance, and Self-Blame." *New Media & Society* 20, no. 12 (2018): 4689-4708.

West, Jessica. *Cyber-Violence against Women*. Battered Women's Support Services, 2014.

Worth, Nancy. "Public Geographies and the Gendered Experience of Saying 'Yes' to the Media." *The Professional Geographer* 72, no. 4 (2020): 547-555.

CHAPTER FIFTEEN

TRANSLATION AS FEMINIST ACTIVISM
Amplifying Diverse Voices through Amargi Feminist Review

By Begüm Acar, Nefise Kahraman, and Senem Kaptan

INTRODUCTION

Volunteer-based translation collectives actively expand transnational debates and cultivate a sense of solidarity beyond national and linguistic borders. What motivates the voluntary labor that goes into the activities of such groups is the belief in the enriching and transformative power of community-engaged work. Translation collectives often undertake activist work that mobilizes their communities and challenges the oppressive narratives of their cultures with their potential to evoke certain sensibilities, such as feminist awareness and advocacy. In Turkey, where transnational feminist debates have always been significant for local feminist activism, feminist translation collectives have played a similar role in serving as vital and vibrant spaces for feminist thought and organizing. This essay will chronicle our journey as a group of feminists who, as students and activists, undertook the work of translating articles in *Amargi Feminist Review* (2006-2015) from Turkish into English with the goal to make available emerging local feminist debates to a transnational audience. The journal was published in relation to Amargi Women's Academy (referred to hereafter as "Amargi"), a grassroots feminist cooperative that was founded by a group of diverse feminist activists in 2001 and based in Istanbul, Turkey.

The word *amargi* means "freedom" and "return to mother/woman" in the ancient Sumerian language, reflecting the core goal of the organization to be a space where women from different walks of life could freely discuss any and all matters. Having operated for eleven continuous years until its closure in 2012,[1] Amargi served as a feminist hub, bringing together activists, scholars, and students from both the national and transnational level. During those years, the organization ran a multiplicity of events, including lectures, seminars, workshops, and discussion groups; expanded feminist scholarship by publishing a series of studies, compilations, and essays;[2] established the Amargi Feminist Bookstore (2007-2011); and, perhaps most importantly, served as a community for women of diverse backgrounds, LGBTQI+ individuals, and other marginalized populations.[3] Seeing patriarchal power relations and gender inequality as the primary markers of everyday life and social injustice, Amargi actively focused on eliminating discrimination and violence through a feminist stance that repudiated militarism, nationalism, and hierarchy.[4]

Despite the presence of the word "academy" within the name of the organization, as well as the presence of activists with ties to the academic world among its founding members, Amargi was not an educational institution in an official sense. Yet, the embrace of the word "academy" within its name was a conscious decision. Sociologist Pınar Selek, who was among the core founders of the cooperative, commented that "we believe [in Amargi] that the institutionalization of knowledge and politics through its alienation from social life is a characteristic of patriarchy."[5] The decision to name the cooperative an "academy" was, therefore, an invitation to challenge and rethink the common perception of knowledge production as something that is done within, and that inherently belongs to, institutionalized settings, such as universities and research centers. Instead, Amargi's foundational manifesto refused the duality between academia and activism, urging for a more critical position that recognized the inextricable link between the everyday experiences of women and LGBTQI+ persons and feminist knowledge production. This position was reflected in one of the foundational mottos of the organization, "Living itself is the most important academic activity." Furthermore, through its other core motto, "We are together with our differences," Amargi embraced and encouraged transversal politics[6]—a political position that sees unity in diversity, promoting dialogue among people of disparate power positions and identities (e.g., class, gender, ability, sexuality) and addressing such differences "with equal respect and recognition."[7]

Amargi Feminist Review, connected to the cooperative through its name and ideological stance, had its roots in similar concerns and the goal to bring together diverse women in what was named a "journal of feminist theory and politics." Highlighting the interconnected nature of these two realms, Pınar Selek, the journal's co-editor, along with feminist scholar Aksu Bora, stated that *Amargi* "was born out of a need to create the opportunity to think on ourselves and also translate the knowledge base within academia to the women's movement and the experience within the women's movement to academia."[8] In expanding on what this would look like in practice, the editorial team highlighted that this means "setting as a priority the strengthening of the loosened ties between feminist theory and politics; not treating theory as a series of abstract thoughts situated before/above politics; not seeing politics as consisting solely of everyday tactics and negotiations and instead making a point to shed theory's light on politics."[9] The journal thus aimed to serve as a place where the artificially produced gap between both theoretical scholarship and political action as well as between academia and activism could be reconciled by upholding women's lives as the primary source of knowledge.

Similar to Amargi's refusal of hierarchies, the journal embraced a model of flat organizing, both in terms of what and who it included among its issues. Within the pages of *Amargi Feminist Review*, life itself was treated as a political act, with topics from local elections to union strikes, from marriage to sexual violence, from education to military service, and from love to friendship all treated as being equally worthy of attention without artificially produced hierarchical priorities. In a similar manner, the journal embraced equity, inclusion, and diversity among its writers as well, underscoring that "*Amargi* is not the type of journal that will be prepared by only those women who produce the most rigorous form of writing and who possess extensive knowledge on a given topic; it was also designed as a journal for women who are within the women's movement and who need to learn how to write."[10] In embracing this stance, the journal reaffirmed the historically important relationship between writing and feminism, and provided a platform that encouraged more women to express themselves in writing. This approach was also made evident in terms of the place translation held within the pages of the journal in an effort to introduce the writings of international authors to feminists in Turkey.

TRANSLATION AS A FORM OF FEMINIST ACTIVISM IN TURKEY

Amargi's embrace of diverse and international voices through translating texts builds on the long tradition of translation as a form of movement building and activism within the feminist movement in Turkey. In fact, this effort predates the founding of

Figure 15.1: Amargi Issue 21, Summer 2011, "Without Seeking Your Forgiveness"—Special issue on forgiveness (and unforgiveness).

modern Turkey, with many women, some of whom were writers and public intellectuals themselves, heavily involved in translating works into and from Ottoman Turkish. *Terakki Muhadderat* (The Progress of Virtuous Women), a newspaper supplement published weekly, was one of the early examples of the journals specifically addressed to a female Muslim readership in the Ottoman Empire. Dating back to the 1860s, *Terakki Muhadderat* featured letters sent by women discussing issues such as education and the place of women in society. The journal is also notable for publishing articles that informed its readers of the feminist activities unfolding in the West. These articles were often enriched with quotations in translation from British newspapers that drew attention to women's struggles in Great Britain.[11]

Feminist scholar Serpil Çakır's comprehensive work on the women's journals published by and for a female readership in the Ottoman Empire provides evidence for the vitality and the wide-reaching impact of those journals for women's cause. Although, today, feminists in Turkey are adequately informed of Ottoman women's feminist activism/activities, this was not always the case. As feminist scholar and activist Şirin Tekeli points out, "We [feminists in modern Turkey] began [our work] with translation because we had no other materials. At the time, we didn't know about the Ottoman women's movement; that history was lost."[12] Tekeli's emphasis on translation as the initiative that set in motion the acceleration of feminist thought and organizing in modern Turkey is only meaningful when considered within the context of modern Turkish history. The lost history that Tekeli evokes refers to the consequence of the transition from an imperial power to a nation state—the dissolution of the Ottoman Empire and the establishment of modern Turkey in 1923. This transition resulted in sweeping nationalist social, political, and economic reforms, which included changing the Ottoman Turkish alphabet, based on Arabic script, to the Latin-based modern Turkish alphabet, thus resulting in the loss of all cultural heritage, including the Ottoman women's movement, that predated modern Turkey. Therefore, turning to translation was, in essence, the way that the modern feminist movement in Turkey found its own language and history.

In modern-day Turkey, there have been several noteworthy platforms prior to *Amargi* that made room for translations in their works and pages. The independent feminist journals *Feminist*, published between 1987–1990; *Kaktüs* (Cactus), published between 1988–1990; and *Pazartesi* (Monday), published between 1995–2005, are some examples.[13] Another notable example of early feminist translation practices can be seen in the work of the feminist collective *Kadın Çevresi* (Women's Circle), founded in 1984 and credited with being the first second-wave feminist organization in Turkey.[14] In a recently published piece in *The Routledge Handbook of Translation and Activism*, feminist activist Ayşe Düzkan, a member of both the *Kadın Çevresi* collective and *Pazartesi*, acknowledges her contribution to the translation of a book published by the collective as her first experience with translation as activism:

> German feminist Alice Schwarzer had interviewed Simone de Beauvoir and collected these interviews in a book. Some of the interviews in the book were copyrighted and we couldn't afford it but we decided to publish the ones dated before the copyright date, under the title *Ben Bir Feministim* (I am a Feminist). We were three women: a physician around her 50s, a friend from high school, and myself. Each of us identified with feminism; each of us translated one part of the book.[15]

Indeed, in addition to its book club through which feminist works were read and discussed, *Kadın Çevresi* had established a publishing house that printed numerous books in translation, such as Juliet Mitchell's *Women's Estate* (*Kadınlık Durumu*), which was collectively translated by six feminist activists. Elaborating on the significance of the work conducted by *Kadın Çevresi*, translation studies scholar and feminist translator Emek Ergün states that "it was as a result of such translational operations of naming and conceptualizing women's experiences of gender oppressions, all facilitated by translation, that a feminist language and consciousness began to develop in Turkey."[16] It would not be wrong to say that the legacy of *Kadın Çevresi* carries on to this day through the rich gender studies scholarship and vibrant feminist movement in Turkey.

Beyond the pages of activist journals, women translators have also long held an important place in acting as astute and critical conveyors of political, literary, and academic knowledge to readers in Turkey, infusing the texts they have translated with a political activist stance. Emek Ergün, the translator of Hanne Blank's *Virgin: The Untouched History* (2007), for instance, opted not to use the patriarchal Turkish correspondence of hymen— "*kızlık zarı*," which literally means "membrane of girlhood" (i.e., virginity) or "maidenhead"—in her translation and instead opted for the term "*himen*." Feminist activist and translator Ayşe Düzkan, who translated *SCUM Manifesto* (1967) by Valerie Solanas in 2002, introducing Solanas to readers in Turkey, followed a similar feminist activist practice and opted to use (among many other examples) "*seks işçiliği*" (sex work) instead of "*fahişelik*" (prostitution).[17] These interventions demonstrate that the agency of the translator holds an important place within the work of feminist translators, marking their choices in how they relay information to the reader. Here, translation is not just seen as a mechanical linguistic process, but a political act and a collective co-construction of texts.

AMARGI TRANSLATORS AND THEIR FEMINIST TRANSLATION PROCESS

The translation process of *Amargi Feminist Review* began in 2008, when three interns in Amargi Women's Academy, Begüm Acar, Gül Varlı, and Miray Çakıroğlu, all of whom were students at the time, came up with the idea to translate selected articles from the journal. The inception of the idea coincided with the time that Amargi Feminist Bookstore, especially with the opening of its coffeeshop, was frequented by international visitors, including activists, researchers, and students. Thus, the bookstore served as a multi-generational, multilingual, and intersectional meeting ground that was home to lively debates where a wide range of issues from sexuality to family were discussed in light of both local and global feminist perspectives. Having witnessed these interactions, the young activists thought that, through translating the articles in *Amargi* into English, the extensive feminist knowledge base

Figure 15.2: Amargi Issue 19, Winter 2010, "All that remains is time"—Special issue on time.

produced in the pages of the journal could reach more people, especially those interested in learning more about the feminist movement and women's everyday lives and struggles in Turkey. Thus began the work of the volunteer translator group.

In many ways, our translation project echoed the workings of the Amargi cooperative, the journal's namesake. As feminists, who were themselves busy with the core questions pertaining to the intricate nature of gender, identity, and politics, we actively reflected on not merely what we were doing, but also *how* we did it. The core group of volunteers espoused a feminist methodology in carrying out the translation project from the very beginning by embracing an inclusive and participatory approach. We first prepared and circulated an open call among the members, friends, and volunteers of Amargi, both the cooperative and the journal, seeking those interested in joining the translation project. This call was accompanied by a survey that asked people what kinds and genres of writing they would be interested in translating; how frequently they could contribute to the translation effort; and whether or not they would like to join the voluntary editorial team to review translated texts prior to publication. The translation project was designed as a collective effort from its inception.

Looking back at the demographic distribution of our initial volunteers, it would not be wrong to claim that *Amargi*'s goal to place women's lives front and center, as well as challenging the artificially produced gap between academia and activism, did find a following. From among the group of people who responded to our initial call for translators, 70% were students, either at the undergraduate or graduate level. While some volunteers had a direct link to the cooperative as activists, others merely knew of Amargi through events or through the journal. The fact that most of us were drawn to this project in spite of having no prior translation experience attests to the appeal of *Amargi*'s political position to its readers. As feminists, it was important for us to see the debates that directly impacted our lives and the spaces that we occupied reach a wider audience of people, including other women whose lives and struggles continued in spaces very similar to or different than ours. We believed that commonality could be established not just through having our experiences reaffirmed through sameness, but also by learning from difference.

This belief in inclusivity in its truest sense also became the guiding principle of our methodology—within our meetings and correspondence, each viewpoint was considered and listened to, with collective partnership and decision-making marking the entire process. Through discussions in our meetings, we chose articles from each issue that we thought would be appealing to an international audience. Those articles were evenly shared amongst ourselves, and once a volunteer translated their article, another member of the collective revised it. While we did have volunteer coordinators to manage and oversee administrative tasks, we set up an organizational model through which the coordination duty would rotate amongst all volunteers. We espoused an open meeting policy, welcoming anyone interested to join us, while meeting notes were shared with those who could not attend. Our meetings served to not only discuss the status of the project and progress made, but also any matter pertaining to the content of the translations, including our methodological choices, as well as issues about our organizational model.

Through collective discussions and brainstorming sessions, we prepared a translation guide, which addressed both style and content. For each of the approximately fifty articles that we translated, we paid particular attention to our expression and the terms we used in order to avoid patriarchal, sexist, militarized, discriminatory, and Orientalizing language. We tried to maintain the unique tone of each feminist writer whose article we were translating, but we also saw translation as a process that entailed the co-production of texts. Our guidelines encouraged collaboration between the translators, editors, and authors as well as providing them with the flexibility to make linguistic and stylistic interventions as they saw fit to produce this co-constructive process. We noted, for instance, that translators were welcome to use gender-neutral pronouns and were encouraged to consult the author of the text on specific linguistic choices (such as the usage of "male/female" vs. "men/women" or the decision to use "she" over "he" throughout a text). We stated that translators may choose to keep the originals of certain gendered terms, instead of using a foreign correspondence, and explain the key cultural context through interventions. Our approach was to always collectively discuss terminology or subjects that we found to be problematic so that we could develop the appropriate methods to address it. In short, we developed our guidelines in order to ensure that our collective effort reflected a feminist approach to translation that was always attuned to the gendered and patriarchal underpinnings of language and linguistic structures.

Selected Works of *Amargi* Translators

"Transmen Compose Voltrans," Author: Aligül Arıkan (translation: Kıvanç Tanrıyar, editing: Begüm Acar), issue 10, fall 2008.

"My Candidacy for the Head of District," Author: Belgin Çelik (translation: Begüm Acar), issue 13, summer 2009.

"No Place Left in the Cemetery of Fallen Women," Author: Gamze Göker (translation: Senem Kaptan, editing: Feride Eralp), issue 2, fall 2006.

"Practicing Theater of the Oppressed with Women," Author: Jale Karabekir (translation: Feride Eralp), issue 9, summer 2008.

"Economic Crisis, Justice and Development Party, and What Kind of Feminism?," Author: Nil Mutluer (translation: Begüm Başdaş), issue 13, summer 2009.

"Politics of Victimhood or Freedom," Author: Pınar Selek (translation: Yelda Şahin Akıllı), issue 4, spring 2007.

"From Literature to Life: Turning into an Author," Author: Sezer Ateş Ayvaz, (translation: Türkan Mamur, editing: Nilay Erten), issue 9, summer 2008.

"For a Feminist Strategy against Poverty," Author: Yıldız Ecevit (translation: Miray Çakıroğlu), issue 6, fall 2007.

"The Fall of Alissa," Author: Yıldız Ramazanoğlu (translation: Nefise Kahraman), issue 10, fall 2008.

"What Does Esmeray Teach Us?", Author: Yeşim Başaran (translation: Kıvanç Tanrıyar), issue 8, winter 2008.

The voluntary nature of our work meant that our project was carried out on a more ad-hoc than a sustained basis, which inevitably produced interruptions and changes in our work pattern. We envisioned, but did not finalize, preparing a collectively produced glossary for the translators, for instance. In a similar manner, we were not able to bring to life the envisioned workshop where we would discuss translation theory and feminist translation practices, nor the series of events where our voluntary translators would discuss firsthand what it meant for them to be a part of this collective project. Furthermore, while we had envisioned publishing our selected translations in the form of an anthology and had sought grant funding to make this possible, including plans to bolster publicity efforts through establishing partnerships with transnational feminist organizations, our application did not receive the funds we had requested. As a result, we decided to make our translations available on *Amargi*'s website and publicized our work through the various *Amargi* networks. The dissolution of the cooperative in 2012 and the closure of the journal in 2015 also meant that our translation effort did not go further than our archived work on the journal website.

REFLECTION AND CONCLUDING REMARKS

One of our volunteer translators, Feride Eralp, fondly described her recollection of the *Amargi* translation project as a "well-intentioned, colossal effort." Indeed, we may have had lofty goals for a project that was carried out entirely through voluntary time and labor, which we, at the time, had described as "a totally amateur work."[18] Yet, the so-called amateur nature of our project also allowed us the freedom to not worry about time constraints or deal with bureaucratic technicalities, which may not have otherwise been possible were this pursued as a professional endeavor. Furthermore, through this project, we not only learned about feminist translation, as well as a diverse range of feminist writing, but also gained extensive experience in conducting collective work, accompanied by critical discussions about the nature of voluntary labor through a feminist perspective. Finally, as women, some of who were discovering and trying to find their

Figure 15.3: Amargi Issue 27, Winter 2013, "The Transformation of Life: Kitchen"—Special issue on neoliberalism in the context of kitchen labor.

place within feminist organizations and activism, our translation project provided us with a continued sense of solidarity and invaluable friendships.

Through our translation effort, we not only aimed to expand transnational debates on gender issues by adding to this conversation what we saw as noteworthy contributions from our local context, but also produced a public archive that amplified feminist voices from Turkey for an audience of activists, students, academics, and engaged communities. In the past decade since we started our collective translation project at *Amargi*, feminist translation as a field has grown in Turkey, with wider and more active reflection on the theory and politics of translating texts as a form of feminist and political activism.[19] It is encouraging to see that our dedicated effort continues today in the work of other feminist platforms, including through independent digital feminist venues such as *5Harfliler* and *Çatlak Zemin*, some of which include former *Amargi* translators, that devote valuable time and labor to translating texts into and from Turkish and widening the scope of our collective feminist consciousness.[20]

While this essay has discussed our introduction to and experiences with feminist translation, this singular experience has significance beyond its impact on our personal lives alone. Specifically, in an environment where we continue to witness persistent global pushback against women's human rights, including their fundamental freedoms and right to bodily autonomy, as well as against the rights of LGBTQI+ persons, feminist translation efforts don't just serve to strengthen feminist solidarity at the transnational level, but also provide access to vital information, especially through digital means, for women, girls, LGBTQI+ individuals, and other marginalized populations who may otherwise not be able to access reliable sources or feel isolated in the face of discrimination or lack of progressive public figures. Therefore, it is our hope that highlighting translation as a political act that extends beyond the realm of the private, as well as a form of public scholarship and means for community engagement, will produce other similar efforts within feminist collectives around the globe.

ACKNOWLEDGMENTS

Even though this essay was written by three volunteer *Amargi* translators, our original translation project was the result of a truly collective effort. We would like to express sincere gratitude to the following volunteers, who contributed to our project at various stages through translating and editing articles; coordinating logistics; and continuing to believe in the importance of our collective effort: Banu Karakaş, Begüm Acar, Begüm Başdaş, Beliz Baldil, Birce Pakkan, Cansu Karamustafa, Derya Bayraktaroğlu, Elif Gazioğlu, Emek Ayşe Yıldız, Esin Düzel, Feride Eralp, Gizem Darendelioğlu, Gizem Sefa, Gül Varlı, Hilal Özçetin, Jale Karabekir, Kıvanç Tanrıyar, Levent Çınar, Lisya Yafet, Miray Çakıroğlu, Nefise Kahraman, Nihan Köse, Nilay Erten, Senem Kaptan, Sevgi Demirkale, Sinem Erdağ, Tania Bahar, Türkan Mamur, Yelda Şahin Akıllı, and Zeynep Demirsu.

NOTES

1. Amargi's closure was the result of a series political divergences, which started in November 2012, when nine Amargi members announced their departure from the collective by stating that "there is no ground left to engage in feminist politics." This declaration was followed by a public farewell note in December 2012 that announced Amargi's closure. For more information and links to both declarations, see Filiz Karakuş, "15 Aralık 2007: Amargi Kitabevi Açıldı." [Amargi Bookstore Opens], *Çatlak Zemin*, last modified December 15, 2019, https://www.catlakzemin.com/15-aralik-2007/.
2. Some of these works include titles such as, *Özgürlüğü Ararken: Kadın Hareketinde Mücadele Deneyimleri* [Searching for Freedom: Experiences of Struggle within the Women's Movement] (2005); *Çalışma Hayatında Kadınların Karşılaştığı Sorunlar ve Hukuki Mücadele Yolları* [Problems Encountered by Women in the Workplace and Possible Legal Remedies] (2008); *Kadınlar*

Arasında: Deneyimlerimiz Hangi Kapıları Açıyor [Amongst Women: What Doors Do Our Experiences Open] (2009). For more information, see Amargi Istanbul, "Amargi Publishing," *Amargi Istanbul*, accessed January 1, 2021, https://amargigroupistanbul.wordpress.com/about-amargi/amargi-publishing/.
3. Filiz Karakuş, "15 Aralık 2007: Amargi Kitabevi Açıldı." [Amargi Bookstore Opens], *Çatlak Zemin*, last modified December 15, 2019, https://www.catlakzemin.com/15-aralik-2007/.
4. Amargi Istanbul, "Information," *Amargi Istanbul*, accessed November 11, 2020, https://amargigroupistanbul.wordpress.com/about-amargi/information/.
5. Özge Gözke, "Amargi: Özgürlük Akademisi" [Amargi: Freedom Academy], *Bianet*, last modified April 9, 2003, https://m.bianet.org/kadin/siyaset/28-amargi-ozgurluk-akademisi.
6. Ülkü Özakın, "Pınar Selek ve Bir Özgürlük Projesi Olarak Amargi," [Pınar Selek and Amargi as a Project of Freedom], last modified January 1, 2011, https://www.yeniduzen.com/pinar-selek-ve-bir-ozgurluk-projesi-olarak-amargi-18989h.htm.
7. For more information on transversal politics, see Nira Yuval-Davis, "What Is 'Transversal Politics'?" *Soundings*, no. 12 (1999): 94–98.
8. Sema Aslan, "Bu Dergiye Herkesin İhtiyacı Olacak" [Everyone Is Going to Need This Journal], *Milliyet*, May 14, 2006, https://www.milliyet.com.tr/kultur-sanat/bu-dergiye-herkesin-ihtiyaci-olacak-532509.
9. Amargi Dergi, "Mutfak" [Kitchen], *Amargi Dergi*, last modified August 10, 2015, http://www.amargidergi.com/yeni/?p=1521.
10. Sema Aslan, "Bu Dergiye Herkesin İhtiyacı Olacak" [Everyone Is Going to Need This Journal], *Milliyet*, May 14, 2006, https://www.milliyet.com.tr/kultur-sanat/bu-dergiye-herkesin-ihtiyaci-olacak-532509.
11. Serpil Çakır, *Osmanlı Kadın Hareketi* [Ottoman Women's Movement] (Istanbul: Metis, 1994), 60–61.
12. Emek Ergün, "Translational Beginnings and Origin/izing Stories: (Re)Writing the History of the Contemporary Feminist Movement in Turkey," in *Translating Women: Different Voices and New Horizons*, eds. Luise von Flotow and Farzaneh Farahzad (New York: Routledge, 2017), 41–55.
13. Ayşe Saki Demirel and Aslı Özlem Tarakçıoğlu, "Feminist Translation Practices in Turkey: The Case of the Feminist Websites 5Harfliler and Çatlak Zemin," *RumeliDe Dil ve Edebiyat Araştırmaları Dergisi*, no. 15 (2019): 295–312, https://dergipark.org.tr/en/pub/rumelide/issue/46260/580614.
14. We use "second-wave" to refer to feminist activism that took place starting with the 1980s in Turkey.

15. Ayşe Düzkan, "Written on the Heart, in Broken English," in *The Routledge Handbook of Translation and Activism*, eds. Rebecca Ruth Gould and Kayvan Tahmasebian (New York: Taylor and Francis, 2020), 217–221.
16. Emek Ergün, "Translational Beginnings and Origin/izing Stories: (Re)Writing the History of the Contemporary Feminist Movement in Turkey," in *Translating Women: Different Voices and New Horizons*, eds. Luise von Flotow and Farzaneh Farahzad (New York: Routledge, 2017), 41–55.
17. Sinem Bozkurt, "Touched Translations in Turkey: A Feminist Translation Approach," *Moment Dergi*, no. 1 (2014): 104–124, https://dergipark.org.tr/tr/download/article-file/427680.
18. Amargi Dergi, "A Special Thanks to Our Volunteers," *Amargi Dergi*, last modified February 25, 2014, http://www.amargidergi.com/yeni/?p=538.
19. A recent volume edited by the translation studies scholar Şehnaz Tahir Gürçağlar, Kelimelerin Kıyısında: Türkiye'de Kadın Çevirmenler [*On the Margins of Words: Women Translators in Turkey*], (Istanbul: Ithaki, 2019), for instance, brings together articles focusing on the biographies of sixteen women translators of Turkey. The volume intends to highlight and honor the pioneering work conducted by women translators while also drawing attention to the absence of research concentrating on women as translators with an aim to fill this gap.
20. Ayşe Saki Demirel and Aslı Özlem Tarakçıoğlu, "Feminist Translation Practices in Turkey: The Case of the Feminist Websites 5Harfliler and Çatlak Zemin," *RumeliDe Dil ve Edebiyat Araştırmaları Dergisi*, no. 15 (2019): 295–312, https://dergipark.org.tr/en/download/article-file/740239.

WORKS CITED

Amargi Dergi. "A Special Thanks to Our Volunteers." *Amargi Dergi*. Last modified February 25, 2014. http://www.amargidergi.com/yeni/?p=538.

Amargi Dergi. "Mutfak" [Kitchen]. *Amargi Dergi*. Last modified August 10, 2015. http://www.amargidergi.com/yeni/?p=1521.

Amargi Istanbul. "Amargi Publishing." *Amargi Istanbul*. https://amargigroupistanbul.wordpress.com/about-amargi/amargi-publishing/.

Amargi Istanbul. "Information." *Amargi Istanbul*. https://amargigroupistanbul.wordpress.com/about-amargi/information/.

Aslan, Sema. "Bu Dergiye Herkesin İhtiyacı Olacak" [Everyone Is Going to Need This Journal]. *Milliyet*. May 14, 2006. https://www.milliyet.com.tr/kultur-sanat/bu-dergiye-herkesin-ihtiyaci-olacak-532509.

Bozkurt, Sinem. "Touched Translations in Turkey: A Feminist Translation Approach." *Moment Dergi* 1, no. 1 (2014): 104-124. https://dergipark.org.tr/tr/download/article-file/427680.

Çakır, Serpil. *Osmanlı Kadın Hareketi* [Ottoman Women's Movement]. Istanbul: Metis, 1994.

Düzkan, Ayşe. "Written on the Heart, in Broken English." In *The Routledge Handbook of Translation and Activism*, edited by Rebecca Ruth Gould and Kayvan Tahmasebian, 217-221. New York: Taylor and Francis, 2020.

Ergün, Emek. "Translational Beginnings and Origin/izing Stories: (Re)Writing the History of the Contemporary Feminist Movement in Turkey." In *Translating Women: Different Voices and New Horizons*, edited by Luise von Flotow and Farzaneh Farahzad, 41-55. New York: Routledge, 2017.

Gözke, Özge. "Amargi: Özgürlük Akademisi." [Amargi: Freedom Academy]. *Bianet*. Last modified April 9, 2003. https://bianet.org/kadin/siyaset/28-amargi-ozgurluk-akademisi.

Karakuş, Filiz. "15 Aralık 2007: Amargi Kitabevi Açıldı." [Amargi Bookstore Opens]. *Çatlak Zemin*. Last modified December 15, 2019. https://www.catlakzemin.com/15-aralik-2007/.

Özakın, Ülkü. "Pınar Selek ve Bir Özgürlük Projesi Olarak Amargi." [Pınar Selek and Amargi as a Project of Freedom]. Last modified January 1, 2011. https://www.yeniduzen.com/pinar-selek-ve-bir-ozgurluk-projesi-olarak-amargi-18989h.htm.

Saki Demirel, Ayşe and Aslı Özlem Tarakçıoğlu. "Feminist Translation Practices in Turkey: The Case of the Feminist Websites 5Harfliler and Çatlak Zemin." *RumeliDe Dil ve Edebiyat Araştırmaları Dergisi*, no. 15 (2019): 295-312. https://dergipark.org.tr/en/download/article-file/740239.

Tahir Gürçağlar, Şehnaz. *Kelimelerin Kıyısında: Türkiye'de Kadın Çevirmenler*. [On the Margins of Words: Women Translators in Turkey]. Istanbul: Ithaki, 2019.

Yuval-Davis, Nira. "What Is 'Transversal Politics'?" *Soundings*, no. 12 (1999): 94-98.

CHAPTER SIXTEEN

LOVE AND MARRIAGE AND THE WORLD'S BEST EDITOR

By Audrey Bilger

My infatuation with public writing started relatively early in my academic career. As much as I valued publishing in scholarly venues, I also longed to be in conversation with a larger audience. In my view, feminist scholars have a mandate to connect with the public because theory can help make sense of the world around us and should be available in forms accessible to a broad readership. I share the view, expressed by bell hooks, that feminist thinkers should not "collude with the formation of a new elite group of women, those college-educated women who would benefit the most from feminist thinking and practice." hooks argues that "the success of feminist movement would be the extent to which the feminist thinking and practice that was transforming our consciousness and our lives would have the same impact on ordinary folks."[1] Writing for general audiences and presenting

Figure 16.1: Michele Kort, superhero. Cartoon by Jason Ho.

feminist theory in accessible terms is an important part of the broader project of contributing to social justice transformation.

In the early 1990s, as I was writing my book on Jane Austen and 18th-century feminist humor, *Laughing Feminism*,[2] I pitched an article to *Ms.* magazine on the myth that women have no sense of humor, a myth I traced back to the 1700s and that persisted into the late 20th century. I regret that I am not a better archivist because I would like to re-read my pitch and the rejection letter I received. If memory serves, the editor let me know that I had not succeeded in convincing them that the story would be relevant to *Ms.* readers and that the topic did not seem particularly timely. Knowing what I came to understand later about writing for the popular press, I realize I probably did not adequately translate my research into terms that conveyed current value. I am sure I made my argument—saying what I had learned in my research—but I neglected to contextualize it in the now—what would have made my argument chime with the times.

This was in 1993, a year before Michele Kort became an editor at *Ms.*, and in retrospect I wonder if she might have nurtured my pitch and helped me find a place in the magazine. Michele had a soft spot for academics. She assisted many of us in developing our voices as public writers. I would eventually write for her, with her, and the two of us edited an anthology together shortly before her untimely death. Our story is bound up with one of the great civil rights wins in US history—marriage rights for lesbian and gay couples—and, working with Michele, I was privileged to be able to write and report on historical developments in real time and to document the moment for posterity.

By the time Michele and I joined forces in 2009, I had been contributing to *Bitch* magazine for a decade and had begun to get a sense of how a piece of public writing can find a broad readership. One of *Bitch*'s founding editors, Lisa Jervis, had been a student-writing tutor for a class of mine at Oberlin College, where I was teaching when I made that first *Ms.* pitch. Lisa and Andi Zeisler started *Bitch*, subtitled "Feminist Response to Pop Culture," as an outlet for feminist media criticism at a time when few publications took an interest in women's points of view at all, let alone in feminism. In 1996, Lisa sent me a copy of the first issue of *Bitch*, a photocopied 'zine at that time, when I was an assistant professor of Literature at Claremont McKenna College. Although I was excited to see what Lisa and Andi were doing with *Bitch*, it took a few years before I felt secure enough in my job—post-tenure, post-coming-out, and battle-tested in the professoriate—to branch out and write for them.

In terms of public writing, in the time after my first rejection by *Ms.*, I had published an interview with novelist Jeanette Winterson in *The Paris Review*.[3] This had been a thrilling assignment—I traveled to London for the interview and met a famous writer—and it made me want to do more. I started out writing interviews for *Bitch*. I interviewed musicians I knew, and I got to connect with cartoonist Lynda Barry for a long conversation (by fax!) about art, creativity, and the demons that haunt us all.[4]

The first think piece I wrote for *Bitch*, "The Common Guy,"[5] an examination of the phrase "you guys," ended up being anthologized in a writing textbook, *Language Awareness*,[6] something that illustrates the permeability of the boundaries between public and academic writing. Over the years, I ran into people who had discovered my piece in classes or told me they had shared photocopies of it with friends. Another *Bitch* essay on women and political humor, "Laughing All the Way to the Polls"[7] got picked up by *Alternet*, and I got an early taste of what happens when one's writing circulates around the internet. The *Alternet* piece went live on a Thursday, and at a party in Los Angeles that weekend, I met someone who recognized my name because she had read my essay. Print publications may take weeks or months—online writing travels quickly.

My writing took a deeply personal turn in 2008, the year I was able to legally marry Cheryl Pawelski (after being a couple for twelve years) in California, prior to the passage of Proposition 8, the ballot initiative that banned marriages between same-sex couples. In the months leading up to the election, I had marched and campaigned against Prop 8, and like many others, I had high hopes that with Barack Obama almost certain to be elected president and California's liberal population, we would defeat the marriage ban. The passage of Prop 8 was a bitter disappointment and a conundrum. What did it mean to be legally married in a state that had voted to deny the right of marriage to lesbian and gay couples?

Naturally, I had to write about this. Because of the urgency of the times, I also wanted to further hone my public writing skills, and so, in March of 2009, I signed up for a seminar called "Write to Change the World," hosted by an organization called the Op-Ed Project. The goal of the Op-Ed Project is to get more women and writers of color onto the opinion pages of major newspapers. In the seminar I attended, there were about fifteen women, and I will never forget spending the morning on the first exercise, which asked each of us to complete the sentence, "Hello, my name is [fill in the blank] and I am an expert in [fill in the blank] because [fill in the blank]." Every woman in the room struggled to claim expertise. They/we squirmed, demurred, and expressed modesty as the facilitators questioned them to elicit, after what seemed in each case like an excruciating eternity, a clear declaration. The worst examples were the three or four of us who were professors. Sure, we stated our areas of specialization, but we resisted the word "expert," and we simply did not see the value of our PhDs outside of the academy. After one of the professors declared at one point, "well, I got my doctorate decades ago," a non-academic participant said, with emphasis, "you have a *P. H. D*—that's a big deal."

For me, this seminar was transformative, and without it, I would not have spent the next few years passionately writing about marriage equality. I needed to be authorized to step outside of what I perceived to be my scholarly niches—18th-century English literature, comic theory, gender studies. The Op-Ed seminar helped me connect the dots between being a scholar with expertise in feminism and the history of marriage and having the right to say something that might matter in the contentious discussions taking place on the national stage around marriage rights. Furthermore, I came to see links between the satirical romances of Jane Austen and the love stories being written by Cheryl and me and other couples whose fate was on the line and possibly on the brink of being legitimized on par with straight couples.

My lived experience as a lesbian who had spent much of my adult life viewing myself as heterosexual, including being married to a man for over a decade, gave me a point of view on what it meant to be a wife that formed the basis for the feminist arguments I made in support of marriage equality over the years. I published my first piece on this topic, "Wife Support," in *Bitch*,[8] contending that married lesbians would enhance, not diminish, the meaning of wife, by removing this role from its binary patriarchal context and reimagining it in a more egalitarian framework. Around the time I was writing this essay, I began conceiving of an anthology that would collect stories from lesbians in the midst of the upheaval that was taking place around the world. In imagining a future in which marriage equality would be law of the land—however improbable that might have seemed in the face of hostility we had experienced for so long—I knew I had to create a record of what it felt like to be in the middle of this cultural change. Because I wanted the collection to be appealing both to an academic gender studies readership and to a more general audience, I asked Michele Kort to be my co-editor, and, much to my delight, she said yes.

My relationship with Michele was a love story in its own right. She was ten years my senior and had come of age in Los Angeles in the 1970s, going to legendary concerts at the Troubadour and spending time among feminist writers, visual artists, and musicians at the Woman's Building arts center. My wife, Cheryl, who works in the music business, had once commissioned Michele to write liner notes for two Judee Sill projects, and so Michele and I had been loosely connected before we worked together. After she agreed to co-edit with me—in an email exchange about some other matter—I went to lunch with her in Beverly Hills, near the *Ms.* offices, and we began to sketch out how we might proceed with our book.

When I think about getting to know Michele, I recall her sense of humor and her laughter. She loved to tease me about my earnestness, lack of sports proficiency, and any indications of academese in my writing. As an editor, she was incredibly sure-footed and confident. Being edited by Michele was a gift. She could cut, rework, ask probing questions, and offer encouragement with ease and solidarity. She loved the written word, and she was a fierce and passionate feminist journalist.

She was also a wonderful teacher, as I discovered first-hand when I had the honor of participating in the *Ms.* Writers Workshop for Feminist Scholars in the spring of 2010. Michele taught us to imagine a broader audience for our work. She talked about public writing as an act of translation, from jargon to more legible prose. Michele and the other facilitators of the *Ms.* workshop stressed that in spite of what some scholars think about writing for a general audience, the point was not to "dumb down" scholarship, but to bring the insights from our research and expertise into conversation with an audience outside of the academy. As anyone who has done this kind of writing can tell you, it is by no means easier to write for the public than to write for specialists. Numerous academic colleagues over the years who have told me they want to try their hand at it, end up giving up in frustration because they cannot find the tone and, in some cases, because they find it difficult to work with editors.

Many of the writers who went through the feminist scholars workshop ended up writing regularly for the then newly launched *Ms.* blog. The blog was Michele's baby. While I know she was proud of her role as senior editor at *Ms.* and committed to being part of the legacy of this iconic publication, she appreciated how blog writing could be more multifaceted and move with the speed of news. By March of 2010, Michele was assigning breaking marriage equality stories to me.

All told, I wrote over seventy pieces for the *Ms.* blog and magazine, many on the overturning of Prop 8 and the federal

Defense of Marriage Act, along with posts and articles on miscellaneous topics, including book and media reviews. Writing for Michele was invigorating, and I have never before or since written with such rapidity. She frequently gave me tight deadlines, as in, *something is happening this morning, can you get a piece to me this afternoon?* One of my favorite things to do was to surprise her with a pitch, as I did when I told her I was going to go after an exclusive interview with Twitter sensation, Feminist Hulk. Not only did I get that interview[9]—by Tweeting out my request, of course—but I snagged a second interview[10] the following year, and then was granted the privilege of revealing Feminist Hulk's identity in a later interview[11] (an English PhD candidate, it turned out). Michele gleefully reported that the first interview was one of the top posts on the blog to date, quickly garnering over 30,000 hits. I will always remember how it felt to be publishing at this rate and the adrenaline that accompanied each new entry.

During this time, I was also contacted by reporters for radio interviews. When NPR reached out to me in August of 2010 to talk with reporter Warren Olney on "To the Point," the booker told me they had come across my writing on the *Ms.* blog and that they valued my perspective on feminism and marriage equality and my highlighting of the issue from a gender equality lens. In my first interview[12] with Olney, we discussed gender and the ruling by a federal judge that found Proposition 8 to be unconstitutional. I ended up doing three more interviews with Olney (March 26, 2013[13]; June 13, 2013[14]; and June 25, 2015[15]) over the following five years. They reached out to me as I kept writing on new developments in the marriage equality story. One of the lessons I had learned from the *Ms.* Feminist Scholars workshop was that if you get your message out in public writing, it can find its way to other forms of media, and my interviews were points of pride not only for me, but for Michele and *Ms.* magazine.

My belief in the value of public writing led me to found the Center for Writing and Public Discourse (CWPD) at Claremont McKenna

College, where I was a tenured professor of Literature, in the fall of 2010. Under my direction, this center hosted workshops for faculty, staff, and students on writing for a general readership and brought in speakers, many of whose work I had encountered through *Ms.* I regularly taught a class on women's magazines, journalism, and feminist humor, and I included a mix of traditional scholarship and popular writing on my syllabuses. For example, in one class I taught a book I had reviewed for the *Ms.* blog, humorist Lizz Winstead's *Lizz Free or Die*,[16] and Winstead accepted an invitation to speak and visit with my class. As a liberal arts college faculty member, I valued the teacher-scholar model, the idea that scholarship invigorates one's teaching and helps to inspire students to think critically and engage more fully with ideas. My public writing and the work of the CWPD lined up perfectly with my role as a teacher-scholar, and students benefitted from seeing how feminist theory could be translated and circulate broadly outside the academy.

Meanwhile, Michele and I were hard at work on our anthology and were pleased to have found a publisher. Seal Press made good sense as a home for the project because of their track record of publishing books that made their way into classrooms and also into the hands of a more general readership. *Here Come the Brides!: Reflections on Lesbian Love and Marriage*[17] was truly a labor of love, born alongside a series of victories for marriage equality. The anthology brought together essays, plays, poetry, cartoons, interviews, and photography to document the state of lesbian marriage in the early 20-teens. We put out a call for contributors that circulated on websites and by email and sought out scholars, artists, journalists, and activists whom we knew would help to ensure a diversity of lived experience and perspectives, including those who were skeptical and even negative about the institution of marriage. Claremont McKenna College provided funding for two CMC students to help with research and interview transcriptions. One of my former students contributed a piece, as did a colleague from the Claremont Colleges and several other academics.

We completed the bulk of the project over the course of 2011. Several times a month, I drove across Los Angeles, from my house in Altadena to Michele's place in Mar Vista, to bring outlines, stacks of submissions, and finally the finished document. In between editing binges, Michele and I walked with her two corgis, Millie and Cricket, around the neighborhoods or got takeout from local restaurants. One of Michele's running jokes was that she and I never got into a fight. That held true for our entire friendship.

In November of 2011, Michele and I were attending the National Women's Studies Association conference in Atlanta as participants on a *Ms.* Writers Workshop panel. We had brought the proofs of *Here Come the Brides!* to review. Unfortunately, Michele was not feeling well, and our proofing sessions were a challenge. Upon returning to L.A., she underwent medical tests and was diagnosed with ovarian cancer.

My memories of this time are clouded with a mixture of worry and joy. Our book came out in 2012, and we put together a series of readings. At the first one, we wore matching wedding veils and had a cake. Our authors were incredibly talented, and the audiences were supportive and appreciative. Michele was going through chemo. The readings were uplifting for her—for both of us. The book was a finalist for the 2013 Lambda Literary Awards, and we attended the ceremony in New York City. Even though we did not win, we were truly honored by the nomination and glad to spend time in New York with loved ones and friends, appreciating what we had accomplished together.

I continued writing for Michele and *Ms.* as marriage equality made its way through various courts around the country and ultimately to the United States Supreme Court. Proposition 8 was declared unconstitutional in June of 2013, and the pendulum of public opinion was swaying in the direction of granting marriage rights to same sex couples. The goal of overturning the federal Defense of Marriage Act had begun to seem more possible. Highlights for me from my writing at that time include getting to interview Prop 8 plaintiffs Kris Perry and Sandy Stier for *Ms.*

Figure 16.2: Michele Kort and Audrey Bilger. Author photo for Here Come the Brides! Photo by Greg Allen.

magazine[18] (this interview was also featured on the *Ms.* blog[19]); making the case on the *Ms.* blog that "Marriage Equality is a Feminist Issue";[20] and summarizing a watershed year in "The Marriage Equality Victories of 2013."[21]

During this same time, Michele was receiving treatments, but hope was hard to preserve. She continued to work for as long as possible, and in her last months, she heard from many of those whom she had edited and supported over the years with expressions of love and gratitude.

On June 26, 2015, the day the United States Supreme Court ruling on *Obergefell v. Hodges* came through, declaring the Defense of Marriage Act unconstitutional and granting federal marriage rights to gay and lesbian couples, I was in Massachusetts, where Cheryl and I had traveled for a music festival. I spent the day in our hotel room, writing a blog post for *Ms.*,[22] waiting to be interviewed by NPR, and bearing the weight of the nearly simultaneous news of the death of my beloved friend, editor, and co-author. Michele lived just long enough to learn of the SCOTUS decision.

Among the many lessons I learned from Michele's editing, uppermost is that a good article needs to make a point. The point I want to stress here is that engaging in public writing is a worthy pursuit. If you are an academic reading this book and thinking you might like to give it a try, I encourage you to seek out allies and pay attention to your editors. Having a supportive editor like Michele in your court is of enormous importance for scholars who engage in writing for the public. The internet can be an ugly place, and comment threads are not for the faint of heart. Within academia, those who engage in public writing face risks in terms of exposure to trolls and also when it comes time for professional evaluations. Keep your friends close—and your editors closer.

In the acknowledgements section of our anthology, Michele wrote to me:

When my dad was particularly grateful to someone, he used the expression, "You're a scholar." Audrey, you're a scholar, in every sense of the word.

Figure 16.3: Michele Kort, Gloria Steinem, and Audrey Bilger, Feminist Majority Foundation gala, May 1, 2012.

These words echo down the corridors of time. Michele, who assisted numerous academic feminists in becoming public writers, who had an appetite for news and new ideas, and whose friendship was priceless to me, was a lover of scholars and was herself a scholar at heart. It is fitting that her papers are housed in the Smith College collection. Michele's influence on feminist writing will live on.

NOTES

1. bell hooks, *Teaching Community: A Pedagogy of Hope* (New York: Routledge, 2003), xi.
2. Audrey Bilger, *Laughing Feminism: Subversive Comedy in Frances Burney, Maria Edgeworth, and Jane Austen* (Detroit: Wayne State University Press, 1998).
3. Jeanette Winterson, interview by Audrey Bilger, *The Paris Review* 145 (1997–98): 68–112.
4. Audrey Bilger, "The! Great! Lynda! Barry!", *Bitch: Feminist Response to Pop Culture* 13 (November 2000): 33–41.
5. Audrey Bilger. "The Common Guy," *Bitch: Feminist Response to Pop Culture* 18 (Fall 2002): 19–20.
6. Paul Escholtz, Alfred Rosa, and Virginia Clark, eds. *Language Awareness*, 10th ed. (Boston and New York: Bedford/St. Martin's, 2009).
7. Audrey Bilger, "Laughing All the Way to the Polls: Political Women's Humor," *Bitch: Feminist Response to Pop Culture* 30 (Fall 2005): 48–53.
8. Audrey Bilger, "Wife Support," *Bitch: Feminist Response to Pop Culture* 45 (Winter 2009): 19–20.
9. Audrey Bilger, "FEMINIST HULK SMASH EXCLUSIVE INTERVIEW WITH MS!", *Ms.* blog. February 21, 2019, msmagazine.com/2010/06/07/feminist-hulk-smash-exclusive-interview-with-ms/.
10. Audrey Bilger, "Feminist Hulk Meets Ms.—Again," *Ms.* blog, March 4, 2019, https://msmagazine.com/2011/06/20/feminist-hulk-meet-ms-magazine-the-sequel/.
11. Audrey Bilger, "Who's Behind the Mask of Feminist Hulk! Only *Ms.* Knows!", *Ms.* blog, August 22, 2011, https://msmagazine.com/2011/08/22/whos-behind-the-mask-of-feminist-hulk-only-the-ms-blog-knows/.
12. Warren Olney's "To the Point," KPCC, August 10, 2010.
13. Warren Olney's "Which Way LA," KPCC, March 26, 2013.
14. Warren Olney's "To the Point," KPCC, June 26, 2013.
15. Warren Olney's "To the Point," KPCC, June 26, 2015.

16. Lizz Winstead, *Lizz Free or Die: Essays* (New York: Riverhead Books, 2013).
17. Audrey Bilger and Michele Kort, *Here Come the Brides: Reflections on Lesbian Love and Marriage* (Berkeley, CA: Seal Press, 2012).
18. Audrey Bilger, "Will Justices Say 'I Do'?", *Ms.* magazine, Winter 2013: 14.
19. Audrey Bilger, "Marriage Equality Wins Again," *Ms.* blog, June 5, 2012, https://msmagazine.com/2012/06/05/newsflash-another-marriage-equality-win-in-california/.
20. Audrey Bilger, "Marriage Equality is a Feminist Issue," *Ms.* blog, December 12, 2012, https://msmagazine.com/2012/12/11/marriage-equality-is-a-feminist-issue/.
21. Audrey Bilger, "The Marriage Equality Victories of 2013," *Ms.* blog, December 20, 2013, https://msmagazine.com/2013/12/20/the-marriage-equality-victories-of-2013/.
22. Audrey Bilger, "How Feminism Helped Pave the Way for Marriage Equality," *Ms.* blog, June 29. 2015, https://msmagazine.com/2015/06/29/feminism-helped-pave-the-way-for-marriage-equality/.

WORKS CITED

Bilger, Audrey. *Laughing Feminism: Subversive Comedy in Frances Burney, Maria Edgeworth, and Jane Austen.* Detroit: Wayne State University Press, 1998.

———. "Feminist Hulk Meets Ms.—Again." *Ms.* blog. March 4, 2019. https://msmagazine.com/2011/06/20/feminist-hulk-meet-ms-magazine-the-sequel/.

———. "FEMINIST HULK SMASH EXCLUSIVE INTERVIEW WITH MS!". *Ms.* blog. February 21, 2019. https://msmagazine.com/2010/06/07/feminist-hulk-smash-exclusive-interview-with-ms/.

———. "How Feminism Helped Pave the Way for Marriage Equality." *Ms.* blog. June 29, 2015. https://msmagazine.com/2015/06/29/feminism-helped-pave-the-way-for-marriage-equality/.

———. "Laughing All the Way to the Polls: Political Women's Humor." *Bitch: Feminist Response to Pop Culture* 30 (Fall 2005): 48–53.

———. "Marriage Equality Is a Feminist Issue." *Ms.* blog. December 12, 2012. https://msmagazine.com/2012/12/11/marriage-equality-is-a-feminist-issue/.

———. "Marriage Equality Wins Again." *Ms.* blog. June 5, 2012. https://msmagazine.com/2012/06/05/newsflash-another-marriage-equality-win-in-california/.

———. "The Common Guy." *Bitch: Feminist Response to Pop Culture* 18 (Fall 2002): 19–20.

———. "The! Great! Lynda! Barry!" *Bitch: Feminist Response to Pop Culture* 13 (November 2000): 33–41.

———. "The Marriage Equality Victories of 2013." *Ms.* blog. December 20, 2013.https://msmagazine.com/2013/12/20/the-marriage-equality-victories-of-2013/.

———. "Who's Behind the Mask of Feminist Hulk! Only Ms. Knows!" *Ms.* blog. August 22, 2011. https://msmagazine.com/2011/08/22/whos-behind-the-mask-of-feminist-hulk-only-the-ms-blog-knows/.

———. "Wife Support." *Bitch: Feminist Response to Pop Culture* 45 (Winter 2009): 19–20.

———. "Will Justices Say 'I Do'?" *Ms. Magazine.* Winter 2013: 14.

Bilger, Audrey and Michele Kort, eds. *Here Come the Brides: Reflections on Lesbian Love and Marriage.* Berkeley, CA: Seal Press. 2012.

Escholtz, Paul Alfred Rosa, and Virginia Clark, eds. *Language Awareness.* 10th ed. Boston and New York: Bedford/St. Martin's, 2009.

hooks, bell. *Teaching Community: A Pedagogy of Hope.* Routledge: New York and London, 2003.

Warren Olney's "To the Point." *KPCC.* August 10, 2010.

Warren Olney's "Which Way LA." *KPCC.* March 26, 2013.

Warren Olney's "To the Point." *KPCC.* June 26, 2013.

Warren Olney's "To the Point." *KPCC.* June 26, 2015.

Winterson, Jeanette. Interviewed by Audrey Bilger. *The Paris Review* 145 (1997–98): 68–112.

Winstead, Lizz. *Lizz Free or Die: Essays.* New York: Riverhead Books. 2013.

CHAPTER SEVENTEEN

SCHOLAR, WRITER, EDITOR, PUBLISHER

Multifaceted Engagements in Feminist Public Writing

By Julie R. Enszer

Audre Lorde, Muriel Rukeyser, Adrienne Rich, Pat Parker, Judy Grahn. I entered adulthood reading these feminist writers. Introduced to many of them as an undergraduate women's studies major, I read them throughout my twenties as I was thinking and feeling my way through the world, learning how to live, how to work and earn money, how to make social change, how to be public about feminism and lesbianism in transformative ways. When I think about writing for a feminist public, I think about these women's work as writers, poets, scholars, and intellectuals. All published, particularly early in their career, with independent presses; in addition to nurturing writers, independent presses hail and cultivate feminist and lesbian audiences. This nexus between author and audience is vital for feminist work. All of these women's writing crossed multiple genres, imagined and welcomed new audiences, and, for most of their lives, their work emerged not through the support of any institution but with the essential energies from grassroots movements of liberation. When I step back to think about my own writing for feminist publics, I recognize these poets and writers and their public practices as central to my own ideas of public feminisms and to constructions of public feminist conversations.

I tend to describe my intellectual life with two adjectives: failed and anachronistic. Though I managed to graduate from my later in life PhD program, I failed to secure a job in academia. Instead, like many other failed academics (scholars who failed to secure jobs in academia), I piece together work. To earn money, I work for a New York publishing house and teach online as an adjunct faculty member in a large Southern flagship university. I rely on my wife and her corporate job for proper health care benefits as a result of the transformative development of federally recognized same-sex marriage. The anachronistic element of my life is that I edit and publish a lesbian-feminist journal founded in 1976. While my title, as editor and publisher, seems glamorous, the daily reality is mundane: I process subscription checks, read submissions, solicit book reviews, move dozens of thirty-five-pound boxes of books around my office, and much more. The journal, *Sinister Wisdom*, is an independent nonprofit organization, unaffiliated with the academy. My work with the journal is uncompensated. Although precarious, this odd work combination provides me modes for engagement in both feminist scholarship and public-facing writing.

From this failed, anachronistic location, I offer three insights about public feminist scholarship. First, writers and scholars in a range of locations, both inside and outside the academy and with fluidity to move among various spaces, invigorate feminist intellectual life, feminist activism, and feminist movements. In particular, scholars in hybrid positions and outside of the academy make vital contributions while simultaneously working to create new worlds and possibilities for feminisms and for women's lives. Their contributions should not be overlooked. Second, a dynamic and collaborative relationship between writers and editors enhances all public writing, and, in feminist public scholarship, editors play an especially vital role. Editors have a unique proximity to publics as they are currently construed as well as perspectives and skills to imagine and conjure new audiences. Editorial insights enhance scholarship and the translation of scholarship to broad public audiences. Understanding the collaborative relationship between scholar and editor enhances the quality of public feminisms. Finally, what feminist scholars teach becomes activism with currency and value for new generations. The power of teaching, particularly what materials feminist scholars use and what values and ideas feminist teachers present, to shape feminist activism to come in the next two or three decades, cannot be underestimated. Teaching histories and legacies of lesbian and feminist print culture, including magazines, journals, periodicals, and book publishing, build future feminist public manifestations. Collectively, these insights suggest strategies to promote more vibrant and robust public feminist conversations today and for many tomorrows.

I. *SINISTER WISDOM*: A FOUNDATION AND GENEALOGY OF PUBLIC FEMINISMS

To begin, two stories. In 1981, under the editorship of Michelle Cliff and Adrienne Rich who bought the journal from the founders, Harriet Desmoines and Catherine Nicholson, *Sinister Wisdom* started offering free subscriptions to women in prison and women in mental institutions. The offer was not trumpeted from rooftops; a single line on the inside front cover announced that the journal was free to women in prison and mental institutions. In the fall of 1983, Cliff reported in her final "Notes for a Magazine" (the editor's message in the journal) that over three hundred women in prison had requested copies of the journal (Michelle Cliff, "Notes for a Magazine," *Sinister Wisdom* 24, Fall 1983, 6). I think, but do not know, that Rich's and Cliff's decision to make the journal free to women in prison extends from conversations that they had with Mohawk writer Beth Brant. Brant was close friends with both Cliff and Rich. She edited *Sinister Wisdom* 22/23: *A Gathering of Spirit*, an issue that featured writing by Native American and indigenous women. Brant corresponded with women in prison and included writings by women in prison in *Sinister Wisdom* 22/23. I cannot trace a clear linkage between Cliff's and Rich's decision and Brant because there are scant archival materials from Brant or Cliff. Yet, from what exists, this story of Brant inspiring the policy seems likely. Today *Sinister Wisdom* continues to provide free subscriptions to women in prison and women in mental institutions as well as publish work by and about women in prison. This practice binds the creative and intellectual work of the journal to women who are among the most disadvantaged and marginalized in contemporary US society, and it ties the journal to an intellectual history actively shaped by women of color.

Melanie Kaye/Kantrowitz edited *Sinister Wisdom* from the winter of 1984, beginning with *Sinister Wisdom* 25, through the summer of 1987, ending with *Sinister Wisdom* 32. Kaye/Kantrowitz and Irena Klepfisz edited another influential issue of *Sinister Wisdom*, *Sinister Wisdom* 29/30: *The Tribe of Dina*. This collection, which like *Sinister Wisdom* 22/23 was later published as a trade book by Beacon Press, gathered voices of Jewish feminists with a focus on Jewish feminists in Israel thinking about peace between Israel and Palestine. *The Tribe of Dina* is part of a constellation of writing that brought visibility to Jewish lesbians and feminists and articulated the centrality of addressing anti-Semitism for intersectional feminism during the 1980s; the collection also highlights the transnational concerns of feminists during the 1970s and 1980s. After Kaye/Kantrowitz left the editorship of *Sinister Wisdom*, she took a teaching job in Vermont for a few years before leaving that job to become the first executive director of Jews for Racial and Economic Justice. During this period of her life, Kaye/Kantrowitz produced influential essays that articulated connections between racism and anti-Semitism and provided important intellectual foundational work for what is now described as intersectionality, a lived experience of multiple oppression.

These two stories provide one foundation and a genealogy of influential writers and theorists of feminisms during the 1980s and beyond. Rich, Cliff, Brant, Klepfisz, and Kaye/Kantrowitz were all prolific writers in a variety of genres from theory, to poetry, to short story, to manifesto. All published widely during the 1970s, 1980s, and 1990s, and feminists read, debated, and discussed their work. All rooted themselves in a variety of organizational locations inside and outside of academia. Their lives and work demonstrate the movement of writers among different locations during the 1980s and the 1990s and how these towering intellectuals embraced different forms of labor as a part of the writing and political practices.

Considering the public feminist works of these five writers, three Jewish women, one Native/Mohawk woman, and one Afro-Caribbean woman, as a foundation for the idea of public feminisms suggests that public feminisms flourish in the presence of porous relationships forged among feminists in multiple locations, inside and outside the academy, prisons, and nonprofit networks. Location is important, but location is not immutable. Movements among different locations corresponding with communication and flexibility creates vibrant forms of feminism. Porousness and flexibility of feminist networks promote the cross pollination of ideas and provides time and space for people from different locations to talk and engage ideas radically as these stories about *Sinister Wisdom* demonstrate.

In my own work as the editor and publisher of *Sinister Wisdom*, I have seen how operating the journal and publishing four issues a year provides a platform to engage other writers and intellectuals as well as to create worlds and conversations into which I want to publish my own creative and intellectual work. The nonprofit structure of volunteers and a board of directors, combined with the necessity of intern labor create a constellation of relationships that are intellectually and emotionally nurturing.

II. COLLABORATIVE EDITORIAL RELATIONSHIPS ENHANCE PUBLIC FEMINIST SCHOLARSHIP

Public feminisms exist in a variety of locations: embodied social action like marches, protests, and demonstrations; in print and online, in written words and in the spaces these words create to be considered and absorbed; in long term practices and actions that lead to greater equality and justice; and, in the types and qualities of our human relationships with one another as well as in our relationships with the broader natural world. Recognizing these myriad locations of public feminisms invites consideration of the variety of skills required. Equally important to the ideas of feminisms are the skills that public feminisms need to thrive. Contemporary women's and gender studies training, whether in colleges and universities or in high schools or other spaces of public education, is most relevant when it not only trains students in a range of feminist theories and ideas but also teaches a range of feminist skills and practices, including editing, organizing information effectively, and collaborative decision-making and problem solving, that they can bring out into the world. Making vibrant connections between the ideas of feminisms and skills to practice public feminisms is a combination that increases the alchemical power of feminisms.

Editing is one of the vital skills in the practice of public feminisms—an under-recognized and under-appreciated one. All writing requires editing for it to reach audiences with clarity, force, and vigor. Editing, like writing, is a process that invites close consideration of words and language for accuracy, veracity, clarity, and candor, values that feminisms extoll. Also, like writing, editing is a practice that is done primarily in solitude, the quiet sanctuary of the mind. In addition to curiosity about language and mastery of many language elements, editing requires time, organization, and technological competence.

Editing, at its best, is a collaborative process where both writer and editor work together to create the best possible piece for the audience. Building these collaborative relationships, however, can be a challenge. Editorial labor is often invisible and devalued. A recent interaction I had with a writer at *Sinister Wisdom* illustrates this devaluation. A scholar submitted a book review that was a provocative assessment of a recent popular lesbian book; the author had an opinion not shared by other reviewers and one that brought value to our communal conversations. I edited the book review, primarily making changes for style based on our journal guidelines, but also asking the writer in two places to provide an additional sentence or two to expand her thinking about two provocative assertions. I returned the review asking the author to provide a revision in ten days to publish the piece in the next issue slated to go to press shortly. The author declined to make any changes to the review; she told me via email that her words stand, and I should publish them as submitted. Working under deadline, I did not have time to engage further, but as a result of this author's arrogance, her ideas are not in public conversations. In fact, most writers who contribute to *Sinister Wisdom* are a joy. They are grateful and appreciative of the editorial work done to produce the journal. I share this anecdote to highlight the burdens that editors face and to invite everyone invested in writing for public audiences to recognize and respect the important roles that editors play. Recognizing and valuing editorial work as a part of public feminisms enhances the value of public feminisms.

In addition to the editorial labor of polishing writing and bringing it into the world, editors have close proximity to audiences, particularly audiences to whom scholars want to speak.

I spend substantial time talking with and listening to readers of and subscribers to *Sinister Wisdom*. I also listen to and read broadly from lesbians in the world. As a result of these activities, I, like other editors, develop visions of what needs to be written for our audiences and our publications. Writers rarely ask me what I think needs to be written for the audience of *Sinister Wisdom* and for lesbian audiences more generally. Rather, I solicit materials. People interested in writing for feminist publics should first read publications thoroughly to understand the editorial vision and the community conversations these publications have. Writers also can cultivate conversations with editors and listen carefully to their visions for what needs to be written as well as absorbing their suggestions for framing and positioning work for audiences. Editors have keen insights into what and how people read. Part of the labor of matching public writing with scholarly work is understanding the needs of editors and audiences and listening to editors to find matches between scholarly research and editorial needs. Ultimately, understanding and respecting the roles of editors in the production of public work enhances it.

III. PUBLIC WRITING IN FEMINIST CLASSROOMS

From observations of public expressions of feminism over the past few decades, particularly representations of feminisms and feminist histories on television, in movies, and other forms of popular culture, it is clear that what feminist scholars teach becomes the foundation for future feminist activism and cultural production. Of course, what feminist scholars teach within women's, gender, and sexuality studies is diverse, multi-faceted, protean. This reality is one of the exciting elements of women's and gender studies. Within this cacophony of teaching and learning, I want to remind people in the field that what is taught in women's and gender studies shapes the next generation of makers, and I want to appeal to teachers to consider teaching histories and legacies of lesbian and feminist print culture, including magazines, journals, periodicals, and book publishing, so that young people see these cultural productions as sites for vibrant engagements.

Over the past decade, feminist zines have been a favorite subject for introductory and advance classes for undergraduates. Zines lend themselves to studying material culture and provide inspiration for final projects in numerous classes. Scholarship by Alison Piepmeier, Adela Licona, and Agatha Beins, among many others, as well as the collecting and curation strategies of Kelly Wooten at Duke University and Jenna Freedman at the Barnard College Library have made zines accessible for scholarly and pedagogical engagements and an exemplar of feminist print culture. My obvious investment is to expand the lens of feminist print culture to include other activities, particularly periodicals and book publishing.

New print and computer technologies have revolutionized periodical and book publishing. Personal computers are present in everyone's lives; print on demand publishing tools make the production of magazines, journals, and books easy for students and everyone. It is easier and cheaper to publish books and magazines than ever before in history. In spite of the opportunities presented in the current publishing landscape, feminist, queer, lesbian publishing is not flourishing. Certainly, it is not dead; more than a handful of vibrant feminist print publications exist and small, hardy publishing houses are nurturing the literary landscape, but it could be much more. Part of the reason for the paucity of new publishing initiatives, compared for example to the 1920s or 1970s, may be that these activities are not actively taught in classes in gender, women's, and sexuality studies. Students do not engage in the imaginary of creating their own journals, magazines, and books. Books form a foundation for knowledge transmission in feminist and queer cultures, but interrogating the making of the books and exploring paths to enter periodical publishing and book-making have not become foundational to women's and gender studies' pedagogy in the same ways that zines have. I invite awareness and new research to change that.

Today, there is actually a small increase in feminist bookstores. New generations of young women are coming into the bookselling trade, and by extension these young women shape conversations about how to make commerce conform with philosophies and ideologies of feminism; they are imagining ways for feminism to engage capitalism and not simply be ravaged by it. The same can happen for periodical and book publishing.

Public feminisms and feminist movements are energized by grassroots media that reach readers, shaping their thinking and engaging broad conversations. Corporate-owned media hobble our intellectual work and our public lives by flattening, commodifying, and minimizing our work. Embracing a full array of feminist print culture—not only zines but also periodicals, journals, magazines, (both in print and online) and books—will build a future for feminist public engagements that are rich and multifaceted. Teaching histories and legacies of lesbian and feminist print culture, including magazines, journals, periodicals, and book publishing, build future feminist public manifestations. This work can enrich us all.

IV. CONCLUSION

During the summer of 2020, a project I worked on was mentioned twice in the *New York Times*. *Sister Love: The Letters of Audre Lorde and Pat Parker* was mentioned by Dwight Garner in an article about letter writing and its delights during the pandemic; then a few weeks later memoirist Sarah Broome mentioned it as a book she had recently read. When I first read the letters between Lorde and Parker, I was in the room where Parker lived, wrote, and died in Pleasant Hill, California. I was riveted by the letters. I knew I wanted to publish them as a small book like *The Delicacy and Strength of Lace*, the letters of James Wright and Leslie Marmon Silko, a book I read as an undergraduate student. I am grateful that Parker's surviving spouse agreed and that the project came together. While I was working on it, many people said that they had read the letters in the archive and that they were not of broad interest. In the immediate aftermath of both Parker's and Lorde's deaths, a publisher rejected them as uninteresting. Perhaps they were not at that time, but to me as someone who never met either woman, the letters were mesmerizing. The letters between Parker and Lorde are intimate, private writing, letters between friends, by two very public poets. Here was a discussion about life, poetry, cancer, family, and death, frank and candid, between two women I admire. Mecca Jamilah Sullivan, who wrote the introduction, felt the same way. These letters became public through my labor and the labors of many who helped assemble, publish, and promote the collection. *Sister Love* found a public audience at one particular moment in time.

Now a new generation is reading and writing and coming into consciousness. What will they find of interest and of use that previous generations have dismissed or known of but not embraced? It is impossible to answer that question, and I am less interested in prognosticating the future than in curating the past. What I do know, however, is three things. First, public feminisms are energized by the presence and support of feminist work in multiple locations: the academy, independent nonprofits, public spaces, public gatherings, independent writers, and all of the different locations where feminists think and live and write and are. Second, thoughtful, engaging, and compassionate editors enhance public feminisms in multiple ways. Third, rich knowledge foundations that include a multiplicity of what has been done in the past and bold challenges for what might be possible in the future—foundations that are expansive, extending, creative, and not circumscribed to what is easy and popular— shape our futures. New public feminisms can be created out of whole cloth, with the right fabric, scissors, thread, old patterns, and new energies.

BIBLIOGRAPHY

Beins, Agatha. "Comparative Perspectives Symposium: Feminist Zines." *Signs* 35, no. 1 (Autumn, 2009): 1–276.

Brant, Beth. *Sinister Wisdom 22/23: A Gathering of Spirit*, Winter 1983.

Cliff, Michelle. "Notes for a Magazine." *Sinister Wisdom* 24, Fall 1983, 6.

Coker, Cait and Kate Ozmet. "Women in Book History: A Bibliography." accessed August 25, 2021. http://www.womensbookhistory.org/.

Enszer, Julie R., editor. *Sister Love: The Letters of Audre Lorde and Pat Parker 1976–1989*. Dover, FL: A Midsummer Night's Press / Sinister Wisdom, 2017.

Kaye/Kantrowitz, Melanie and Irena Klepfisz. *Sinister Wisdom 29/30: The Tribe of Dina*, 1986.

Kaye/Kantrowitz, Melanie and Irena Klepfisz. *The Tribe of Dina*. Boston, MA: Beacon Press, 1989.

Kaye/Kantrowitz, Melanie. *The Issue Is Power: Essays on Women, Jews, Violence, and Resistance*. San Francisco, CA: Aunt Lute, 1992.

Licona, Adela. *Zines in Third Space: Radical Cooperation and Borderlands Rhetoric*. Albany, NY: State University of New York Press, 2013.

Meagan. "Is the Resurgence of Feminist Bookstores in the South a Moment or a Movement?" *Autostraddle*, November 7, 2019. https://www.autostraddle.com/resurgence-of-feminist-bookstores-in-the-south-a-moment-or-a-movement/.

Piepmeier, Alison. *Girl Zines: Making Media, Doing Feminism*. New York: NYU Press, 2009.

Wright, Anne and Joy Harjo. *The Delicacy and Strength of Lace: Letters Between Leslie Marmon Silko and James Wright*. Minneapolis, MN: Graywolf Press, 2009.

PART IV

FEMINIST PEDAGOGIES FOR COMMUNITY ENGAGEMENT

In this final section, chapter authors relate their experiences with teaching in multivalent ways. In "The Activist Possibilities of Wikipedia: Praxis, Pedagogy, and Potential Pitfalls," Jenn Brandt explores how Wikipedia can serve as an educational tool and platform for putting knowledge into practice. Riddhima Rajesh Sharma's "Teaching and Learning through 'Doing': Reflections and Strategies of Using Open Access Digital Tools for Feminist Pedagogy and Praxis" reflects on the author's process of "unlearning and relearning" as she created FemPositive, a digital feminist platform launched in India. In "RBG, Public Pedagogy, and Online Activism," Suzanne Leonard explores the symbiotic relationship between pedagogy, writing, and activism alongside a discussion of her public feminisms and online activism course. Michelle Larkin's essay, "There is No Just Future without Intersectional Sustainability: Feminist Pedagogy for Tackling Privilege and Centering Praxis in Sustainability Education" offers a compelling critique of sustainability education, praxis, and policy through the lens of intersectional pedagogy. Lastly, Nick Sanders, Grace Pregent, and Leah Bauer discuss their work in a writing center that provides services to the wider public in their Lansing, Ml community in "Orienting Public Pedagogues: A Black Feminist Approach to Community-Engaged Writing Center Work."

CHAPTER EIGHTEEN

THE ACTIVIST POSSIBILITIES OF WIKIPEDIA

Praxis, Pedagogy, and Potential Pitfalls

By Jenn Brandt

The syllabus for the course discussed in this chapter can be accessed on Fulcrum at https://doi.org/10.3998/mpub. 12682117.

INTRODUCTION

In January 2015, the National Women's Studies Association partnered with Wiki Education[1] on the NWSA Wikipedia Initiative, a campaign to increase information about women's studies and feminist topics on Wikipedia, as well as to make existing WGSS content more robust in terms of citations and accuracy. This partnership was designed in response to the gender gap[2] and gender bias[3] on Wikipedia, where it is estimated that the majority of Wikipedia editors are white males, and where articles about women and topics related to them are often missing or

Wikipedia editors are predominantly male

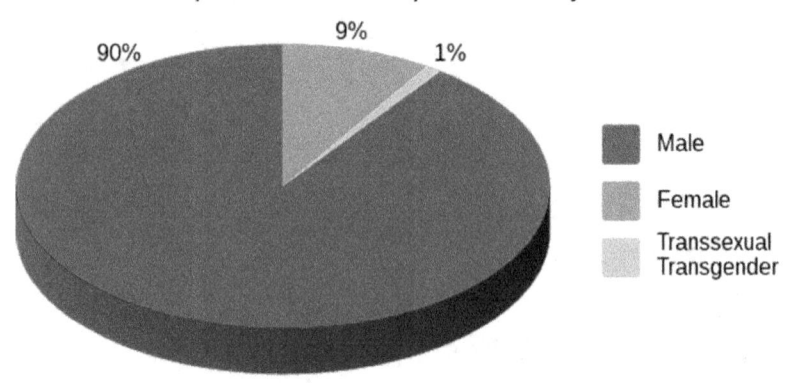

- Male: 90%
- Female: 9%
- Transsexual Transgender: 1%

Figure 18.1: Wikimedia Commons. "Wikipedia Editors Are Predominantly Male EN." File: Wikipedia editors are predominantly male EN.svg–Wikimedia Commons, November 20, 2014.

incomplete. These gaps relate to larger questions of systemic bias on Wikipedia[4] and the underrepresentation of marginalized groups on the site. Partnerships such as the NWSA Wikipedia Initiative are working to remedy this situation, and as a result of the efforts of this effort, by the end of the spring 2020 semester, the NWSA Wikipedia Initiative has resulted in over 8100 students in over 385 courses adding 6.08 million words to Wikipedia, while editing over 8.47 thousand articles and creating 1300 new ones.

Drawing from my experiences as both a NWSA/Wiki Education Fellow[5] and teaching as part of the NWSA Wikipedia Initiative, this chapter discusses the challenges and rewards for both students and faculty when using Wikipedia in the classroom. While many

Figure 18.2: "Campaign: National Women's Studies Foundation." Wiki Education [Screenshot by Jenn Brandt], January 23, 2022.

350 PUBLIC FEMINISMS

academics turn their students away from Wikipedia, the site has potential to be both an engaging pedagogical tool, as well as a public space for academic activism.

COURSE DESCRIPTION AND IMPLEMENTATION

Background

Informed by my training as an interdisciplinary scholar in the fields of English, popular culture studies, and gender and women's studies, in the spring of 2018 I developed and taught "Identity, Rhetoric, and Culture," a senior-level seminar for undergraduates. Cross-listed between the Women's and Gender Studies Program and the English Department's minor in Professional and Public Writing, the first six weeks of the course focused on introducing students to theories on gender, identity, and rhetorical communities in preparation for the course's two main assignments, with the second half of the semester focused on the Wikipedia assignment. In addition to evaluating current Wikipedia content, students received training through Wiki Education[6] on skills such as fact-based, neutral writing; research; media literacy and source evaluation; critical thinking; and collaboration.

I designed "Identity, Rhetoric, and Culture" with the Wikipedia project in mind, and planned the course for a full two semesters before implementation. Two semesters of planning are certainly not required; however, I encourage faculty to become familiar with Wikipedia's editorial policies before teaching with it. Although my course was a new design, Wikipedia can easily be adapted into a number of existing courses across the curriculum. While faculty can certainly teach with Wikipedia without Wiki Education's assistance, I found the organization's partnership beneficial, as it provided free resources and training for my students, as well as a helpful "dashboard," where I could track students' progress and contributions. Making sure students are familiar with the Wikipedia platform is important, as research suggests that both

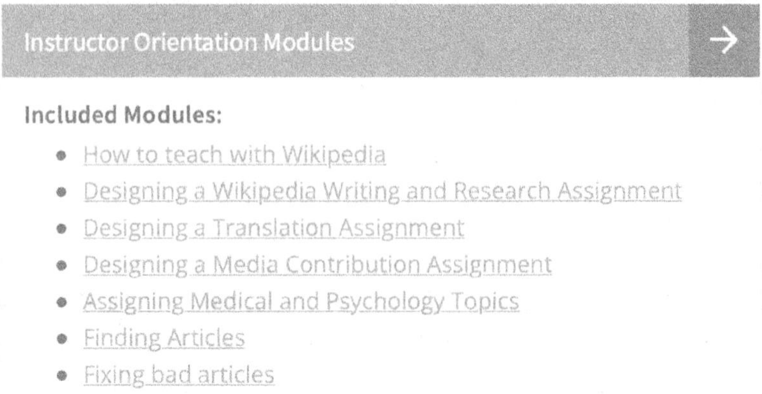

> **Instructor Orientation Modules** →
>
> Included Modules:
> - How to teach with Wikipedia
> - Designing a Wikipedia Writing and Research Assignment
> - Designing a Translation Assignment
> - Designing a Media Contribution Assignment
> - Assigning Medical and Psychology Topics
> - Finding Articles
> - Fixing bad articles

Figure 18.3: "Instructor Orientation Modules." Wiki Education [Screenshot by Jenn Brandt], January 23, 2022.'

confidence[7] and unfamiliarity with the conventions and "rules" of Wikipedia[8] contribute to Wikipedia's gender gap. There are also a number of resources specifically designed for instructors using Wikipedia in the classroom.[9]

During this time, I was also participating in a pilot program that Wiki Education designed to train scholars to edit and write Wikipedia articles on socially and politically relevant topics. I had already committed to teaching with Wikipedia before signing up for the Fellows program, and I saw this as a good opportunity to learn alongside my students. I was the only fellow teaching with Wikipedia during the program, which provided me with a unique experience in my dual roles of instructor and fellow.[10] In this way I shared my experiences as a fellow in class, being open with my own struggles and successes editing Wikipedia content.

Becoming familiar with Wikipedia is crucial to the success of teaching with the site, but one does not need to be in a formal training program in order to teach with Wikipedia. Having a basic understanding of how Wikipedia actually works and hands-on experience as an editor—which anyone can do—is necessary for

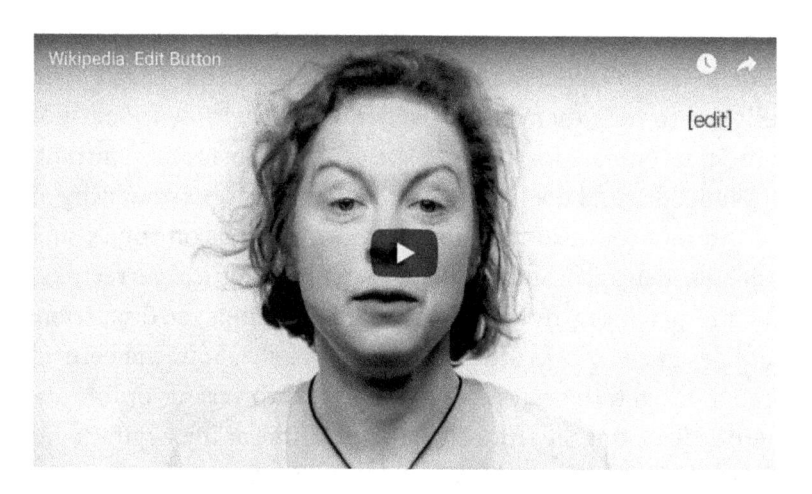

Figure 18.4: Wikimedia Foundation. "Wikipedia: Push the Edit Button." YouTube. [Screen shot by Jenn Brandt], September 23, 2010. https://www.youtube.com/watch?v=25hWh1Pa44M.

troubleshooting in class, anticipating areas where students might struggle, and maintaining credibility in the classroom. That being said, one by no means has to be an expert in Wikipedia in order to teach with it.

Implementation

Although I did not introduce the Wikipedia assignment until week five of the semester, students were aware of it from day one, and I frequently brought Wikipedia into class discussion when appropriate during the first month of the course. This was strategic, as I wanted students to become comfortable with considering Wikipedia in an academic context before embarking on making any edits. High school teachers and college professors, either unfamiliar with how Wikipedia works or weary of students using Internet sources, often discourage students from using Wikipedia. Students were also a bit confused when they first heard about the assignment, unclear about the work that would be required and unsure how Wikipedia fit into a women's studies course. To that end, during the first month of the semester, students completed a number of low-stakes writing assignments designed to help them think deeper about their own identities, in order to prepare for later considerations of bias and neutrality on Wikipedia, and the larger, gendered implications of writing on the Internet. We also read and discussed articles on topics such as gender-neutral pronouns, code switching, political correctness, and Internet misogyny and trolling. These readings and discussions were designed to help students think broadly about the course's larger aims and the ways identity factors into various online and rhetorical writing situations. Taking the time at the beginning of the semester to address the relationship between bias and identity as it relates to writing and rhetoric was not only important to the course's overall aims and goals, but also served to help students see the potential for their own implicit biases and to hopefully prevent students from unintentionally contributing to the patriarchal environment of Wikipedia. In this way I wanted the course to consider Wikipedia as an opportunity for "investigation of, and participation in, public knowledge curation with attention to the ways particular community norms and values are encoded in its discourse practices and digital tools."[11] My goal was to situate our work in Wikipedia into larger conversations about gender and identity and their role in knowledge formation, as well as the types of identity-based gatekeeping that takes place in both discourse communities and online spaces. This was important in getting students to understand the activist potential of editing Wikipedia.

When introducing the Wikipedia assignment, I prepared a number of lectures to supplement our class discussion. At the outset, we spent a class period discussing what, exactly, Wikipedia is. I began class by having students brainstorm everything they know, everything they think they know, and everything they want to know about Wikipedia. This discussion was not only useful in helping me gauge students' familiarity with the site, but also in helping them generate a discussion on their own understanding of how knowledge is created and disseminated, along with reflection on their comfort levels with various Internet platforms and sources of information. From there, we discussed Wikipedia's "five pillars,"[12] or, its fundamental principles: it's an online encyclopedia; its content is free; it has a neutral point of view; editors should treat each other with respect; and Wikipedia has no "firm" rules, its policies and guidelines evolve over time. After establishing what Wikipedia "is," we went on to discuss the demographics of Wikipedia editors[13] and users, referring back to our previous readings on identity and rhetoric. Students were sent home with the assignment to create a Wikipedia account and familiarize themselves with the site and our class's Wiki Education dashboard.[14]

The following week, I introduced students to the Wikipedia assignment as it related to our course goals, emphasizing the skills students would develop over the duration of the assignment. These included writing for a wide and diverse audience in order to share ideas publicly; deepening the writing practice through drafting, revising, editing, and peer review; and understanding the ethical standards and point of view necessary to write for Wikipedia. As part of this discussion, the class reviewed their prior knowledge on rhetorical analysis and appeal. This helped situate the type of research that would be necessary in order to appropriately edit Wikipedia, as well as to deepen student understanding of the neutral point of view necessary on the site. Although it has been argued that Wikipedia "privileges patriarchal methodologies and epistemologies,"[15] I found that Wikipedia's policies were a good case study to not only consider standpoint theory and feminist epistemologies, but also a way to extrapolate and think more broadly about the Internet, media, and debates regarding "fake news." In this way, the course stressed critical thinking in addition to considering feminism's activist potential with respect to public writing.

As students began to consider articles for editing, a number of in-class and take-home activities were assigned. In class, students were to look up a Wikipedia article on any topic of interest to them. The more familiar they were with the topic of their chosen article, the better, as the goal was to have them assess the article's content for thoroughness, accuracy, organization, and comprehension, as well as for possible bias. This included paying attention to the page's references and citations. Students also looked over their chosen page's history[16] to see how recently it had been updated, as well as the article's talk page,[17] to see if there were any ongoing discussions or debates. After students had time to look over their chosen articles, I pulled a few of them up on the classroom projector for the entire class to see, giving students a chance to discuss what they found.

This class period was also dedicated to making sure that students were comfortable with the first few training modules and understood how to access their personal sandboxes,[18] workspaces to practice with the Wikipedia editing tools and to draft contributions. The sandbox is an interesting space to explore with students because, although it is their personal workspace, it is not private. Anyone can view, or edit, a sandbox according to the same procedures that apply to any other Wikipedia page. The sandbox serves as a great reminder that all work done on Wikipedia is a form of public writing. As a class we talked about the importance of following proper rules of citation and copyright, even on work that was in a draft state. Students could also practice leaving messages on the talk pages of their classmates' sandboxes as a way to introduce talk page etiquette[19] and practice with the editing code.

While some students quickly identified articles to work on, others needed more help. Given the topic of our course, I suggested students consult Wikipedia's index[20] of articles related to feminism. As students narrowed their choices, a more detailed evaluation of articles took place. In particular, students were asked to consider the neutrality of the article, the thoroughness of the article's content, and the quality of citations. During this time, I shared with students my own progress editing the Wikipedia articles for Women's Studies[21] and author Margaret Atwood.[22] I discussed my process for finding appropriate citations for Atwood's page, as well as the sexist and racist language I found on the talk page for Women's Studies. A particularly sobering incident occurred when the Women's Studies page was vandalized with anti-Semitic language, but I was able to point to students how quickly the offensive material was removed by editors, thus hitting home the importance of having more feminists and people from marginalized communities active on the site.

DISCUSSION

While certainly rewarding, teaching with Wikipedia requires a level of flexibility. The first half of the course was fairly standard, with lectures, in-class writing activities and assignments, and culminated with students completing annotated bibliographies for their articles. This last piece was important as all information included on Wikipedia needs to be cited to a credible and relevant secondary source, preferably peer-reviewed (unless linking to a credible news outlet). This is a potentially problematic aspect of Wikipedia, as it privileges certain knowledges when one considers the way that women and people of color have been historically left out of academic conversations. Although an annotated bibliography is a common assignment, in this case it took on a different relevancy as we discussed the importance of credible sources as they relate to the Internet, particularly in our contemporary political climate and in an era of "fake news," but I also emphasized citing women and other minority voices. Given that our course was themed around the intersections of gender and identity, students were encouraged to think about these connections not only as they related to their topics, but also with respect to the information and authors they cited. This led to broader questions and discussions regarding sexism, racism, and homophobia on the Internet, as well as the "neutrality" of algorithms and search engines. In particular, the work of Safiya Noble, and her monograph *The Algorithms of Oppression* (from which students read excerpts), was especially useful. These discussions deepened students' engagement with the course and course theme as the relevance and importance of the work they were doing became increasingly apparent.

One visible instance of this occurred fairly early in the semester as students were selecting articles to improve. In searching for possible pages to edit, a student discovered that the page for Media and Gender[23] prominently featured a photograph of a topless female newscaster.[24] The student's rationale for removing the picture was straightforward in that a photo of a topless woman was neither necessary nor the most appropriate image for the page's subject matter. The photo was removed without incident, but some quick investigation revealed that the image appeared on other pages as well. When I attempted to remove the image from the article on the Sexual Revolution[25], to my surprise, I was met with some resistance. Another editor argued that finding an image offensive

Figure 18.5: "Media and Gender." Wikipedia. Wikimedia Foundation, April 6, 2018. https://en.wikipedia.org/wiki/Media_and_gender.

was not reason enough to remove it and flagged me for censorship. My rationale for its removal from the Sexual Revolution page was similar to my student's, especially considering the photograph was from 2008 and the article covers the time period of the 1960s–1980s. Ultimately the photo was removed, but this debate resulted in interesting online and in-class discussions on the topic of nudity, censorship, and the objectification of women. It also provided me with my own personal example of how editors can be met with hostility by others in the Wikipedia community, especially when dealing with issues of gender and sex.

While this particular example dealt with visual rhetoric, it prepared the class to think more deeply about the ways language shapes and frames the gendered dynamics of Wikipedia and the dissemination of information. For example, a student chose to work on the page for Rosemarie Aquilina[26] and had to make decisions on the kinds of personal information relevant to include about Judge Aquilina. In particular, the class had a spirited discussion on whether or not it was necessary to mention that Judge Aquilina's youngest children were conceived via IVF. In order to think deeper about the gendered implications of this information and, more broadly, of Wikipedia entries, we discussed not only Aquilina's page, but also the pages of male judges, looking for disparities, as well as looking at the language used on the pages of other individuals involved in the case against Larry Nassar and the USA Gymnastics sex abuse scandal.[27] While at the outset of the semester I could not have anticipated these classroom conversations, they became instrumental in the course's success.

Therefore, it was during the second half of the semester that the structure of the course became looser. I could not prepare for class in the traditional sense, as it was difficult to predict the online interactions or issues students would experience as they began to edit their articles. Although I always had goals and objectives for each class meeting, I made sure to allocate time for questions and also create a space for students to address any concerns they were having. Most of these questions or concerns were a direct result of the "real-world" feedback students were experiencing from other Wikipedia editors, which added an additional audience component to the work they were doing. While most Wikipedia editors are friendly and helpful, it was still jarring for some students to realize that people outside of our classroom space were reading their work. This not only encouraged them to take the assignment seriously, but also lent additional credibility to things I had been saying to them in class, particularly to those who proceeded to use sources or make edits I advised against.

For example, whereas one student completed the annotated bibliography and had good sources to support the edits he was making to his chosen page, he failed to properly cite his additions in his sandbox. Although this was pointed out to him by both me and in peer review, he persisted in moving his additions from the sandbox to the main page without citations. Not unexpectedly, his additions were quickly removed by an outside Wikipedia editor. The student was both surprised and frustrated to see that an independent party confirmed the comments he had been receiving in class, resulting in a learning experience that worked on multiple levels. Another student was cautioned about making edits to an article on video game journalism,[28] a highly controversial topic on Wikipedia and the Internet due to the #GamerGate controversy. We reviewed the article's history and talk page to discuss strategies for successfully entering this conversation. Even though the student felt prepared to take on the subject, she quickly realized that outside editors would be watching her work and tracking her additions closely. Despite warnings that her chosen page would be more difficult to edit than most and, therefore, potentially require more work, the student persisted with mixed results. Although the majority of her edits were removed, it was still a beneficial learning process with respect to the larger discussion on "ethics" in journalism and online sexism and misogyny. Perhaps the most unexpected "controversy" arose on edits made to Alice Walker's article.[29] The page is currently under active arbitration due to what Wikipedia refers to as Walker's ongoing comments regarding the Arab-Israeli conflict.[30] Although Walker's stance on Israel and its occupation of Palestinian lands were outside of the scope of the student's additions and edits, she engaged in numerous exchanges on the article's talk page with other editors about Walker's work as an activist more broadly. In addition to the opportunity to consider the ways that activism is conceived of and understood by the general public, these exchanges also led to a closer consideration of the ways a subject matter's race plays into the discussions surrounding them and their representation on Wikipedia, as well as Wikipedia's stance on neutrality given the language it uses to describe and label Israel's occupation of the West Bank.

Thus, interacting with Wikipedia's processes and outside editors became a crucial component of the course for many students. Not only did these interactions facilitate a more rewarding writing experience, but they also provided useful context to some of the course's broader themes of gender and identity. Given the course's focus on public writing and online rhetoric, these interactions were invaluable to the learning experience. A number of students engaged in extended dialogues with other Wikipedia editors over the edits they were making. One student made a number of additions to the artist Halsey's page,[31] discussing the performer's activism and participation in the 2018 Women's March. In addition to elaborating on Halsey's involvement, the student included information on celebrity activism. Although this information was well-researched and written, it was deemed outside the scope of the article. At first the student was discouraged that her work was removed by another editor, but then realized it was better suited for different Wikipedia pages. Ultimately, the student was able to not only contribute to the Halsey page, but also to the articles on the 2018 Women's March and the #MeToo Movement.

Overwhelmingly, students' experiences were positive. In addition to the desire to write well for a public audience, the fact that students chose articles that were of interest to them personally made them take greater ownership of their work. While most students selected to edit existing pages, one student in the course created an entirely new page on bisexual literature.[32] Although it was not her intention at the start of the semester to create a new article, once she realized there was not a Wikipedia entry for the topic, her own passion and belief in the importance of the subject matter compelled her to go above and beyond her (and my own) expectations. As the semester progressed and she worked on her article, she became a more vocal participant in class discussions, in spite of earlier skepticism about the course.

She, along with many of her classmates, also commented that they routinely discussed and shared the work they were doing for the course with family and friends. The public nature of Wikipedia, along with the general public's familiarity with it, make it an accessible assignment for students to demonstrate their knowledge and skills not only with their personal networks, but also to potential employers. Conversations with other Wikipedia editors furthered the "real-world" feedback provided by the course, and a number of students enjoyed seeing the impact of their work by tracking page views of their articles.

CONCLUSION

Using Wikipedia in the classroom provides a number of both tangible and pedagogical benefits. Wikipedia is the fifth-most visited website in the world,[33] and provides information to countless individuals globally. Helping to make Wikipedia a more accurate, diverse, and comprehensive site allows students to use their classroom learning for real-world good. In turn, student engagement and satisfaction are increased as they see and share the application of their study. Not only can they point out their contributions to their peers, friends, and family, as well as to potential employers, but they can also see the impact of their work through Wikipedia's "page view statistics" feature.

Incorporating a Wikipedia assignment not only helps in the development of student writing, but with critical thinking skills as students consider the factors that contribute to knowledge creation and dissemination to various audiences. In particular, the importance of brevity, clear communication, and relevant and reliable sources is stressed. A Wikipedia assignment not only provides students with a different way of thinking about their own writing, but also a more nuanced understanding and approach to information on the Internet. Discussions about algorithms, neutrality, and various identity designations are deepened as students engage in their own forms of public writing via Wikipedia. Additionally, considering Wikipedia as a text unto itself is a fruitful exercise. Using various Wikipedia features such as a page's edit history or page view statistics[34] provides useful information on a given topic, as well as greater context for a subject matter's relevance, cultural import, and history. As a living document, students can discover when certain information is added or removed from an article, track its views to other cultural and political events, and more deeply grasp the evolution of a subject over time.

Wikipedia is a well-known website, with millions of people visiting it every day. Empowering students to actively engage with a website they regularly use is a win-win. It not only benefits students by training them to critically engage with the media they use, but is also a way for academics to perform works of public good. Faculty and students have access to books, periodicals, and resources through institutional libraries that most Wikipedia editors don't, and, therefore, are a vital resource for making Wikipedia better. Instead of complaining about Wikipedia and our students' reliance on it—something faculty routinely do—incorporating a Wikipedia assignment is a more productive and meaningful way to teach ourselves and our students to engage with online spaces and shift conversations through public writing.

NOTES

1. See wikiedu.org for more information on Wiki Education.
2. See https://meta.wikimedia.org/wiki/Gender_gap for more information on the gender gap on Wikipedia.
3. See "Gender Bias on Wikipedia," *Wikipedia*, Wikimedia Foundation, December 24, 2020, https://en.wikipedia.org/wiki/Gender_bias_on_Wikipedia.
4. See "Systemic Bias," *Wikipedia*, Wikimedia Foundation, January 9, 2021, https://en.wikipedia.org/wiki/Wikipedia:Systemic_bias.
5. Wikipedia Fellows is an initiative of Wiki Education designed to train subject-matter experts to contribute to Wikipedia. For more information on the initiative and the initial cohort, see Ryan McGrady's "Announcing the Wikipedia Fellows Pilot Cohort," *Wiki Education*, July 9, 2018, https://wikiedu.org/blog/2018/01/18/announcing-the-wikipedia-fellows-pilot-cohort/.
6. All of Wiki Education's student training modules can be found at https://dashboard.wikiedu.org/training/students.
7. Julia B. Bear and Benjamin Collier, "Where are the Women in Wikipedia? Understanding the Different Psychological Experiences of Men and Women in Wikipedia," *Sex Roles* 74 (2016): 259.
8. Leigh Gruwell, "Wikipedia's Politics of Exclusion: Gender, Epistemology, and Feminist Rhetorical (In)action," *Computers and Composition* 37 (2015): 125.
9. See https://wikiedu.org/teach-with-wikipedia/ for resources and to sign up to teach with Wiki Education.
10. See Jenn Brandt, "Women's Studies Scholar Improves Wikipedia While Her Students Follow Along," *Wiki Education*, September 9, 2019, https://wikiedu.org/blog/2018/05/31/womens-studies-scholar-improves-wikipedia-while-her-students-follow-along/ for my experiences as part of the Fellows program.
11. Melanie Kill, "Teaching Digital Rhetoric: Wikipedia, Collaboration, and the Politics of Free Knowledge," in *Digital Humanities Pedagogy: Practices, Principles, and Politics*, ed. Brett D. Hirsch (Cambridge, UK: Open Book Publishers, 2012): 390.
12. For further discussion of Wikipedia's five pillars, see "Five Pillars," *Wikipedia*, Wikimedia Foundation, December 27, 2020, https://en.wikipedia.org/wiki/Wikipedia:Five_pillars.

13. For further information on registered Wikipedia editors, see "Who Writes Wikipedia?," *Wikipedia*, Wikimedia Foundation, December 22, 2020, https://en.wikipedia.org/wiki/Wikipedia:Who_writes_Wikipedia%3F.
14. The course's Wiki Education dashboard, which includes links to the assignment's timeline, student contributions, and training modules, can be accessed at https://dashboard.wikiedu.org/courses/High_Point_University/Rhetoric,_Identity,_and_Culture_(Spring_2018)/home.
15. Leigh Gruwell, "Wikipedia's Politics of Exclusion: Gender, Epistemology, and Feminist Rhetorical (In)action," *Computers and Composition* 37 (2015): 118.
16. Each article on Wikipedia has an associated "history" page, which details the pages creation and edits. For more information on article histories and their usefulness in researching with Wikipedia, see "Help: How to Read an Article History," *Wikipedia*, Wikimedia Foundation, December 11, 2020, https://en.wikipedia.org/wiki/Help:How_to_read_an_article_history.
17. In addition to its history page, Wikipedia article's also have "talk" pages where editors can discuss changes proposed and made to the article. For more on talk pages, see "Help: Talk Pages," *Wikipedia*, Wikimedia Foundation, January 9, 2021, https://en.wikipedia.org/wiki/Help:Talk_pages.
18. Instructions for creating and using Wikipedia sandboxes can be found here: "About the Sandbox," *Wikipedia*, Wikimedia Foundation, October 27, 2020, https://en.wikipedia.org/wiki/Wikipedia:About_the_sandbox.
19. Specific rules for editing an article's talk page can be found here: "Talk Page Guidelines," *Wikipedia*, Wikimedia Foundation, January 7, 2021, https://en.wikipedia.org/wiki/Wikipedia:Talk_page_guidelines.
20. See "Index of Feminism Articles," *Wikipedia*, Wikimedia Foundation, August 16, 2020, https://en.wikipedia.org/wiki/Index_of_feminism_articles.
21. See "Women's Studies," *Wikipedia*, Wikimedia Foundation, January 8, 2021, https://en.wikipedia.org/wiki/Women%27s_studies.
22. See "Margaret Atwood," *Wikipedia*, Wikimedia Foundation, January 6, 2021, https://en.wikipedia.org/wiki/Margaret_Atwood.
23. See "Media and Gender," *Wikipedia*, Wikimedia Foundation, December 29, 2020, https://en.wikipedia.org/wiki/Media_and_gender.
24. Screenshot of page before student removed the photo. Author altered the image for inclusion in this chapter by including a "black bar" across the reporter's chest.
25. See "Sexual Revolution," *Wikipedia*, Wikimedia Foundation, December 20, 2020, https://en.wikipedia.org/wiki/Sexual_revolution.
26. See "Rosemarie Aquilina," *Wikipedia*, Wikimedia Foundation, December 31, 2020), https://en.wikipedia.org/wiki/Rosemarie_Aquilina.

27. See "USA Gymnastics Sex Abuse Scandal," *Wikipedia*, Wikimedia Foundation, January 11, 2021, https://en.wikipedia.org/wiki/USA_Gymnastics_sex_ab use_scandal.
28. See "Video Game Journalism," *Wikipedia*, Wikimedia Foundation, November 28, 2020, https://en.wikipedia.org/wiki/Video_game_jou rnalism.
29. See "Alice Walker," *Wikipedia*, Wikimedia Foundation, January 7, 2021, https://en.wikipedia.org/wiki/Alice_Walker.
30. Wikipedia's arbitration committee has created a series of edit guidelines for any pages that may contain material related to the Arab-Israeli conflict. For more details, see "Arbitration/Index/Palestine-Israel Articles," *Wikipedia*, Wikimedia Foundation, July 12, 2020, https://en.wikipedia.org/wiki/Wikipe dia:Arbitration/Index/Palestine-Israel_articles.
31. See "Halsey (Singer)," *Wikipedia*, Wikimedia Foundation, January 6, 2021, https://en.wikipedia.org/wiki/Halsey_(singer).
32. See "Bisexual Literature," *Wikipedia*, Wikimedia Foundation, December 16, 2020, https://en.wikipedia.org/wiki/Bisexual_literature.
33. Gray, Alex. "These Are the World's Most Popular Websites." *World Economic Forum*, 10 April 2017, https://www.weforum.org/agenda/2017/04/most-popu lar-websites-google-youtube-baidu/.
34. Wikipedia keeps track of page views, which can be used trace an article's popularity or how visits to a page have changed over time. For more information, see "Pageview Statistics," *Wikipedia*, Wikimedia Foundation, September 13, 2020, https://en.wikipedia.org/wiki/Wikipedia:Pageview_statistics.

WORKS CITED

"About the Sandbox." *Wikipedia*. Wikimedia Foundation. October 27, 2020. https://en.wikipedia.org/wiki/Wikipedia:About_the_sandbox.

"Alice Walker." *Wikipedia*. Wikimedia Foundation. January 7, 2021. https://en.wikipedia.org/wiki/Alice_Walker.

"Arbitration/Index/Palestine-Israel Articles." *Wikipedia*. Wikimedia Foundation. July 12, 2020. https://en.wikipedia.org/wiki/Wikipedia:Arbitration/Index/ Palestine-Israel_articles.

Bear, Julia B. and Benjamin Collier. "Where Are the Women in Wikipedia? Understanding the Different Psychological Experiences of Men and Women in Wikipedia." *Sex Roles* 74 (2016): 245–265.

"Bisexual Literature." *Wikipedia*. Wikimedia Foundation. December 16, 2020. https://en.wikipedia.org/wiki/Bisexual_literature.

Brandt, Jenn. "Women's Studies Scholar Improves Wikipedia While Her Students Follow along." *Wiki Education*. September 9, 2019. https://wikiedu.org/blog/2018/05/31/womens-studies-scholar-improves-wikipedia-while-her-students-follow-along/.

"File: Wikipedia Editors Are Predominantly Male EN.svg." File: Wikipedia editors are predominantly male EN.svg. Wikimedia Commons. November 20, 2014. https://commons.wikimedia.org/wiki/file:Wikipedia_editors_are_predominantly_male_EN.svg#/media/File:Wikipedia_editors_are_predominantly_male_EN.svg.

"Five Pillars." *Wikipedia*. Wikimedia Foundation. December 27, 2020. https://en.wikipedia.org/wiki/Wikipedia:Five_pillars.

"Gender Bias on Wikipedia." *Wikipedia*. Wikimedia Foundation. December 24, 2020. https://en.wikipedia.org/wiki/Gender_bias_on_Wikipedia.

Gray, Alex. "These Are the World's Most Popular Websites." *World Economic Forum*. 10 April 2017. https://www.weforum.org/agenda/2017/04/most-popular-websites-google-youtube-baidu/.

Gruwell, Leigh. "Wikipedia's Politics of Exclusion: Gender, Epistemology, and Feminist Rhetorical (In)action." *Computers and Composition* 37 (2015): 117–131.

"Halsey (Singer)." *Wikipedia*. Wikimedia Foundation. January 6, 2021. https://en.wikipedia.org/wiki/Halsey_(singer).

"Help: How to Read an Article History." *Wikipedia*. Wikimedia Foundation. December 11, 2020. https://en.wikipedia.org/wiki/Help:How_to_read_an_article_history.

"Help: Talk Pages." *Wikipedia*. Wikimedia Foundation. January 9, 2021. https://en.wikipedia.org/wiki/Help:Talk_pages.

"Index of Feminism Articles." *Wikipedia*. Wikimedia Foundation. August 16, 2020. https://en.wikipedia.org/wiki/Index_of_feminism_articles.

"Instructor Orientation Modules." Wiki Education Dashboard. Accessed January 10, 2021. https://dashboard.wikiedu.org/training/instructors.

Kill, Melanie. "Teaching Digital Rhetoric: Wikipedia, Collaboration, and the Politics of Free Knowledge." In *Digital Humanities Pedagogy: Practices, Principles, and Politics*, edited by Brett D. Hirsch, 389–405. Cambridge, UK: Open Book Publishers, 2012.

"Margaret Atwood." *Wikipedia*. Wikimedia Foundation. January 6, 2021. https://en.wikipedia.org/wiki/Margaret_Atwood.

McGrady, Ryan. "Announcing the Wikipedia Fellows Pilot Cohort." *Wiki Education*. July 9, 2018. https://wikiedu.org/blog/2018/01/18/announcing-the-wikipedia-fellows-pilot-cohort/.

"Media and Gender." *Wikipedia*. Wikimedia Foundation. December 29, 2020. https://en.wikipedia.org/wiki/Media_and_gender.

"Pageview Statistics." *Wikipedia*. Wikimedia Foundation. September 13, 2020. https://en.wikipedia.org/wiki/Wikipedia:Pageview_statistics.

"Rosemarie Aquilina." *Wikipedia*. Wikimedia Foundation. December 31, 2020. https://en.wikipedia.org/wiki/Rosemarie_Aquilina.

"Sexual Revolution." *Wikipedia*. Wikimedia Foundation. December 20, 2020. https://en.wikipedia.org/wiki/Sexual_revolution.

"Systemic Bias." *Wikipedia*. Wikimedia Foundation. January 9, 2021. https://en.wikipedia.org/wiki/Wikipedia:Systemic_bias.

"Talk Page Guidelines." *Wikipedia*. Wikimedia Foundation. January 7, 2021. https://en.wikipedia.org/wiki/Wikipedia:Talk_page_guidelines.

"USA Gymnastics Sex Abuse Scandal." *Wikipedia*. Wikimedia Foundation. January 11, 2021. https://en.wikipedia.org/wiki/USA_Gymnastics_sex_abuse_scandal.

"Video Game Journalism." *Wikipedia*. Wikimedia Foundation. November 28, 2020. https://en.wikipedia.org/wiki/Video_game_journalism.

"Who Writes Wikipedia?" *Wikipedia*. Wikimedia Foundation. December 22, 2020. https://en.wikipedia.org/wiki/Wikipedia:Who_writes_Wikipedia%3F.

Wikimedia Commons. "Wikipedia Editors Are Predominantly Male EN." File: Wikipedia editors are predominantly male EN.svg. Wikimedia Commons. November 20, 2014. https://commons.wikimedia.org/wiki/File:Wikipedia_editors_are_predominantly_male_EN.svg#/media/File:Wikipedia_editors_are_predominantly_male_EN.svg.

Wikimedia Foundation. "Wikipedia: Push the Edit Button." *YouTube*. YouTube. September 23, 2010. https://www.youtube.com/watch?v=25hWh1Pa44M&feature=youtu.be.

"Women's Studies." *Wikipedia*. Wikimedia Foundation. January 8, 2021. https://en.wikipedia.org/wiki/Women%27s_studies.

CHAPTER NINETEEN

TEACHING AND LEARNING THROUGH "DOING"

Reflections on Using Open Access Digital Tools for Feminist Pedagogy and Praxis

By Riddhima Sharma

INTRODUCTION

"This campaign meant a lot to me," a student wrote in their end of semester reflection essay about how the social media project they did for my Introduction to Women's, Gender, and Sexuality Studies class helped them find a sense of community on Instagram, learn about the nuances of the body positive movement, various body image issues, and find a sense of self-love and acceptance. Their project was a visual Instagram campaign which aimed to talk about body image, stereotypes, and underlined the need to normalize, accept, and celebrate all kinds of bodies. Like this student, several years ago I experienced several such moments when so many concepts and theories from my college classroom began making sense to me when I was working on developing a digital feminist platform called FemPositive that I co-founded in India in 2014. My feminist praxis through FemPositive continues to be one of the most fulfilling ways in which I have learned, unlearned, and relearned feminisms. This essay is a critical reflection on my work in building FemPositive and teaching in an American classroom to think through ways in which feminist pedagogy and praxis intermingle to facilitate a critical learning environment committed to action. I hope for this essay to be useful for readers in thinking about one of the many ways to bridge feminist theory and praxis in their classrooms and outside it.

I begin with my first academic encounter with Indian feminisms which pushed me to reflect on the politics of inclusion and exclusion in curricula of particular histories and feminist ideas of access to knowledge which formed the foundations of FemPositive. I then map the ways in which FemPositive not only became a means to put theory into action for me, but itself became a continuous learning space rooted in action. And then re-entering the classroom as an educator, I reflect on some of the ways in which I worked with my students to connect the feminist theories we were learning with action outside of the classroom. Both my work with FemPositive and in the classroom with students I delineate in this essay have been intentionally focused on bringing, or at least thinking about bringing, feminist education, critical thinking, and self-reflexivity out of the classroom into more broadly accessible community spaces and our day-to-day lives. While doing this work comes with challenges and limitations, I argue the need to keep taking small steps towards bridging access to knowledge and embodying feminist ideas of supplementing theory with social justice praxis.

FEMPOSITIVE: LEARNING THROUGH DOING

In 2013, alongside my law degree, I pursued a one-year certificate course in women's studies at the Research Centre for Women's Studies, SNDT Women's University which was my first academic encounter with feminisms and women's histories in India. Until then, the only little exposure to feminism I had was about Western feminist movements and the American "waves" of feminism in my undergrad political science courses. I was twenty-three years old at the time, thrilled about all the history, women, literature, and movements I was getting to learn about but was also sad because I wished I had learnt about this sooner in life. If it took me so many years to learn the histories of feminisms in India because they were missing from school syllabi, there was a good chance that many other folks were unaware too. The importance of knowledge sharing, access to education, and critical learning which have been so central to feminist movements and which formed some of the key themes in the graduate certificate course turned into something I became deeply interested in. Therefore, when I finished the certificate course in 2014, I not only wanted to learn more about feminisms but also wanted to find ways to share all the feminist histories and literature I had learnt about in the course with more people.

Facebook was a social media platform where a lot of political conversations were taking place at the time. Several of the popular feminist pages and groups I came across on the platform were largely Global North centric in their discourses, and housed knowledge around Global North feminist leaders, movements, and histories. Indian feminist pages and knowledges, while present in these spaces, were not as visible. I found this to be an exciting opportunity to utilize Facebook to share and make visible, Indian feminist histories and contemporary issues. After a few months of planning with a friend of mine, Chirag Kulshrestha, we started a Facebook page called FemPositive, through which we hoped to connect with and build a feminist learning community of South Asian folks. Some of the goals I had in starting this digital feminist platform included:

a) Leveraging social media to find and build a community of folks across all identities who are interested in learning about feminisms (as a student, I had no resources to do anything fancy like start a "real" organization/non-profit).

b) Educating myself by setting aside some time every week to researching and sharing resources/texts to the FemPositive page.
c) Potentially crowdsourcing an accessible reading list for folks who might be interested in learning about feminist histories, movements, and figures in South Asia broadly and India specifically, but perhaps didn't have access to one.

My personal feminist journey and the evolution of FemPositive were and continue to be tightly knit together. When I started FemPositive, my knowledge of and my politics around feminisms were extremely narrow and limited. As a *Brahmin* (upper caste), cisgender, able-bodied woman, I had the privilege to not think about the intersections of caste, sexuality, disability, and class in my feminist praxis. My work with FemPositive over the last six years was critical for me to learn about the nuances and intersections of privilege, power, and oppression. It has also been a space to reflect on my position within this matrix of power and domination. Working to recognize my privileges, and actively unlearning exclusionary ideas and behaviors became crucial to relearn what it means to embody feminist values of self-reflexivity, inclusivity, equity, allyship, and everyday praxis.

Two projects have been at the center of my personal journey of unlearning and relearning and, therefore, also instrumental to FemPositive's development. A few months into launching the FemPositive Facebook page, we put together a poster series called #FeministReads. This series was geared towards building a repository of feminist texts by sharing weekly feminist book recommendations by South-Asian authors, particularly women, in the form of posters. This project was a first step towards imagining what open access feminist knowledges might look like. Figure 19.1 below is a sample of what the #FeministReads posters look like, with an image of the book cover on the left, and an abstract or book description on the right. A couple of huge limitations of this project, which was built through a blend of personal research and crowdsourcing through friends and colleagues, was that it was mostly English language texts and the fact that all we could do was share book titles and not the texts themselves (except in some cases where texts were available in open access digital formats). So, any potential impact of this project was limited to broadly English-speaking folks who either had access to libraries where they could find these books or had the resources to purchase them.

Thinking through ways of bridging these gaps of a social media based #FeministReads repository, and to offer possibilities of realizing a feminist learning community that we envisioned, we

Feminist Read of the Week

I, PHOOLAN DEVI

I, Phoolan Devi: The Autobiography of India's Bandit Queen - Phoolan Devi

"What others called a crime, I called justice" – Phoolan Devi
A female Robin Hood, a modern day Count of Monte Cristo - Phoolan Devi, the notorious Bandit Queen of India, has become a living legend. Enduring cruel poverty and degradation, Phoolan Devi survived the humiliation and horrifying gang rape to claim retribution for herself and all low-caste women of the Indian plains.
In a three-year campaign which rocked the government, she delivered justice to rape victims and stole from the rich to give to the poor, before negotiating surrender on her own terms. Throughout her years of imprisonment without trial Phoolan Devi remained a beacon of hope for the poor and downtrodden, and in 1996, amidst both popular support and media controversy, she was elected to the Indian Parliament. For over a decade journalists, biographers and film-makers have found the power and scope of Phoolan Devi's myth irresistible. Now finally she tells the story of her life through her eyes and in her own voice.

www.fempositive.org | www.facebook.com/fempositive

Figure 19.1: A poster from the #FeministReads repository.

partnered with Vacha Charitable Trust, a non-profit organization that worked with women and girls, to collaboratively host and facilitate a monthly feminist reading group at their office library in Mumbai. Launched in December 2016, we titled the sessions "Women: Written, Unwritten" to invite participants to explore together the rich history of women's writing and resistance which had been marginalized or erased from our primary education. The process of putting together and running this reading group was one that greatly influenced the way I think about feminist education and critical learning environments even before I had read bell hooks or Paulo Freire.

Firstly, choosing texts that we would read and how we would share them with participants required thinking about not only which were the most foundational texts, but also questions of which texts were most accessible, especially in terms of writing style and language. We chose short stories and poetry collections because we wanted the reading itself to take place collectively during the session, being particularly mindful of limitations on who can do

Figure 19.2: A picture from the second edition of "Women: Written, Unwritten" in collaboration with Vacha Charitable Trust where we read Savitribai Phule's poems from her collection of poems titled "Kavya Phule" (first published in Marathi in 1854) in Marathi, Hindi, and English.

Figure 19.3: A picture of Tarabai Shinde's Stri-Purush Tulana (A Comparison Between Women and Men—first published in Marathi in 1882) in Marathi and English from the third edition of "Women: Written, Unwritten."

prereading and come, and to explore the collaborative learning possibilities of reading a text together. Secondly, we thought about who our potential participants and co-learners could be. While sending out messages and emails to folks in our networks was one option, we also chose to publish a Facebook event page to invite folks who followed FemPositive and Vacha on social media and may be interested in joining us. The response was wonderful, not only in terms of the comments/messages we received when we put out the event on our Facebook page and networks, but also in how sincerely folks wanted to engage in such a space. Several folks who were consistently engaged with our page and were located in Mumbai joined us for one or more sessions. We were able to do this because we had a community of over 4000 folks following the page, and a promising daily organic engagement on our posts so it seemed right to publish and share updates on our activities/events on Facebook. It is also important to note that at that time, the Facebook algorithms were not as unforgiving and reaching people organically through liking/commenting on the page and sharing posts to one's personal profile were viable ways to promote one's page or events. Thus, we managed to reach and engage with a small but very passionate group of folks without paid Facebook promotions or ads. Today, however, the social media landscape has transformed drastically across platforms and organic community building has become a lot more difficult, which is why we now have smaller communities of around 1500 followers on Instagram and Twitter, which are now more popular platforms used by social justice movements.

Each month's session had anywhere between six to twenty participants who were a mix of known and unknown folks, old and young, from different walks of life, who had all come together to read, learn, and reflect together. Finally, we had structured the two-hour session to read together in the first half (often going around in the circle to read a passage/poem out loud), pause to reflect individually, and then discuss the text, its context, the author and their background, the emerging themes, how we felt, and the questions the text raised. This loose structure enabled us to learn collaboratively. Being on the same page (sometimes quite literally), our reactions, questions, and discussions came out very organically. Our diverse positionalities brought out different sets of questions, insights, and other nuances which led to passionate, critical discussions. Issues we discussed ranged from defining feminism or other concepts from the texts, life, and contexts of the authors, to unpacking themes and issues from texts and their relevance in contemporary India and in our personal contexts. For instance, reading Savitribai Phule's poems in our second Women: Written, Unwritten session (captured in Figure 19.2 above) generated a discussion on the intersections of caste and gender and Savitribai Phule's central role in advocating for girls' education and how most of us had never heard of her. It also led to a discussion on the politics of invisibility of women's histories and contributions in Indian education and why it has increasingly become important to find alternative ways to make this knowledge accessible. So, while the texts themselves were the starting point for our discussions, they were often doorways into deeper reflections.

FemPositive encouraged me to rethink the ways in which we learn and share knowledge. The possibilities of teaching and learning outside formal classrooms, in collective learning spaces like feminist reading groups, or on social media platforms were exciting. FemPositive's collective learning space particularly, became a model for me when I started teaching in a classroom, first as a guest lecturer at a couple of institutions in Mumbai and later as a graduate teaching instructor at Bowling Green State University, which I joined in 2018 to pursue my doctoral studies. Especially because FemPositive had grown out of my learnings in a feminist classroom, and later the platform itself became another kind of learning space, I wanted to introduce an element of practical learning to my Introduction to Women's, Gender, and Sexuality Studies classroom.

Because of the way I had taken up parts of what I learnt in my certificate course around feminist ideas of education and access to build FemPositive, it was important to me that my students find something relatable in our course which they could put to use in their day-to-day lives. A lot of times we would be confronted with the question of "What does feminism have to do with me?" in our reading group sessions, and on our Facebook page where folks who did not identify as women or were not actively in the non-profit/women's studies spaces felt that feminisms and feminist theory were not meant for them or their discipline/profession. Untangling these questions helped me become more aware of how important it is to talk about the entrenched intersecting privileges and oppressions in every sphere of our lives, and thus the need for feminist thought and praxis in every space. These lessons especially became crucial when I entered the university classroom in the United States as a graduate instructor teaching diverse groups of students, many of whom had similar questions— what has feminism got to do with them, their lives, or the career they're pursuing? And how—if it all—can they use what they learn in our classroom in their lives?

FEMINIST CLASSROOMS: PUTTING THEORY INTO ACTION

Coming to the university classroom from a digital and community feminist organizational background, my approach to teaching was very much located within the discourse of connecting feminist education to action. The works of Savitribai Phule— India's first woman teacher and anti-caste leader whose work centered around education as a means to ending interlocking oppressions of caste and gender in India, and bell hooks, whose scholarship around education's radical transformative potential for liberation, continue to influence my scholarship, pedagogy and commitment to a feminist politics of allyship, social justice, and praxis. Savitribai's pioneering work in starting the first school for girls and children of marginalized castes in India in 1849 was a radical act of resisting caste and gender-based oppression, which was also reflected in her written works such as *Kavya Phule* (1854), a collection of poems in Marathi. One of her poems, translated to English titled "Rise, To Learn and Act," imbues this call to action for marginalized caste communities to educate themselves and break the shackles of caste oppression, "Awake, arise and educate, Smash traditions-liberate!" (Braj Ranjan Mani and Pamela Sardar, eds., *A Forgotten Liberator: The Life and Struggle of Savitribai Phule* (New Delhi: Mountain Peak, 2008), 66.). In *Teaching to Transgress: Education as the Practice of Freedom* (1994) hooks argues that education as the practice of freedom must enable a process of building bridges between theoretical knowledge and praxis. A critical feminist pedagogy engages both teachers and students in actively critiquing, and resisting intersectional systems of oppression to foster critical learning beyond hierarchical boundaries. These two scholars' works echo in my pedagogical practice, particularly in my conscious efforts to bridge theory and praxis in the classroom and outside it.

Being committed to the goals of making feminist scholarship accessible (and relatable!), I hoped to engage my students in thinking about how they could translate their learning experiences in the classroom into an accessible social justice "action" project in their fields of interest. While developing my syllabus for the Introduction to Women's, Gender, and Sexuality Studies course, I came across an assignment developed by an alumna of my program, Kate Schaab, called the feminist action project, which was aimed towards encouraging students to put their critical learning into practice by first, analyzing a number of existing feminist online/offline community activist projects around their chosen topic and then, coming up with their own creative "solution" in the form of an educational/awareness/knowledge sharing project. I adapted this assignment for my class with an added optional component of designing their action project as a social media campaign (I made this one of two options—the other being designing a workshop module—during the COVID-19 pandemic when our school year was completely online/remote).

FemPositive was, in many ways, my own long-term feminist action project, providing the perfect example to share with my students and to frame our thinking about this assignment in the classroom. While FemPositive was a way to put what I had learnt during my certificate course to action, it also quickly became a project to further engage in digital and offline collective learning. Feminist education and praxis were not neatly separate from one another but were intrinsically connected to each other. So, when I introduced the feminist action project to my classroom, I did not just imagine it being an exercise of implementing what they were learning, but as a co-constitutive process of learning through "doing." This project gave students the opportunity to deep dive into a specific area or topic in the course that resonated with them and build a more nuanced understanding of feminist theory and praxis in the process of developing their project.

I have taught this course for four semesters (fall 2019 to spring 2021) and had some interesting experiences in having my students develop their own feminist action projects. From developing feminist workshop modules, planning social media awareness campaigns, to creating websites and artworks, my students came up with creative ways to engage their feminist education outside the classroom, within the student and non-academic communities. The workshop module and social media campaign were the most popularly chosen by students. The workshop module meant developing a workshop outline on a feminist issue of one's choice. For example, one student had developed a comprehensive workshop module, including a complete PowerPoint presentation, around preventing domestic violence through education. Their target audience was students from pre-K to 12th grade, which they broke down into smaller groups. Their workshop plan included details of what they would teach each progressive grade of students starting from learning about one's own body, consent, and emotions, to introducing subjects of sexual violence in the higher grades in order to create awareness. Another student developed a plan for a STEM camp for young girls as well as coded and designed a mock website for it. Yet another student designed a comprehensive workshop module on busting the myth of the sex binary using the work of feminist biologists.

Because digital tools like social media are popularly used today for socializing as well as activism and organizing, I was particularly interested in how I could encourage students to think creatively about using these platforms for their projects. Especially during the pandemic when I was teaching online, I encouraged students to choose between developing a workshop module or a social media campaign. A student who had a personal YouTube vlog created an informative video discussing privilege and oppression. The idea was to translate these concepts into relatable language to inform their subscribers on feminist issues and concepts. One student who was interested in the possibilities of digital streaming in facilitating inclusive representation of queer folks focused their project on developing a potential queer character for a hypothetical Netflix show. Several students utilized Instagram's visual nature to design feminist awareness campaigns around topics like women leaders in American history, women in STEM and other fields, or issues like gender stereotyping and why it is harmful, or sexual harassment in various contexts. Here I would like to note that while during the course students had the option to either directly create a page and post a couple of sample posts on their chosen social media platforms or share a detailed plan along with proposed sample posts, invariably students removed the pages/posts after the end of the semester.

Reflections

In the semesters where I had my students work on a feminist action project, there were some students who chose to develop their campaigns using digital tools, and several others who chose to develop different offline, community-based campaigns and workshops. An underlying theme across the projects was the need to make feminist theories and histories, as well as contemporary issues and movements more broadly accessible, and apply their critical thinking skills to develop different models of engagement around feminist issues beyond the classroom and academia. The reflections I offer here draw from my experiences of working with my students during the course of developing their projects and the reflections they shared on their experience of developing such a project.

Firstly, because these introductory courses fulfill certain core requirements for various undergraduate programs, the classes usually have a mix of students from various programs and majors having a wide range of interests. Working on the feminist action project was a way for students to find a subject area within the course themes that intersected with their interests and engage in a more focused study of these intersections to develop their project. For many students this meant studying a variety of initiatives and projects utilizing different tools and strategies including digital media tools. This was a productive exercise in exploring the discourse and activism around a particular feminist issue in detail. To see students use a critical feminist and intersectional lens in looking at a topic/subject they are close to, was a fulfilling experience for me as an educator and also introduced me to different, exciting work taking place in US-based feminist movements. For instance, a student who developed a workshop module on building inclusive workplaces through a disability awareness training used a disability and feminist lens to visualize and address the issue of workplace inclusivity. Their central interest was in disability studies and special education and they spent time researching disability through a gender perspective which helped them deepen their understanding of inclusivity through an intersectional lens.

Secondly, an important part of this project was identifying particular feminist issues they were interested in and focusing on a particular aspect or knowledge gap which they want to bridge with their feminist action project. This, I truly believe, brought out some of the most creative ideas from students because it was an opportunity for them to ponder over some critical questions. This included questions around issues such as the lack of access to information around women's contributions to STEM fields, or the lack of comprehensive sexuality education in schools, or the invisibility of feminist histories and figures, among many other things. They were then encouraged to explore how they could use their skills and knowledge to do something about this? Who would their target audience/participants? How can they best present their chosen issues to them to educate or and perhaps inspire action? What happened in this step is that students were able to shift their thinking about our course materials from a theoretical standpoint as materials that we are simply studying with no context in our present lives, to actually seeing these concepts, histories, and issues play out around us and having an opportunity to contribute, even if only through a short class project, to these discourses. For example, one student was interested in exploring how they could use their privilege for building feminist allyship via their action project. A practical way they thought of doing this was to help make visible small businesses in their hometown through a social media campaign. As a feminist scholar passionate about and committed to connecting my scholarship and pedagogy with everyday praxis, an action-based project like this was very helpful to engage my students in connecting learning with action.

Finally, the completed projects my students turned in that addressed particular feminist issues and gaps through a specific "solution" they came up with, outlined and in several cases, developed actual mock plans for, were very well thought out and developed with care. The solutions looked very different for different students based on their strengths, interests, and imagination. While several students developed extended outlines or step-by-step plans of a workshop module or social media campaign around a topic, others actually submitted a draft of what their workshop presentation would look like. I have struggled with evaluating how much and how well my students have learnt in a course like this. How do you "measure" how well students have grasped the concepts and ideas you tried to work your way through with them? For me, the nuance, care, and reflexivity with which students developed their action projects provided a good indication of how well they had understood, were critically aware of, and tried to embody what we were learning in class in their specific contexts and positionalities. I specifically looked at the depth of their understanding of their chosen topic for their action project and by extension, their understanding of intersectional feminisms. I looked for these in the kinds of resources they chose for their workshop or how sensitive they were of their positionality in taking up a specific issue for their project or how nuanced their social media project was.

Learning With and From Students

An aspect of this process which I had not anticipated being helpful in the fall of 2019 when I first taught this course, was the possibility of students' action projects not only becoming examples for future cohorts to study, but also the potential of these projects becoming a repository of pedagogical resources developed by and for students. A few different students from my classes have guest lectured on and discussed their action projects and experiences with my subsequent classes. This was a chance to actually test out their action project solutions with their peers. The presenting students were very enthusiastic about sharing their work and candid reflections of doing this project retrospectively. The students listening in had the opportunity to ask questions to folks who had already been through this process. This exchange was important because at first, students tended to feel overwhelmed or lost about the idea of doing what seemed like a massive project, but which in reality, was to help them look at this course from an action-oriented perspective. In some other cases, I requested permission from students to share their action project as part of specific modules where I thought students could benefit from the resources put together by the previous cohort.

Challenges

While this entire process has been deeply fulfilling for me as a feminist and educator, there were certainly some limitations to what I imagined was a perfect, wonderful loop of critical learning, researching, knowledge sharing, resource/campaign building, and teaching. Several of my students who had used digital media tools like Instagram, Twitter, YouTube, and even built a website to develop their projects did not (or could not) preserve, archive, or continue these projects after completing the course for various reasons (which they aren't really required to do). So, this leaves the question of whether a project like this can inspire students to think about and pursue longer term online/offline community engaged feminist campaigns, to one's imagination. Despite these limitations and challenges, this assignment was a great way to help students think about our course materials and concepts in present context, draw connections between theory and their personal or collective experiences, and finally to build an understanding of how to develop and execute a social justice-oriented feminist project.

LOOKING AHEAD WITH HOPE

After several years, I continue to grapple with the same questions of access to feminist knowledge, but with a deeper focus on the potential and constraints of digital media platforms. Starting FemPositive was a way to put my education to practice with the goal of making feminist learning possible outside formal classroom spaces. It has been a small project, but reaching even twenty people in the span of six years has been a milestone for this project and for me. Similarly, with the feminist action projects of my students, even if they took small steps in making a plan, envisioning their workshop or campaign, or actually implemented it even if for a brief period, is a breakthrough for us.

As I begin yet another semester of teaching and working with my students to relate what we're learning to our contemporary socio-political conditions and prod their minds to think about what they can do in their own small ways through an action project, I continue to feel energized. Not just by the possibility of what might happen in this classroom, but by the hope of what kind of individuals all of them might go on to become and how what they learn here might translate into feminist praxis in their lives.

BIBLIOGRAPHY

"FemPositive." Facebook. Accessed July 14, 2022. https://www.facebook.com/fempositive.

hooks, bell. *Teaching to Transgress: Education as the Practice of Freedom.* New York: Routledge, 1994.

Mani, Braj Ranjan, and Pamela Sardar, eds. *A Forgotten Liberator: The Life and Struggle of Savitribai Phule.* New Delhi: Mountain Peak, 2008.

Mohanty, Chandra Talpade. "On Race and Voice: Challenges for Liberal Education in the 1990s." *Cultural Critique*, no. 14 (1989): 179–208. Accessed September 2, 2020. doi:10.2307/1354297.

CHAPTER TWENTY

RBG, PUBLIC PEDAGOGY,
AND ONLINE ACTIVISM

By Suzanne Leonard

SATURDAY, SEPTEMBER 19, 2020
It is with a heavy heart that I begin to write. Ruth Bader Ginsburg, the heretofore indomitable Supreme Court Justice, champion of the rights of women and other marginalized groups, died last night. I heard the news at 7:29 pm from a friend, about nine minutes after the announcement was made. And then, I spent hours on Facebook, Twitter, and text, posting expletives, crying, and commiserating with other despairing friends, acquaintances, colleagues, and strangers. I forgot to put my five-year-old daughter to bed. In the clear light of day, I have been feeling guilty for it all, for the anger, the neglect, the vitriol I feel towards Mitch McConnell and Donald Trump who immediately said they would replace her before 2021, and for the opening of, I admit, a second bottle of wine.[1] I am wondering how I can possibly write this article, which is already overdue, when frankly I feel so sad and hopeless.

And then it occurred to me—this article is actually about what happened on the night that RBG died. It's about how new media allows us to share emotions, create communities, and spur actions. My experience, I realize, was a profound expression of collective mourning amongst people who care deeply about social justice and human rights (And as I later learned, on the night Ginsberg passed, the word "fuck" trended widely on social media. *The Cut* ran a story that evening with the headline: "Women are Texting Each Other One Word.").[2] Unlike the multiple and sustained happenings in so many streets following the murder of George Floyd, and the protests that have continued as incidences of police brutality against people of color have continued to mount, there was something both acutely present and yet completely ephemeral about the evening of Ginsburg's death. Despite these differences, I would like to bring these various discourses under the umbrella of public feminism. As does the volume in which this essay appears, I refer to activities in streets, on phones, in classrooms, in print publications, and via social media. In spite of their differences in tone, character, and scale, all must be understood as works of intersectional public feminism.

MOVING FORWARD

The same day I began this article, I received a text from the Women's March, urging that supporters stage events to honor Ginsburg. When I clicked on the attached link, I was forwarded a set of instructions, explaining how to publicize, organize, and conduct a vigil. Armed with this outline, I enlisted my daughter to make a sign (she chose "fight, fight" as a slogan) and got to work. While created for this particular event, the Women's March roadmap I received is in fact highly replicable for other activist gatherings, insofar as it describes exactly how to publicize the event on social media, and included a selection of appropriate images. Describing the event, the write-up our local town newspaper noted in its opening sentence that residents were given less than eight hours' notice.[3] We had about thirty participants, mostly older women, some men, and at least two girls, brought there by their mothers. People spoke eloquently and from the heart about Ginsburg, detailing the countless ways in which she had inspired them or impacted their lives, and shared their fears for the future. Someone noted that, for years, people had been sending Ginsburg care packages, vitamins and healthy foods, just to keep her alive. We pledged that, like her, we would eat our kale.

For context, I live in a predominantly white, seaside town with a population of approximately 18,000, located less than ten miles outside of downtown Boston. We have a town square that is publicly available for gatherings, and I knew that we could likely come together there without needing permission or a permit. About a month prior, I helped organize a "read-in" in the same location to protest the gutting of services provided by our town library, and the

Figure 20.1: Signs reading "Fight, Fight" and "Now It's Our Turn" at the RGB vigil held in Metcalf Square in Winthrop, Massachusetts on September 19, 2020.

laying off of the majority of its staff during COVID-19. I knew some of our town council members, one of whom came to the vigil. I am fairly comfortable with public speaking, and I am also a white, middle-aged woman of some means. I have no doubt that my relative position of privilege in my town helped the event to gain some traction.

I am also, of course, no stranger to feminism in academia: I am the director of my university's Master's Program in Gender and Cultural Studies, am well versed in feminist scholarship, and publish widely in the field of feminist media studies. Particularly since the election of Donald Trump in 2016, my social media feeds, email accounts, professional and personal conversations have all served as conduits for conversations about we can *do* to combat blatant misogyny and racism. What I am relatively new to, however, is the burgeoning field of public feminism, which I have now come to believe is perhaps the most efficacious path to sustaining the movement's momentum. Although I did not exactly realize it at the time that I organized the vigil, a lecture that I attended on public feminisms, and a course that I subsequently taught in the wake of that lecture, moved me from the classroom to the streets, proverbially, and also literally. The rest of this essay will be about that process, detailing how a year ago I knew very little about what I now see as the future of feminism. As I will explore in this piece, I now try to embody the values of public feminism in my teaching, scholarship, and activism. The RBG vigil was hence both a culmination and also a beginning.

Ultimately, and as I will discuss, I conceptualized and instructed a two-credit, elective course in the spring semester of 2020 at Simmons University, titled "Public Feminisms, Online Activism, and Social Change." Much like the anecdotes I have shared, its genesis likewise came from a collective community; as a result, I would like to spend some time detailing how I came to teach this course and why. In November of 2019, I attended the annual National Women's Studies Association's conference in San Francisco in order to publicize Simmons' Gender and Cultural Studies Master's Program. I was there armed with flyers and buttons, trying to make connections and promote a revamped program, one that focused less on erudite theory and more on public praxis.

In that spirit, I attended a panel session titled "Writing for the Popular Press: A Workshop for Feminist Scholars." I realized later that the session was sponsored by *Ms.* magazine, intended to highlight their website and garner both readers and writers. Included on the panel were Janell Hobson, a regular contributor to *Ms.*, as well as Carrie Baker, one of this volume's editors. Presenters spoke about their experiences writing for *Ms.*, discussed how they birthed story ideas, and *Ms.* staffers circulated information about how we all could become more involved. As I sat in the audience, I wondered: was there a way of training students in these acts of popular feminist critique? As an English professor, I have long used op-eds as a way of teaching students how to efficiently and effectively make an argument. Given the fact that op-eds make for great pedagogy, why not assign one, on a favored feminist cause or observation, to my undergraduates?

As this question germinated, I also saw multiple panels at the NWSA which underlined the importance of public feminism. Perhaps none as fun and lively, however, as the one featuring the founders of the Crunk Feminist Collective, a collection dedicated to creating spaces "of support and camaraderie for hip hop generation feminists of color, queer and straight, in the academy and without."[4] In that room were some of the progenitors of what we might call the "new" mediatized feminism, the kind that relies on internet technologies to spread its words, images, and insights. Theirs was a sort of feminized criticism that intersected with popular culture, and did so from a slightly more academic standpoint than its more corporate corollaries, say, *Jezebel*, *Refinery 29*, *Autostraddle*, or *Bitch*. And while the wave framing of feminism is not necessarily a metaphor I espouse, it is worth mentioning that for many the "fourth" wave of feminism is distinguished by its relationship to social media and other online platforms.[5] At the conference, I also scrambled to keep track of what seemed to me an exciting outpouring of new books on the relationships between new media (particularly Twitter) and social justice. There was particular enthusiasm about Keith P. Feldman and Abigail De Kosnik's edited collection, *#identity: Hashtagging Race, Gender, Nation, and Sexuality* and also *#HashtagActivism: Networks of Race and Gender Justice*.[6]

As I sat in the conference's Friday plenary session on "Laboring and the Politics of Re/Production," I also received a fortuitous email from my department chair, offering the opportunity to teach a two-credit course on a topic of my choosing (in lieu of a course of mine that was currently under enrolled). I quickly wrote the following course description for "Public Feminism, Online Activism, and Social Change":

> The goals of this seminar are twofold. Firstly, students will be introduced to the flourishing world of public feminism, in the form of intersectional feminist publications (Crunk Feminist Media Collective, *Teen Vogue*, *Ms.* online, *Signs* Feminist Intellectuals Project, *Scholar & Feminist Online*, *Refinery29*, *Teen Vogue*, Bitch. com) as well as activist campaigns such as #SayHerName, #BeenRapedNeverReported, #SolidarityIsForWhiteWomen, #ThighHighPolitics, #NoMeCuidanMeViolan, #TransIsBeautiful, #CelebrateMySize, etc. Second, the course will lead students to a demonstrable outcome, in the form of writing or producing a work of online activism that can be submitted for wider dissemination. Instruction will be given on how to write public-facing blogs, op-eds, and comment pieces in ways that are succinct and rhetorically effective.

From this description, I developed a course that I was fortunate enough to teach in person until mid-March 2020, and online for the rest of the semester. For the remainder of this article, I will summarize what I saw as the main "clusters" I developed for the course, listing readings, assignments, and desired outcomes. I should say, however, that in some cases each cluster could be a class of its own. I will then offer some advice and tips for readers hoping to organize their own courses on this subject.

CLUSTER #1: ACTIVISM AT YOUR COLLEGE/UNIVERSITY

This cluster is meant to help students position themselves as agents of change in their own communities, and to recognize the unique opportunities and challenges in their surroundings. Allison Dahl Crossley's book *Finding Feminism: Millennial Activists and the Unfinished Gender Revolution* (which I discovered at the NWSA book exhibit) profiles undergraduate students at four colleges and universities, and presents a sociological study of how they found pathways for agitation and alteration.[7] Additionally, the unit includes an article on Emma González, the high school student who became an icon for gun control rights following the mass shooting at Marjory Stoneman Douglas High School in Parkland, FL.[8] By profiling activists that are roughly the same age as my students, I endeavored to have them assess and critique their own experiences, specifically in order to locate potential avenues for action in their local communities.

Assignment: Write a four to five page "letter" to Dahl, explaining how your experiences as students and activists compare to those she documents. Do you relate to the subjects, actions taken, or attitudes expressed by her subjects? (Feel free to quote Dahl or her subjects in your response.) Relatedly, how does the campus climate at your college or university compare to the ones she documents? What are the areas on your campus where you would like to see change?

Instructor Tip: I found it useful to start with this sort of local assignment, where students conceptualized their own communities as spaces where they could be effective change agents. This assignment immediately positioned them as actors, and asked them to imagine the ways they might intervene.

CLUSTER #2: FEMINIST WRITING MODELS AND STRATEGIES

After seeing the Crunk Feminist Collective present at NWSA, and modeling my course so much after Crunk's formats, it seemed imperative that students also study their groundbreaking style and scholarship. Because my goal was to introduce my students to pithy but effective pieces of writing—rather than do a deep dive into a selected topic area—I asked students to read widely in the collected volume of Crunk essays.

Read: Come to class having read any ten essays from the *The Crunk Feminist Collection* (They are short!).[9] Pick at least one that includes a list as a way to express its main ideas. Bring your books to class so we can read more essays together.

In Class Activity: Diagram and discuss two representative entries from *The Crunk Feminist Collection*. Practice writing fabulous first lines.

Instructor Tip: Make sure to devote appropriate class time to this assignment. I asked students to examine two representative articles. For each, they reproduced the opening line; offered a brief summary of the argument; listed the examples used; noted particularly effective turns of phrases; and shared the article's "useful takeaways". We mapped these components out on the board so that they could understand the mechanics of argument construction. This was an extremely useful exercise but it was not fast.

CLUSTER #3: CASE STUDY OF TWITTER AS FEMINIST PRAXIS IN CASES OF SEXUAL VIOLENCE

The work of the class was focused in part on how social media—and Twitter in particular—has been used in order to foment change. I have edited the reading list to reflect how I would teach the course if I were to instruct it again, focusing specifically on

Twitter and sexual violence. I did not have this framing device when I first taught the course, and believe the unit could have used more coherence, which I have imposed here.

Read: "Introduction: Digital Feminist Interventions" and "Twitter as a Pedagogical Platform" by Kaitlynn Mendes, Jessalynn Keller, Jessica Ringrose, from *Digital Feminist Activism: Women and Girls Fight Back Against Rape Culture*;[10] "#MeToo and the Politics of Collective Healing: Emotional Connection as Contestation" by Jacquelyn Arcy and Allison Page;[11] and "#WhyIStayed: Virtual Survivor-Centered Spaces for Transformation and Abolishing Partner Violence" by Julia Havard.[12]

Assignment and In Class Activity: Pick a hashtag that has been personally impactful to you or your communities. Explain what the hashtag is designed to convey, show examples using visuals, and describe how it has influenced public conversations.[13]

Instructor Tip: Interactivity is crucial for this lesson, especially as Twitter is such a moving target. I was fortunate to be able to host Brooke Foucault Welles (co-author of *#HashtagActivism: Networks of Race and Gender Justice*) in person and Jessalynn Keller via Skype for this conversation, both of whom have done extensive research on Twitter. Student presentations were also an excellent way to share knowledge and content.

CLUSTER #4: RESEARCHING FEMINIST WEBSITES

Having students research feminist websites was a means to tee up the final writing assignment, and so that students became fluent in the tone and positionalities of their chosen media outlet. More important than what site they picked to investigate was the extent to which they could describe, and hopefully sync with, its communicative strategies.

Assignment: Pick a site like *Bitch, Gal-Dem, Jezebel, Ms. Online, Autostraddle, Teen Vogue*, etc., and read at least five representative articles that attempt to do feminist work. Try to discern patterns in tone, topic, and structure. After this exercise, write a four-to-five-page response that describes not only the articles' content but also their commonalities. What sorts of interventions does this site value? In your response, please indicate ideas that you would like to work up for possible submission to this site.

Instructor Tip: This is a crucial assignment to include before students attempt to write their own pieces.

CLUSTER #5: WRITING YOUR PIECES AND SHARING THEM PUBLICLY

A publishable, polished piece of writing was meant to be the culminating assignment for the course. After consultation with me, students drafted and then revised their publications for submission. We also planned to present student writings in a public forum.

Assignment: Fill out the op-ed worksheet, detailing your selected publication and intended intervention (*Added as an appendix*).

Instructor Tip: Students often require coaching on how to refine a topic so that it works as a short-format piece. They also need to be encouraged to write what they know, as students who did produced the most successful pieces. Perhaps the most important question I asked on the op-ed worksheet was: Why are you the best person to write on this topic?

FINAL REFLECTIONS

Obviously, the interruption of COVID-19 posed unexpected challenges for this class. However, I was interested to see how many of my students pivoted in terms of their topic choices once in-person classes ceased. I received two quite excellent pieces that focused on systematic injustices that predated the pandemic but were exacerbated by it: "Zoombombing Should Come as No Surprise" and "The Scope of Racial Violence During the Pandemic Extends Beyond Asian-Americans: How a Facebook Group Showed Me Some Ugly Realities About My Own Community." One of my students did, in fact, succeed in having her essay published: "My Journey through Bi-Racial, Bi-Cultural Feminism," was written by a student from Taiwan and posted on an English-language website in May of 2020.[14] Less important than their publication success, however, was the idea that the course helped my students to hone their views and communicate them in effective, succinct, and relatable ways.

Admittedly, as an English professor, I prioritized—and trained my students on—effective written communication. A specialist in a different discipline might choose to teach a course on public feminisms differently. For example, a data scientist might help students to map clusters of ideas to think about how they take hold.[15] A sociologist or political scientist specializing in movement organizing might study how The Women's March—as an event, ideology, and/or organization—has shifted and progressed, particularly in the wake of initial criticism about its racial exclusivity. A communications specialist might interrogate how public protests such as those surrounding the deaths of George Floyd, Breonna Taylor, and Ahmaud Arbery are depicted in the popular press. And so on.

Participating in public engagement and teaching public feminisms are activities that have provided me stability mentally, intellectually, and emotionally in difficult times. Indeed, current political and juridical realities—and the many battles we face with a divided Senate and a stacked Supreme Court— call for this kind of involvement, in the sense that scholars have a duty to intervene in public discourse and to bring their knowledge and skills to bear on public conversations. One of the many privileges of my work as a professor is that I see my opportunities for outreach as manifold, both helping students to write and speak about topics they are passionate about, and in ways that are rhetorically effective, and also by doing this work myself. Failing to use, and share, such knowledge risks not just American democracy, but also, frankly, life on the planet. The invocation alluded to in my course title—Public Feminism, Online Activism, and Social Change—has become a touchstone for me both personally and professionally. I hope that in sharing my newfound skills and practices, and the ways I have tried to translate them to my students, you might feel just a bit more stable, too.

NOTES

1. That promise was indeed brought to fruition with the rushed confirmation of Amy Coney Barrett to the Supreme Court, a mere eight days before the 2020 presidential election. As a member of the court's conservative supermajority, she played a significant role in the Dobbs decision of 2022, which overturned Roe vs. Wade.
2. The Cut, "Women are Texting One Another One Word," *The Cut*, September 18, 2020, https://www.thecut.com/article/ruth-bader-ginsburg-dies-women-respond-with-common-text.html.
3. Kate Anslinger, "Residents Show Up to Honor RBG," *Winthrop Transcript*, September 24, 2020, https://winthroptranscript.com/2020/09/24/residents-show-up-to-honor-rbg.
4. Crunk Feminist Collective, https://www.crunkfeministcollective.com/about/.
5. For a discussion of the wave formulation of feminism, see Linda Nicholson, "Feminism in Waves: Useful Metaphor or Not?," *New Politics* 12, no. 4 (2010), https://newpol.org/issue_post/feminism-waves-useful-metaphor-or-not/.
6. Keith P. Feldman and Abigail De Kosnik, eds., *#identity: Hashtagging Race, Gender, Nation, and Sexuality* (Ann Arbor, MI: University of Michigan Press, 2019); Sarah J. Jackson, Moya Bailey, and Brooke Foucault Welles, *#HashtagActivism: Networks of Race and Gender Justice* (Cambridge, MA: MIT Press, 2020).

7. Alison Dahl Crossley, *Finding Feminism: Millennial Activists and the Unfinished Gender Revolution* (New York: New York University Press, 2017).
8. Emily Bent, "This Is Not Another Girl-Power Story: Reading Emma González as a Public Feminist Intellectual," *Signs* 45, no. 4 (2020): 795–816.
9. Brittany Cooper, Susana Moore, and Robyn Boylorn, eds., *The Crunk Feminist Collection* (New York: Feminist Press, 2017).
10. Kaitlynn Mendes, Jessalynn Keller, and Jessica Ringrose, *Digital Feminist Activism: Women and Girls Fight Back Against Rape Culture* (Oxford: Oxford University Press, 2019).
11. Jacquelyn Arcy and Allison Page, "#MeToo and the Politics of Collective Healing: Emotional Connection as Contestation," *Communication, Culture, and Critique* 13, no. 3 (2020): 333–348.
12. Julia Havard, "#WhyIStayed: Virtual Survivor-Centered Spaces for Transformation and Abolishing Partner Violence," in *#identity: Hashtagging Race, Gender, Nation, and Sexuality*, eds. Keith P. Feldman and Abigail De Kosnik (Ann Arbor, MI: University of Michigan Press, 2019), 137–151.
13. For a descriptive write-up of what she calls hashtag syllabi, "bricolage iterations of reading lists created by or circulated among educators on Twitter," see Meredith D. Clark, "Remaking the #Syllabus: Crowdsourcing Resistance Praxis as Critical Public Pedagogy," *Communication, Culture, and Critique* 3 (2020): 222–241.
14. Katrina Yang Farrell, "My Journey Through Bi-Racial, Bi-Cultural Feminism," *CommonWealth Magazine*, May 19, 2020, https://english.cw.com.tw/article/article.action?id=2717.
15. See especially Catherine D'Ignazio and Lauren F. Klein, *Data Feminism* (Cambridge, MA: MIT Press, 2020).

WORKS CITED

Anslinger, Kate. "Residents Show Up to Honor RBG." *Winthrop Transcript*, September 24, 2020. https://winthroptranscript.com/2020/09/24/residents-show-up-to-honor-rbg.

Arcy, Jacquelyn and Allison Page. "#MeToo and the Politics of Collective Healing: Emotional Connection as Contestation." *Communication, Culture, and Critique* 13, no. 3 (2020): 333–348.

Bent, Emily. "This Is Not Another Girl-Power Story: Reading Emma González as a Public Feminist Intellectual." *Signs* 45, no. 4 (2020): 795–816.

Clark, Meredith D. "Remaking the #Syllabus: Crowdsourcing Resistance Praxis as Critical Public Pedagogy." *Communication, Culture, and Critique* 13, no. 2 (2020): 222–241.

Crossley, Alison Dahl. *Finding Feminism: Millennial Activists and the Unfinished Gender Revolution*. New York: New York University Press, 2017.
Cooper, Brittney, Susana Moore, and Robyn Boylorn, eds. *The Crunk Feminist Collection*. New York: Feminist Press, 2017.
Crunk Feminist Collective. https://www.crunkfeministcollective.com/.
D'Ignazio, Catherine and Lauren F. Klein. *Data Feminism*. Cambridge, MA: MIT Press, 2020.
Feldman, Keith P. and Abigail De Kosnik, eds. *#identity: Hashtagging Race, Gender, Nation, and Sexuality*. Ann Arbor, MI: University of Michigan Press, 2019.
Havard, Julia. "#WhyIStayed: Virtual Survivor-Centered Spaces for Transformation and Abolishing Partner Violence." In *#identity: Hashtagging Race, Gender, Nation, and Sexuality*, edited by Keith P. Feldman and Abigail De Kosnik, 137–151. Ann Arbor, MI: University of Michigan Press, 2019.
Jackson, Sarah J., Moya Bailey, and Brooke Foucault Welles. *#HashtagActivism: Networks of Race and Gender Justice*. Cambridge, MA: MIT Press, 2020.
Mendes, Kaitlynn, Jessalynn Keller, and Jessica Ringrose. *Digital Feminist Activism: Women and Girls Fight Back Against Rape Culture*. Oxford: Oxford University Press, 2019.
Nicholson, Linda. "Feminism in Waves: Useful Metaphor or Not?" *New Politics* 12, no. 4 (2010). https://newpol.org/issue_post/feminism-waves-useful-metaphor-or-not/.
The Cut. "Women Are Texting One Another One Word." *The Cut*, September 18, 2020. https://www.thecut.com/article/ruth-bader-ginsburg-dies-women-respond-with-common-text.html.
Yang Farrell, Catrina. "My Journey Through Bi-Racial, Bi-Cultural Feminism." *CommonWealth Magazine*, May 19, 2020. https://english.cw.com.tw/article/article.action?id=2717.

APPENDIX 1 PUBLIC FEMINISMS
Worksheet / Op-Ed Outline

Proposed Publication:
Ideal Word Count (based on the publications' specifications):
Proposed Title:
Tagline (If any):
First Sentence (Remember to make this catchy!):
Three Sentence Abstract: What are the main takeaways of your intervention?
Why are you the best person to write on this topic?
What additional reading/resources/interviews you will need to embark upon before you can start writing?

CHAPTER TWENTY-ONE

THERE IS NO JUST FUTURE WITHOUT INTERSECTIONAL SUSTAINABILITY
Feminist Pedagogy for Tackling Privilege and Centering Praxis in Sustainability Education

By Michelle Larkins

Sustainability can be a complicated subject to teach in higher education. A sense of urgency accompanies this curriculum as we face interconnected challenges of climate change, food insecurity, poverty, and public health. Other difficulties stem from the breadth of everyday issues sustainability can be applied to, and confusion over exactly what sustainability means, as a framework and set of practices. This ubiquity is a result of the widespread interest in sustainability and subsequent variations on the theme through which scholars, institutions, governments, and market actors differentiate themselves. Sensemaking in the classroom is made more complex by the technical jargon and bureaucracy that comes along with the practice of sustainable development. And herein lies another conundrum—sustainability and sustainable development have become interchangeable terms—whereas, originally the latter was a strategic economic pathway to achieving the former. My own thinking is guided by the idea of just sustainabilities, "The need to ensure a better quality of life for all, now and into the future, in a just and equitable manner, whilst living within the limits of supporting ecosystems."[1] I am drawn to this definition (and its practice) from my position as a feminist scholar who explores connections between environmental justice and sustainability—sustainability must connect to social justice and equity, must recognize the diversity and plurality of needs and livelihoods, and must pursue these outcomes for all human communities and ecosystems. Why spend time worrying about definitions? Because definitions are an act of boundary-making,[2] that can serve to limit or include individuals or communities, and guide policy and decision-making across scales of governance. In this way, we can understand that whosoever defines the scope of the problem, also defines the scope of available solutions.[3] If the unmet needs or experiences of your community are not recognized as part of the sustainability problem set, it is less likely that measures to address those inequities will be offered as sustainability solutions.

I am fortunate to work with intelligent young people every day, and in many of our initial conversations they've shared with me that they never knew that sustainability "cared" about social justice, or that sustainable solutions must account for differing community experiences that intersect with race, gender, and class identities. My students have the privilege of education, and hopefully will leave their university experience with the understanding that sustainability cannot be divorced from equity or justice, just as it cannot be divorced from concepts of ecological limits. However, as a feminist educator I am committed not only to work with my students, but in community engagement (a two-way flow of learning and benefit) on sustainability issues and solutions. Taking this approach, sustainability needs to be practiced in an inclusive manner that encourages authentic participation and change. Together, as a learning community, my students and the partners we work with are interested in what is said, and therefore unsaid, about what sustainability is. What is sustainable; for whom, why, and how? And, whose livelihoods, landscapes, and communities are to be recognized, valued, and sustained?

Within this essay, I draw upon two recent professional experiences to discuss why limited definitions of sustainability can be harmful, and why intersectional approaches—approaches that recognize the structures of power and their reinforcement, the multiple and interconnecting identities of stakeholders, and that sustainable solutions are embedded in local contexts—to sustainability are needed in our learning communities to foster meaningful engagement and just transformations. First, I reflect on my service as the lead faculty member of an interdisciplinary team that drafted new university-wide learning outcomes in sustainability for all undergraduates. Second, I discuss the design of two new courses for the Applied Sustainability major at Pacific University, *Community Engaged Research,* and *Gender and the Environment.* To ground this discussion, I first offer a brief background on the field of sustainability, and its emergence in higher education.

SUSTAINABILITY AS A FIELD

Conceptually, sustainability began to emerge in earnest in English language academic works in the decades of the 1970s and 1980s. Greater international political attention was garnered with the publication of the United Nations commissioned Brundtland Report in 1987, from where the oft cited, "development which meets the needs of current generations without compromising the ability of future generations to meet their own needs" originates.[4] Following this milestone, these frameworks chart a parallel course, and there is a rich literature tracing sustainability/sustainable development as a scientific and governance approach—albeit mostly from a US/European perspective.[5] Beginning in the 1990s, the pedagogical practices of Education for Sustainability (EfS) and Education for Sustainable Development (ESD) were introduced.[6] Both of these frameworks highlight experiential learning, the importance of cultural context and local knowledge, and a need for reflexivity in learners.[7] Later work examines the application of coupled human and natural systems[8]—the idea of interactions and co-evolution between human communities and ecosystems— to sustainability teaching; other scholars advocate for more of an emphasis on civic participation and engagement[9] to balance technoscientific approaches. Critical approaches to sustainability, that emphasize the need for reconnection to the practices of environmental and social justice, and that delineate between Western[10] and Indigenous knowledge traditions, are increasing in number. This has resulted in an evolving specialization of academic fields, such as sustainable design, agriculture, energy, and engineering, to name just a few. To this last point, the Association for the Advancement of Sustainability in Higher Education (AASHE) found 421 undergraduate programs with a focus in sustainability in their most recent census.[11]

Internationally, the Sustainable Development Goals—a seventeen-item charter for achieving global sustainability by 2030—were adopted by world leaders at a United Nations Summit in September, 2015. The metrics and indicators within these goals are broadly represented on the websites of non-governmental organizations, think tanks, and some multinational corporations; the SDGs (as they are abbreviated by many practitioners) are arguably the most comprehensive and ambitious international development schema to date, covering broad issues such as water quality and access, climate change, food insecurity, and community resilience. As an example of their technical specificity, Goal One, to end poverty everywhere in all its forms, has seven targets, twelve indicators, forty-eight publications, and 804actions. More jargon comes in the form of the "5 Ps" framework to which the SDGS align; people, planet, prosperity, peace, and partnerships; this framework is explained in sub-documents, but not on the main landing page.[12]

At the point of student experience, these expert articulations and distinctions have been slower to permeate. To be clear, I have no expectation that a typical undergraduate student would be well versed in these theories. However, most have formed an opinion of what the term means before arriving at college. When students enter my classroom, they may have a general recognition of the representation of sustainability as a Venn diagram connecting the social, ecological, and economic spheres. Most often their greatest familiarity is with environmentally friendly activities—composting, recycling, plastics reduction—less so with anything collective. These perceptions could be attributed to the fact that the widespread interest in sustainability I mention above is not limited to academics and policy-makers. Distinct from the SDGs, across the United States sustainability has become increasingly mainstream, perhaps even a buzzword. Another definition here is important, Merriam Webster describes a buzzword as, "an important-sounding usually technical word or phrase often of little meaning used chiefly to impress laymen." Corporations have sustainability pledges, clothing brands and durable goods manufacturers present eco-conscious options for a price, and restaurants and grocery stories present food choices alongside sustainability adjacent labels of "local, farm to table, fair trade, ethically sourced, or organic." Amongst these platforms exist myriad interpretations (sometimes even co-optations) of sustainability; variations of ideological orientations, intentions, and scale. In short, everyday experiences have exposed my students to the fashion of sustainability, but not the function. Problematically, in many of these instances, sustainability has become a performance of consumer choice and socioeconomic privilege. Like the faulty logic of *voting with your fork*[13] that can be found in some food advocacy projects (if you buy local, organic tomatoes, more local, organic tomatoes will be sold and sustainable agriculture will prosper) consumptive sustainability reserves access for the highest socioeconomic classes, popularizes solutions or trends that reflect only the needs of these classes, reduces the potential for other groups to participate in the benefits or design of sustainability (e.g. wellbeing or healthy communities), and can be used to prop up prejudiced statements that suggest lower socioeconomic groups do not care about sustainability.

As a feminist educator, exploring these connections to socioeconomic class with my students is important. Earned criticisms of mainstream feminist and gender rights movement platforms highlight how the concerns of only certain social classes were visible, and thus, the fight for "progress" and "equality" were only for select groups of women. In order to become transformative and just, feminism(s) and sustainability(ies)—and their intersections—must disrupt class privilege, acknowledging how socioecological and socioeconomic inequities are reproduced and upheld when multiple standpoints are not included. When I refer to the complexity of teaching sustainability, it is in the twin efforts of helping students to wade through the politicking and jargon of sustainability as theory/sustainability as governance, and to undo commodified exposures to sustainability. And this is of central concern in this essay—what are the ways in which we can disrupt the norm that sustainability is an option only for privileged communities and identities, and how can we re-center collective praxis. Challenging these privileged narratives of sustainability in and beyond our classrooms is a practice of feminist activism, because in doing so, we make space for counter narratives— experiences and strategies that enable new possibilities for inclusive human community.[14] Representative sustainability can be radical, especially when the focus shifts from accumulating knowledge, to sharing and practicing knowledge where we live, work, and play.

Eric Neumayer wrote on the concept of weak versus strong sustainability,[15] exposing the dangerous logic in the former, where technological innovation and modernization could offset the decline in natural resources, without having to reduce overall consumption. Strong sustainability by contrast recognizes the intrinsic values of ecosystem services, biodiversity, and the wellbeing of human and biological communities that can be borne only of natural resources (instead of manufactured substitutes). It is an obvious bias, but I believe that we all need a practical understanding of sustainability in order to move toward a just future, and to begin carrying out those principles in the present. To borrow Neumayer's convention, we need to practice sustainability in its strongest form. However, I would argue that what constitutes "strong" must be about much more than economic theorems.

Earlier, I introduced Julian Agyeman's concept of just sustainabilities, developed with Robert Bullard and Bob Evans; critical because it recognizes that sustainability is not a one size fits all approach. Rather, sustainability is embedded in specific places, cultures, and contexts. If we are to practice strong sustainability in this sense, as educators and members of our own communities we need to recognize the plurality of sustainable solutions. My ideas about sustainability, and the energy I bring to my classes are also informed by my position as a feminist scholar who uses the theory and practice of intersectionality. Intersectional approaches build upon the collective experiences of women of color in the Civil Rights Movement, and the later legal theories of Kimberle Crenshaw,[16] and writings of Black womanist scholar Patricia Hill Collins.[17] Together these scholars articulated the unique standpoints of Black women; outlining distinct experiences and oppression in the criminal justice system that were beyond gender, and the erasure of Black women's experiences and accomplishments in mainstream feminist and gender studies. Central to this framework is the recognition of lived realities as knowledge (moving beyond just theory); it has become a pathway to understand that oppressive practices intersect with race, gender, class, and other identities that are marginalized by the ruling class to produce distinct experiences of injustice, and that these same complex identities inform what justice (or sustainability) looks like. Intersectionality also acknowledges the complexity and the structural significance of interactions between institutions of power and marginalized identities, and demands that we take action on these ideas, not just write about them. To embody a strong plural sustainability, we need a way to recognize that we are not all starting at the same place and that the impacts of unsustainable practices have been disproportionately borne. We also need to examine how some social groups are or are not able to engage around issues of sustainability because of race, class, gender, and geographic privilege, and challenge representations of sustainability that reinforce individualist, market centric, and technoscientific positions—positions that advance Western ways of knowing and undermine the sociality of sustainability. We can't forget that there are political projects guiding how knowledge is produced and shared, and that universalist notions of science and feminism have shaped which narratives are recognized. To practice intersectionality as an educator requires a commitment to making knowledge public and comprehensible, creating space to learn and share multiple ways of knowing, and to engage with communities in sustainability actions.

I want to now turn to a discussion of how this type of a strong sustainability approach can be translated to student experience inside and outside the classroom, based on my own work at Pacific University.

COMING TO PACIFIC

Pacific University is a small liberal arts college near Portland, Oregon, with approximately 1800 undergraduate students, and 2100 graduate students. We are a minority serving institution, where 25% of our students are first generation (the first in their families to attend college), and the incoming undergraduate class in Fall 2021 was comprised of close to 30% transfer students from local community colleges. I was hired at Pacific University at the beginning of the 2017/2018 academic year to direct their co-curricular sustainability center, a position which included developing and teaching courses for a nascent sustainability major, creating student programming, and strengthening community relationships. Early in 2018, the faculty voted to require two credits of sustainability designated coursework for all undergraduates. This would involve drafting a statement of purpose, as well as student learning outcomes (statements that describe the knowledge, skills, and abilities a student will gain after successful completion of a course) that faculty across social science, arts and humanities, and natural science disciplines would need to include in their individual courses for the class to be certified as meeting the Pacific sustainability standard. It was exciting to lead this team; however, this effort could only succeed if the other teaching faculty embraced our work. We started by asking: where were our blind-spots, who were our faculty champions across campus who would want to teach these new/revised courses, and what was the current sustainability narrative on Pacific's campus?

Before this undertaking, I had just finished a collaborative project[18] that examined the framing of sustainability in US colleges through major textbooks and readers. It was premised on the fact that most faculty, even those of us trained in interdisciplinary departments, may feel more comfort in one or two pillars of sustainability (i.e., ecological, social, economic) and thus educators who are teaching introductory courses that favor breadth over depth, may draw heavily upon textbooks and readers. As I mentioned previously, more and more colleges are adding sustainability curriculum. For some, an introductory course will be their sole exposure to sustainability content, and we know that next to the instructor, assigned texts carry authority for most college students.[19] What we found was scant attention to engagement and theories of social action, with little to no recognition of the politics of difference—crucial for understanding how social privilege and disadvantage structure opportunities for some while closing the window of engagement for others.[20] Thus, in moving forward with a universal requirement for undergraduate sustainability coursework that would be taught by dozens of faculty, I was keen on making sure that Pacific's standard would recognize equity and inclusion, and avoid the technoscientific/sustainable development positions discussed earlier.

In conversations with fellow educators at my university, there were competing concerns that sustainability as a concept is too vague, ubiquitous, and conversely not inclusive enough. Many shared a frustration over the lack of clarity. It was both that the inter/trans-disciplinary nature of sustainability can be especially arduous to grapple with; and that ecocentric and technocratic representations of sustainability abound, drawing close comparison to the failure of the mainstream environmental field to recognize the contributions and needs of communities of color, low socioeconomic status, women, Indigenous communities, and members of other marginalized identities. This last concern was compounded by the fact that the majority of faculty and courses that were slated for consideration for the sustainability designation were housed in the environmental sciences department. One of the most pervasive narratives on our campus was that sustainability teaching and learning was the purview of the natural science fields, and that connections between sustainability and social justice/civic engagement were not well emphasized. Through faculty development workshops we posed a new question, "How does our sustainability teaching dismantle or reinforce privilege on our campus?" to be able to move away from representations of sustainability as something that succeeds or fails based on consumer actions. In addition to sharing the ideas of other sustainability scholars, faculty worked through environmental privilege exercises, understanding how representing sustainability as "environmental sustainability" disenfranchised some students. This process culminated in our faculty adopting a statement grounded in just sustainabilities, and a set of learning outcomes that included students engaging with sustainability as practice, not just theory. In the 2020/2021 academic year, Pacific had over forty-five courses (inside and outside of the environmental sciences) that had been created or revised to meet these standards, and our student body was being exposed to a sustainability that is plural, equitable, and transdisciplinary.

Pacific's Sustainability Statement and Student Learning Outcomes

Sustainability is a conceptual framework and set of practices that recognize the complexity, embeddedness, and interconnections between ecological integrity, social equity, and economic vitality; and actively works toward ethical, transdisciplinary solutions across local and global scales that advance the wellbeing of people and places now and in the future.

Upon completion of this requirement students will be able to:

- Evaluate sustainability issues and solutions using an approach that focuses on the intersections between complex human and natural systems.
- Describe the three aspects of sustainability (environmental, economic, and social) and give examples of how at least two of the three are interrelated.
- Articulate how sustainability relates to their lives as community members, workers, and individuals and how their actions impact sustainability.

RE-CENTERING PRAXIS IN THE CLASSROOM AND THE COMMUNITY

The Applied Sustainability major had been in existence for two years when I joined Pacific, and it was (and still is) housed in the Environmental Science Department. One of my duties at Pacific was to design four new courses to complement current offerings and faculty specializations. To advance a strong and intersectional sustainability for students in this major, I designed two new courses; the first focused on research methodology, and the second on gender and the environment. In both of these classes, my goal was to encourage students to collapse barriers between the university and community members in our region.

Community Engaged Research

All students at Pacific are required to complete a senior research thesis. Given our applied focus, it was critical that our program expose students to community engaged research methods. Not only do they need to understand the ethical principles of engagement, but we need to create distance from approaches where research is performed "on" communities. Within our program, students learn how to move through a collaborative design process wherein questions and aims are co-constructed. The overarching goal of this course is to increase the applicability of research findings to community well-being. Research design in these projects, which are location or case-specific, place significance on local ways of knowing. Community guests help to animate this course, by sharing their previous experience working with research teams, and articulating how an engaged approach creates meaning for them personally and/or their constituents. I also share my own experiences as a graduate student and faculty member who practices this approach. For example, I talk with them about how I volunteered in a community organization for a year to build rapport, before I as an outsider could begin to work with community members to think about how to increase safe access for new Latinx migrants and monolingual Spanish speakers to food and environmental resources. Engagement takes time and trust. Above all, and from the position of teaching our sustainability courses informed by feminist pedagogy, I discussed the importance of cross-cultural engagement, shared instances where I had to exercise deep reflection on my position/privilege, and consider how this has been paramount to effectively communicating needs to improve outcomes.

A collective victory is the ways in which students are now framing their senior research projects as work *with* community, and in their efforts to create significant artifacts that community partners wish to receive and that authentically support their work. For example, a student project from 2020 included creation of a concept note and materials for grant applications to establish a food literacy and year-round market space in our community, following the loss of a local CSA (community supported agriculture) operator that aggregated produce from small Latinx owned farms in our region. In partnership with a local food justice organization (FJO), and under the auspices of my class, the student crafted a case study to argue for why our small town needed an affordable market that supported local farmers and provided access to nutritious foods in our community (our town has the second highest poverty rate in the county), and their research included identifying which tracts in our town could qualify as opportunity zones—information which has helped the FJO apply for economic development funds and technical assistance grants. Before graduating, the student was able to participate in interviews for grant selection, and help to design inclusive neighborhood input sessions (in English and Spanish). Another student worked with local government to render designs and an energy analysis for a village of tiny eco-houses to meet the needs of some of our houseless population. Given the success of this course, a new learning outcome for the major has been added:

- Understand and apply principles of community engagement in accordance with disciplinary standards, to develop equitable interventions for sustainability issues, and communicate these solutions to diverse audiences through culturally appropriate modes.

Gender and the Environment

The purpose of this course is to expose students to how the environment and the impact of unsustainable practices are differentially constructed and experienced, through a lens of intersectionality. Distinct from a frame of ecofeminism (which examines how women and nature are treated in a male-dominated world),[21] students in this class examine how interlocking identities such as race, gender, class, sexual orientation, and citizenship interplay in issues of environmental justice, green gentrification, international development, agriculture, and outdoor recreation; how communities shape local and transnational calls for justice; and how empowerment strategies vary.

At the most basic level, adding this course to the required curriculum demanded that our students start to grapple with the politics of sustainability; to ask the hard questions about why "we" continue industrial or agricultural practices that irrevocably harm human and environmental communities, and who determines that these communities can be sacrificed. As a graduate student at Michigan State University, I was fortunate to be part of a program that focused on *Gender, Justice, and Environmental Change,* the first of its kind in the United States. As a teacher, I wanted students to be exposed to these frameworks sooner, to be able to draw on these principles in their lives and careers, to understand that it is not only our bodies that are gendered, but professions, institutions, politics, and policies.

Beyond the theoretical, students propose and conduct community roundtables, bringing together members of the local region to discuss what they are learning and to hear from others how their environmental experiences have been framed. Pictured below, is a group that was convened by my students to discuss the intersections of environmental activism, gender, and age (the activists all came to their current projects after turning sixty).

These community roundtables have been an important space for students to understand the implications of "gendering",

Figure 21.1: Students and Community Activists after Roundtable Discussion.

how this process of othering is used to construct hierarchies that determine exclusion and inclusion of social, economic, and environmental benefits. For example, in the group above, our discussion included stories of how activism could only come in retirement because of time demands and the need to work full-time; of choices to become a mother, or not have children because of their environmental convictions; of expectations of community "mothering" or "grand-mothering" they were confronted with when joining city organizations. Most important, these roundtables ensure that students' understanding is not framed by a deficit model, painting community members as powerless victims. Instead, these conversations have allowed for theories to be refuted, for alternatives to be discussed, and for building greater awareness between all of us.

Students leave this course with an understanding of the radical nature of intersectional sustainability frameworks compared to other theoretical traditions, based in the recognition of the coupling of human and natural systems, and the impacts of the institutions of race, class, and gender.[22] This course gives students a space to explore the plurality and sociality of sustainability; to examine how some social groups are or are not able to engage around issues of sustainability, ways they are or are not permitted by cultural "elites" or "experts" to engage, or the discipline they may face for doing so by those who perceive their action as a social threat. Moreover, students can describe how different social positions frame experiences, motivations to activism, and activism tool-kits,[23] and are prepared to critically apply these recognitions and understandings within future academic settings and to their own praxis as scholars/citizens. To this last point, students keep a portfolio where they discuss how the readings and experiences of the week are reflected in their interactions with friends and family, how it changes/informs what they are learning in other classes, and where they see these themes represented in media.

CONCLUSION

Representations of sustainability proliferate, but in my experience with undergraduates in the United States, most have concluded that "practicing" sustainability is a personal consumption choice (perhaps out of their league), and that sustainability is unconcerned with issues of environmental or social justice. New and related terminology is emerging, such as resiliency,[24] just futures, and transitions[25] that are exciting but which still require a solid understanding of what is sustainable—for whom, why, and how? And, whose livelihoods, landscapes, and communities are to be recognized, valued, and sustained? To move toward these just futures, we need to practice strong sustainability in our classrooms and our communities. This means we must foreground the experiences of excluded communities and identities (human and non-human), and examine the potential for the reproduction of social, material, and geographic inequalities in technoscientific solutions and governance frameworks. Last but not least, as teachers we must continue to be engaged practitioners, and encourage our students in this process. The inability to understand how community engagement and praxis fits into the sustainability transition process is a dire shortcoming that will hinder students' personal development and stifle the sustainable transition writ large. An intersectional sustainability, is a just sustainability.

NOTES

1. Julian Agyeman, Robert Doyle Bullard, and Bob Evans, eds., *Just Sustainabilities: Development in an Unequal World* (MIT press, 2003).
2. Fridolin Simon Brand and Kurt Jax, "Focusing the Meaning (s) of Resilience: Resilience as a Descriptive Concept and a Boundary Object," *Ecology and Society* 12, no. 1 (2007).
3. Lois Marie Gibbs and Murray Levine, *Love Canal: My Story* (Suny Press, 1982).
4. World Commission on Environment and Development, *Our Common Future*, Oxford Paperbacks (Oxford: Oxford University Press, 1987).

5. Ben Purvis, Yong Mao, and Darren Robinson, "Three Pillars of Sustainability: In Search of Conceptual Origins," *Sustainability Science* 14, no. 3 (2019): 681–695.
6. David W. Orr, *Ecological Literacy: Education and the Transition to a Postmodern World* (Suny Press, 1992).
7. John Huckle, Stephen Sterling, and Stephen R. Sterling, eds., *Education for Sustainability* (Earthscan, 1996).
8. Jianguo Liu, Thomas Dietz, Stephen R. Carpenter, Marina Alberti, Carl Folke, Emilio Moran, Alice N. Pell, et al., "Complexity of Coupled Human and Natural Systems," *science* 317, no. 5844 (2007): 1513–1516.
9. Efrat Eizenberg, and Yosef Jabareen, "Social Sustainability: A New Conceptual Framework," *Sustainability* 9, no. 1 (2017): 68.
10. Western ways of knowing, or Western epistemology, is characterized by the justification of knowledge through approaches that can be tested or verified through quantitative/experimental means, an emphasis on objectivity and the removal of bias by divorcing the knower from what is known.
11. Association for Advancement of Sustainability in Higher Education. https://hub.aashe.org/browse/topics/curriculum/.
12. The Sustainable Development Goals, United Nations Home Page. https://www.undp.org/content/undp/en/home/sustainable-development-goals.
13. Christine Parker, "Voting with Your Fork? Industrial Free-Range Eggs and the Regulatory Construction of Consumer Choice," *The Annals of the American Academy of Political and Social Science* 649, no. 1 (2013): 52–73.
14. Lee Anne Bell, *Storytelling for Social Justice: Connecting Narrative and the Arts in Antiracist Teaching* (Routledge, 2019).
15. Eric Neumayer, *Weak Versus Strong Sustainability: Exploring the Limits of Two Opposing Paradigms*, (Edward Elgar Publishing, 2003).
16. Kimberlé Crenshaw, "Mapping the Margins: Intersectionality, Identity Politics, and Violence against Women of Color," *Stanford Law Review* 43 (1990): 1241.
17. Patricia Hill Collins, "Black Feminist Thought in the Matrix of Domination," *Black Feminist Thought: Knowledge, Consciousness, and the Politics of Empowerment* 138 (1990): 221–238.
18. Michelle Larkins, Wynne Wright, and Shari Dann, "Sustainability and Engagement: Strange Bedfellows in the Undergraduate Textbook," *International Journal of Sustainability in Higher Education* (2018).
19. Reed Geertsen, "The Textbook: An ACIDS Test," *Teaching Sociology* (1977): 101–120.
20. Michelle Larkins, Wynne Wright, and Shari Dann, "Sustainability and Engagement: Strange Bedfellows in the Undergraduate Textbook," *International Journal of Sustainability in Higher Education* (2018).

21. Greta Gaard, *Ecofeminism* (Temple University Press, 2010).
22. Laura Pulido, "A Critical Review of the Methodology of Environmental Racism Research," *Antipode* 28, no. 2 (1996): 142–159; Robert Melchior Figueroa, "Indigenous Peoples and Cultural Losses," in *The Oxford Handbook of Climate Change and Society* (2011): 232–249; David Schlosberg, "Theorising Environmental Justice: The Expanding Sphere of a Discourse," *Environmental Politics* 22, no. 1 (2013): 37–55.
23. Kyle Powys Whyte, "The Recognition Dimensions of Environmental Justice in Indian Country," *Environmental Justice* 4, no. 4 (2011): 199–205; Dorceta E. Taylor, "The Rise of the Environmental Justice Paradigm: Injustice Framing and the Social Construction of Environmental Discourses," *American Behavioral Scientist* 43, no. 4 (2000): 508–580;Terry Mizrahi and Margaret Lombe, "Perspectives from Women Organizers: Views on Gender, Race, Class, and Sexual Orientation," *Journal of Community Practice* 14, no. 3 (2006): 93–118.
24. Marcus J. Collier, Zorica Nedović-Budić, Jeroen Aerts, Stuart Connop, Dermot Foley, Karen Foley, Darryl Newport, Siobhán McQuaid, Aleksander Slaev, and Peter Verburg, "Transitioning to Resilience and Sustainability in Urban Communities," *Cities* 32 (2013): S21-S28; Dayton Marchese, Erin Reynolds, Matthew E. Bates, Heather Morgan, Susan Spierre Clark, and Igor Linkov, "Resilience and Sustainability: Similarities and Differences in Environmental Management Applications," *Science of the Total Environment* 613 (2018): 1275–1283.
25. Raphael J. Heffron and Darren McCauley, "What is the 'Just Transition'?," *Geoforum* 88 (2018): 74–77.

WORKS CITED

Agyeman, Julian, Robert Doyle Bullard, and Bob Evans, eds. *Just Sustainabilities: Development in an Unequal World*. Cambridge, MA: MIT Press, 2003.

Bell, Lee Anne. *Storytelling for Social Justice: Connecting Narrative and the Arts in Antiracist Teaching*. Abingdon: Routledge, 2012.

Brand, Fridolin Simon, and Kurt Jax. "Focusing the Meaning (s) of Resilience: Resilience as a Descriptive Concept and a Boundary Object." *Ecology and Society* 12, no. 1 (2007).

Collier, Marcus J., Zorica Nedović-Budić, Jeroen Aerts, Stuart Connop, Dermot Foley, Karen Foley, Darryl Newport, Siobhán McQuaid, Aleksander Slaev, and Peter Verburg. "Transitioning to Resilience and Sustainability in Urban Communities." *Cities* 32 (2013): S21–S28.

Collins, Patricia Hill. "Black Feminist Thought in the Matrix of Domination." *Black Feminist Thought: Knowledge, Consciousness, and the Politics of Empowerment* 138 (1990): 221–238.

Crenshaw, Kimberle. "Mapping the Margins: Intersectionality, Identity Politics, and Violence against Women of Color." *Stanford Law Review* 43 (1990): 1241.

Eizenberg, Efrat, and Yosef Jabareen. "Social Sustainability: A New Conceptual Framework." *Sustainability* 9, no. 1 (2017): 68.

Figueroa, Robert Melchior. "Indigenous Peoples and Cultural Losses." In *The Oxford Handbook of Climate Change and Society*, edited by John S. Dyzek, Richard B. Norgaard, and David Shlosberg. 232–249. Online edition. Oxford Academic, 2012.

Gaard, Greta. *Ecofeminism*. Philadelphia, PA: Temple University Press, 2010.

Geertsen, Reed. "The Textbook: An ACIDS Test." *Teaching Sociology* 5, no. 1 (1977): 101–120.

Gibbs, Lois Marie, and Murray Levine. *Love Canal: My Story*. Albany, NY: Suny Press, 1982.

Heffron, Raphael J., and Darren McCauley. "What Is the 'Just Transition'?" *Geoforum* 88 (2018): 74–77. https://hub.aashe.org/browse/topics/curriculum/ https://www.undp.org/content/undp/en/home/sustainable-development-goals.

Huckle, John, Stephen Sterling, and Stephen R. Sterling, eds. *Education for Sustainability*. London: Earthscan, 1996.

Larkins, Michelle, Wynne Wright, and Shari Dann. "Sustainability and Engagement: Strange Bedfellows in the Undergraduate Textbook." *International Journal of Sustainability in Higher Education* 19, no. 2 (2018).

Liu, Jianguo, Thomas Dietz, Stephen R. Carpenter, Marina Alberti, Carl Folke, Emilio Moran, Alice N. Pell, et al. "Complexity of Coupled Human and Natural Systems." *science* 317, no. 5844 (2007): 1513–1516.

Marchese, Dayton, Erin Reynolds, Matthew E. Bates, Heather Morgan, Susan Spierre Clark, and Igor Linkov. "Resilience and Sustainability: Similarities and Differences in Environmental Management Applications." *Science of the Total Environment* 613 (2018): 1275–1283.

Mizrahi, Terry., and Maragaret Lombe. "Perspectives from Women Organizers: Views on Gender, Race, Class, and Sexual Orientation." *Journal of Community Practice* 14, no. 3 (2006): 93–118.

Neumayer, Eric. *Weak Versus Strong Sustainability: Exploring the Limits of Two Opposing Paradigms*. Northampton, MA: Edward Elgar Publishing, 2003.

Orr, David W. *Ecological Literacy: Education and the Transition to a Postmodern World*. Albany, NY: Suny Press, 1992.

Parker, Christine. "Voting with Your Fork? Industrial Free-Range Eggs and the Regulatory Construction of Consumer Choice." *The Annals of the American Academy of Political and Social Science* 649, no. 1 (2013): 52–73.

Pulido, Laura. "A Critical Review of the Methodology of Environmental Racism Research." *Antipode* 28, no. 2 (1996): 142–159.

Purvis, Ben, Yong Mao, and Darren Robinson. "Three Pillars of Sustainability: In Search of Conceptual Origins." *Sustainability Science* 14, no. 3 (2019): 681–695.

Schlosberg, David. "Theorising Environmental Justice: The Expanding Sphere of a Discourse." *Environmental Politics* 22, no. 1 (2013): 37–55.

Taylor, Dorceta E. "The Rise of the Environmental Justice Paradigm: Injustice Framing and the Social Construction of Environmental Discourses." *American Behavioral Scientist* 43, no. 4 (2000): 508–580.

Whyte, Kyle Powys. "The Recognition Dimensions of Environmental Justice in Indian Country." *Environmental Justice* 4, no. 4 (2011): 199–205.

World Commission on Environment and Development. *Our Common Future*. Oxford Paperbacks. Oxford: Oxford University Press, 1987.

CHAPTER TWENTY-TWO

ORIENTING PUBLIC PEDAGOGUES
A Black Feminist Approach to Community-Engaged Writing Center Work

By Nick Sanders, Grace Pregent, and Leah Bauer

INTRODUCTION

During the fall 2019 semester, a group of community members, academic administrators, faculty, and students gathered together for the primary purpose of advising the Writing Center at Michigan State University (MSU). This advisory council was intentionally designed to work across and challenge "academic" and "public" boundaries and traditional hierarchical and patriarchal constructs, particularly since the Writing Center's mission and programming hinges upon a broad understanding of community and community literacy and a deep belief in partnering with others, across campus and community, to enact social change.[1]

During this gathering, a community member on the council, Angelo Moreno, adult services librarian at the East Lansing Public

Library (ELPL), called on the Writing Center administration and on us to think critically about how we might share our resources with East Lansing by collaborating with the ELPL. Moreno emphasized that though the city of East Lansing benefits from the presence of a Research 1 institution overall,[2] many members of the community are not beneficiaries of these resources.[3] Though the Writing Center has a long history of collaborating with community partners, especially within Lansing and East Lansing, this call prompted us to question who we were working with and how.[4] We asked: How might we reach a broader range of community members from early childhood, through phases of fundamental literacy development, to adult continuing learners? What could this formal collaboration with the East Lansing Public Library look like, and how could it be informed and driven by shared values?

We were three of the members of the council that semester: Leah Bauer, an undergraduate writing consultant in the Writing Center and a senior theater major; Grace Pregent, associate director of the Writing Center and affiliate faculty in Writing, Rhetoric, and American Cultures (WRAC); and Nick Sanders, a graduate writing center consultant. We were redesigning a community-engaged learning course—WRA 395: The Theory and Practice of Consulting—that we would teach together in the spring. We immediately pivoted to regarding *how* we were approaching our course design and began intentionally scaffolding the origins of the Community Writing Center (CWC).

Today, the Community Writing Center, or CWC, exists to bring writing and literacy celebration and support to members of the community, from young children working on projects to community members applying for grants and employment to writers working on letters, stories, and websites. The CWC is a reciprocal community-university partnership with the mission of amplifying the voices, stories, and literacies of members of the East Lansing community. As an integral community partnership, the

Figure 22.1: The Writing Center.

CWC is guided by the East Lansing Public Library's core values of community, accessibility, innovation, and knowledge[5] as well as the Writing Center's long-standing commitment to community engagement and "working with and developing multiple literacies"[6] in and beyond the university. The CWC also supports the values and priorities of the College of Arts and Letters at MSU: "Equity, Openness, and Community."[7] We work with community members either face-to-face in the East Lansing Public Library or through open videoconference hours. Additionally, we provide feedback through email on any writing project.[8] We have also developed workshops on creative writing, grant writing, and a full summer youth writing workshop series.

Additionally, as three white[9] teachers tasked with developing civically conscious, community-engaged tutors, we recognize the ways our whiteness shapes and constrains our classroom and community engagement. In particular, we recognize how historical, political, and ideological frames (e.g., schooling, religion, location, media, etc.) have reinscribed whiteness in dominant, normative ways, while maligning and harming people of Color.[10] Indeed, whiteness has overwhelmingly framed contemporary conversations and norms in higher education and community engagement and has thus confined our worldviews as instructors and community-engaged practitioners. While we engage the ongoing work of unlearning and divesting whiteness, we are simultaneously critical of how community-engagement and service learning programs "commodif[y] people of Color for the benefit of white people and white-serving institutions."[11] Indeed, the Lansing area population breakdown is approximately 54% white, 22% Black/African American, and 6% multiracial (non-Hispanic),[12] and yet the racial demographics of our university is significantly more majority white (74%).[13] We must acknowledge the legacy of white supremacy that necessitates the political project of Black feminism and recognize that our identities as white people, whether we intend to or not, are implicated in the violence of white supremacy. Therefore, this positioning urgently calls for our shared responsibility to disrupt whiteness and to redress structures that do harm to our colleagues and students of Color, particularly those within spheres of our direct influence, such as those in our tutor education course.

Following Sara Ahmed's essential critique of the narcissism of whiteness studies,[14] we are deliberate and accountable in centering Black feminist thinkers, activists, and leaders. As Black queer feminist Audre Lorde[15] has written, white women in particular must use their anger, anger often expressed as white rage[16] and through microaggressions against women of Color, in "the service of our [Black feminist] vision ... for it is in the painful process of this translation that we identify who are our allies with whom we have grave differences, and who are our genuine enemies."[17] Put another way, it is essential for white people to work with other white people on antiracism in ways that are accountable to communities of Color but also do not recruit our colleagues of Color into harmful spaces where white people reckon with their racial violence. Furthermore, such a perspective is also extended to avoid tokenizing people of Color. We fully reject a checkbox approach to equity and justice work and, simultaneously, practice accountability in our personal and professional lives.

By engaging Black feminist thinkers and teachers, we continually had critical, structural conversations about the systems of whiteness at our Predominately White Institution (PWI)—and about how to divest from them. Our students—and the broader university—are majority, though not solely, white, which calls us to practice deep reflection and introspection around the systems of white supremacy in writing centers and higher education and to work to break patriarchal institutional structures in doing so. Collectively, given our context, we feel that it is also our shared responsibility to name and disrupt the violence of whiteness in our writing center and community writing center by honoring and centering the contributions of Black feminists.

In this chapter, we situate Black feminist theory and theorists such as Kimberlé Crenshaw, Deborah King, Constance Haywood, and April Baker-Bell as guiding forces in the redesign of our course. We then offer reflections from students and ourselves from these community-engaged learning experiences, such as working with young adults on school assignments, community professionals on websites and grants, and local writers on fiction and nonfiction pieces. These reflections have contributed both to our students' and our own emerging identities and practices as public pedagogues. Central to this mission, however, was cultivating our and our students' critical consciousness around the ways social systems inscribe inequity and bolster whiteness. At the same time, this work also called us to center joy and celebration in how we engage community members. We conclude by considering how Black feminism will influence our ongoing strategic planning as we work toward the sustainability of our community-based work.

BLACK FEMINISM AND COMMUNITY-ENGAGEMENT IN WRA 395

Both the curriculum and community-engagement components of our WRA 395 course, a tutor education course, are guided by Black feminism and our writing center's commitment to linguistic, racial, and disability justice. While the writing center at Michigan State has historically enacted commitments of social justice, the center's recently codified language statement[18] and accessibility statement calls for a deep and enduring commitment to language justice and action to challenge the ongoing reproduction of standard English "as the only corrective form" in academic and community settings. Like other calls for linguistic justice,[19] our writing center's commitment to language advocacy represents stances toward enacting a more just, equitable, and loving approach to the work of students in the center as well as work with and among various community partners. Black feminism helps demonstrate these commitments around language, race, and embodiment. However, as white teachers, we also have to develop reflective and accountable practices to decenter and challenge whiteness, while honoring Black feminist scholars to disrupt and dismantle white patriarchal institutional structures.

We are oriented to the work of Black feminism as a core intellectual and activist tradition centering Black women's experiences and stories in a white-supremacist and capitalist world. Black feminism, as a framework, offers robust analytical schemas to unearth how oppressions reproduce, compound, and interact to dismantle systems of oppression. On her visit to the podcast *How to Survive the End of the World*, Alexis Pauline Gumbs notes that "Black feminism is a rigorous love practice, that it is profoundly inclusive. I think about the Combahee River Collective statement [1977], which said that if Black women were free, everyone else would have to be free because our freedom requires the destruction of all systems of oppression[s]."[20] One of the core understandings in Gumbs' words is the way gender and race are not separate categories but multiply with each other—in addition to class, disability, sexuality, etc. As represented in one of the foundational documents for Black feminism, "Combahee River Collective: A Black Feminist Statement," a key feature of Black feminist thought remains the acknowledgment that oppressions are simultaneous, interlocking, and dynamic.

This brings us to one of the two key ideas shaping our course through the lens of Black feminism: *intersectionality*. Analyzing employment discrimination in the 1970s, Black feminist legal scholar and theorist Kimberlé Crenshaw described intersectionality that reflected the interactions among race and gender as systems, an understanding which Crenshaw argued was paramount for social justice movement work.[21] Ijeoma Oluo writes of intersectionality as "the belief that our social justice movements must consider all of the intersections of identity, privilege, and oppression that people face in order to be just and effective."[22] Crenshaw's understanding of intersectionality vitally expands Oluo's by its emphasis on structures—politics, law, and universities, for example—and the critique of those structures. With intersectionality, Crenshaw refers to the ways that interlocking and multiple social systems inform social identities and how the "multidimensionality" of Black women's experiences is reduced and ignored by the "single- axis" treatment of gender and race prevalent in law and other policy.[23] Intersectionality, therefore, reflects the ways our various identities are shaped by interlocking social systems and informs how we move through the world or how our movements in the world are constrained. This is the foundation for the work of our class, so in our syllabus, via Oluo, we provided students with reflective prompts to consider their own experiences, including, "Am I shifting some focus and power away from the most privileged in the conversation?" and "Could the identity differences between me and the person I'm talking to contribute to our differences of opinion or perspective?"[24] Our syllabus describes how intersectionality informs the general course design, which is not a linear overview of topics but brings into tension ideas from its five main focus areas to "combine, compound, mitigate, and contradict each other."[25] As a guide for our course design and delivery, intersectionality is a way of understanding how each of our five main focus areas, and their related topics, interact and shape the different ways people understand themselves and understand and critique systems of power and how these structures position people.

Because the cornerstone of our course is reflection on our identities and the identities of the clients we work with, intersectionality and Black feminism inform not only the course design, but the community-engagement as well.

A second course throughline anchored in Black feminist theory is the idea of *reciprocity*. From a Black feminist lens, reciprocity compels us to develop understandings of communities and values, while recognizing the historical ways universities have broken trust with the communities in which they exist. To frame the idea of reciprocity in the course, our students read a blog piece by Constance Haywood[26] that works to see reciprocity as aligning values, interrogating positionality, and reconsidering motivation in community work. As Haywood writes, "we should see reciprocity as always being contingent upon the desires and goals of the communities we engage, as these—whatever they may be—should be our goals and values as well." In other words, by naming the values of our community partners, practicing deep and empathetic listening, and continually reconsidering our identities and positions, we can ensure that reciprocity helps guide the work of the community writing center.

Taken together, Black feminist theories, particularly around intersectionality and reciprocity, frame our community-engagement course by focusing on humans working and living with other humans. Intersectionality—the recognition that people have intersecting identities that shape how they perceive, understand, and move through the world—helps us engage and orient students to pay attention to difference and embodiment. Bridging intersectionality with reciprocity—aligning the values of ourselves with others and interrogating our motivations—works to enable students to reflect and interrogate their own values and the values of our community partners. In what follows, we show how our students, and we ourselves, grappled with these ideas in the context of their community-engagement course.

STUDENT REFLECTIONS

Throughout the course, our learning community read, interrogated, and responded to Black feminist ideas of embodiment, story, and identity. Through the recursive course design, we and our students gradually enacted a public pedagogy in the community-engaged experience. The students[27] consisted of an interdisciplinary group of undergraduates from across the university in programs

Figure 22.2: First day of the community writing center at the East Lansing Public Library.

such as English Education, Professional Writing, Philosophy-Prelaw, and Political Science, and they situated their learning within their respective prior knowledges and experiences.

In their frequent reflections on course readings and conversations, many of the students wrote about grappling with, quite simply, what feminist pedagogy *looks like* in practice as they began engaging with community members at the ELPL. Students initially wrote about feeling "productively frustrated" when facing their "preconceived ideas and feelings surrounding privilege and systematic oppression." While they connected immediately with the concept of feminist pedagogy, many also recognized the tension between how they had been taught to perceive "correct" learning and writing practices and how they were being asked to act as feminist consultants now within those harmful academic frameworks. One student, Michael, with increasing concern, asked in a response paper how he might "find the line where teaching a student goes from simply correcting passive voice to enforcing white hegemony." He ended his response paper asking, "WHEN IS WRITING JUST INCORRECT BECAUSE OF GRAMMATICAL ERRORS, AND WHEN IS IT AN EXPRESSION AND CULMINATION OF ONE'S IDENTITY AND EXPERIENCES?"[28] When another student, Olivia, reflected on her experience with a community member, she wondered "How could I correct his grammar without sending the message that Arabic is not as worthy of a language as English was?" Olivia's reflection here represents her understanding of how systems, in particular white supremacy, shape and dictate how languages are valued and devalued. This reflection is significant as it showcases how she was un/learning ideas about language in the moments of working with community members.

Students were constantly aware of the system they were working within, and that they would be asked in many ways to uphold that system, correcting grammar for white academic standards. It became one of the most frequent topics of conversation during class time and in many written reflections. At first, this fear of accidentally enforcing patriarchal methods and standards was often panic-inducing; attempting to simultaneously "correct" students' and other community members while meeting their needs seemed paradoxical. They wondered how they could be student-centered consultants and not do what the students ask of them? Is it more important to challenge harmful standards even if deviating from those standards may have real-world consequences, not for us, but for those who trust us with their work? Prompted reflections became looser and less formal in style as they honestly bared their anxieties to us, exposing the deep care they each held for the integrity of an individual's unique voice and truth. Students also frequently interrogated their own relationships and previously unexamined beliefs and privileges, admitting that it was uncomfortable but eye-opening work. In one of her earlier reflections, one student, Lauren, admitted that "much work is still needing to be done in order to learn the appropriate means of approaching communities that of which I do not belong." Lauren's recognition of the structural systems shaping her involvement, particularly to communities she does not belong, further emphasizes Crenshaw's theory of intersectionality as a structural critique in action.

The eventual shift away from their own personal anxieties toward their encounters with community members became the turning point in many of their conceptions of feminist pedagogy in action and their role as consultants. In discussing how her perspective on feminist pedagogy and her own anxieties had developed during the course, Jennifer shared that "This mindset I have, of fear and failure, is a product of a patriarchal academia. Feminist pedagogy should try to undermine this by fostering and accepting mistakes, failures, and struggles as an integral part of the learning process for both tutors and students. In doing so, all individuals would be freed from the binary of correct or incorrect, good or bad, or patriarchal or feminist." Accepting that feminist pedagogy allowed Jennifer to embrace her own humanity and showed how that pedagogy could be used to center humanity in her consultations with others. In his final reflection, Michael wrote that "we must address what the student wants regardless of if that counters our writing center discourse"; he embraced the paradox by admitting that "Enacting feminist pedagogy is blurrier than [he] first expected." Focusing on the student, the person, similarly helped him to escape the confines of theory and see the flexible human interaction as the most important focus, leaving his or our agenda behind. Lauren, who was at first overwhelmed, dove wholeheartedly into the work she knew she had to do, and by the end of the semester was posing complex questions about advocacy and challenging ideologies; she surmised that "Feminist pedagogy demands that we take a moment of reflection in order to consider the world around us not only through our own lenses of understanding but also through the lenses of those within and outside of our own communities." Our students were eventually able to connect to feminist pedagogy not just as a theory, but as a way of entering a space and interacting with others that could be personal, malleable, and at times blurry, but always focused on understanding. They chose to listen, to reflect, to meet their clients' needs and respect their agency to choose, and to confront the selves that they brought with them to these interactions. Feminist pedagogy came to mean something different to each of them since their understanding and use of it was born out of their unique prior knowledges and their connections to and experiences with community members.

Through their community-engagement experience in the community writing center, students returned to the idea of reciprocity not only as a foundational idea for their work in community-engagement but also in how they approached their identities as novice consultants in our writing center. As we mentioned above, we framed the community-engagement component of the course through being in community and naming and aligning the values of community partners as a key dimension of reciprocity. We were working to push back against and challenge reciprocity as a transactional research practice (e.g., if you do this, we will do this) and push toward seeing it more as a way of being and way of doing work with others.

Students demonstrated their commitment to this embodied work as they reflected on practices of listening, cultivating empathy and trust, and the roles of advocacy within spaces like the community writing center and our university writing center. These responses represented both a functional understanding of the what and how of reciprocity (e.g., how values shape reciprocal practices and strategies) and also a larger consideration of the roles and functions of reciprocity within a global community. That is, students named an orientation that centered embodiment, difference, and identity as guiding understandings of their community-engagement work. In the words of one of our consultants, Fatima, "my multiple identities are all equally valued." Meeting community members as they are, as complete messy humans, and bringing their whole selves, also as messy complicated humans, continued to be an important theme for students in our course.

Students also identified learning with and from members of the community as part of the reciprocal relationship being developed between our university and the local library. Jennifer, for instance, discussed the concept of listening as a powerful act of resistance and empowerment. Listening also served as an important practice for students in the course they reflected on how they were thinking about supporting community members as opposed to regulating their writing and identities. From our perspective, the learning that students named here was foundational for them to see their role as support and that they, too, would often learn and be changed by members of the community. Jason, using an extended metaphor of reciprocity from mathematics (e.g., that we all have something in common, just like reciprocals of 10 have '10' in common), showed us that care was a profound practice within the community engagement part of the course. As he wrote, "Instilling and acting with care for you, we walk away with one-tenth of the other," echoing Michael's reflection of continuously learning from community members in the community writing center.

As these examples pinpoint, students' work to see how reciprocity was a feminist practice, also developed deeper understandings about the nature of learning in writing centers. The ways students named their learning and the questions that they had based on their community-engaged experiences also provided them space to unpack their own identities as learners. Fatima, for instance, powerfully wrote: "Our writing is a reflection of ourselves, and to push our own experiences, and processes and versions of standard English on to someone else would be unfair. At the end of the day our job is to make sure that they feel their voice is being heard through whatever it is they are trying to write." Like Fatima, D. brought together her own experiences outside of the social pressures of the classroom. She wrote:

> My final project intensified my awareness of how powerful my voice is, and how valid and valuable my opinions and experiences are. This experience helped me better understand the writing center's and the library's vision, mission, and goals by reminding me of the significance of passing on knowledge and strengthening literacy beginning within my current community. I now realize that there is more to life and learning than receiving a grade ... Clients need to be heard and feel understood without the invasion of racial tension or discomfort within the writing center. These changes can be accompanied by collective action, by working within the system and challenging its core principles and values for people of various nationalities and ethnicities. This course has highlighted that consulting—and life for that matter—is all about the way you choose to respond.

D. and Fatima's words powerfully demonstrate the roles of reciprocity and feminist pedagogy not only within the community writing center but for us as humans living and working with others. They also serve as a comparison for how students from different backgrounds navigated the framework of feminist pedagogy, occasionally diverging in focus as they gravitated toward aspects that best supported their growth as writers and consultants. Our white students began reckoning very early on with their own whiteness, their power as consultants, and anxiety over upholding systems that have traditionally served them. They also expressed concern about entering communities to which they felt they did not belong, and how they might do so without causing harm. Most of their final reflections centered around feminist pedagogy as a way to exist with more intentionality and care and how to encourage others to exist and express themselves freely, reframing the practice of consulting as a reciprocal relationship. While students of color also grappled with the confines of academia and how to best enact feminist pedagogy, their relationship to the theory was often much more personal and uplifting. Their reflections often moved freely between the writing center's theory and their individual histories with language, writing, and identity, and eventually merged the two into consultant philosophies grounded in their own experiences. Feminist pedagogy became not only a way to approach others in consultations, but a way to reconsider the power and validity of their own voices and multiple identities and nurture that empowerment in others.

OUR REFLECTIONS AND LOOKING FORWARD

Through the experience of becoming a community of teachers, we worked alongside our students through moments of anxiety about our course design and initiating this new partnership with the East Lansing Public Library. We found that the frameworks of Black feminism helped us negotiate moving together in a socially just direction as consultants, administrators, teachers, and community partners. Together, we continuously reframed how we think about communities and the positionality of the writing center with multiple, overlapping communities within and beyond the boundaries of the university. We also necessarily let go of expectations about what this partnership could look like, and allowed for uncertainty.

In some ways, we developed a radical listening practice in which we fostered staying in moments of productive discomfort with each other, our students, and our partners, allowing for differences and misunderstanding to be named and deliberated over and for possibilities to form out of this deliberation. Working both with a new model of teaching as a trio of faculty, graduate student, and undergraduate student and with a new classroom model centered around building a community writing center, we often found ourselves in modes of uncertainty similar to our students', unable to answer questions definitively about enacting feminist pedagogy in specific situations or even what the community writing center would look like as it began to take shape. Our classes became an open dialogue where students could pose questions and answer each other. They could unpack their interactions at the CWC and consider how their own perspectives had changed through closer reading or practice. We offered our own past experiences and prior knowledge as teachers and consultants and tried to reframe our preconceived notions of successful community engagement. Collectively, we began to understand our discomfort as stemming from being in a community space outside of our university community. We worked to push through that discomfort by expanding our expectations and challenging our fear of doing "nothing" for the first few weeks in the community writing center. In that sometimes uncomfortable but much more exciting space, we greeted strangers, passed out candy, read a book to a 3-year-old, helped middle schoolers with their novels and seniors with websites, and spent time exploring the ELPL and building community with each other and the library staff. Centering reciprocity and Black feminism allowed us to decenter our own anxieties, stay in discomfort, and find value in those interactions and lift the varied goals of the community along with our own.

As we look forward, Black feminism—and in particular intersectionality and reciprocity—continues to guide our partnership and strategic planning with our local library. In continuing our relationship with the library and community, we are devoted to keeping with our commitments to introspection and reciprocity. For instance, our current undergraduate consultant who completed the course has designed an orientation experience for incoming CWC consultants that focuses on identity, intersectionality, and reciprocity as defining features of working in the community writing center. We're grateful to have the ongoing opportunity to engage in intentional partnership building with the East Lansing Public Library and to continue amplifying and honoring the diverse literacies, languages, and experiences of our community members.

NOTES

1. We are particularly inspired by the understanding of "community" as articulated in the mission and vision of the Coalition for Community Writing. The Coalition is an international organization motivated by "the transformative potential of partnering people across higher education, social innovation, and the public sector to use writing toward social change" and actively "reimagining how communities write themselves; how writing is used as a tool for public awareness and expression, for dialogue across difference, and for community building; and how higher education and communities can collaborate toward these ends." https://communitywriting.org/mission-goals/.
2. Within the US university system, Research 1 institutions tend to refer to universities with high research activity which often are heavily resourced monetarily. Since our university is positioned in communities and is highly resourced, we find it an important place for community-engagement and particularly equity-driven community work.
3. See also Ellen Cushman, "The Rhetorician as an Agent of Social Change," *College Composition and Communication* 47, no. 1 (1996): 7-28.

4. The Writing Center at MSU has a longstanding history of community partnerships and relationships. Among others, see Patricia Lambert Stock, "Reforming Education in the Land-grant University: Contributions from a Writing Center," *The Writing Center Journal* 18, no. 1 (1997): 7–29; Troy Hicks, "Multiliteracies across Lifetimes: Engaging K-12 Students and Teachers through Technology-based Outreach," *Multiliteracy Centers: Writing Center Work, New Media, and Multimodal Rhetoric* (2010): 151–170; and Trixie Smith, "'Oh, I Get By With A Little Help From My Friends': Short-Term Writing Center/Community Collaborations," in *WAC Partnerships Between Secondary and Postsecondary Institutions*, eds. Jacob S. Blumner and Pamela B. Childers (Fort Collins, CO: The WAC Clearinghouse and Parlor Press, 2016), 155–166.
5. East Lansing Public Library, "About Us," accessed August 2, 2022, https://www.elpl.org/about-us/.
6. Writing Center @ MSU, "Vision Statement," accessed August 2, 2022, https://writing.msu.edu/about/vision-statement/.
7. Michigan State University's College of Arts and Letters, "College Values and Priorities," https://cal.msu.edu/about/values-priorities/.
8. Approximately six weeks into the pilot, Michigan State University announced an immediate move to remote instruction. Days later, Michigan Governor Gretchen Whitmer, responding to the COVID-19 pandemic, signed Executive Order 2020-9 to temporarily close "places of public accommodation," (e.g., libraries). At this time, we began working with community members in virtual spaces though we anticipate returning to face-to-face engagements in the future.
9. We are deliberate in our capitalization of "Black" and lower-casing of "white." We do so to recognize the socially constructed nature and material consequences of race created through whiteness. Likewise, following Cherly Matias, we also capitalize "Color" when referring to students, people, and colleagues of Color.
10. See Zeus Leonardo, *Race, Whiteness, and Education* (New York, Routledge, 2009); Cherly E. Matias, *Feeling White: Whiteness, Emotionality, and Education* (Rotterdam, Sense Publishers, 2016); Ruha Benjamin, *Race After Technology: Abolitionist Tools for the New Jim Crow* (Cambridge, Polity Books, 2019).
11. Lauren N. Irwin and Zak Foste, "Service-Learning and Racial Capitalism: On the Commodification of People of Color for White Advancement," *The Review of Higher Education* 44, no. 4 (2021): 425.
12. "Lansing, MI," *Data USA*, December 29 2020, https://datausa.io/profile/geo/lansing-mi#about.

13. Office of Inclusion and Intercultural Initiatives, "Diversity at MSU: 2018–2019 Student and Workforce Data Report," Michigan State University, May 2020, https://inclusion.msu.edu/_assets/documents/about/annual-reports/2018-19-Diversity-at-MSU-Student-and-Workforce-Report-Final-RevisedJune2020.pdf.
14. Sara Ahmed, "Declarations of Whiteness: The Non-Performativity of Anti-Racism," *Boarderlands E-Journal* 3, no. 2 (2004).
15. Audre Lorde, "The Uses of Anger," *Women's Studies Quarterly* 25, no. 1/2 (1997): 278–285.
16. Carol Anderson, *White Rage: The Unspoken Truth of our Racial Divide* (New York: Bloomsbury, 2016)
17. Lorde, "The Uses of Anger," 280.
18. Writing Center @ Michigan State University, "Language Statement," accessed August 2, 2022, https://writing.msu.edu/language-statement/.
19. April Baker-Bell, *Linguistic Justice: Black Language, Literacy, Identity, and Pedagogy* (New York: NCTE/Routledge, 2020); Vershawn Ashanti Young, "'Nah, We Straight': An Argument Against Code Switching," *JAC* 29, no. 1/2 (2009): 49–76; Rosina Lippi-Green. *English with an Accent: Language, Ideology, and Discrimination in the United States* (New York: Routledge, 2012); Geneva Smitherman, *Talkin and Testifyin: The Language of Black America* (Boston: Houghton Mifflin, 1977); Jonathan Rosa, *Looking like a Language, Sounding like a Race: Raciolingusitc Ideologies and the Learning of Latinidad* (New York: Oxford University Press, 2019).
20. Autumn Brown, adrienne maree brown, and Alexis Pauline Gumbs, "A Breathing Chorus with Alexis Pauline Gumbs," *How to Survive the End of the World*, December 19, 2017, podcast audio, https://www.endoftheworldshow.org/blog/2017/12/19/a-breathing-chorus-with-alexis-pauline-gumbs; The Combahee River Collective, "A Black Feminist Statement," in *Words of Fire: An Anthology of African-American Feminist Thought*, ed. Beverly Guy-Sheftall (New York: The New Press, 1995).
21. Kimberlé Crenshaw, "Demarginalizing the Intersection of Race and Sex: A Black Feminist Critique of Antidiscrimination Doctrine, Feminist Theory and Antiracist Politics," *University of Chicago Legal Forum*, no. 1(1989): 139–167.
22. Ijeoma Oluo, *So You Want to Talk about Race* (Seal Press: 2018), 74.
23. Crenshaw, "Demarginalizing the Intersection of Race and Sex," 23.
24. Oluo, 80.
25. Oluo, 75.

26. Constance Haywood, "'I Do This for Us': Thinking Through Reciprocity and Researcher-Community Relationships," *Digital Rhetoric Collaborative*, last modified December 10, 2018, https://www.digitalrhetoriccollaborative. org/2019/12/10/i-do-this-for-us-thinking-through-reciprocity-researcher-community-relationships/.
27. All students cited in this chapter have provided written consent and indicated how they would like to be referenced. Additionally, we also offered students an opportunity to change anything that we quoted to adequately represent their ideas, yet no students decided to change their quoted writing. The following list represents how they preferred to be addressed in this chapter: Michael B., Jennifer Bell, Fatima Konare, D. Thomas, Lauren House, Jason G., and Olivia Gundrum.
28. We have preserved the all-caps as they appear in Michael's response paper. We feel this helps represent his ideas and the complex questions he was working through.

WORKS CITED

Ahmed, Sara. "Declarations of Whiteness: The Non-Performativity of Anti-Racism." *Boarderlands E-Journal* 3, no. 2 (2004).

Anderson, Carol. *White Rage: The Truth of Our Racial Divide*. New York: Bloomsbury, 2017.

Baker-Bell, April. *Linguistic Justice: Black Language, Literacy, Identity, and Pedagogy*. New York: NCTE/Routledge: 2020.

Benjamin, Ruha. *Race After Technology: Abolitionist Tools for the New Jim Crow*. Cambridge, UK: Polity Press, 2019.

Brown, Autumn, brown, adreinne maree, and Alexis Pauline Gumbs. "A Breathing Chorus with Alexis Pauline Gumbs." *How to Survive the End of the World*. December 19, 2017. Podcast audio. https://www.endoftheworldshow.org/blog/2017/12/19/a-breathing-chorus-with-alexis-pauline-gumbs.

Combahee River Collective. "A Black Feminist Statement." In *Words of Fire: An Anthology of African American Feminist Thought*, edited by Beverly Guy-Sheftall, 231–240. New York: The New Press, 1991.

Crenshaw, Kimberle. "Demarginalizing the Intersection of Race and Sex: A Black Feminist Critique of Antidiscrimination Doctrine, Feminist Theory, and Antiracist Politics." *University of Chicago Legal Forum* 1989, no. 1 (1989): 139–168.

Cushman, Ellen. "The Rhetorician as an Agent of Social Change." *College Composition and Communication* 47, no. 1 (1996): 7–28.

Data USA. "Lansing, Michigan." *Data USA.* https://datausa.io/profile/geo/lansing-mi#about.

Haywood, Constance. "'I Do This for Us': Thinking Through Reciprocity and Researcher-Community Relationships." *Digital Rhetoric Collaborative* (2019). https://www.digitalrhetoriccollaborative.org/2019/12/10/i-do-this-for-us-thinking-through-reciprocity-researcher-community-relationships/.

Hicks, Troy. "Multiliteracies across Lifetimes: Engaging K-12 Students and Teachers through Technology-Based Outreach." In *Multiliteracy Centers: Writing Center Work, New Media, and Multimodal Rhetoric*, edited by David Sheridan and James Inman, 155–170. New York: Hampton Press, 2010.

Irwin, Lauren N. and Zac Foste. "Service-Learning and Racial Capitalism: On the Commodification of People of Color for White Advancement." *The Review of Higher Education* 44, no. 4 (Summer 2021): 419–446.

King, Deborah. "Multiple Jeopardy, Multiple Consciousness: The Context of a Black Feminist Ideology." *Signs* 14, no. 1 (Autumn, 1989): 42–71.

Leonardo, Zeus. *Race, Whiteness, and Education.* New York: Routledge, 2009.

Lippi-Green, Rosina. *English with an Accent: Language, Ideology and Discrimination in the United States.* New York: Routledge, 2012.

Lorde, Audre. "The Uses of Anger: Women Responding to Racism." *Women's Studies Quarterly* 25, no. 1/2 (1997): 278–285.

Matias, Cheryl. *Feeling White: Whiteness, Emotionality, and Education.* Rotterdam: Sense Publishers, 2016.

Office of Inclusion and Intercultural Initiatives. "Diversity at MSU: 2018–2019 Student and Workforce Data Report." Michigan State University, May 2020. https://inclusion.msu.edu/_assets/documents/about/annual-reports/2018-19-Diversity-at-MSU-Student-and-Workforce-Report-Final-RevisedJune2020.pdf.

Oulo, Ijeoma. *So You Want to Talk About Race.* New York: Seal Press, 2018.

Rosa, Johnathan. *Looking Like a Language, Sounding Like a Race: Raciolingusitc Ideologies and the Learning of Latinidad.* New York: Oxford University Press, 2019.

Smith, Trixie. "'Oh, I Get by with a Little Help from My Friends': Short-Term Writing Center/Community Collaboration." In *WAC Partnerships Between Secondary and Postsecondary Institutions*, edited by Jacob S. Blumner and Pamela B. Childers, 155–166. Fort Collins, CO: The WAC Clearinghouse, 2016.

Smitherman, Geneva. *Talkin and Testifyin: The Language of Black America.* Detroit: Wayne State University Press, 1977.

Stock, Patricia Lambert. "Reforming Education in the Land-Grant University: Contributions from a Writing Center." *The Writing Center Journal* 18, no. 1 (1997): 7–29.

Young, Vershawn Ashanti. "'Nah We Straight': An Argument Against Code Switching." *Journal of Advanced Composition (JAC)* 29, no. 1/2 (2009): 49–76.

CONCLUSION

LOOKING FORWARD

By Aviva Dove-Viebahn and Carrie N. Baker

In 2018, landslide election victories for women candidates in the United States led many news outlets to declare it the Year of the Woman, a throwback moniker from 1992 when a record-breaking number of women were newly elected to Congress after Anita Hill's testimony at Clarence Thomas's Supreme Court nomination hearings.[1] The 2018 election season more than doubled the number of women in the Senate, with fourteen new Senators joining the ten already in office. In the House of Representatives, the thirty-six newly elected women brought the total of congresswomen up to 102, a landmark forty-three of whom were women of color. Scholars, activists, and pundits attribute these sizeable gains for women candidates to factors ranging from the mobilization of progressive voices during the first two years of Donald Trump's presidency, driven by Women's Marches and related events; continuing and renewed commitment to social justice sparked by the #BlackLivesMatter movement; and outrage over the confirmation of Brett Kavanagh to the US Supreme Court in October of that year. While we are still far from gender parity in the highest echelons of US political power, the election of Vice President Kamala Harris and further electoral wins for women candidates down-ballot in 2020 suggest a continued upward momentum for the inclusive growth of roles for women and people of color in politics and beyond. Increasing diversity in politics is only one benchmark of a potential progressive turn and only a representational one at that; candidates who are women or people of color do not necessarily always enact policies that offer better support or solutions to those in marginalized communities—from communities of color and LGBTQIA+ individuals to immigrants or those living in poverty. However, these political shifts suggest, at the very least, a more widespread understanding of the need for inclusivity along gendered and racial lines when it comes to the desires of voters.

This is an era of reckoning—one in which feminist scholars are perfectly positioned to engage publicly and decisively in politics, culture, and social life by bringing their historical, material, and theoretical knowledge to bear in their communities, from the local to the global. Carrying forward with the gains of the past and present, feminist scholars' involvement in social justice movements, activism, academia, and public pedagogy can take myriad forms, as evidenced by the essays included in this volume. The long history and enduring future of our collective desires for and dreams of equality come starkly to the fore in these essays, whose authors have found, and continue to seek, new ways to translate their research, teaching, and other forms of knowledge into work that benefits and inspires the public. There is certainly a place for and tremendous value in academic and scholarly research within the academia; however, this collection demonstrates how work that exceeds the bounds of academia or otherwise stretches the conventional notion of "scholarship" can maintain its intellectual rigor while simultaneously reaching across thresholds imagined or actual between scholarly institutions and the communities they inhabit.

The Trump administration brought with it a significant backlash against women, people of color, LGBTQIA+ individuals, and other marginalized communities—the ramifications of which were felt not just in the United States, but around the world, and are persisting beyond the defeat of Trump.[2] While the political gains for women in 2018 and 2020 indicate a renewed dedication on the part of many progressives to galvanize around and support feminist candidates and policies, the challenge to achieve social justice is far from over in politics and beyond, including the workplace, education, health care, urban and rural infrastructure, and more. Women, people of color, LGBTQIA+ individuals, immigrants, and those living in poverty in the United States and globally still encounter significant obstacles to their political, cultural, and economic freedom and equality due to all manner of factors, from implicit bias and lack of institutional support to outright sexism, racism, homophobia, capitalist exploitation, hate, or violence—as the essays in this collection attest. These challenges are all the more reason for feminist scholars to engage broader publics.

During the summer 2020 during protests sparked by the police murders of George Floyd and Breonna Taylor, many activists took to the streets. Many more took to the digital sphere via social media, online news, and blogs. These virtual spaces of discourse were especially appealing for their immediacy, widespread reach, and relative safety amidst what was also the height of the COVID-19 pandemic. Both the physical protests and their digital echoes—videos, photos, details, and speeches shared all over the world through Twitter, Instagram, Facebook, and the 24-hour news cycle—helped reinvigorate and mainstream the #BlackLivesMatter movement.[3] Although certainly not enough has been done to combat the forces of racism and misogyny that allowed Taylor to be shot in her sleep or Floyd to be killed in custody, there is little question that the very public outrage at their deaths would not have had the same impact without the extensive work of activists and writers who rapidly disseminated information about Taylor and Floyd, as well as the subsequent protests. As public scholars, we need to look to these cultural moments where change must be made and recognize how our academic work can and should inhabit mainstream and activist spaces.

Our collection offers one such inroad into the digital public sphere as a place for feminist scholars to consider and interrogate ways for academia to bear on activism. For those of us who teach or mentor youth, our students are navigating an increasingly complex socio-political world and are continuously seeking the tools so they can be prepared, in the words of the Campus Compact's 30th Anniversary Action Statement we discussed in the introduction, "for democratic citizenship" while "building partnerships for change."[4] When pedagogy and social justice inform one another, we can also access vital opportunities for those we serve and support to both build on the feminist work that's come before us and forge new paths toward greater inclusivity and equality. The terms of our engagement as public scholars, writers, activists, teachers, and community members are always changing. And yet, the drive to merge and bridge academia and scholarly knowledge with, in, and for our communities—locally, regionally, nationally, or globally—remains a steadfast tenet of public feminisms, now and into the future.

VALUING PUBLIC FEMINISMS IN HIGHER EDUCATION

Feminist public engagement can provide many benefits to scholars, including opportunities to share knowledge, scholarship and pedagogies with a broader audience, gain new knowledge, and learn new skills.[5] Public writing and speaking encourages scholars to communicate in a more accessible and engaging way—skills scholars can take back into their scholarship and teaching. Public engagement can deepen our understanding of issues that we teach and research by connecting us with activists, policymakers, artists, and others from whom we can learn.[6] Public writing can even lead to new scholarship. For example, one of this volume's editors wrote an article on youth sex trafficking for *Ms.* in 2010 that inspired deeper study and resulted in a scholarly book.[7] In her book, *The Public Professor: How to Use Your Research to Change the World,* economist Lee Badget documents how scholars are not only making a significant public impact through sharing their research, but also gaining significant rewards from public engagement. "Many professors have gotten new research questions, new perspectives, new ideas, new sources of data, and occasionally even new funding opportunities by interacting with the broader public," reports Badgett.[8] But will university and college administrators, department chairs, and tenure committees value public engagement when making promotion decisions?

While over 450 colleges and universities have pledged in the Campus Compact's 30th Anniversary Action Statement to "reinvigorate higher education for the public good," it is less clear whether administrators, department chairs, and faculty committees value this work when they make decisions on hiring, tenure and promotion. The president of the American Council of Learned Societies, Joy Connolly, recently wrote an article in *Inside Higher Ed* titled, "We Need to Rethink What Counts for Tenure Now." In this article, Connolly questions prevailing standards at many universities that still focus primarily on the publication of scholarly books and articles for tenure. She asks, "If the purpose of research is to enrich understanding, why is the central requirement for tenure at research universities so inflexible?" She continues, "COVID-19 has vividly focused our energies on the key question of how to connect with learners—in the first instance, our students. What if we also think critically about other audiences of learners: Ourselves as scholars and the broader public, and about how our connections with these audiences can shape what we most value about scholarship and what work we choose to reward?"

Connolly advocates a "flexible approach to defining what counts in the production and circulation of knowledge" and questions "the ever-higher value being placed on highly specialized research."[9]

Connolly is not alone in calling for valuing public engagement. Scholarly associations in several fields have issued statements urging educational institutions to value public work and making recommendations about how to do so. In 2013, the National Women's Studies Association addressed the issue of how to evaluate publicly-engaged scholars for tenure and promotion in a report by the Field Leadership Working Group:

> The field studies cultures, movements, and strategies of resistance and with an eye toward realizing social justice; its practitioners conduct research and design curricula that address the persistence and tenacity of inequalities as well as their changing forms. Women's and gender studies faculty may collaborate with community partners and organizations—local, national, and global—in transformational action research and advocacy. Therefore, assessment measures should account for collaboration in ways that do not devalue such profiles on the grounds that they signal less rigorous work or lower levels of "productivity." Indeed, collaborative work is often more challenging than solitary scholarship, and this labor should be recognized in such assessments. This recognition requires developing innovative assessment techniques.[10]

The report recommends that departments and external evaluators widen the scope of what counts as models of research, teaching, and service, accountings for a more expansive sense of where and how such work should take place, and find ways to recognize and value a wider range of contributions in various forms.

Other scholarly associations have also addressed the issue of how to assess public scholarship. The American Sociological Association's 2016 report, "What Counts? Evaluating Public

Communication in Tenure and Promotion," proposed that universities consider "public communication" in tenure and promotion cases and in overall faculty assessment, suggesting three criteria for evaluation: the content of the writing, its quality and rigor, and its public impact.[11] The American Historical Association provide their own criteria for evaluation of the "publicly engaged academic historian" in a report originally adopted in 2010 and revised in 2017:

> The scholarly work of public historians involves the advancement, integration, application, and transformation of knowledge. It differs from "traditional" historical research not in method or in rigor but in the venues in which it is presented and in the collaborative nature of its creation. Public history scholarship, like all good historical scholarship, is peer reviewed, but that review includes a broader and more diverse group of peers, many from outside traditional academic departments, working in museums, historic sites, and other sites of mediation between scholars and the public.[12]

This report contains detailed guidelines on how university administrators, department chairs, and tenure and promotion committees should evaluate publicly engaged faculty members for tenure and promotion. Some funders have gone a step further, requiring that funded research have a broader impact. For example, the National Science Foundation now requires grantees to spell out the "broader impacts" of projects. NSF has two criteria for proposals: intellectual merit and broader impacts. Broader impacts include "the benefits of the proposed activity to society" and how the applicant will "disseminate their research broadly to enhance scientific and technological understanding."[13] Campus Compact also offers a collection of resources and policies on how to assess engaged scholarship in the review, promotion, and tenure process.[14]

In our own experience, we have found that our public engagement has enriched our scholarship and teaching, and has been valued by our institutions in hiring and promotion decisions. We have both done extensive public writing, which has raised our visibility and status on campus and helped us gain teaching positions and promotions. For Aviva, public writing helped her obtain a tenure-track teaching job by diversifying her job application materials and demonstrating public engagement, which made her a stronger candidate. For Carrie, her public writing led to scholarship that supported promotion to full professor. We are not alone. Gina Ulysse, a professor of Feminist Studies at the University of California, Santa Cruz, says that writing for the popular press led to the publication of her book, *Why Haiti Needs New Narratives*, which helped her gain promotion to full professor at Wesleyan University.[15] Janell Hobson, professor and chair of the Department of Women's, Gender, and Sexuality Studies at the University at Albany, reports that in her research statement to support her application for promotion to full professor, she referred to her public writing as evidence of the impact of her work, noting that a *Ms.* magazine article that she wrote about Beyoncé was widely taught in college courses and cited in academic articles. According to Hobson, all of her external reviewers valued her public writing. This work has made her a national scholar with national impact, which contributed to her successful promotion.[16] We believe that scholars at all levels—from undergraduates and graduate students to newly minted assistant professors and beyond—can find valuable ways to contribute in the public sphere while also supporting the missions of the educational institutions of which they are a part.

A CALL TO ACTION

At a time of multiple crises when science and facts are questioned more and more, and social justice is under increasing attack, the need for feminist scholars to find ways to communicate effectively to a broader public is more urgent than ever. As inequality has grown, and the crises of COVID-19, climate change, and police violence take a particularly hard toll on women, people of color, LGBTQIA+ people, and people living in poverty, the voices of feminist scholars in the public sphere are more necessary than ever. We call on scholars throughout the academy to reach out beyond their classrooms, labs, and libraries to engage a broader public in collaborative and mutually beneficial relationships that can lead to new knowledge and much-needed solutions to the most pressing problems of our day. Failing to do so leaves open the door for attacks on science, higher education, and knowledge itself. The recent controversy over "critical race theory" is a case in point. Conservatives, led by Donald Trump, have caricatured and attacked critical race theory to mobilize a base that seeks to hold, maintain, and regain political power despite being a minority of voters.[17] Scholars need to find better ways to explain and advocate their theory and knowledge to a broader public. We call on feminist scholars to continue to use art and public programming, activism and policy advocacy, public writing and community education in ever more expanded and creative ways to reach people across a broad range of communities to engage in uncomfortable and difficult conversations about our country's history, the ongoing impacts of social injustices, and the complex problems we face today and in the future. We must embrace creative tools, such as storytelling and visual representation, as well as broader platforms, from social media to the streets, to share what we know and offer solutions for a fairer, more just society.

NOTES

1. Elaine Kamarack, "2018: Another 'Year of the Woman,'" *Brookings*, November 7, 2018; Li Zhou, "The Striking Parallels Between 1992's 'Year of the Woman' and 2018, Explained by a Historian," *Vox*, November 2, 2018; and Maya Salam, "A Record 117 Women Won Office, Reshaping America's Leadership," *The New York Times*, November 7, 2018.

2. See, for example, Julie Moreau, "Trump in Transnational Perspective: Insights from Global LGBT Politics," *Politics & Gender* 14, no. 4, 619–648, doi:10.1017/S1743923X18000752; Robbie Gramer, "Trump Officials Seek to Push Social Conservative Values in International Agreements," *Foreign Policy*, September 30, 2020; and Richard Wine, "The Trump Era Has Seen a Decline in America's Global Reputation," *Pew Research Center*, November 19, 2020.

3. Jose A. Del Real, Robert Samuels, and Tim Craig, "How the Black Lives Matter Movement Went Mainstream," *The Washington Post*, June 9, 2020; Nate Cohn and Kevin Quealy, "How Public Opinion Has Moved on Black Lives Matter," *The New York Times*, June 10, 2020.

4. "30th Anniversary Action Statement of Presidents and Chancellors," Campus Compact, March 20, 2016.

5. Carrie N. Baker, Michele Berger, Aviva Dove-Viebahn, Karon Jolna, and Carmen Rios, "Amplifying the Voices of Feminist Scholars in the Press," *Feminist Formations* 32, no. 2 (Summer 2020): 29–51

6. Laura W. Perna, *Taking It to the Streets: The Role of Scholarship in Advocacy and Advocacy in Scholarship* (Baltimore: Johns Hopkins University Press, 2018); M.V. Lee Badgett, *The Public Professor: How to Use Your Research to Change the World* (New York: New York University Press, 2016).

7. Carrie N. Baker, "Jailing Girls for Men's Crimes," *Ms.*, Summer 2010, 36–41; Carrie N. Baker, *Fighting the US Youth Sex Trade: Gender, Race, and Politics* (New York: Cambridge University Press, 2018).

8. Badgett, *The Public Professor*, 8.

9. Joy Connolly, "We Need to Rethink What Counts for Tenure Now," *Inside Higher Ed*, April 9, 2020.

10. "Women's Studies Scholarship: A Statement by the National Women's Studies Association Field Leadership Working Group," 2013, https://cdn.ymaws.com/www.nwsa.org/resource/resmgr/resources/tenure_statement_2013.pdf.

11. ASA Subcommittee on the Evaluation of Social Media and Public Communication in Sociology, "What Counts? Evaluating Public Communication in Tenure and Promotion," August 2016, https://www.asanet.org/sites/default/files/tf_report_what_counts_evaluating_public_communication_in_tenure_and_promotion_final_august_2016.pdf; Amy Schalet, "Should Writing for the Public Count Toward Tenure?," *The Conversation*, August 18, 2016.

12. "Tenure, Promotion, and the Publicly Engaged Academic Historian," adopted by the Organization of American Historians Executive Board on April 8, 2010; by the National Council of Public Historians Board of Directors on June 3, 2010; and by the American History Association Council on June 5,

2010; revisions approved by AHA Council on June 4, 2017, at https://www.historians.org/jobs-and-professional-development/statements-standards-and-guidelines-of-the-discipline/tenure-promotion-and-the-publicly-engaged-academic-historian.

13. National Science Foundation, "Merit Review Broader Impacts Criterion: Representative Activities," https://www.nsf.gov/pubs/2002/nsf022/bicexamples.pdf.
14. Campus Compact, "Engaged Scholarship and Review, Promotion, and Tenure," May 11, 2009, https://compact.org/resource-posts/trucen-section-b/.
15. Gina Athena Ulysse, *Why Haiti Needs New Narratives: A Post-Quake Chronicle* (Middletown, CT: Wesleyan University Press, 2015), xix–xxviii; Interview with Gina Ulysse, August 31, 2018 (on file with authors).
16. Interview with Janell Hobson, September 10, 2018 (on file with authors).
17. Marik Von Rennenkampff, "Trump Blasts 'Critical Race Theory' But Is America's Most Dangerous Critical Theorist," *The Hill*, October 25, 2020.

WORKS CITED

ASA Subcommittee on the Evaluation of Social Media and Public Communication in Sociology. "What Counts? Evaluating Public Communication in Tenure and Promotion." August 2016. https://www.asanet.org/sites/default/files/tf_report_what_counts_evaluating_public_communication_in_tenure_and_promotion_final_august_2016.pdf.

Badgett, M.V. Lee. *The Public Professor: How to Use Your Research to Change the World*. New York: New York University Press, 2016.

Baker, Carrie N. *Fighting the US Youth Sex Trade: Gender, Race, and Politics*. New York: Cambridge University Press, 2018.

———. "Jailing Girls for Men's Crimes," *Ms.*, Summer 2010: 36–41.

Baker, Carrie N., Michele Tracy Berger, Aviva Dove-Viebahn, Karon Jolna, and Carmen Rios. "Amplifying the Voices of Feminist Scholars in the Press." *Feminist Formations* 32, no. 2 (Summer 2020): 29–51.

Campus Compact. "Engaged Scholarship and Review, Promotion, and Tenure." May 11 2009. https://compact.org/resource-posts/trucen-section-b/.

Campus Compact. "30th Anniversary Action Statement of Presidents and Chancellors." *Campus Compact*, March 20, 2016. https://compact.org/actionstatement/statement/.

Cohn, Nate and Kevin Quealy. "How Public Opinion Has Moved on Black Lives Matter." *The New York Times*, June 10, 2020. https://www.nytimes.com/interactive/2020/06/10/upshot/black-lives-matter-attitudes.html.

Connolly, Joy. "We Need to Rethink What Counts for Tenure Now." *Inside Higher Ed*, April 9, 2020. https://www.insidehighered.com/advice/2020/04/09/covid-19-demands-reconsideration-tenure-requirements-going-forward-opinion.

Del Real, Jose A., Robert Samuels, and Tim Craig. "How the Black Lives Matter Movement Went Mainstream." *The Washington Post*, June 9, 2020. https://www.washingtonpost.com/national/how-the-black-lives-matter-movement-went-mainstream/2020/06/09/20ibd6e6-a9c6-11ea-9063-e69bd6520940_story.html.

Gramer, Robbie. "Trump Officials Seek to Push Social Conservative Values in International Agreements." *Foreign Policy*, September 30, 2020. https://foreignpolicy.com/2020/09/30/trump-officials-anti-abortion-sexual-orientation-usaid-oecd-evangelical-values/.

Interview with Gina Ulysse. August 31, 2018 (on file with authors).

Interview with Janell Hobson. September 10, 2018 (on file with authors).

Kamarack, Elaine. "2018: Another 'Year of the Woman'." *Brookings*, November 7, 2018. https://www.brookings.edu/blog/fixgov/2018/11/07/2018-another-year-of-the-woman/.

Moreau, Julie. "Trump in Transnational Perspective: Insights from Global LGBT Politics." *Politics & Gender* 14, no. 4 (2018), 619–648. doi:10.1017/S1743923X18000752.

National Science Foundation. "Merit Review Broader Impacts Criterion: Representative Activities." *National Science Foundation*, 2002. https://www.nsf.gov/pubs/2002/nsf022/bicexamples.pdf.

NWSA Field Leadership Group. "Women's Studies Scholarship: A Statement by the National Women's Studies Association Field Leadership Working Group." *NWSA*, 2013. https://cdn.ymaws.com/www.nwsa.org/resource/resmgr/resources/tenure_statement_2013.pdf.

Perna, Laura W. *Taking It to the Streets: The Role of Scholarship in Advocacy and Advocacy in Scholarship*. Baltimore: Johns Hopkins University Press, 2018.

Salam, Maya. "A Record 117 Women Won Office, Reshaping America's Leadership." *The New York Times*, November 7, 2018. https://www.nytimes.com/2018/11/07/us/elections/women-elected-midterm-elections.html.

Schalet, Amy. "Should Writing for the Public Count Toward Tenure?" *The Conversation*, August 18, 2016. https://theconversation.com/should-writing-for-the-public-count-toward-tenure-63983.

"Tenure, Promotion, and the Publicly Engaged Academic Historian." *Organization of American Historians Executive Board*, April 8, 2010. Revised June 4 2017. https://www.historians.org/jobs-and-professional-development/statements-standards-and-guidelines-of-the-discipline/tenure-promotion-and-the-publicly-engaged-academic-historian.

Ulysse, Gina Athena. *Why Haiti Needs New Narratives: A Post-Quake Chronicle*. Middletown, CT: Wesleyan University Press, 2015.

Von Rennenkampff, Marik. "Trump Blasts 'Critical Race Theory' But Is America's Most Dangerous Critical Theorist." *The Hill*, October 25, 2020. https://thehill.com/opinion/white-house/522600-trump-blasts-critical-race-theory-but-is-americas-most-dangerous-critical.

Wine, Richard. "The Trump Era Has Seen a Decline in America's Global Reputation." *Pew Research Center*, November 19 2020. https://www.pewresearch.org/fact-tank/2020/11/19/the-trump-era-has-seen-a-decline-in-americas-global-reputation/.

Zhou, Li. "The Striking Parallels Between 1992's 'Year of the Woman' and 2018, Explained by a Historian." *Vox*, November 2, 2018. https://www.vox.com/2018/11/2/17983746/year-of-the-woman-1992.

Author Biographies

Begüm Acar works as the coordinator of the Gender and Women's Studies Center at Sabancı University. Begüm studied Sociology and Comparative Literature, and continues her graduate study in Musicology. Begüm has volunteered in feminist organizations at both national and international levels and taken part in campaigns and research projects specially on femicide, local elections, peace, and women's labor. She is a member of Ritimkolektif—women's rhythm group.

Carrie N. Baker is the Sylvia Dlugash Bauman professor of American Studies and a professor in the Program for the Study of Women and Gender at Smith College. She has published three books, *The Women's Movement Against Sexual Harassment* (Cambridge University Press, 2008), which won the 2008 NWSA Sara A. Whaley book prize, *Fighting the US Youth Sex Trade: Gender, Race, and Politics* (Cambridge University Press, 2018), and *Sexual Harassment Law: History, Cases and Practice* (Carolina Academic Press, 2020), coauthored with Jennifer Ann Drobac and Rigel C. Olivieri. She earned her JD and PhD in Women's Studies from Emory University. She is a frequent writer for *Ms.* magazine, where she serves as co-chair of the *Ms.* Committee of Scholars, and has a monthly column in the *Daily Hampshire Gazette* (Northampton,

Massachusetts). She engages the broader public as a member of the Scholars Strategy Network and Women's Media Center's SheSource, and is an alumna of WMC's Progressive Women's Voices, a media and leadership training program.

Sharon L. Barnes earned a PhD in English from The University of Toledo in 1998. Her focus of study was on Feminist and Literary Theory and Twentieth-Century American Women Writers, with a special emphasis on African-American woman poet Audre Lorde. After a stint at Kent State University, she returned to UT in 2000, where she currently chairs the Department of Women's & Gender Studies. She teaches courses in the sexuality studies minor, Feminist Theory, and Global Issues in Women's Studies. She is a long-time supporter of Toledo's Take Back the Night, one of the largest anti-violence against women events in the region.

Leah Bauer (she/they) graduated from Michigan State University in May 2020 with a BFA Acting Major and Arabic Minor, and is a former consultant, undergraduate representative, and co-teacher for the MSU Writing Center. They are personally interested in empathetic social justice theatre, and community-based, queer, anti-capitalist activism and education.

Audrey Bilger, Ph. D., currently serves as the 16th president of Reed College in Portland, Oregon. She was appointed to this position in 2019 and is Reed's first woman president. Her previous position was at Pomona College, in Claremont, California, where she served as vice president for academic affairs and professor of English.

Bilger's work focuses on comedy, Jane Austen, the English novel, feminist theory, popular culture, and gender and sexuality. Her book, *Here Come the Brides! Reflections on Lesbian Love and Marriage*, co-edited with Michele Kort, was a 2013 Lambda Literary Award finalist. She is the author of *Laughing Feminism: Subversive Comedy in Frances Burney, Maria Edgeworth, and Jane Austen*. She serves on the *Ms.* magazine Committee of Scholars. Her work has appeared in *Ms., The Paris Review, The San Francisco Chronicle*, and *The Los Angeles Times*.

Michael Borshuk is Associate Professor of African American Literature and Director of the Humanities Center at Texas Tech University in Lubbock, Texas. He is the author of *Swinging the Vernacular: Jazz and African American Modernist Literature* and the editor of the forthcoming *Jazz and American Culture*.

Jenn Brandt is associate professor and program coordinator of Women's Studies at California State University, Dominguez Hills. Her research explores the relationship between contemporary narratives of identity and institutional structures of inequality. She is particularly interested in the ways in which politics shape and reflect contemporary culture. She is the co-author of *An Introduction to Popular Culture in the US: People, Power, and Politics*, and her work has appeared in a number of edited collections and peer-reviewed journals including *Studies in Twentieth and Twenty-First Century Literature, Critique: Studies in Contemporary Fiction*, and the *Journal of Graphic Novels and Comics*.

Aviva Dove-Viebahn is an assistant professor of Film and Media Studies at Arizona State University and a contributing editor for the Scholar Writing Program at *Ms.* magazine, which frequently carries her essays and reviews in both its print and online editions. She's currently working on a book project exploring representations of feminine intuition, as a contested and ambivalent form of gendered power and knowledge, in contemporary television.

Mariam Durrani is an assistant professor of Anthropology at Hamilton College where she teaches courses on Linguistic Anthropology, Muslim Youth, Gender and Sexuality, Feminist Anthropology, and Migration/Transnationalism. Durrani's forthcoming book project examines the "Muslim youth subject" through an ethnography about processes of transnational racialization for Pakistani and Pakistani-heritage college students in Lahore and New York City. As a social justice advocate and public anthropologist, she publishes her research on academic and public platforms. Her anti-racism scholarship includes a chapter, "The Gendered Muslim Subject: Language, Islamophobia, and Feminist Critique", in *The Oxford Handbook of Language and Race* (2020) and another chapter, "Communicating and Contesting Islamophobia", in *Language and Social Justice: Case Studies on Communication and the Creation of Just Societies* (Routledge, 2019). Durrani has written editorial essays for *Anthropology News, Religion Dispatches,* and *Chapati Mystery*. She can be found on Twitter at @mariamdurrani.

Zoë Antoinette Eddy is a mixed heritage Indigenous (Anishinaabe) anthropologist. She received her PhD in Social Anthropology and Archaeology from Harvard University in 2019. Her research focuses on global Indigeneity, gender, environmental politics, community engagement, and Indigenous reclamation of history and culture through art and performance. She also works in museums to attempt to find ways to destabilize institutional conventions through Indigenous curation strategies. She currently works as an assistant teaching professor at The Global School at Worcester Polytechnic Institute; she is also a Harvard University research affiliate. Outside of her academic work, she is a poet, activist, and performance artist involved in the MMIWG2S movement. She is committed to public engagement, community anthropology, and Indigenous interventions.

Julie R. Enszer, PhD, is a scholar and a poet. Her book manuscript, *A Fine Bind*, is a history of lesbian-feminist presses from 1969 until 2009. Her scholarly work has appeared or is forthcoming in *Southern Cultures, Journal of Lesbian Studies, American Periodicals, WSQ,* and *Frontiers*. She is the author of four poetry collections, *Avowed, Lilith's Demons, Sisterhood,* and *Handmade Love*. She is editor of *The Complete Works of Pat Parker*, winner of the 2017 Lambda Literary Award for Lesbian Poetry, *Sister Love: The Letters of Audre Lorde and Pat Parker 1974–1989*, and *Milk & Honey: A*

Celebration of Jewish Lesbian Poetry, a finalist for the 2012 Lambda Literary Award in Lesbian Poetry. Enszer edits and publishes *Sinister Wisdom*, a multicultural lesbian literary and art journal, and is an adjunct instructor of Women's Studies at the University of Mississippi. You can read more of her work at www.JulieREnszer.com.

Calla Evans is a PhD student in Communication and Culture at Ryerson University on traditional territories of the Anishinaabe, Mississaugas, and Haudenosaunee peoples. Her current research maps the boundaries of Fat Instagram and explores the activism possibilities of visual social media towards liberation for fat folx. Previously she has explored the intersection of Fat Studies and Fashion Studies and how those at the largest end of the fat spectrum experience a lack of access to social spaces due to limited clothing availability. She is a research assistant at both the Centre for Fashion Diversity & Social Change and the Creative Communities in Collaboration research lab. She also teaches in the School of Creative Industries at Ryerson University. Calla is committed to research that blurs the line between academia and activism, drawing on her lengthy career as a feminist documentary photographer.

Lynée Lewis Gaillet, distinguished university professor and chair of the English department at Georgia State University, is author of numerous articles and book chapters addressing Scottish rhetoric, writing program administration, composition/rhetoric history and pedagogy, publishing matters, and archival research methods. She is a recipient of a National Endowment for the Humanities (NEH) Award and an International Society for the History of Rhetoric (ISHR) Fellowship. Her book projects include: *Scottish Rhetoric and Its Influence, Stories of Mentoring, The Present State of Scholarship in the History of Rhetoric, Scholarly Publication in a Changing Academic Landscape, Publishing in Community, Primary Research and Writing: People, Places, and Spaces, On Archival Research, Writing Center and Writing Program Collaborations,* and *Remembering*

Differently: Re-figuring Women's Rhetorical Work. Gaillet is a former president of The Coalition of Feminist Scholars in the History of Rhetoric and Composition, and a former executive director of the South Atlantic Modern Language Association.

Lindsay Garcia (she/her) is a socially-engaged performance artist and assistant dean of the college for junior/senior studies and recovery/substance-free student initiatives at Brown University. She received her PhD in American Studies from William & Mary and her MFA from Purchase College, State University of New York. Her research and artwork employ a queer, feminist, and critical race approach to non-humanity. Garcia has published her research in academic and art world publications and exhibited her artwork internationally at museums, galleries, and film festivals.

Nefise Kahraman is a literary scholar and translator with a PhD in Comparative Literature from the University of Toronto. She holds a BA in Translation Studies from Boğaziçi University, Istanbul. She established a literary translation collective, *Translation Attached*, in 2015. Based in Toronto, *Translation Attached* is devoted to translating literary texts from Turkish into English. Nefise continues to organize its activities, such as weekly literary translation workshops and events. Alongside English and Turkish, she also works in Persian and French.

Senem Kaptan is a researcher and educator, with a PhD in Anthropology from Rutgers University. Currently, Senem works as the coordinator of the RISE Juvenile Justice Higher Education Initiative at Middlesex College, and previously worked at the Women's International League for Peace and Freedom (WILPF), conducting research and advocacy to advance feminist peace. Senem stepped into the world of feminist translation by translating Janet Kaplan's interview with Marina Abramović for *cin ayşe*, a feminist fanzine in Turkey, and is the translator of the feature-length documentary, *İki Tutam Saç: Dersim'in Kayıp Kızları*.

Jack Kendrick is a recent graduate of Smith College, where he studied Mathematics and Computer Science. Jack is currently a PhD student in Mathematics at the University of Washington. Jack works with Transforming HWCs as a campus research associate.

Alex Ketchum, PhD, has been the faculty lecturer of the Institute for Gender, Sexuality, and Feminist Studies of McGill University since 2018. She organizes the SSHRC funded, Feminist and Accessible Publishing and Communications Technologies Speaker and Workshop Series. This research is supported by her multi-year SSHRC Insight Grant, *Disrupting Disruptions: The Challenge of Feminist and Accessible Publishing and Communications Technologies*, 1965–present. For more about her work, see http://www.alexketchum.ca.

Michelle Larkins is an assistant professor in Environment and Sustainability at Fort Lewis College, in Durango, Colorado. Her research focuses in two primary areas: intersectional approaches to environmental justice, particularly working with communities on food and natural resource livelihood concerns; and equitable and inclusive approaches to the teaching and learning of sustainability and environmental studies. Dr. Larkins earned her PhD from Michigan State University in 2017, where she worked with Latinx *promotoras* and other women environmental justice leaders in Colorado and New Mexico to understand the impact of gender, ethnicity, place, and migration on food justice outcomes. Prior to joining Fort Lewis College, she was on the faculty at Pacific University in Oregon.

Don Lavigne is an associate professor of Classics and affiliate faculty member in Women's and Gender Studies at Texas Tech University in Lubbock, Texas. His research concerns gender and sexuality in ancient Greek and Roman poetry in general and, in particular, the way gender is used to construct poetic voices.

Renee Lemus has a PhD in Ethnic Studies. She is a proud Xicana, descendant of Mexican immigrants, with deep roots in her culture and a passion for social justice. She lives in Long Beach with her husband and two children. She currently works as a professor in the field of Women's Gender and Sexuality Studies. She also cohosts the podcast Las Doctoras where she and her co-host Dr. Cristina Rose discuss ways to heal from the historical impacts of colonization. Her work is grounded in a feminist perspective centering the experience of BIPOC and advocates for the structural change required to eradicate white supremacy, capitalism, and cis-hetero-patriarchy. Through her lived experience and her academic background, she is particularly passionate about reproductive justice and the framework it offers for liberation. She also feels deeply guided by spirituality and ancestral wisdom which offers a holistic approach to social justice.

Suzanne Leonard is professor of English and director of the Master's Program in Gender and Cultural Studies at Simmons University in Boston. She is the author of *Wife, Inc.: The Business of Marriage in the Twenty-First Century* (2018) and *Fatal Attraction* (2009). She is also co-editor of *Fifty Hollywood Directors* (2014) and *Imagining We in the Age of I: Romance and Social Bonding in Contemporary Culture* (2021).

Megan Nanney is the diversity research associate at East Carolina University. Their research, which has been published in *Gender & Society, Advances in Gender Research, Research in Higher Education,* and *Sociology Compass,* focuses on the institutionalization of diversity and inclusion in higher education. Megan's current project examines transgender admission policies and student experiences in historically women's colleges. Megan also serves on the Executive Council for Sociologists for Trans Justice and is one of the founders of Transforming HWCs.

Nazneen Patel, a native New Yorker, born in Queens and raised in New Jersey, studied Political Science and South Asian Languages & Civilizations at The University of Chicago. She pursued an

MA in South Asian Studies (Historical Anthropology focus) at the University of Pennsylvania and has since left academia to become a K-12 public school educator. She has taught elementary and middle school in Philadelphia and NYC and is currently an Instructional Coach in Brooklyn. Nazneen's work in education is based on a fundamental belief in "education as social justice." Her focus is on developing anti-racist teachers through transformative coaching, developing curriculum that centers on BIPOC as well as leading equity and integration initiatives inside educational institutions.

Grace Pregent (she/her/hers) is the interim director of the Writing Center at Michigan State University and affiliate faculty in the Department of Writing, Rhetoric, and American Cultures, as well as in Global Studies. Her work focuses on rhetorical narrative theory, globalization and higher education, and community-based literacy.

Gabrielle Rodriguez Gonzalez is a Puerto Rican-Dominican Mount Holyoke student from Hialeah, Florida. They've worked across English, Education, Film, Theater, and Latinx Studies departments at the college to fulfill their interests in creating worlds that critique cemented choices and their nonsensical nature. They've headed the Film Society, been a senator for all four years of their college career, created two short films, and won the James Baldwin-created Word! Festival in 2021. Gabrielle was the lead intern at Rontu Literary Agency and is currently editing their debut novel. In their spare time, Gabrielle consults for Transforming HWCs as a research and content editor.

Jose Roman is a freelance translator and virtual assistant, currently working at Mastering Diabetes; he is a former Civil Engineer student. Born in Venezuela, Jose Roman decided to drop his studies, being less than a year away from obtaining his Engineering degree, and flee from his home country due to the political and humanitarian crisis, in search of a place where his safety and access to public services would be guaranteed. He currently resides in Lima, Peru with his partner, where they are building a new home and have rescued two kittens. Given that Peru has no LGBTQ+ rights, and same-sex marriages aren't legal yet, they find themselves building their life back from scratch and planning if Peru will be their new forever home or just a place to be safe while they find a new home that can guarantee not only their human rights but their rights as members of the LGBTQ+ community.

Cristina Rose (QWOC Feminista-Artivist-Pin@y-Muxer-Traveler-Survivor) is a mama, an artist, a full-time lecturer in Women's Studies at CSU, Dominguez Hills, and a co-host of the Las Doctoras podcast. Grand-daughter of Priscilla of New Mexico and Concepcion of Cebu, Cristina works to explore and integrate these epistemologies in her research, writing, and family. With a PhD from the California Institute of Integral Studies and a student of Voices of Our Nation's Arts, her publications such as "Sacred Heart of Mango" and "mumbling of prayers (at the basilica of la virgen)" appear in *Regeneración Tlacuilolli, Label Me Latina/o,* and *Verses Typhoon Yolanda*. Cristina is the eldest child in her family, is a first-generation college student, and identifies as queer she/siya. Follow her work @drcristinarose and cristinagolondrina.com.

Jessica Rose is a PhD Candidate at Georgia State University. As a rhetorician, she is interested in feminist rhetorics, multimodal rhetorics, public discourse, and archives. Her scholarship explores the ways in which literacies, culture, and composition intersect, especially in environments where communication critically impacts social mores. Archival methods and methodologies feature prominently in her scholarship and her pedagogy, as it is her most ardent belief that early development of archival literacy catalyzes curiosity and critical thinking among students. Her publications include the thesis, "The Rhetoric of the iPhone: A Cultural Gateway of Our Transforming Digital Paradigm," the collaborative chapter "Misogyny in Higher Education" from

Misogyny in American Culture: Causes, Trends, and Solutions reference set, and the co-authored chapter, "Archiving Our Own Historical Moments: Learning from Disrupted Public Memory" from the forthcoming edited collection, *Nineteenth Century American Activist Rhetorics* (2020).

Nick Sanders (he/him/his) is a third-year doctoral student in the Department of Writing, Rhetoric, and American Cultures at Michigan State University and graduate coordinator of the community writing center. Nick's professional interests work to promote equity-driven public and institutional cultures around teaching and learning. His work examines the intersections of anti-racist pedagogy and administration, transformative learning, and critical whiteness studies.

Zainab Shah is a writer from Lahore currently living in Brooklyn. Her essays have been published in *BuzzFeed*, *SAVEUR Magazine*, and *The Best Food Writing Anthology 2015*. You can find her on Twitter @zainabshah.

Riddhima Sharma is a doctoral student at Bowling Green State University. She is the founder of a digital feminist platform, FemPositive, that works towards building a more informed movement for gender justice through online and offline campaigns in India. She has previously taught courses in Gender, Law, and Public Policy at the Research Centre for Women's Studies, SNDT Women's University, Mumbai as visiting faculty and led numerous workshops around Gender, Digital Media, gender-based violence and law in India. Presently, her research interests lie at the intersections of digital media, feminist movements, and pedagogy in South Asia.

Elizabeth A. Sharp, is the director of Women's and Gender Studies and professor of Human Development and Family Studies at Texas Tech University in Lubbock, Texas. Her research focuses on ideologies of gender and families. She recently engaged in a multi-year transdisciplinary research project, integrating social science data and live performance.

Susan. M. Shaw is professor of Women, Gender, & Sexuality Studies at Oregon State University. Her research focus is on feminist theologies and women in religion. She is a regular contributor to *Ms. Magazine* online and *Baptist News Global*. She formerly blogged for *Huffington Post*, and she has published with *The Conversation, Inside Higher Education*, and *the Berkley Forum*. She is author of *Reflective Faith: A Theological Toolbox for Women* and *God Speaks to Us, too: Southern Baptist Women on Church Home and Society*. She is co-author with Grace Ji-Sun Kim of *Intersectional Theology: An Introductory Guide* and with Janet Lee of *Gendered Voices, Feminist Visions: Classic and Contemporary Readings*. She is the editor of *Women's Lives around the World: A Global Encyclopedia* and the forthcoming *Women and Religion: Global Lives in Focus*.

Helis Sikk (she/her) is a visiting assistant professor of gender studies at Brown University. She received her PhD in American Studies from William & Mary and her MA from the University of Wyoming. Her research takes a feral multidisciplinary approach in exploring the relationships between queerness, affect, the built environment, communities, media, and visual cultures. She is the co-editor of *The Legacies of Matthew Shepard* (Routledge 2019), a collection of essays that documents the cultural legacy of Matthew Shepard. Sikk is currently working on her monograph, *Mainstreaming Violence: Affect, Activism, and Queer Politics of Representation*, which traces the affective genealogy of anti-LGBTQ+ violence since the 1960s.

Jess Smith currently teaches in the Department of English at Texas Tech University in Lubbock, Texas. Her work can be found in *Prairie Schooner, Waxwing, 32 Poems, The Rumpus*, and other journals. She received her MFA from The New School and is the recipient of scholarships from the Sewanee Writers' Conference and the Vermont Studio Center.

Dana Weiser is an associate professor in Human Development and Family Sciences and a faculty affiliate in Women's and

Gender Studies at Texas Tech University in Lubbock, Texas. Her work examines how family experiences shape young adults' later relationship experiences and sexual behaviors, with a particular focus on infidelity and sexual violence.

Allison Whitney is an associate professor of Film and Media Studies in the Department of English at Texas Tech University in Lubbock, Texas. Her research focuses on the intersection of technological history with gender, race, and sexuality in genre cinema. She also conducts oral history research on the film culture of West Texas.

Kimberly A. Williams (she/her) is a long-time community activist turned award-winning author and teacher. She directs the Women's & Gender Studies Program at Mount Royal University where she teaches courses on feminist, queer, and critical race theories, men and masculinities, feminist approaches to health and health care, and the global sex trade industry. Having earned her PhD in Women's Studies from the University of Maryland, in the traditional territories of the Pamunkey and Piscataway, Dr. Williams is a white settler trying to live unsettled in Treaty 7 territory, on the hereditary homelands of the Blackfoot Confederacy, the Îyârhe Nakoda and Tsuut'ina Nations, and of the Métis Nation of Alberta, Region III. Learn more at kawilliamsphd.com.